Studies in European Economic Law and Regulation

Volume 2

For further volumes:
http://www.springer.com/series/11710

Chris Downes

The Impact of WTO SPS Law on EU Food Regulations

Springer

Chris Downes
European Consulting Company (ECCO)
Brussels
Belgium

ISSN 2214-2037 ISSN 2214-2045 (electronic)
ISBN 978-3-319-04372-2 ISBN 978-3-319-04373-9 (eBook)
DOI 10.1007/978-3-319-04373-9
Springer Cham Heidelberg New York Dordrecht London

Library of Congress Control Number: 2014931499

Printed on acid-free paper

Springer is part of Springer Science+Business Media (www.springer.com)

Acknowledgements

I would first like to thank the University of Kent Law School for its generous financial support of my doctoral research completed in 2011 from which this book emanates. A special word of thanks to my supervisor Professor Harm Schepel at the university who first encouraged me to undertake a doctoral thesis, little knowing, it has to be said, that the subject would be SPS measures. His confidence in the completion of this research project was touching and his quizzical reflections highly instrumental in staving off some of the more fruitless lines of research.

I am indebted to the numerous officials of EU institutions, whose provision of information and ideas have contributed, often unwittingly, to the development of this research: in particular, Enrique Beltrán Poveda, Niall Gerlitz and Jean-François Roche. I am also grateful to Selma Doyran of the Joint FAO/WHO Food Standards Programme, for her help in tracking down various elusive documents. Simon Pettman and David Pineda of the International Alliance of Dietary Supplements Associations generously took time to provide extremely valuable insights into global food supplement regulations. I would also like to acknowledge the support of all my colleagues at ECCO, most notably Alain Galaski for his healthy attitude towards working life which has provided me with the flexibility to pursue this research, Frances Hunt for sharing her expertise on food additives and Laurent Reverdy for his good-humoured tolerance of my idiosyncratic working practices. Michael Downes's sterling efforts to reacquaint me with the niceties of the English language have been enormously appreciated, as has James Downes's technical assistance.

Hannah, Lukas and Anton: thank you for your patience during those periods behind the computer and your forgiveness when the true conceit of the claim that Daddy has been 'writing a story' will become clear. To Ann, my boundless appreciation for your support, love and our friendship.

Table of Cases

WTO Cases

Contents

About the Author

Dr. Chris Downes has 15 years of experience working as a consultant on issues related to EU food law. He is currently Manager, International Trade & Regulatory Affairs at The European Consulting Company (ECCO), a Brussels-based consultancy specialising in food and trade policy. He is a guest lecturer on international economic law at the University of Kent, teaching at their Brussels campus.

Abbreviations

AB	Appellate Body
ADI	Acceptable Daily Intakes
AJIL	American Journal of International Law
ALOP	Appropriate Level of Protection
ASEAN	Association of South East Asian Nations
CAC	Codex Alimentarius Commission
CCFA	Codex Committee on Food Additives
CCFAC	Codex Committee on Food Additives and Contaminants
CCNFSDU	Codex Committee on Nutrition and Foods for Special Dietary Uses
CML Rev	Common Market Law Review
CNFR	Current Novel Food Regulation
DG Sanco	European Commission, Directorate General for Health & Consumers
ECJ	European Court of Justice
EJIL	European Journal of International Law
EL Rev	European Law Review
Envtl L	Environmental Law
EP	European Parliament
EU	European Union
FAO	Food and Agriculture Organisation
FVO	Food and Veterinary Office (European Commission)
GAIN	Global Agriculture Information Network
GATT	General Agreement on Tariffs and Trade
GM	Genetically Modified
GMO	Genetically Modified Organism
GMP	Good Manufacturing Practice
GSFA	General Standard on Food Additives
HACCP	Hazard Analysis Critical Control Point
INS	International Numbering System
IPPC	International Plant Protection Convention
IR	International Relations

JCMS	Journal of Common Market Studies
JECFA	Joint FAO/WHO Expert Committee on Food Additives
JWT	Journal of World Trade
KFDA	Korean Food and Drug Administration
LL	Liberty Link
MEP	Member of the European Parliament
Mercosur	Mercado Común del Sur (Southern Common Market)
MLR	Modern Law Review
MRA	Mutual Recognition Agreements
NA & EP	Notification Authority & Enquiry Point
NAFTA	North American Free Trade Agreement
NNFR	New Novel Food Regulation
PPM	Process and Production Method
RDI	Reference Daily Intakes
SPS	Sanitary and Phytosanitary
SPS Agreement	World Trade Organisation Agreement on the Application of Sanitary and Phytosanitary Measures
TBT	Technical Barriers to Trade
UK FSA	UK Food Standards Agency
US FDA	US Food and Drug Administration
USDA	US Department of Agriculture
VCLT	Vienna Convention on the Law of Treaties
VJIL	Virginia Journal of International Law
VMS	Vitamin and Mineral Food Supplements
WHO	World Health Organisation
WTO	World Trade Organisation

Chapter 1
Introduction

Abstract This introductory chapter explains the anomaly in assessments of the SPS Agreement that prompted further investigation into its impact on EU food regulations: the view of legal commentators that the regime significantly intrudes on domestic policy-making and the common understanding of EU officials that its influence is marginal. The chapter provides context for the analysis that follows, briefly introducing the Agreement, its origins, provisions and key implications for national regulators and outlining the legal and political context in which European food regulators operate. It then familiarises the reader with two important international venues for the development of food norms: the WTO Committee on Sanitary and Phytosanitary Measures and Codex Alimentarius. It concludes with an outline of the structure of the book and provides some guidance to readers.

1.1 Why Another Book About the WTO SPS Agreement?

A vast amount has already been written about the World Trade Organisation (WTO) Agreement on the Application of Sanitary and Phytosanitary Measures (SPS Agreement), the primary WTO text governing domestic food regulation.[1] Too much, perhaps. Reviewing a recent addition to the literature on the subject, Jacqueline Peel notes (barely suppressing a sigh, one suspects) that 'one might reasonably question the utility of another book devoted to the topic'.[2] My sense that this well-trodden ground merited further investigation stemmed from an incident in spring 2005.

Academic study of the Agreement at that time drew confident conclusions from early SPS-related case law that national regulators would henceforth face considerable constraints in developing new regulatory measures. With this in mind, I visited Rue Breydel in Brussels—home to the European Commission's service responsible for consumer protection and health (DG Sanco)—to represent the views of an industry group on a food law proposal under discussion. Well armed, I felt, with a convincing set of arguments drawn from SPS law, I contested the WTO compatibility of the new regulation. Somewhat bemused, the official concerned informed me

[1] Agreement on the Application of Sanitary and Phytosanitary Measures, opened for signature 15 April 1994, 1867 UNTS 493 (entered into force 1 January 1995) (SPS Agreement).

[2] J Peel, 'Review: *Regulating Health and Environmental Risks under WTO Law: A Critical Analysis of the SPS Agreement*. By Lukasz Gruszczynski' (2011) 23 *Journal of Environmental Law* 157.

C. Downes, *The Impact of WTO SPS Law on EU Food Regulations*, Studies in European Economic Law and Regulation 2, DOI 10.1007/978-3-319-04373-9_1,

that his limited knowledge of the SPS Agreement left him in no position to judge the case presented, and the discussion moved swiftly on. This rather dismissive attitude is not unusual. In the course of researching this book, I have pressed numerous officials dealing with different aspects of European food law for their views about the influence of the SPS Agreement on their work. Grappling with highly political and emotive food issues, the demands of domestic economic interests, the irreconcilability of diverging national cultural preferences, as well as dodging inter-institutional skirmishes, international legal obligations are consistently reported to be marginal to their everyday concerns.

In one sense, such responses are not surprising. One would not realistically expect all European Union (EU) officials to be well versed in international law, nor the presumptions of academics to be perfectly reproduced in the day-to-day realities of policy-making. Nevertheless, the disparity between academic and administrative perceptions of the SPS Agreement's significance raised questions in my mind about the validity and relevance of much scholarly work on this topic. What, if anything, has been the real impact of the SPS Agreement? Do international lawyers simply overestimate the influence that multinational agreements place upon domestic actors? Or does international law constrain the European decision-making process in a way that is not immediately obvious even to those directly involved? This book attempts to offer some answers to these questions.

A not unreasonable consideration at this point is whether it is worth dwelling too extensively on how scholars perceive the operation of an international treaty. In other words, why should we care how lawyers choose to characterise the SPS Agreement?

There are three ways in which academic work on the SPS Agreement may have broader ramifications. A first consideration is legal commentators' contribution to wider public acceptance of the WTO. Academic criticism of the SPS Agreement helps sustain the commonly held perception of an organisation that, in pursuit of free trade, silences valid public concerns. The resulting public frustration can spill over in a dramatic fashion as in Seattle in 1999, where the WTO's approach to growth hormones in beef was a prominently cited grievance in the violent street protests.[3] Regardless of one's views on the issue in question, it would be perverse if public anger was the product of an entirely erroneous understanding of the body's influence. Secondly, an overblown conception of the invasiveness of the SPS Agreement in national policy-making may galvanise legal reform.[4] If the evaluation that propels a call to rewrite the SPS Agreement is inaccurate, the remedies proposed are unlikely to be suitable. Any changes to the legal framework, and the efforts required to negotiate them, may then prove unnecessary or even harmful. If we wish to improve the system, we first have to understand its real impact. Finally, there is the behaviour of policy-makers themselves. If national administrators are encouraged to believe that their policy options will be unduly constrained by international law,

[3] J Madeley, 'There's a Food Fight in Seattle' *New Statesman* (22 November 1999) www.newstatesman.com/node/136187.

[4] For examples of proposals for revising the SPS Agreement, see n 78 in Chap. 3 below.

this may change the way they interact with other countries in international bodies, such as Codex Alimentarius, aimed at facilitating and managing the global food trade.[5] However, should international rules be shown not unduly to impinge upon national policy-making, potentially beneficial cooperation and compromise within these bodies need not be eschewed. The question of how we represent the power and influence of a legal regime is therefore not of purely academic interest.

More recently, particularly following the *US—Continued Suspension* dispute, scholars have tended to downplay the potential intrusiveness of the SPS Agreement.[6] In one way, this dilutes the anomaly that initially prompted this research. Yet, if anything, this latter trend towards a less negative appraisal of the SPS Agreement only accentuates the rather curious relationship between lawyers, law and social reality. How can a single dispute transform our appreciation of a treaty and the role it plays in international society? Does the revised view of the SPS Agreement imply that its significance has been wrongly understood over the preceding decade? Will the outcome of subsequent dispute settlement cases once more reverse the swing of the scholarly pendulum? More than ever, we need to understand the actual impact of the SPS Agreement.[7]

As indicated by Peel, the SPS Agreement has been extensively treated elsewhere. Nevertheless, for the benefit of readers not so familiar with the role of the Agreement, the remainder of this Introduction aims to situate the analysis that will follow. Section 1.2 briefly introduces the Agreement, its origins, provisions and key implications for national regulators. Section 1.3 describes how legal commentators have customarily characterised the SPS Agreement and its impact on domestic policy-making, the intriguing demonisation of the regime that initially provoked this study. As the focus of this book is largely on the Agreement's impact on the EU food

---

[5] There is some evidence of this, for example, in Codex Alimentarius meetings on food additives, in which EU representatives have recently started to adopt norms with a caveat (known as 'note 161') that accepts international standards only 'subject to national legislation'. See Codex Alimentarius Commission Document ALINORM 10/33/12, para 70–75. For a detailed discussion, see C Downes, 'Only a Footnote? The Curious Codex Battle for Control of Additive Regulations' (2012) 7 *European Food and Feed Law Review* 232.

[6] See, e.g. L Gruszczynski, *Regulating Health and Environmental Risks under WTO Law: A Critical Analysis of the SPS Agreement* (Oxford, OUP, 2010) 273 (concluding that 'the SPS Agreement is actually able to provide a workable mechanism that seriously takes into account the complex nature of science and scientific risk assessment and does not compromise the legitimate regulatory choices of WTO members'); B Mercurio and D Shao, 'A Precautionary Approach to Decision Making: The Evolving Jurisprudence on Article 5.7 of the SPS Agreement' (2010) 2 *Trade Law and Development* 195, 223 (noting that the Agreement 'is capable of being flexibly interpreted so as to both protect policy space and national regulations and at the same time protect against creeping protectionism'); S Cho, 'International Decisions, *United States—Continued Suspension of Obligations in the EC—Hormones*' (2009) 103 AJIL 299, 302 (pointing to the Appellate Body's (AB) 'ostensible effort to broaden a regulating member's policy space'). Others remain doubtful. See, e.g. J Peel, 'Of Apples and Oranges (and Hormones in Beef): Science and the Standard of Review in WTO Disputes under the SPS Agreement' (2012) 61 ICLQ 47 (pointing to the intrusive nature of the AB's approach in *Australia—Apples* subsequent to the *US—Continued Suspension* dispute).

[7] See Gruszczynski (n 6) 274 (noting that 'the impact of the SPS Agreement on the practice of WTO Members definitely merits a separate and detailed study').

policy, Sect. 1.4 will then provide a short scene-setting introduction to the legal and political context in which European regulators operate. Section 1.5 familiarises the reader with two important international venues for the development of food norms—the WTO Committee on Sanitary and Phytosanitary Measures (SPS Committee) and Codex Alimentarius—on which Part III of this book will focus. The Introduction concludes with an outline of the structure of the book and provides some guidance to readers (Sect. 1.6).

1.2 What Is the SPS Agreement?

1.2.1 Background

Concerns about the safety of imported food and suspicions of protectionism have been recurring features of trade in agricultural products for almost 150 years.[8] Before the Uruguay Round came into effect in 1995, all technical regulations fell within the scope of the General Agreement on Tariffs and Trade (GATT) Standards Code, which sought to outlaw technical standards that unnecessarily obstructed international trade.[9] However, the Code failed to provide an adequate framework for distinguishing necessary from unnecessary measures.[10] This ambiguity, combined with deficient enforcement, rendered the GATT largely ineffective at disciplining non-tariff measures.[11] From the outset of the Uruguay Round of negotiations launched to reform the GATT, technical regulations in the context of agricultural trade were singled out for attention.[12] Although there was no explicit mandate to do so, the Working Group charged with the task of addressing this issue quickly concluded that a separate code specific to agricultural measures was required.[13] Consequently, the Uruguay Round replaced the Standards Code with two separate agree-

[8] See T Epps, *International Trade and Health Protection* (Cheltenham, Edward Elgar, 2008) 17 (providing an interesting history of some of these disputes).

[9] Agreement on Technical Barriers to Trade, 12 April 1979, 1186 UNTS 276, GATT, BISD, 26th Supp 8 (1980).

[10] SJ Rothberg, 'From Beer to BST: Circumventing the GATT Standards Codes Prohibition on Unnecessary Obstacles to Trade' (1990) 75 *Minnesota Law Review* 505, 516–517.

[11] DG Victor, 'The Sanitary and Phytosanitary Agreement of the World Trade Organisation: An Assessment After Five Years' (2000) 32 *New York University Journal of International Law and Politics* 865, 874.

[12] GATT, Ministerial Declaration of Uruguay Round (GATT Doc MINDEC 20 September 1986), s D, Agriculture, iii (setting the aim of 'minimizing the adverse effects that sanitary and phytosanitary regulations and barriers can have on trade in agriculture, taking into account the relevant international agreements').

[13] GATT Doc MTN.GNG/NT5/WGSP/2 (14 November 1988) para 12. The prominent differences in European and US thinking on the use of growth hormones in meat were undoubtedly a factor in this decision. See DA Wirth, 'The Role of Science in the Uruguay Round and NAFTA Trade Disciplines' (1994) 27 *Cornell International Law Journal* 817, 823–824.

ments, one oriented towards sanitary and phytosanitary measures (SPS Agreement), and a further one aimed at regulating non-sanitary measures (Technical Barriers to Trade or TBT Agreement[14]).

In the context of the hard-fought liberalisation of agricultural trade, the SPS dimension of the Uruguay Round negotiations was relatively straightforward. There were limited changes between the draft text adopted in late 1990 and the final text adopted some 18 months later, once the deadlock on market access issues had been broken.[15] In the light of post-agreement conflicts, one popular narrative of the negotiations is that the EU[16] did not hold its ground in negotiations, culminating in a text that leaned manifestly towards the US regulatory philosophy.[17] However, in practice, all the major agricultural exporters, the EU included, were important players in discussions from the outset.[18] The EU had not only major defensive interests relating to the ongoing dispute on growth hormones in meat, but frustrated ambitions concerning the exports of wine.[19] The greatest resistance to the proposed text in the latter stages in fact came from the US delegation,[20] largely due to public fears of a drop in US food standards.[21] This issue was ultimately addressed by allowing individual Members to introduce measures more stringent than required by international standards. The one matter that was not conclusively resolved in the final text was the legitimacy of non-scientific concerns as a basis for setting sanitary

[14] Agreement on Technical Barriers to Trade, opened for signature 15 April 1994, 1868 UNTS 120 (entered into force 1 January 1995).

[15] TP Stewart, *The GATT Uruguay Round: A Negotiating History (1986–1994)* (The Hague, Kluwer Law International, 1999) 41. See also J Croome, *Reshaping the World Trading System: A History of the Uruguay Round* (Geneva, WTO Secretariat, 1995) 235–237.

[16] For simplicity, and at the risk of anachronism, the name 'European Union' (abbreviated to 'EU') will be used throughout this book, although until December 2009, and the entry into force of the Lisbon Treaty, the European Communities (EC) was the formal Member of the WTO. The same approach will be adopted when discussing regulatory developments predating the existence of the European Union.

[17] Drezner, for example, claims that 'the SPS Agreement was a low-priority issue for the European Union during the Uruguay round' and 'was not a major player in the SPS negotiations'. DW Drezner, *All Politics Is Global: Explaining International Regulatory Regimes* (Princeton, Princeton University Press, 2008) 162–163.

[18] See MTN.GNG/NT5/WGSP/1 (28 October 1988).

[19] At a key moment in discussions, the EU was facing restrictions on exports of wine to the US due to the presence of the pesticide procymidone. As Codex was in the process of adopting a residue limit for the pesticide, the EU keenly understood the potential benefits of reinforcing the role of international standards in the new agreement. See D Prévost and P van den Bossche, 'The Agreement on the Application of Sanitary and Phytosanitary Measures' in PFJ Macrory, AE Appleton and MG Plummer (eds), *The World Trade Organization: Legal, Economic and Political Analysis* (Berlin, Springer, 2005) 243.

[20] Stewart (n 15) 42.

[21] See H Rowen, 'Are Food Imports Safe?' *Washington Post* (31 May 1990).

measures,[22] an ambiguity that today remains one of the most significant challenges for policy-makers.[23]

1.2.2 Key Disciplines

The Agreement's core principles and aims are relatively simple. The SPS Agreement affirms the basic right of WTO Members to take measures to protect 'human, animal or plant life or health' (Article 2.1).[24] It also reiterates the obligations established in the GATT Agreement not to 'arbitrarily or unjustifiably discriminate' between Members, and prohibits applying measures in a manner that constitutes 'a disguised restriction on international trade' (Article 2.3). A distinguishing prerequisite for SPS measures is that they must generally be based on scientific principles and adequate scientific evidence (Article 2.2). To ensure that this is the case, a particular emphasis is placed upon substantiation through appropriate risk assessment (Article 5). This requirement is not absolute. Where there is insufficient scientific evidence to maintain a measure in this way, Members may provisionally act on the basis of 'available pertinent information' (Article 5.7).

Science has an obvious prominence throughout the SPS Agreement, but is not the only relevant factor in developing measures. In assessing the risk of determining the appropriate measure, Members must (under Article 5.3) also take into account economic factors (including, for example, 'the relative cost-effectiveness of alternative approaches') and strive to minimise negative trade effects (Article 5.4). There is also a more complex requirement to ensure consistency in the level of protection offered across SPS measures (Article 2.5). A further overarching obligation for WTO Members is to advance international harmonisation, both by basing domestic measures on international standards (Article 3.1) and through active involvement in international organisations (Article 3.4). While striving for harmonisation, the SPS Agreement does not necessarily require homogeneity of measures. Members must also accept the measures of other Members, regardless of their particular regulatory form, provided that they meet the level of protection deemed acceptable to the importing Member. The SPS Agreement hereby opens up the opportunity for inter-Member scrutiny and discussion of respective policies (Article 4).

As well as bringing discipline to WTO Members' development of sanitary measures, the SPS Agreement seeks to illuminate this process by introducing a commitment to transparency (Article 7 and Annex B). The latter includes a requirement for each Member to notify any new measures under consideration and ensure publication of all measures in force. A large number of SPS measures involve the control, inspection and approval of food. Article 8 and Annex C seek to improve

[22] See Epps (n 8) 27.

[23] See discussion in Chaps. 4 and 5 below.

[24] As the focus in this study is on food policy, provisions specifically oriented towards plant or animal health (such as SPS Agreement Art 6 relating to pest- or disease-free areas) are not considered.

the operation of these procedures: for example, by ensuring that they are no more burdensome in timing and information requirements than is absolutely necessary. In order to manage the operation of the SPS Agreement and advance its objectives, the Agreement establishes a Sanitary and Phytosanitary Committee made up of WTO Members. The Committee is charged to undertake activities required to advance the objectives of the Agreement, such as liaising with international organisations, monitoring harmonisation and facilitating communication between Members (Article 12). So that it can deal with the different levels of development of country Members, a commitment is made to provide technical assistance to other Members (Article 9) and to offer special and differential treatment to cater for the special needs of developing-country Members (Article 10).

1.2.3 What Are the Implications for Domestic Policymakers?

What do these disciplines actually mean for the national management of food policy? When trying to apply the basic principles outlined above to scientifically contentious and politically divisive areas of food policy, the vagueness of many of the SPS provisions soon becomes apparent.[25] Nevertheless, the dispute-settlement cases that have been brought before the WTO over the last 15 years, although limited in number, have brought clarity to a number of articles in a way that provides policy-makers with some idea of the scope of the requirements imposed. These have been dealt with expertly and comprehensively elsewhere.[26] As an introduction to the types of dilemma that the SPS Agreement creates for national administrations, a number of examples are given below of questions that have been explored by dispute-settlement bodies:

Does the SPS Agreement Allow a WTO Member to Choose What Risk Is Acceptable?

It remains the 'prerogative'[27] of WTO Members to establish what they consider to be an appropriate level of protection for their own citizens. This may be set as high as the Member chooses—potentially at 'zero risk'[28]—even in cases where the subject of the measure has already been treated in an internationally agreed

[25] The AB has vented its frustration about the difficulties in interpreting some aspects of the Agreement. See *EC—Measures concerning Meat and Meat Products* (*Hormones*), Appellate Body Report (adopted 16 January 1998) WT/DS26/AB/R, WT/DS48/AB/R, para 175 (in which the AB noted that 'Article 3.3 is evidently not a model of clarity in drafting and communication').

[26] For the fullest and most up-to-date analysis at the time of writing, see Gruszczynski (n 6).

[27] *Australia—Measures Affecting Importation of Salmon (Australia—Salmon),* Appellate Body Report (adopted 20 October 1998) WT/DS18/AB/R, para 199.

[28] *Australia—Salmon,* Appellate Body Report, para 125.

standard.[29] However, freedom is circumscribed somewhat by an 'implicit obligation' clearly to determine the level of protection, although not necessarily in quantitative terms.[30] A Member's chosen level of protection is paramount even where different to the actual level of protection provided by the applied measure.[31] This distinction is particularly important in a situation where other Members are seeking to demonstrate inconsistency between Members' measures under Article 5.5 and to suggest adequate and less trade-restrictive alternatives. The level of protection to be met in this instance is that determined by the Member and not that which may be inferred from the chosen measure.[32]

How Closely Does a WTO Member's Measure Have to Relate to the Available Science?

A greater constraint on national regulatory freedom arises from the obligation that measures be 'based on' risk assessment. To meet the demands of the SPS Agreement, there must be 'a rational relationship between the measure and the risk assessment'.[33] Rationality does not imply the need to adhere to mainstream scientific thinking. A minority scientific view can be considered a valid basis for a measure, provided 'the divergent opinion [is] coming from qualified and respected sources'.[34] Nevertheless, evidence pointing to potential general risk is not adequate. In order for a Member to draw upon the available science, it must be 'sufficiently specific to the case at hand'.[35] The adequacy of the scientific basis would have to be judged on a case-by-case basis.[36]

[29] *Hormones*, Appellate Body Report, para 172.

[30] *Australia—Salmon,* Appellate Body Report, para 205.

[31] *Australia—Salmon,* Appellate Body Report, para 197 (in which Australia characterised its appropriate level of protection as 'very conservative', whereas the prohibition in place ensured 'zero risk').

[32] *Australia—Salmon,* Appellate Body Report, para 203. However, if the Member has failed to sufficiently determine its level of protection, this may be inferred from the measure actually applied. See paras 206–207.

[33] *Hormones*, Appellate Body Report, para 193.

[34] *Hormones*, Appellate Body Report, para 194.

[35] *Hormones*, Appellate Body Report, para 200 (in which the general studies demonstrating an overall risk of cancer associated with hormones were not found to be an adequate basis for the EU's restrictions) and *Japan—Apples*, Appellate Body Report, para 202 (finding the 'general discussion' of fire blight in Japan's risk assessment not to constitute risk assessment within the meaning of Art 5.1).

[36] *Japan—Measures Affecting Agricultural Products*, Appellate Body Report (adopted 22 February 1999) WT/DS76/AB/R, para 84.

What Can WTO Members Consider an Appropriate Risk Assessment?

The requirement to draw on risk assessment, in turn, places under scrutiny the adequacy of the scientific evaluation used by a Member to justify measures. Risk assessment has been defined as 'a process characterized by systematic, disciplined and objective enquiry and analysis, that is, a mode of studying and sorting out facts and opinions'.[37] A Member does not have to undertake its own assessment, but can rely on an evaluation carried out by another Member or international body.[38] Article 5.2 provides a list of elements that can be taken into account in risk assessment, but this is not exhaustive. Factors 'not susceptible to quantitative analysis' can be equally relevant to a risk assessment.[39] Members are obliged to take into account risk assessment techniques developed by relevant international organisations, but are not compelled to replicate a particular form of risk assessment, which may be shaped in part by the level of protection chosen by the individual Member.[40] The risk that a Member seeks to analyse cannot be purely theoretical,[41] and the assessment again has to be adequately focused on that specific risk.[42]

When Can the WTO Member Take Provisional Measures?

In many cases, regulators find that scientific evidence is inconclusive, or that new research may bring into question previous understandings of risk. The Agreement creates the thankless task for a WTO Member or adjudicator of determining whether evidence is sufficient to be assessed in the normal way (under Article 2.2 and 5.1) or insufficient to permit the use of provisional measures (not based on risk assessment). The quantity of evidence, in itself, is not deemed to be determinant as 'a lot of scientific research has been carried out on a particular issue, without yielding reliable evidence'.[43] Nor is the fact that the science is controversial.[44] Furthermore, the existence of either an international standard or a broad scientific consensus does not mean *per se* that 'sufficient' scientific evidence is available within the mean-

[37] *Hormones,* Appellate Body Report, para 187.

[38] *Hormones,* Appellate Body Report, para 190.

[39] *Hormones,* Appellate Body Report, para 187.

[40] *United States/Canada—Continued Suspension of Obligations in the EC—Hormones Dispute (US—Continued Suspension),* Appellate Body Report (adopted 31 March 2008) WT/DS320/R, WT/DS321/R, paras 534 and 685.

[41] *Hormones*, Appellate Body Report, para 186.

[42] It is not sufficient, under Art 5.1, to undertake just *some* evaluation of the likelihood of the spread of disease, as Australian quarantine authorities were considered to have done in *Australia—Salmon*, if this evaluation leads only to 'general and vague statements'. *Australia—Salmon,* Appellate Body Report, para 129.

[43] *Japan—Measures Affecting the Importation of Apples*, Appellate Body Report (adopted 26 November 2003) WT/DS245/AB/R, para 185.

[44] *US—Continued Suspension*, Appellate Body Report, para 677.

ing of Article 5.7.[45] The finely determined requirement for recourse to Article 5.7 in cases of scientific controversy is that 'a qualified and respected scientific view … puts into question the relationship between the relevant scientific evidence and the conclusions in relation to risk thereby not permitting the performance of a sufficiently objective assessment of risk'.[46]

How Far Can a Member Deviate from International Standards?

Where a Member's measure 'conforms to' international standards, there is a (rebuttable) presumption of SPS consistency (Article 3.2).[47] However, a Member can choose either to 'base' a measure on international standards—incorporating some elements of the standard, but not others[48]—or to introduce an entirely unrelated measure which provides a higher level of protection than would be provided by the international standard. Where it does so, however, it must be supported by adequate risk assessment.[49] It is not entirely clear whether a measure providing a higher level of protection may nevertheless be considered to be based on an international standard, a claim that would potentially strengthen a Member's defence against a complainant.[50] A Member has an incentive to conform to international standards, but a failure to do so does not imply that the burden of proof is upon that Member to justify its deviation from the standard.[51]

As these examples indicate, the Agreement establishes a fundamental tension between, on the one hand, the national regulator's freedom to choose the measures deemed appropriate, and on the other, a notable scientific evidentiary burden. This book will explore the extent that this tension, so evident in abstraction, has in practice coloured the domestic regulatory process.

---

[45] *US—Continued Suspension*, Appellate Body Report, paras 695–696. In this case, the Panel had held that there is a need for a Member to bring forward a 'critical mass' of scientific evidence in order to demonstrate that previously sufficient scientific information is now insufficient. However, the AB ruled (at para 705) that the threshold implied, equivalent to a 'paradigm shift', was far too 'inflexible'.

[46] *US—Continued Suspension*, Appellate Body Report, para 677.

[47] A conforming measure is one that 'would embody an international standard completely and, for practical purposes, converts it into a municipal standard'. *Hormones*, Appellate Body Report, para 170.

[48] *Hormones*, Appellate Body Report, para 163.

[49] *Hormones*, Appellate Body Report, para 177.

[50] For a detailed discussion, see Gruszczynski (n 6) 96–100.

[51] *Hormones*, Appellate Body Report, para 102.

1.3 How the SPS Agreement's Influence Is Generally Portrayed

The particular focus of this book on the SPS Agreement's impact on domestic policy-making brings with it a danger of overstating the importance of this dimension in the research to date. Many analysts, it should be noted from the start, are not predominantly concerned with the question of 'impact'. In some cases, commentators primarily aim to explain the content and functioning of SPS law.[52] Such analysis does not endeavour to draw far-reaching conclusions about the effect of the Agreement.[53] Other studies focus on the detail of a single WTO dispute, not necessarily exploring its wider implications for domestic regulations.[54] Alternatively, the author's primary interest may lie in a specific area of food policy,[55] the overall operation of the WTO[56] or an aspect of the policy-making process.[57] In each case, the SPS Agreement forms a significant factor of the analysis undertaken, but the impact of law on domestic policy falls beyond the scope of these studies.

While clearly not all writers choose to reflect on the significance of the Agreement for national regulators, it is nevertheless a regularly recurring theme. Some commentators are hesitant about positing a direct link between international legal

[52] Pauwelyn's assessment of the SPS regime is exemplary in this respect, highlighting the significant aspects of the text, describing dispute-settlement findings and explaining the implications of the latter for an understanding of the Agreement's provisions. J Pauwelyn, 'The WTO Agreement on Sanitary and Phytosanitary (SPS) Measures As Applied in the First Three SPS Disputes' (1999) 2 JIEL 641. For this type of evaluation of Codex Alimentarius, see TP Stewart and DS Johanson, 'The SPS Agreement of the World Trade Organisation and International Organisations: The Roles of the Codex Alimentarius Commission, International Plant Protection Convention, and International Office of Epizootics' (1999) 26 *Syracuse Journal of International Law and Commerce* 27.

[53] Pauwelyn emphasises that 'no attempt is made to critically assess what has been decided [in dispute settlement]'. Pauwelyn (n 52) 642.

[54] For discussion of the *EC—Biotech* dispute, see S Poli, 'The EC's Implementation of the WTO Ruling in the Biotech Dispute' (2007) 32 EL Rev 705; S Lester and D Bodansky (ed), 'International Decisions: *European Communities-Measures Affecting the Approval and Marketing of Biotech Products*' (2007) 101 AJIL 453. On the *Hormones* dispute, see D Wüger, 'The Never-Ending Story: The Implementation Phase in the Dispute between the EC and the United States on Hormone-Treated Beef' (2002) 33 *Law and Policy in International Business* 777.

[55] See, e.g. JMM Akech, 'Developing Countries at Crossroads: Aid, Public Participation, and the Regulation of Trade in Genetically Modified Foods' (2006) 29 *Fordham International Law Journal* 265; AE Appleton, 'The Labelling of GM Products Pursuant to International Trade Rules' (2000) 8 *New York University Environmental Law Journal* 566; C Carlarne, 'From the USA with Love: Sharing Home-Grown Hormones, GMOs, and Clones with a Reluctant Europe' (2007) 37 *Environmental Law* 301.

[56] See PXF Cai, 'Between Intensive Care and the Crematorium: Using the Standard of Review to Restore Balance to the WTO' (2007) 15 *Tulane Journal of International and Comparative Law* 465 (discussing SPS jurisprudence at length in a study of the standard of review in the WTO dispute settlement process).

[57] J Atik, 'Science and International Regulatory Convergence' (1996) 17 *Northwestern Journal of International Law and Business* 736 (on the role of science in regulation).

obligations and domestic policy. For example, Kalderimis considers that attention paid to WTO compatibility will '*likely* define the [Genetically Modified Organism (GMO)] health policies of a number of countries'[58] and Peel argues that WTO rulings '*may* have far-reaching effects for the area of sanitary and phytosanitary (SPS) risk management'.[59] Others are far less diffident in claiming to have identified a decisive factor in policy formation. SPS rules are pronounced to have 'a significant impact'[60] and 'great implications'.[61] They are viewed as able to 'strike down domestic health regulation'[62] and 'constrain ... the domestic policy objectives member countries may pursue, and what policy tools member countries may use'.[63] The power of the SPS regime to impinge upon domestic control causes some dismay. It is perceived to undermine the existing practice of food regulation by 'unmistakably elevat[ing] the policing of trade restrictive measures above the ability of national governments to address risk'.[64] This will 'strip national regulators of their discretion',[65] 'choke the ability of a sovereign nation to decide how best to promote the values of its people'[66] and 'gobble all domestic laws that have any impact on in-

[58] D Kalderimis, 'Problems of WTO Harmonisation and the Virtues of Shields over Swords' (2004) 13 *Minnesota Journal of Global Trade* 305, 326 (emphasis added).

[59] J Peel, 'A GMO by Any Other Name… Might be an SPS Risk!: Implications of Expanding the Scope of the WTO Sanitary and Phytosanitary Measures Agreement' (2006) 17 EJIL 1009, 1011 (emphasis added).

[60] BA Silverglade, 'The WTO Agreement on Sanitary and Phytosanitary Measures: Weakening Food Safety Regulations to Facilitate Trade?' (2000) 55 *Food and Drug Law Journal* 517.

[61] MD Carter, 'Selling Science under the SPS Agreement: Accommodating Consumer Preference in the Growth Hormones Controversy' (1997) 6 *Minnesota Journal of Global Trade* 625, 655.

[62] J Bohanes, 'Risk Regulation in WTO Law: A Procedure-Based Approach to the Precautionary Principle' (2002) 40 *Columbia Journal of Transnational Law* 323, 356. See also O Aginam, 'Food Safety, South-North Asymmetries and the Clash of Regulatory Regimes' (2007) 40 *Vanderbilt Journal of Transnational Law* 1099, 1111 (claiming that WTO Members 'are often compelled to abandon the obligations they undertook in other pre-existing international regimes'); A Szajkowska, *Regulating Food Law: Risk Analysis and the Precautionary Principle as General Principles of EU Food Law* (Wageningen, Wageningen Academic Publishers, 2012) 59 (arguing that 'the system of trade rules aims to limit discretion as much as possible').

[63] LM Wallach, 'Accountable Governance in the Era of Globalization: The WTO, NAFTA, and International Harmonization of Standards' (2002) 50 *University of Kansas Law Review* 823, 827; DG Victor (n 11) 937 (claiming that the policy-maker's 'freedom is constrained'); See also G Skogstad, 'Internationalization, Democracy, and Food Safety Measures: The (Il)Legitimacy of Consumer Preferences' (2001a) 7 *Global Governance* 293, 295 (noting that '[t]he EU, in particular, finds compromised its policy autonomy and its capacity to render governments accountable').

[64] AO Sykes, 'Domestic Regulation, Sovereignty, and Scientific Evidence Requirements: A Pessimistic View' (2002) 3 *Chicago Journal of International Law* 353, 368.

[65] RA Pereira, 'Why Would International Administrative Activity Be Any Less Legitimate?—A Study of the Codex Alimentarius Commission' (2008) 9 *German Law Journal* 1693.

[66] S Keane, 'Can the Consumers' Right to Know Survive the WTO: The Case of Food Labelling' (2006) 16 *Transnational Law and Contemporary Problems* 291, 331.

ternational trade'.[67] Indeed, 'it is hard to imagine a greater intrusion on conventional notions of sovereignty.'[68]

What is striking is not only the certitude expressed by many of these analysts about the regime's impact, but the tone in which they convey their observations. Far from showing lawyerly detachment, their language is frequently tinged with menace, even violence, suggesting that the WTO has set in motion a change of dramatic proportions. The SPS Agreement acts as a 'wrecking ball',[69] initiating a 'clash of regulatory regimes',[70] and 'hangs like the proverbial sword of Damocles over national risk regulators'.[71] The enforcement of WTO rules is a 'procrustean' process[72] that 'cuts close to the heart of state sovereignty and domestic authority'[73] and leaves national measures like a 'fly caught in a spider's web'.[74] As Bloche has noted, the portrayal of the WTO agreements as 'implacable threats … constitutes pessimism bordering on panic'.[75] Given its recurrence, it is difficult to dismiss this language as mere rhetorical extravagance, an attempt to add a little colour to the insipid world of sanitary measures. Rather, the linguistic choices betray a deeper unease about the damaging grip of the SPS Agreement on national governance.[76]

Part I of this book explores why an international agreement, perceived to be of marginal importance by many regulators, has stirred such emotions among legal writers.

1.4 The EU Food Policy Context

The typical narrative of the development of EU food law—the domestic regulatory setting predominantly treated in this book—describes a clear shift in focus over time, from ensuring the operation of the Single Market to guaranteeing consumer

[67] D Schramm, 'The Race to Geneva: Resisting the Gravitational Pull of the WTO in the GM Labelling Controversy' (2007) 9 *Vermont Journal of Environmental Law* 93, 125.

[68] AT Guzman, 'Food Fears: Health and Safety at the WTO' (2004) 45 VJIL 1, 26.

[69] Shramm (n 67) 110.

[70] Aginam (n 62).

[71] A Arcuri, 'Food Safety at the WTO after Continued Suspension' in A Antoniadis, R Schütze and E Spaventa (eds), *The European Union and Global Emergencies–A Law and Policy Analysis* (Oxford, Hart Publishing, 2011). This echoes the language of Kalderimis who defines the defence of values in the SPS regime in terms of 'swords and shields'. Kalderimis (n 58).

[72] D Winickoff et al., 'Adjudicating the GM Food Wars: Science, Risk, and Democracy in World Trade Law' (2005) 30 YJIL 81, 93.

[73] Guzman (n 68) 24.

[74] HS Shapiro, 'The Rules That Swallowed the Exceptions: The WTO SPS Agreement and its Relationship to GATT Articles XX and XXI' (2007) 24 *Arizona Journal of International and Comparative Law* 199, 212.

[75] MG Bloche, 'WTO Deference to National Health Policy: Towards an Interpretive Principle' (2002) 5 JIEL 825, 827.

[76] See Cai (n 56) 538 (describing the 'generalised sense of outrage from thwarted sovereignty').

health and safety.[77] Over its first three decades of law-making, the EU's primary goal was to create a functioning internal market unencumbered by divergent national cultural and regulatory traditions. The initial strategy adopted was the development of 'vertical' directives: essentially, recipes for individual products, commencing with cocoa and chocolate in 1973. Early ambitions for this exercise were thwarted[78] by the technical complexity of establishing compositional rules, by the underlying diversity of national interests, and by the requirement of unanimous support of Member States for each vertical directive.[79] There was a change in strategic direction in 1985 with the launching of the Commission's 'New Approach' to legislating on foodstuffs, which recognised that defining the compositional requirements of individual foods was not essential to permitting free movement of trade.[80] This approach built on the rulings of the European Court of Justice (ECJ), most famously the findings in *Cassis de Dijon*, in which the Court confirmed that products 'lawfully produced and marketed' in the exporting state must be admitted into the importing state unless they were legitimate reasons (such as public health) for not doing so.[81] Nevertheless, because Member States could not be relied upon to respect this principle of mutual recognition in areas where domestic standards existed, the harmonisation process remained important[82] and was facilitated by the transition from unanimous to qualified majority voting in Council.[83] New legislative initiatives were driven by the economic imperatives of the market, rather than any coherent concept of food safety.[84]

This situation changed dramatically with the Bovine Spongiform Encephalopathy (BSE) crisis in 1996 when the consumption of infected beef was linked to the human neurodegenerative new variant Creutzfeldt–Jakob disease. The outbreak

---

[77] See, e.g. A Alemanno, *Trade in Food: Regulatory and Judicial Approaches in the EC and the WTO* (London, Cameron May, 2007) Chap. 1; BMJ van der Meulen, 'The System of Food Law in the European Union' (2009b) 14 Deakin Law Review 305, 313–320; RK O'Rourke, *European Food Law* (London, Sweet and Maxwell, 3rd edn, 2005); D Holland and H Pope, *EU Food Law and Policy* (The Hague, Kluwer Law International, 2004). Although this characterisation fairly reflects the overall trend, it underplays the attention paid to consumer health issues in the early years. See, e.g. D Welch, 'From "Euro Beer" to "Newcastle Brown", A Review of European Community Action to Dismantle Divergent "Food" Laws' (1983) 22 JCMS 47 (describing a 1976 Directive on eruric acid with entirely health-related aims).

[78] Of the around 50 vertical directives on different food sectors envisaged between 1969 and 1973, only 14 had been adopted by 1985. European Commission, 'Completion of the Internal Market: Community Legislation of Foodstuffs' ('Completion of Internal Market'), COM(85) 603 final, 3.

[79] See Alemanno (n 77) 53 and Welch (n 77) 57.

[80] European Commission, 'Completion of Internal Market' (n78) 5.

[81] Case 120/78, Rewe-Zentrale AG [1979], para 14. For comments on the implications of this case, see Alemanno (n 77) 39–42. Notwithstanding the importance of *Cassis de Dijon*, the principles articulated must be seen as the culmination of previous ECJ judgements and 'not a revolutionary case'. Welch (n 77) 62.

[82] Alemanno (n 77) 57.

[83] The Single European Act [1987] OJ L169/1, Art 100A.

[84] E Vos, 'EU Food Safety Regulation in the Aftermath of the BSE Crisis' (2000) 23 *Journal of Consumer Policy* 227, 231.

revealed in the starkest manner the institutional weaknesses in the management of European food safety. The European Parliament Committee created to establish the causes for the crisis produced a devastating account of mismanagement and deliberate manipulation.[85] The Commission responded quickly with a Green Paper establishing three central principles drawn from the BSE experience: separation of the responsibilities for science and legislation, detachment of the legislative and inspection functions, and greater transparency throughout the decision-making process.[86] The Commission took immediate steps to implement these principles, but further food-safety scandals, such as the Belgian dioxin contamination in 1999 (in which toxic oils had been found to have been deliberately fed to chickens), maintained pressure for wholesale reform.[87] The European Commission's 2000 White Paper on food safety provided a new vision for European food law, establishing the need for an independent scientific body and a plan of action including over 80 legislative measures.[88] Equally importantly, it provided the necessary impetus for this rapid overhaul.[89]

The most significant legislative output of this initiative was the General Food Law Regulation 178/2002 (GFL),[90] a comprehensive legal framework for food policy extending across all stages of production (known alternatively as the 'farm to fork' or 'plough to plate' approach). The GFL establishes consumer safety as a central objective of food law, but also protects against deceptive trade practices and ensures that accurate information is provided.[91] It places primary responsibility for legal compliance upon food (and feed) businesses, supported by a system of controls organised by Member States.[92] Risk analysis forms the basis of food law, the risk assessment element of which is undertaken by a newly established European Food Safety Authority (EFSA).[93] The Regulation formally introduces the

[85] Among the failings identified were: inadequate scientific resources, inappropriate political pressure from the UK government, uncoordinated responses between various Commission directorates, and a Commission 'policy of disinformation'. European Parliament, 'Report on alleged contraventions or maladministration in the implementation of Community law in relation to BSE, without prejudice to the jurisdiction of the Community and national courts' (A4-0020/97, 7 February 1997) in particular s A.I.C.

[86] European Commission, 'Commission Green Paper: The General Principles of Food Law in the European Union', COM (97) 176.

[87] O'Rourke (n 77) 6–7.

[88] European Commission, 'White Paper on Food Safety', COM (1999) 719 final.

[89] Chalmers notes that BSE-related failure 'was to achieve what years of harmonisation of laws had failed to manage. A new European politics of risk emerged'. D Chalmers, '"Food for Thought": Reconciling European Risks and Traditional Ways of Life' (2003) 66 MLR 532, 534. See also Holland and Pope (n 77) 21 (describing the Commission's vigorous pursuit of its White Paper timetable).

[90] Regulation (EC) 178/2002 of the European Parliament and of the Council laying down the general principles and requirements of food law, establishing the European Food Safety Authority and laying down procedures in matters of food safety [2002] OJ L31/1 (GFL).

[91] GFL, Art 5.

[92] GFL, Arts 17, 19 and 20.

[93] GFL, Art 6 (on risk analysis) and Chap. III (on EFSA).

'precautionary principle' into food law, a risk-management option which allows decision-makers to act in cases where potential risk exists, but where insufficient scientific data is available to undertake a full risk assessment.[94] Greater emphasis is also placed on the traceability of food, although the general obligation on operators is limited to identifying the immediately preceding and following steps in the food supply.[95] In addition, the new framework strives to improve transparency, encouraging increased involvement of stakeholders throughout the legislative process, with a view to securing consumer confidence in food law.[96]

The post-White Paper approach to food safety is a radical break with the past: food-safety concerns rather than Single Market demands henceforth dictate the legislative agenda.[97] To this end, and with the guidance of European Food Safety Authority, the EU systematically develops and updates legislation establishing limits for undesirable substances—such as pesticide residues and contaminants—in foodstuffs. Further legislative work is dedicated to authorising, again following scientific assessment, the marketing of various categories of food, including food additives, sweeteners, colours, novel foods and genetically modified organisms (GMOs): the SPS measures considered in Part II of this book fall predominantly within these areas of food law. In addition, the Commission may, where necessary, adopt emergency measures to respond to emerging food-safety incidents. Identification of such incidents is enhanced under the GFL by an improved Rapid Alert System which shares information among Member States in order to facilitate swift responses.[98] A final substantial field of work, but less relevant to the SPS context, is the regulation of information provided to the consumer, notably in the form of food labelling and nutrition and health claims.

As will already be clear, domestic events largely dictated the direction and pace of regulatory change in the EU. It has been claimed that the WTO also influenced the new legal framework,[99] but if so, this is in rather subtle ways. The GFL makes no direct reference to the SPS Agreement and related obligations,[100] but does enhance the status of international standards, which are to be 'taken into consideration' in the

---

[94] GFL, Art 7.

[95] GFL, Art 18.

[96] GFL, Chap. III, s 4.

[97] For example, one of the most notorious areas of non-harmonisation remains food supplements, but the Commission has initiated no new regulatory measures to address this failing. See European Commission, 'Staff Working Document—Situation in the Different Sectors', Accompanying Document to the Report from the Commission 27th Annual Report on Monitoring the Application of EU Law (SEC (2010) 1144) 386–387, ec.europa.eu/eu_law/docs/docs_infringements/annual_report_27/sec_2010_1143_en.pdf.

[98] GFL, Chap. IV, s 1.

[99] G Skogstad, 'The WTO and Food Safety Regulatory Policy Innovation in the European Union' 39 JCMS (2001) 485, 498.

[100] The closest the GFL comes to doing so is a recognition that the EU 'supports the principles of free trade in safe feed and safe, wholesome food in a non-discriminatory manner'. GFL, rec 23.

development of food law.[101] The language of the Regulation also, in places, mirrors that of international texts.[102] However, the GFL can be considered in many ways to have reinforced differences between EU and WTO approaches to food safety. For instance, it foresees a place for 'other legitimate factors' in developing food regulation ostensibly at odds with the strictly scientific approach enshrined in the SPS Agreement.[103] Likewise, the GFL provides a stronger legal basis for the use of the precautionary principle, whose articulation had already proved controversial in the WTO context.[104] While the EU's establishment of independent scientific advice has certainly strengthened its capacity to provide a WTO-compatible legal defence of its SPS measures, the pre-eminence of the consumer over the market in the new regulatory scheme may, if anything, have exacerbated existing tensions between European and WTO regulatory approaches.[105] It is these tensions between the SPS Agreement and EU food policy[106] that will be further investigated in Part II.

1.5 International Food Norm Generation

As van der Meulen has noted, several international organisations are now implicated in determining the way in which food is regulated nationally, essentially establishing a meta-framework for the governance of food safety.[107] The case studies presented in Part III of this book focus on two primary venues for norm generation: the SPS Committee and Codex Alimentarius. This section introduces the reader to these institutional settings.

---

[101] SPS Agreement Art 4. However, the EU can be considered somewhat to have diluted SPS obligations in this respect. See n 31 in Chap. 3 below.

[102] See, e.g. B van der Meulen, 'Science Based Food Law' (2009a) 1 *European Food and Feed Law Review* 58, 61 (noting 'that little doubt can exist that [SPS Agreement Art 5] has served the EU legislature as an example'). A concrete example is the definition of food, which is drawn from the Codex definition. See van der Meulen (n 77) 323.

[103] Alemanno (n 77) 404. The relationship between SPS rules and non-scientific considerations will be treated at length in Chap. 4.

[104] The Commission was far from timid in its strategy on this point: '[T]he Community has the objective to clarify and strengthen the existing WTO framework for the use of the precautionary principle in the area of food safety, in particular with a view to finding an agreed methodology for the scope of action under that principle.' 'Commission White Paper on Food Safety' (n 12) para 110.

[105] For an overview of the differences between the two, see Alemanno (n 77) pt IV.

[106] Member States have been unusually willing to relinquish national power over food policy. See O'Rourke (n 77) 9 (pointing in particular to the benefits for Member States of not being 'placed in the "firing line" by irate consumers concerned that they have put their health at risk'). For this reason, and given that harmonisation of foodstuffs is now highly advanced, it is legitimate to reflect, as Part II below will do, upon the impact of SPS law on EU policy objectives writ large rather than at a Member-State level.

[107] B van der Meulen, 'The Global Arena of Food Law: Emerging Contours of a Meta-Framework' (2010) 3 *Erasmus Law Review* 217.

1.5.1 SPS Committee

The SPS Committee, established under Article 12 of the SPS Agreement, is charged with facilitating the implementation of the Agreement and 'the furtherance of its objectives'. The Committee generally meets three times per year[108] and is composed of WTO Member delegations, comprising relevant officials of national food authorities or their Geneva-based colleagues, and invited observers.[109]

The SPS Committee broadly performs five functions. The first is to act as a conduit for the exchange of information on national regulatory developments. Detailed procedures for regulating this flow of information have been introduced and refined by the Committee.[110] The impact of these arrangements is in one sense undeniable. As of September 2013, 149 of the 159 WTO Members had established a single national 'notification authority' responsible for implementing notification procedures.[111] In total, these authorities had notified in excess of 12,000 sanitary and phytosanitary measures.[112] Yet, viewed globally, fulfilment of the SPS transparency commitments remains patchy,[113] and doubts remain as to whether non-notification owes more to a deliberate policy of concealment or to simple administrative neglect.[114] The SPS Committee also shares, as a standing item on its meetings' agenda, information about Member initiatives to secure recognition of the equivalence of SPS measures.[115] Oversight of this information sharing has been greatly enhanced since 2007 by the creation of an online SPS Management Information System, which permits rapid and targeted research.[116]

In addition to exchanging information, the Committee serves as a platform for the discussion of specific sanitary measures considered by WTO Members to be impinging upon trade. The number of new 'specific trade concerns' brought to the attention of the Committee each year has varied between 10 and 42.[117] Raising

[108] This has become the standard practice, although the Committee rules foresee a minimum of two meetings per year. WTO Document G/SPS/1 (4 April 1995) para 4.

[109] The standards setting bodies—Codex Alimentarius, International Plant Protection Convention (IPPC) and World Organization for Animal Health (OIE)—have a 'close working relationship' with the Committee, while other bodies such as the Agency for International Trade Information and Cooperation or the West African Economic and Monetary Union are invited on an *ad hoc* basis. See G/L/943, para 10–11 (11 November 2010).

[110] G/SPS/7/Rev.3 (20 June 2008).

[111] G/SPS/GEN/804/Rev.6 (7 October 2013) para 2.2.

[112] ibid para 3.3.

[113] 25 % of all regular notifications have been made by the US alone, while 33 % of Members have failed to submit any notification at all. See ibid para 15 and Table 1 respectively.

[114] RH Steinberg, 'The Hidden World of WTO Governance: A Reply to Andrew Lang and Joanne Scott' (2009) 20 EJIL 1063, 1064 (criticising the failure of Lang and Scott to weigh up 'the possibility that committee representatives may be strategically providing incomplete or inaccurate information'). Chap. 6 s 6.2 below provides some insights into the EU's behaviour in this respect.

[115] For a discussion of equivalence, see Chap. 6, s 6.3 below.

[116] The public part of this system is accessible via spsims.wto.org.

[117] G/SPS/53 (3 May 2010) para 90.

an issue in this way provides no guarantee of resolution. Nevertheless, approximately one third of those concerns raised since 1995 have been fully or partially resolved.[118] Moreover, efforts are underway to introduce a new procedure that will faciliate dialogue and the resolution of such problems with the help of the good offices of the Chairperson.[119] The contention of specific national regulations within the Committee has a dual function. Most obviously, it exposes Members perceived to be erring in their SPS duties to broader international scrutiny and applies pressure to justify their actions. But by debating the legitimacy of measures, Members also refine their collective understanding of the meaning and implications of the SPS framework.[120]

A third task of the Committee is 'to carry out the functions necessary to implement the provisions' of the regime.[121] Given this mandate, there is considerable scope for the Committee to seek operational solutions to the obstacles that arise during implementation, namely the creation of rules and procedures to clarify and facilitate the operation of the SPS regime.[122] In addition to the work on transparency referred to above, the Committee has developed a procedure to enhance transparency of special and differential treatment,[123] elaborated guidelines on the application of Article 5.5[124] and adopted a Decision on Equivalence.[125] The legal status of these procedures may be ambiguous,[126] but adopted by consensus, they serve *de facto* as the rules by which the behaviour of WTO Members is assessed.[127]

A fourth assignment of the Committee under Article 12.4 is to monitor harmonisation and the use of international standards. The Committee's work in this area has been unclear from the outset, not least as a similar (albeit largely unused) 'acceptance procedure' was already in place within Codex Alimentarius. Members

---

[118] ibid para 92 (noting also that the resolution of other issues may have occurred without being reported to the Committee).

[119] Disscussions relating to the implementation of SPS Agreement Art 12.2 have advanced, but the discussed procedure has not yet been adopted by the Committee. See G/SPS/W/259/Rev.7 (9 September 2013) for the latest recommendation.

[120] Through this process, Members 'arrive at settled (though not necessarily authoritative from the point of view of dispute settlement bodies) understandings'. J Scott, *The WTO Agreement on Sanitary and Phytosanitary Measures. A Commentary* (Oxford, OUP, 2007) 54.

[121] SPS Agreement Art 12.1.

[122] The pressure to fulfil this function is maintained through a built-in obligation (foreseen under Art 12.7) to review the operation of the Agreement. In April 2010, the Committee completed its third review in just over a decade. See generally G/SPS/53 (n 117).

[123] G/SPS/33 (2 November 2004).

[124] G/SPS/15 (18 July 2000).

[125] G/SPS/19 (26 September 2001).

[126] See ns 13–18 in Chap. 2 below and related text.

[127] Consider, most significantly, the approach of the Panel in *US—Poultry*, who noted that while the SPS Committee's Decision on Equivalence is not binding, 'we do consider that this Decision expands on the Member's own understanding of how Article 4 relates to the rest of the *SPS Agreement* and how it is to be implemented'). *United States—Certain Measures Affecting Imports of Poultry from China*, Panel Report (adopted 29 September 2010) WT/DS392/R, para 7.136.

consequently sought to avoid any unnecessarily duplication of this work.[128] As a result, the provisional procedure adopted for monitoring harmonisation focused on identifying specific problems associated with standards, either the non-use of existing standards by Members or the problematic non-existence of standards.[129] There are two obvious problems with this approach. Firstly, the standard-related problems that are identified also constitute 'specific trade concerns' and Members generally present them as such, rather than making recourse to the monitoring procedure.[130] Secondly, even were it not underutilised as at present,[131] the limited scope this procedure offers for identifying problems cannot really serve the original aims of assessing the progress of harmonisation. This is not to argue that the procedure as currently designed has no purpose. Steering Codex work's through emerging disputes can be extremely valuable.[132] However, reservations among Members about the current monitoring process are clear and a number of proposals for amendments have been put forward.[133] In particular, the revision of the notification procedures from 1 December 2008 to explicitly include information on the relevance of international standards to new measures offers a potential basis for reconceiving the Committee's work in this area.[134]

Finally, the SPS Committee has an important didactic role, providing technical assistance, primarily to developing-country Members, which can strengthen their capacity to meet SPS obligations. The Secretariat encourages WTO Members to identify their assistance needs and has organised over 250 workshops, seminars and other activities since 1994.[135] Such initiatives provide a very practical example of how SPS values and disciplines are inculcated into national regulatory systems.[136]

---

[128] See generally G/SPS/W/82 (23 June 1997).

[129] G/SPS/11/Rev.1 (15 November 2004) para 6.

[130] G/SPS/25 (1 July 2003) para 4.

[131] Between 2009 and 2012, for example, only one issue was referred to the Committee under the procedure, and even the legitimacy of this issue was questioned, as concerning regional rather than international standards. See G/SPS/54 (3 November 2010) para 15.

[132] For example, in a case involving Sri Lanka's exports of cinnamon to the EU, the absence of a Codex Standard on sulphur dioxide was identified as the cause of trade disruption and the Committee's requests to Codex on this issue were undoubtedly instrumental in resolving this dispute. See G/SPS/42 (4 August 2006) paras 4–9.

[133] A workshop on the relationship between the SPS Committee and the international standard-setting organisations held in October 2009 highlighted these issues. See the summary report G/SPS/R/57 (22 February 2010).

[134] The EU has proposed the creation of a 'new inventory mechanism' using information garnered by the new notification format. See G/SPS/GEN/970 (21 October 2009) para 8.

[135] G/SPS/GEN/521/Rev.8 (4 March 2013) para 4.

[136] The Committee's training efforts are aimed at 'those with responsibilities in the food safety, animal health or plant protection area within their national administrations…and other officials responsible for coordination of WTO trade issues and SPS matters within their governments.' G/SPS/GEN/521/Rev.5 (8 March 2010) para 9.

1.5.2 Codex Alimentarius Commission

The Codex Alimentarius Commission (CAC) was established in 1963, a joint initiative of the Food and Agriculture Organisation (FAO) and the World Health Organisation (WHO) aimed at developing and simplifying work on international standards.[137] The adopted food standards and other texts together form the Codex Alimentarius. Membership of the Commission is open to all those countries that are members of either of the two parent organisations.[138] While formally dependent on these organisations, in practice the CAC works relatively autonomously.[139] Regional membership is also permitted, although as yet, the EU is the only member of this sort, enjoying the right to present either an EU position (reflecting existing legislation) or a negotiated 'common position', depending on the issue under discussion.[140] Meetings are also attended by a large number of observers, representing 47 international governmental organisations and 135 non-governmental organisations (NGOs).[141] For the most part, the latter are industry bodies, a presence that has been a constant source of concern for commentators,[142] but which is downplayed by those most closely involved.[143]

Through its association with the SPS Agreement, the aim of the CAC's work is generally perceived to be to enhance international trade. Strictly speaking, Codex's work has a dual function of 'protecting consumers' health and ensuring fair practices in the food trade'. It is, then, through the publication of these standards that

[137] See the Report of the Joint FAO/WHO Conference on Food Standards held in October 1962, which established the framework for Codex's work (ALINORM 62/8) 5.

[138] See, Joint FAO/WHO Food Standards Program, *Codex Alimentarius Commission Procedural Manual* (Rome, FAO/WHO, 19th edn, 2010) (*Codex Manual*) 6.

[139] As Masson-Matthee points out, Codex Alimentarius Decisions are not submitted to the FAO and WHO although formally required to do so under the statutes, allowing the Commission to proceed on the basis of Member agreement. MD Masson-Matthee, *The Codex Alimentarius Commission and its Standards* (The Hague, TMC Asser Press, 2007).

[140] For an explanation of the EU's complex internal process of coordinating Codex positions, see ML Maier, 'The Regulatory State Goes Global: EU Participation in International Food Standard-Setting by the Codex Alimentarius Commission' (GARNET conference on 'The European Union in International Affairs', Brussels, April 2008) papers.ssrn.com/sol3/papers.cfm?abstract_id=1567705.

[141] An updated list of Members is available at www.codexalimentarius.net/web/organizations.jsp.

[142] Criticism of the underrepresentation of consumer interests in the Codex Committees has been a consistent theme of the literature on Codex. See, e.g. E Smythe, 'In Whose Interests? Transparency and Accountability in the Global Governance of Food: Agri-Business, the Codex Alimentarius and the World Trade Organization' in J Clapp and DA Fuchs (eds), *Corporate Power in Global Agrifood Governance* (Cambridge, MA, MIT Press, 2009) 98–99.

[143] An evaluation of the body undertaken in 2002 based on responses of Codex participants found that international NGO's involvement in decision-making was 'about right'. WB Traill et al., 'Report of the Evaluation of the Codex Alimentarius and Other FAO and WHO Food Standards Work' (Rome, FAO/WHO, 15 November 2002) www.fao.org/docrep/meeting/005/y7871e/y7871e00.htm.

Codex enhances harmonisation and facilitates international trade.[144] The distinction is a subtle one, but is important in demonstrating that Codex's priorities are dictated primarily by public-health needs and not trade problems.[145] Within this remit, the CAC has the responsibility for determining priorities, guiding the preparation of standards and ensuring the adoption and publication of final standards.[146] An Executive Committee assists the CAC in this task, managing the Commission's programme of standards development and making proposals. This Committee is made up of a group of 17 geographically representative Members.[147] The Commission is supported by a Secretariat provided by the FAO and a series of Codex committees and task forces.[148] Responsibility for chairing, organising, and financing each of these subsidiary bodies is given to a particular Codex Member who acts as a host country on a permanent basis.[149] These bodies are in turn supported by scientific expert bodies, most notably the Joint Expert Committee on Food Additives (JECFA), the Joint Meeting for Pesticide Residues (JMPR) and the joint FAO/WHO Expert Meetings on Microbiological Risk Assessment (JEMRA).

A defining feature of Codex's work is the emphasis placed on consensus as the basis of decision-making. According to its rules of procedure, the Commission 'shall make every effort to reach agreement on the adoption or amendment of standards by consensus'. Recourse may be made to voting, but 'only if … efforts to reach consensus have failed'.[150] Following the adoption of the SPS Agreement and the higher profile of Codex standards, there was a concern that the consensus approach would disintegrate. However, following a flurry of votes such as the controversial one on the milk hormone, Bovine Somatotropin (BST) in 1997, consensus was re-established as the norm.[151] The procedure for setting Codex standards is a complex affair, involving eight steps from the initial decision by the Commission to initiate work on a standard to the final decision (and potential vote) in Step 8. In between, a draft standard will be reviewed at least twice by the relevant Codex Committee, although it is not uncommon for draft texts to be returned to earlier steps for further

[144] See *Codex Manual* (n 138) 17 (General Principles of the Codex Alimentarius) para 1.

[145] However, as described above (see n 132), the SPS Committee will occasionally flag up issues deemed to be requiring attention by Codex.

[146] *Codex Manual* (n 138) 4 (Statutes of the Codex Alimentarius Commission) Art 1(c) and (d).

[147] *Codex Manual* (n 138) 9 (Rules of Procedure) Rule V.

[148] They include various types of committees: general subject committees (dealing with specific areas of food law, such as food labelling or pesticide residues), commodity committees (responsible for single products such as fruit or fish), coordinating committees (aimed at promoting issues specific to a given region) and *ad hoc* intergovernmental taskforces (assigned a specific task on a temporary basis, such as antimicrobial resistance). The review of active and dissolved committees can be found at www.codexalimentarius.net/web/committees.jsp.

[149] *Codex Manual* (n 138) 5 (Statutes of the Codex Alimentarius Commission) Art 9.

[150] *Codex Manual* (n 138) 14 (Rules of Procedure of the Codex Alimentarius Commission) Rule XII.

[151] The exception to this trend was a vote on the labelling of Emmental cheese in 2007. See DE Winickoff and DM Bushey, 'Science and Power in Global Food Regulation: The Rise of the Codex Alimentarius' (2010) 35 *Science, Technology and Human Values* 356.

reflection. While a laborious process, this procedure provides ample opportunity for Member comment and is therefore integral to the aims of adopting standards by consensus. An accelerated five-step procedure can be used with the agreement of the Commission, for example, where urgent problems related to trade or public health arise.[152] While the work of developing standards in Committee is often painstaking and tedious to those directly involved,[153] it has over the years excited considerable interest and criticism from the general public.[154]

1.6 Structure of the Book and Guidance to Readers

1.6.1 Structure

The book is divided into three parts. Part I illustrates and seeks to understand the scholarly criticism described above that emerged from the first decade or so of studying the SPS Agreement. Why did a near-consensus form among legal commentators on the constraining effect of the SPS regime and its negative implications on domestic policy-making? To answer this question, Part I takes a closer look at the way in which SPS obligations are studied by legal commentators. Chapter 2 first considers the process of evaluating the impact of SPS rules. It identifies three central analytical choices—field of enquiry, conception of how law functions and evaluative perspective—that underlie and ultimately shape any such assessment. A taxonomy of these choices is set out, providing a framework for characterising and categorising existing academic work in the field. Using this framework, Chap. 3 then proceeds with a review of legal literature on the SPS Agreement. This reveals a tendency towards analysis with three notable characteristics. Firstly, the field of enquiry is generally confined to the Agreement's text and related jurisprudence. Secondly, commentators predominantly adopt an assumption that international law will directly regulate the behaviour of states. Finally, in evaluating the functioning of the SPS Agreement, commentators tend to focus on its significance for national sovereignty, values and interests, largely sidelining its impact in terms of the Agreement's trade goals. This review concludes that it is the combination of these analytical choices that explains legal commentators' expectations about the SPS's influence over domestic policy-making and suggests that alternative analytical approaches could enhance understanding of the Agreement's effects.

To examine whether common claims about the SPS Agreement's impact are justified, Part II takes a fresh look at the role of SPS obligations in the development of EU food policy. Chapter 4 tests the prominent criticism that the SPS regime

[152] *Codex Manual* (n 138) 22 (General Principles of the Codex Alimentarius, Procedures for the Elaboration of Codex Standards and Related Texts) Introduction.

[153] This view is based on personal experience as Observer to meetings of the Codex Committee on General Principles in 2002 and 2004.

[154] See discussion of Codex's work on food supplements in Chap. 7, s 7.4 below.

instigates a policy-making culture that elevates science at the expense of other important social and cultural factors, re-examining both theoretical arguments and EU practice.[155] It finds that EU food policy in fact remains highly sensitive to social-value judgements, even where the scientific basis for such measures, and thus compatibility with WTO rules, remains tenuous. Chapter 5 examines in greater detail one specific regulatory measure, the management of 'novel foods' in the EU, in order to tease out the potential and limits of the WTO's influence on the policy-making process. The EU experience as recounted suggests that while influential, the Agreement's effect is more subtle and complex than is generally assumed.

Part III continues to evaluate the impact of the SPS Agreement on domestic policy makers, but focuses on the extent to which the Agreement has contributed to the transnational governance of food by converging international regulatory practices and facilitating dialogue between trading partners. With reference to EU practice, Chap. 6 considers the impact of two procedural SPS Agreement commitments—transparency and equivalence—that have been hitherto little discussed in the WTO SPS literature. It finds that although in some respects the EU may not fully comply with the obligations articulated in SPS rules, the Agreement has nevertheless set in motion new and important patterns of behaviour between trading partners that can have significant implications for domestic SPS measures. It suggests that sustained interaction between WTO Members is creating a new practice of cooperation and critical self-reflection on food policy. Chapter 7 reflects on the substantive impact of transnational governance, tracing the uptake of Codex Alimentarius norms across domestic legislation worldwide in two contested areas of food policy: food additives, and vitamin and mineral supplements. A complex picture emerges: the levels of attention paid to international norms vary widely across both countries and issues. The study confirms that international standards can contribute importantly to domestic regulations, but that their influence is neither automatic nor uniform.

This book therefore argues that evaluating and critiquing the SPS Agreement's impact simply in terms of its constraint on, and threat to, national sovereignty risks overlooking important aspects of its functioning. In particular, it emphasises the value of appreciating the regime's role as a catalyst for transnational governance of food regulations: shared knowledge, reflection, dialogue and potential problem-solving. A fuller awareness of both the possibilities and limits of transnational governance can enrich our overall assessment of the SPS regime and inform debate on textual, procedural or institutional reform.

1.6.2 Guidance to Readers

Were the reader to share my curiosity in the various topics—the epistemology of legal scholars, the dissemination of international norms through domestic policy-making, the fraught balance of risk and non-risk factors in EU food policy, the role

[155] Many of the case studies analysed in Parts II and III below have benefited from the insights of officials involved in the relevant dossiers. However, arguments are supported by citation of publicly available documents as far as possible.

and impact of international standards bodies, the EU's idiosyncratic regulation of certain food sectors—addressed in this volume, I could only advise them to read avidly and methodically through the entire book. However, accepting that such a predisposition is unlikely (and probably undesirable), the following pointers may be helpful. For scholars of international economic law, particularly those with a specific interest in the SPS Agreement, I would hope that Part I provides a thought-provoking reflection on how the SPS Agreement is analysed and resulting perceptions of the influence of WTO rules. Part II should also usefully complement, and to a certain extent challenge, existing accounts of SPS law. As Part II progresses and Part III continues, I can imagine some of the more legally inclined balking (although quite mistakenly I would argue) at the detailed accounts of domestic food regulations and policy practices. By contrast, for practitioners with an interest in food policy, the more academic considerations of Part I may seem alarmingly obscure and can be skipped with an entirely clear conscience. The latter two parts of the book illustrate the major influences of WTO law in domestic policy-making, and provide, through detailed case studies, an accessible introduction to SPS rules. Scholars from other disciplines, for example, those with an interest in risk regulation or the generation and dissemination of international norms more generally may well find valuable insights in Parts II and III respectively.

1.6.3 A Few Caveats

While ambitious, the reassessment that this book proposes is inevitably a partial one. Firstly, this research predominantly reflects on the impact of SPS law. Clearly, other WTO texts, most notably the TBT Agreement, may be instrumental in shaping domestic food regulation. Yet as specifically designed to address food regulations, one could reasonably expect the WTO's impact, if any, to be exerted through the SPS Agreement. Moreover, the book is restricted to just one area of the SPS Agreement's scope, namely food safety. The possibility cannot be discounted that greater attention to other fields of animal and plant health would significantly disrupt the portrayal of the Agreement set out below.[156] Secondly, though the final chapter strives to give a more global account of the influence of the SPS Agreement, the primary focus is predominantly, and unashamedly, on Europe. A detailed account of the experiences of the EU's trading partners in managing the expectations of the SPS Agreement would undoubtedly complement the work undertaken here. This book also studiously sidesteps the ongoing SPS Committee debate and burgeoning academic work on private non-governmental standards,[157] although the

[156] Indeed, Jacqueline Peel has highlighted the seemingly different approach or 'double standard' taken by the Appellate Body when faced with human health or quarantine risk issues. Peel (n 6) 449–452.

[157] See, e.g. SJ Henson, 'The Role of Public and Private Standards in Regulating International Food Markets' (2008) 4 Journal of International Agricultural Trade and Development 63; L Fulponi, 'Private Voluntary Standards in the Food System: The Perspective of Major Food Retailers in OECD Countries' (2006) 31 Food Policy 1. 'SPS-related private standards' has now become a

question of how the WTO manages to discipline these, either within or outside the SPS Agreement, will clearly be highly significant for the future efficiency of international agricultural trade. Finally, this study has resisted any inclination to address the crucial and ultimately most interesting question: whether the SPS Agreement's role in facilitating and controlling global trade is a contribution or an obstacle to the sustainable and secure production of food. Notwithstanding the efforts of this book, there is, Peel would no doubt be aghast to hear, much more to be written about the WTO Agreement on Sanitary and Phytosanitary Measures.

References

Aginam O, 'Food Safety, South-North Asymmetries and the Clash of Regulatory Regimes' (2007) 40 *Vanderbilt Journal of Transnational Law* 1099.

Akech JMM, 'Developing Countries at Crossroads: Aid, Public Participation, and the Regulation of Trade in Genetically Modified Foods' (2006) 29 *Fordham International Law Journal* 265.

Alemanno A, *Trade in Food: Regulatory and Judicial Approaches in the EC and the WTO* (London, Cameron May, 2007).

Appleton AE, 'The Labelling of GM Products Pursuant to International Trade Rules' (2000) 8 NYU *New York University Environmental Law Journal* 566.

Arcuri A, 'Food Safety at the WTO after Continued Suspension: A Paradigm Shift?' in A Antoniadis, R Schütze and E Spaventa (eds), *The European Union and Global Emergencies—A Law and Policy Analysis* (Oxford, Hart Publishing, 2011).

Atik J, 'Science and International Regulatory Convergence' (1996) 17 *Northwestern Journal of International Law and Business* 736.

Bloche MG, 'WTO Deference to National Health Policy: Towards an Interpretive Principle' (2002) 5 JIEL 825.

Bohanes J, 'Risk Regulation in WTO Law: A Procedure-Based Approach to the Precautionary Principle' (2002) 40 *Columbia Journal of Transnational Law* 323.

Cai PXF, 'Between Intensive Care and the Crematorium: Using the Standard of Review to Restore Balance to the WTO' (2007) 15 *Tulane Journal of International and Comparative Law* 465.

Carlarne C, 'From the USA with Love: Sharing Home-Grown Hormones, GMOs, and Clones with a Reluctant Europe' (2007) 37 *Environmental Law* 301.

Carter MD, 'Selling Science under the SPS Agreement: Accommodating Consumer Preference in the Growth Hormones Controversy' (1997) 6 *Minnesota Journal of Global Trade* 625.

Chalmers D, '"Food for Thought": Reconciling European Risks and Traditional Ways of Life' (2003) 66 MLR 532.

Cho S, 'International Decisions. *United States—Continued Suspension of Obligations in the EC—Hormones*' (2009) 103 AJIL 299.

Downes C, 'Only a Footnote? The Curious Codex Battle for Control of Additive Regulations' (2012) 7 *European Food and Feed Law Review* 232.

Drezner DW, *All Politics Is Global: Explaining International Regulatory Regimes* (Princeton, Princeton University Press, 2008).

Epps T, '*International Trade and Health Protection*' (Cheltenham, Edward Elgar, 2008).

Fulponi L, 'Private Voluntary Standards in the Food System: The Perspective of Major Food Retailers in OECD Countries' (2006) 31 *Food Policy* 1.

regular discussion point in SPS Committee meetings, see e.g. G/SPS/R/70 (8 May 2013) 23–24; G/SPS/R/71 (28 August 2013) 19–20.

Gruszczynski L, *Regulating Health and Environmental Risks under WTO Law: A Critical Analysis of the SPS Agreement* (Oxford, OUP, 2010).
Guzman AT, 'Food Fears: Health and Safety at the WTO' (2004) 45 VJIL 1.
Henson SJ, 'The Role of Public and Private Standards in Regulating International Food Markets' (2008) 4 *Journal of International Agricultural Trade and Development* 63.
Holland D and Pope H, '*EU Food Law and Policy*' (The Hague, Kluwer Law International, 2004).
Kalderimis D, 'Problems of WTO Harmonisation and the Virtues of Shields over Swords' (2004) 13 *Minnesota Journal of Global* 305.
Keane S, 'Can the Consumers Right to Know Survive the WTO?: The Case of Food Labeling' (2006) 16 *Transnational Law and Contemporary Problems* 291.
Lester S and Bodansky D (ed), 'International Decisions: *European Communities-Measures Affecting the Approval and Marketing of Biotech Products*' (2007) 101 AJIL 453.
Maier ML, 'The Regulatory State Goes Global: EU Participation in International Food Standard-Setting by the Codex Alimentarius Commission' (GARNET conference on 'The European Union in International Affairs', Brussels, April 2008).
Masson-Matthee MD, '*The Codex Alimentarius Commission and its Standards*' (The Hague, TMC Asser Press, 2007).
Mercurio B and Shao D, 'A Precautionary Approach to Decision Making: the Evolving Jurisprudence on Article 5.7 of the SPS Agreement' (2010) 2 *Trade Law and Development* 195.
O'Rourke R, '*European Food Law*' (London, Sweet and Maxwell, 3rd edn, 2005).
Pauwelyn J, 'The WTO Agreement on Sanitary and Phytosanitary (SPS) Measures As Applied in the First Three SPS Disputes' (1999) 2 JIEL 641.
Peel J, 'A GMO by Any Other Name… Might be an SPS Risk!: Implications of Expanding the Scope of the WTO Sanitary and Phytosanitary Measures Agreement' (2006) 17 EJIL 1009.
Peel J, 'Review: *Regulating Health and Environmental Risks under WTO Law: A Critical Analysis of the SPS Agreement*. By Lukasz Gruszczynski' (2011) 23 *Journal of Environmental Law* 157.
Peel J, 'Of Apples and Oranges (and Hormones in Beef): Science and the Standard of Review in WTO Disputes under the SPS Agreement' (2012) 61 ICLQ 47
Pereira RA, 'Why would International Administrative Activity Be Any Less Legitimate?—A Study of the Codex Alimentarius Commission' (2008) 9 *German Law Journal* 1693.
Poli S, 'The EC's Implementation of the WTO Ruling in the Biotech Dispute' (2007) 32 EL Rev 705.
Prévost D and van den Bossche P, 'The Agreement on the Application of Sanitary and Phytosanitary Measures' in PFJ Macrory, AE Appleton and MG Plummer (eds), *The World Trade Organisation: Legal, Economic and Political Analysis* (Berlin, Springer, 2005).
Rothberg SJ, 'From Beer to BST: Circumventing the GATT Standards Codes Prohibition on Unnecessary Obstacles to Trade' (1990) 75 *Minnesota Law Review* 505.
Schramm D, 'The Race to Geneva: Resisting the Gravitational Pull of the WTO in the GMO Labelling Controversy' (2007) 9 *Vermont Journal of Environmental Law* 93.
Scott J, '*The WTO Agreement on Sanitary and Phytosanitary Measures. A Commentary*' (Oxford, OUP, 2007).
Shapiro HS, 'The Rules That Swallowed the Exceptions: The WTO SPS Agreement and Its Relationship to GATT Articles XX and XXI' (2007) 24 *Arizona Journal of International and Comparative Law* 199.
Silverglade BA, 'The WTO Agreement on Sanitary and Phytosanitary Measures: Weakening Food Safety Regulations to Facilitate Trade?' (2000) 55 *Food and Drug Law Journal* 517.
Skogstad G, 'Internationalization, Democracy, and Food Safety Measures: The (Il)Legitimacy of Consumer Preferences' (2001a) 7 *Global Governance* 293.
Skogstad G, 'The WTO and Food Safety Regulatory Policy Innovation in the European Union' (2001b) 39 JCMS 485.
Smythe E, 'In Whose Interests? Transparency and Accountability in the Global Governance of Food: Agri-Business, the Codex Alimentarius and the World Trade Organization' in J Clapp and DA Fuchs (eds), *Corporate Power in Global Agrifood Governance* (Cambridge, MA, MIT Press, 2009).

Steinberg RH, 'The Hidden World of WTO Governance: A Reply to Andrew Lang and Joanne Scott' (2009) 20 EJIL 1063.
Stewart TP, '*The GATT Uruguay Round: A Negotiating History (1986–1994)*' (The Hague, Kluwer Law International, 1999).
Stewart TP and Johanson DS, 'The SPS Agreement of the World Trade Organisation and International Organisations: The Roles of the Codex Alimentarius Commission, International Plant Protection Convention, and International Office of Epizootics' (1999) 26 *Syracuse Journal of International Law and Commerce* 27.
Sykes AO, 'Domestic Regulation, Sovereignty, and Scientific Evidence Requirements: A Pessimistic View' (2002) 3 *Chicago Journal of International Law* 353.
Szajkowska A, '*Regulating Food Law: Risk Analysis and the Precautionary Principle as General Principles of EU Food Law*' (Wageningen, Wageningen Academic Publishers, 2012).
Traill WB, Bedouin R, Gourlie K, Husch J and Lustre A, 'Report of the Evaluation of the Codex Alimentarius and Other FAO and WHO Food Standards Work' (FAO/WHO, 15 November 2002).
van der Meulen BMJ, 'Science Based Food Law' (2009a) 1 *European Food and Feed Law* 58.
van der Meulen BMJ, 'The System of Food Law in the European Union' (2009b) 14 Deakin Law Review 305.
van der Meulen B, 'The Global Arena of Food Law: Emerging Contours of a Meta-Framework' (2010) 3 *Erasmus Law Review* 217.
Victor DG, 'The Sanitary and Phytosanitary Agreement of the World Trade Organisation: An Assessment After Five Years' (2000) 32 *New York University Journal of International Law and Politics* 865.
Vos E, 'EU Food Safety Regulation in the Aftermath of the BSE Crisis' (2000) 23 *Journal of Consumer Policy* 227.
Wallach LM, 'Accountable Governance in the Era of Globalization: The WTO, NAFTA, and International Harmonization of Standards' (2002) 50 *University of Kansas Law Review* 823.
Welch D, 'From "Euro Beer" to "Newcastle Brown": A Review of European Community Action to Dismantle Divergent "Food" Laws' (1983) 22 JCMS 47.
Winickoff DE and Bushey DM, 'Science and Power in Global Food Regulation: The Rise of the Codex Alimentarius' (2010) 35 *Science, Technology and Human Values* 356.
Wirth D, 'The Role of Science in the Uruguay Round and NAFTA Trade Disciplines' (1994) 27 *Cornell International Law Journal* 817.
Wüger D, 'The Never-Ending Story: The Implementation Phase in the Dispute between the EC and the United States on Hormone-Treated Beef' (2002) 33 *Law and Policy in International Business* 777.

Part I
What Lawyers Expect from the SPS Agreement and Why

Chapter 2
Evaluating the Impact of International Law: A Taxonomy of Analytical Choices

Abstract The SPS Agreement is commonly adjudged by legal commentators to place a constraint on domestic policy-makers and therefore threaten WTO members' legitimate policy preferences. This chapter takes a first step to understanding why this view has come to dominate writing on SPS rules. It identifies and discusses three major analytical choices—field of enquiry, conception of how law functions and evaluative perspective—that, consciously or not, shape the evaluation of the *impact* of law. Firstly, the analyst decides the appropriate object of study (field of enquiry), for example, formal texts, domestic legal practice or the social effects of regulations that will significantly inform the conclusions drawn about the rules under study. Secondly, a conception of how international law functions will determine expectations as to the consequences of the legal regime. In particular, those viewing law as 'regulating' domestic actors will anticipate different outcomes to those focussing on the 'generative' potential of law to instil new ideas and behaviour. Finally, the commentator may choose to study the impact of international rules from the 'ascending' perspective of the State, for example, its implications on sovereignty or national values, or alternatively from the 'descending' perspective of the legal regime, that is, the furthering of its stated goals. This choice of perspective will bring to fore different aspects of the functioning of rules. The chapter finally draws together these dimensions to form a taxonomy of analytical choices which creates a framework for assessing commentary on the SPS Agreement.

2.1 Introduction

The view of the World Trade Organisation (WTO) Agreement on the Application of Sanitary and Phytosanitary Measures (SPS Agreement) as a constraint on, and potential threat to, domestic policy-making is a prominent theme among legal commentators.[1] What lies at the root of this scholarly anxiety surrounding the SPS Agreement? Howse and Mavroidis explain the disquiet as follows:

[1] See Chap. 1, s 1.3 above.

C. Downes, *The Impact of WTO SPS Law on EU Food Regulations,* Studies in European Economic Law and Regulation 2, DOI 10.1007/978-3-319-04373-9_2,

> Many of the controversies about the effect of WTO law on domestic regulation have been influenced by the view that the law as it stands may well impede the ability of governments to regulate new and uncertain risks to health and the environment.[2]

If, as these authors imply, consternation about the SPS Agreement results from the particular 'view' adopted over a decade of study, we may speculate as to the possible consequences of an alternative perspective. In order to understand the claim that the SPS Agreement constrains domestic policy-making, we should first seek greater insight into the reasoning that sustains the view of it that is generally taken.

With this end in mind, Part I of this book scrutinises existing scholarly study of the Agreement, and in particular the views of law that inform it, before turning to a direct evaluation of the Agreement's impact in Parts II and III. As the approach taken in Part I is unusual in legal scholarship, it perhaps requires further explanation. After all, if we are concerned with the impact of international law, surely the answers lie 'out there' and not in extended academic introspection? Self-reflection may be justified on a number of grounds, however. The notion that commentators of diverse origins, backgrounds and intellectual persuasions share a common view of law seems improbable, and therefore is an intriguing topic for further investigation in itself. At the very least, we need to verify whether there is indeed a scholarly way of approaching the Agreement, which can explain the divergence noted between academic and bureaucratic perceptions of the regime. If such a common approach is identified, we need to then reflect on how this may colour our understanding and expectations of the Agreement. In turn, this will help, in Parts II and III of this book, to stake out new ground, rather than succumbing to what Joel Trachtman has described as 'one of the pathologies of international economic law', namely 'to cover ground that has already been covered'.[3] Given that the SPS Agreement has proved bizarrely inspirational in recent years and the scholarly output relatively large, the danger of duplicating the work of others is particularly acute. To escape this pathology therefore requires a more detailed examination of both the subject of study and the assumptions underlying it.

Chapter 2 strives to facilitate such a review by identifying the fundamental analytical choices associated with any attempt to define the influence of the SPS Agreement. The question at the heart of this enquiry—what is the Agreement's impact on domestic policy-making?—seems simple enough, but cannot be addressed, even superficially, without assuming a position on three analytical dimensions. Firstly, a commentator must choose what evidence is relevant to an understanding of the Agreement's effect. For example, is it enough to examine the text of the Agreement itself, or must we scrutinise domestic behaviour in order to assess its significance? A decision about the appropriate *field of enquiry* will determine the basic scope of any analysis. Secondly, in order to comment on the effect of international law on domestic

---

[2] R Howse and PC Mavroidis, 'Europe's Evolving Regulatory Strategy for GMOs—The Issue of Consistency with WTO Law: Of Kine and Brine' (2000) 24 *Fordham International Law Journal* 317.

[3] JP Trachtman, 'International Economic Law Research: A Taxonomy' in C Picker, I Brunn and D Arner (eds), *International Economic Law: The State and Future of the Discipline* (Oxford, Hart Publishing, 2008) 43.

policy, a view must be taken on how the two interrelate. Without a hypothesis about this relationship, the possibility of impact can be neither postulated nor dismissed. A *conception of how law functions* therefore forms a second dimension of any analysis. A third choice when examining the influence of the Agreement is to decide on what impact one wishes to assess. Does the analyst's interest lie in the extent to which the Agreement has attained its intended goals or is it rather what it implies for a state's capacity to manage domestic SPS issues? While the investigation of the former may reveal something of the latter (and *vice versa*), the nature of the enquiry will differ significantly according to this third dimension, the *evaluative perspective* adopted. The seemingly simple question posed above thus spans three complex issues: how does law really influence state behaviour, what should we be evaluating and how?

This chapter examines the main alternatives available to analysts in each of the three dimensions identified. In so doing, it sets out a taxonomy of analytical choices, using which we can start to characterise and categorise existing legal study of the SPS Agreement.

2.2 Focus of Research: Field of Enquiry

Embarking upon a study of the SPS Agreement and its relationship with domestic policy-making, a primary consideration will be where one's enquiry should begin and end. This decision may be influenced by simple practicalities. What information is freely available? How much time does such a study merit? In addition, however, the scope of analysis chosen will probably reflect a deeper conviction, instinctive or elaborated, as to what elements are relevant to understanding a legal regime. This section considers three alternative approaches to this issue: formalism, empiricism and critical theory.

2.2.1 Formalism

Formalism views law as 'a body of rules with fixed determinate meaning', and its practitioners strive for the 'identification of a definitive assessment of "what international law says"'.[4]

For a formalist, an understanding of the SPS Agreement is to be found primarily in the texts of the Agreement[5] and the decisions arising from the World Trade

[4] SJ Anaya, 'Divergent Discourses about International Law, Indigenous Peoples, and Rights over Lands and Natural Resources: Toward a Realist Trend' (2005) 16 *Colorado Journal of International Environmental Law and Policy* 237, 244.

[5] See Art 31 of the Vienna Convention on the Law of Treaties: 'A treaty shall be interpreted in good faith in accordance with the ordinary meaning to be given to the terms of the treaty in their context and in the light of its object and purpose.' Vienna Convention on the Law of Treaties, 23 May 1969, S Exec Doc L, 92-1 (1970), 1155 UNTS 331 (entered into force on 27 January 1980) (VCLT).

Organization's (WTO) dispute-settlement mechanism.[6] As one moves beyond these sources, however, views can diverge sharply as to what is relevant to ascertaining the meaning of the Agreement. Some consider the WTO to be a 'self-contained' legal system, one that is 'closed' from obligations arising from international law.[7] Others reject this notion, arguing that the WTO 'is not a secluded island but part of the territorial domain of international law'.[8] According to this view, not only the immediate WTO Agreements, but all sources contained in Article 38(1) of the Statute of the International Court of Justice can be relevant to the meaning of WTO texts.[9] Moreover, measures which are *prima facie* legal according to WTO provisions may nevertheless be illegal where in breach of other international agreements.[10] Whatever the textual merits of either argument, as has been noted (and lamented[11]), the trend in dispute-settlement bodies is towards the latter 'incorporative' approach to non-WTO law.[12]

In addition to this long-standing debate, formalists face the added complexity in interpreting the SPS Agreement of the evident importance, but ambiguous legal status, of two related normative sources. The first is Codex Alimentarius standards,[13]

[6] Although not *de jure* having precedential quality, the jurisprudence is widely construed to be critical *de facto* to interpretation. See R Bhala, 'The Precedent Setters: *De Facto Stare Decisis* Fact in WTO Adjudication (Part Two of a Trilogy)' (1999) 9 *Journal of Transnational Law and Policy* 1.

[7] The expression 'self-contained' has been the general shorthand for describing this perspective on WTO law. See JP Kelly, 'Judicial Activism at the World Trade Organization: Developing Principles of Self-Restraint' (2002) 22 *Northwestern Journal of International Law and Business* 353, 357. The WTO Dispute Settlement Understanding (DSU) lends itself to this view of WTO law, stressing throughout that dispute settlement applies to the 'covered agreements' and 'serves to preserve the rights and obligations of Members under the covered agreements' (Art 3(2)), but also see Arts 7(2) and 11. Understanding on Rules and Procedures Governing the Settlement of Disputes, 15 April 1994, UNTS, vol 1869, 401.

[8] J Pauwelyn, 'The Role of Public International Law in the WTO: How Far Can We Go?' (2001) 95 AJIL 535, 552. See also A Lindros and M Mehring, 'Dispelling the Chimera of Self-Contained Regimes: International Law and the WTO' (2005) 16 EJIL 857.

[9] In brief, Art 38(1) sources are international conventions, international custom, general principles of law, judicial decisions and the teachings of publicists. Statute of the International Court of Justice, 26 June 1945, 59 Stat 1055, 33 UNTS 993. Palmeter and Mavroidis argue that the terms of reference established by Art 7 of the DSU (to 'address the relevant provisions in any agreement or agreements signed by the parties to the dispute') establishes this article as 'the WTO substitute, *mutatis mutandis*, for Article 38'. D Palmeter and PC Mavroidis, 'The WTO Legal System: Sources of Law' (1998) 92 AJIL 398, 399.

[10] Pauwelyn (n 8) 551 (giving the example of a trade right that must be foregone due to the agreement of a later environmental rule).

[11] JP Kelly, 'Naturalism in International Adjudication' (2008) 18 *Duke Journal of Comparative and International Law* 395, 412.

[12] See JL Dunoff, 'The WTO in Transition: Of Constituents, Competence and Coherence' (2001) 33 *George Washington International Law Review* 979, 992; Lindros and Mehring (n 8) 866–873.

[13] The focus here is only on food-related standards and not the other international standards referred to in SPS Annex A, para 3.

non-binding in themselves, but 'hardened'[14] by their inclusion in the SPS Agreement as an appropriate reference point in considering the legality of sanitary measures. The second is decisions agreed by the Committee on Sanitary and Phytosanitary Measures (SPS Committee), the body formally mandated to 'carry out the functions necessary to implement the provisions of this Agreement'.[15] Adopted by consensus, some of the latter closely resemble formal legal texts, establishing clear obligations (of what Members *shall* do), while others deliberately constrain their own legal significance.[16] Both standards and SPS Committee decisions appear to be integral to establishing the propriety of WTO Member actions, while their legal standing remains questionable. The Vienna Convention on the Law of Treaties (VCLT) offers some partial solutions to this dilemma for formalists. For example, depending on the interpretation required, Codex standards could be 'informative' sources which help in the interpretation of the SPS Agreement's 'ordinary meaning',[17] while SPS Committee decisions may constitute 'subsequent agreement between the parties' under VCLT Article 31(3)b.[18]

For present purposes, the puzzle of precisely which norms are valid in the appreciation of SPS Agreement obligations need not be resolved. Whilst one approach may be more true to formalism than another,[19] even the more inclusive method is still formalist. In other words, whether drawing exclusively from dispute settlement reports or extrapolating from Codex standards, there is a common premise that the meaning and significance of the SPS Agreement is to be derived from such written sources.

2.2.2 *Empiricism*

For some scholars, the narrow interpretation of legal sources alone provides an unnecessarily arid view of law. Why undertake an abstract evaluation of a WTO treaty, when that text only has real meaning in the domestic context in which it is

---

[14] For a discussion of the implications of 'soft' and 'hard' norms, see H Hillgenberg, 'A Fresh Look at Soft Law' (1999) 10 EJIL 499, 504. See also GC Shaffer and MA Pollack, 'Hard vs. Soft Law: Alternatives, Complements, and Antagonists in International Governance' (2010) 94 *Minnesota Law Review* 706.

[15] SPS Agreement Art 12.1.

[16] For an extensive discussion on the legal status of SPS decisions, see J Scott, *The WTO Agreement on Sanitary and Phytosanitary Measures. A Commentary* (Oxford, OUP, 2007) 70–72.

[17] VCLT Art 31(1). This was the approach taken by the *EC—Biotech* panel, for example, in defining 'pests'. See *EC—Measures affecting the Approval and Marketing of Biotech Products (EC—Biotech)*, Panel Report (adopted 29 September 2006) WT/DS/291–293/R, para 7.238. For a critique of the Panel's methods in this respect, see MA Young, 'The WTO's Use of Relevant Rules of International Law: An Analysis of the Biotech Case' (2007) 56 ICLQ 907, 918.

[18] See Scott (n 16) 73 and fn 141.

[19] Ultimately, as Koskenniemi notes, 'anything can be labelled 'formalism' because the term is purely relational'. M Koskenniemi, 'What is International Law?' in MD Evans (ed), *International Law* (Oxford, OUP, 2003) 101.

(or is not) enacted?[20] Instead, we should consider the 'multifaceted ways in which legal norms are disseminated, received, resisted "on the ground"'.[21] Alternatively labelled New Legal Realism, the 'new' New Haven School and sociolegalism, such scholarship broadly shares a shift of analytical focus from law as derived from legal texts, towards law's meaning within society.[22] The generic term of 'empiricism' will be used here to describe this second field of enquiry. Escaping the shackles of formalist thinking is seen by many as liberating. Empirical study is believed to bring 'new facts, [allowing us to] see existing ideas through a different lens'[23] and furnish a 'better understanding of the world in which law operates'.[24] How would an empirical study of the SPS Agreement differ from a formalist one? There are three aspects to the answer.

Firstly, a view that 'international law is happening all around'[25] naturally leads empirical researchers to turn to non-formal sources. There appear to be no particular limitations as to where empiricists should turn their attention. Statements that reveal important attitudes towards law, evolutions in policy-making,[26] the behaviour of actors in the domestic system,[27] and the interrelationship of state and non-state law-making[28] illustrate just some of the possible avenues for exploring legal impact. Indeed, an eclectic approach is itself viewed as an important catalyst in fostering new insights.[29]

Secondly, lawyers must find new methods for managing the newly generated data. A qualitative approach—describing in depth the impact of law using data in specific cases—is felt to provide a heightened level of scrutiny of the issue

---

[20] GC Shaffer, 'A New Legal Realism: Method in International Economic Law Scholarship' in C Picker, I Brunn and D Arner (eds), *International Economic Law: The State and Future of The Discipline* (Oxford, Hart Publishing, 2008) (*International Economic Law*) 41.

[21] Paul Schiff Berman, 'Law and Globalisation' (2005) 43 *Columbia Journal of Transnational Law* 485, 492.

[22] See BG Garth, 'Introduction: Taking New Legal Realism to Transnational Issues and Institutions' (2006) 31 *Law and Social Inquiry: Journal of the American Bar Foundation* 939 (on new legal realism); LA Dickinson, 'Toward a "New" New Haven School of International Law?' (2007) 32 YJIL 547; Berman, ibid (on sociolegal scholarship).

[23] SD Franck, 'Empiricism and International Law: Insights for Investment Treaty Dispute Resolution' (2008) 48 VJIL 767, 771.

[24] Shaffer (n 20) 42.

[25] JK Levit, 'Bottom-Up Lawmaking through a Pluralist Lens: ICC Banking Commission and Transnational Regulation of Letters of Credit' (2008) 57 *Emory Law Journal* 1147, 1150.

[26] See, e.g. SH Cleveland, 'Human Rights Sanctions and International Trade: A Theory of Compatibility' (2002) 5 JIEL 133.

[27] R Goodman and D Jinks, 'International Law and State Socialisation: Conceptual, Empirical, and Normative Challenges' (2005) 54 *Duke Law Journal* 983, 995 (discussing the exploitation of human rights norms by private citizens).

[28] Levit (n 25).

[29] Describing the new generation of empirical work, Dickinson notes that 'these scholars seem to share a common commitment not to adhere too strictly to any particular method or model, but to try and to understand the complexity and plurality of the forces at work in the world.' Dickinson (n 22) 552.

concerned.[30] Although such studies are relatively infrequent in international law, well-documented economic institutions such as the WTO are viewed as particularly amenable to such research.[31] This type of study is certainly more favoured than a quantitative empirical approach which applies statistical methods, such as regression, to available data. The latter is treated with some caution even by advocates of empirical research,[32] and with considerable scepticism elsewhere.[33]

Thirdly, empirical-based work is often associated with a commitment among its practitioners to improving the functional operation of international law. Indeed, Garth argues that this type of research is 'by definition concerned with promoting social change'.[34] There is certainly a normative drive to much empirical work, be it advancing policy reform,[35] institutional change[36] or simply reasserting the importance and effectiveness of international law.[37] However, while new legal realists may share a belief in the transformative power of international law, it is not clear why this should necessarily be the case. Empirical accounts are equally capable of undermining the status of international law.[38]

2.2.3 *Critical Theory*

Critical theory, the third field of enquiry discussed here, shares the doubts of empiricists about the value of formalism. However, instead of assessing the operation

---

[30] Franck (n 23) 786.

[31] M Hoffman and K Topulos, 'Tyranny of the Available: Under-Represented Topics, Approaches, and Viewpoints' (2008) 35 *Syracuse Journal of International Law and Commerce* 175, 195.

[32] See OA Hathaway, 'The New Empiricism in Human Rights: Insights and Implications' (2004) 98 *American Society of International Law Proceedings* 206, 207 and Shaffer (n 20) 34.

[33] See DJ Bederman, 'Constructivism, Positivism, and Empiricism in International Law' (2007) 89 *Georgetown Law Journal* 469 (criticising Anthony Arendt's attempt at quantitative analysis); G Verdirame, '"The Divided West": International Lawyers in Europe and America' (2007) 18 EJIL 553, 561 (lamenting the tendency of these studies to 'restate the obvious, confirm the well known or repeat the commonsensical'). For a concrete example of the limitations of empirical studies, see JW Yackee, 'Conceptual Difficulties in the Empirical Study of Bilateral Investment Treaties' (2008) 33 *Brooklyn Journal of International Law* 405.

[34] Garth (n 22) 944.

[35] See Hathaway (n 32) 210 (asserting that empirical research 'must be linked to concrete policy recommendations').

[36] See, e.g. GC Shaffer, 'The World Trade Organization Under Challenge: Democracy and the Law and Politics of the WTO's Treatment of Trade and Environment Matters' (2001) 25 *Harvard Environmental Law Review* 1 (discussing the creation of a World Environment Organisation); R Goodman and D Jinks, 'How To Influence States: Socialization and International Human Rights Law' (2004) 54 *Duke Law Journal* 621, 703 (seeking to 'improv[e] the capacity of global and domestic institutions to harness the process through which human rights cultures are built').

[37] Dickinson sees the creation of a counter-narrative to growing scepticism towards international law as an integral element of this empiricism-based scholarship. Dickinson (n 22) 552.

[38] Consider, for example, the sceptical portrayal presented in JL Goldsmith and EA Posner, *The Limits of International Law* (Oxford, OUP, 2005).

of law in reality, critical theorists strive to lay bare the realities that led to, and are ultimately concealed by, law. They attempt to

> undo the naturalness of conventional ways of thinking about law and proceed to show us that the way we conceptualize it binds us to ... commitments which may or may not be ones that we like to make.[39]

Such critiques have a dual focus. There is firstly an analysis of law itself: that is, the way that law captures and reasserts a certain understanding of social reality.[40] Secondly, the lawyers who perpetuate the 'conventional ways of thinking' are also the subject of critical analysis.[41] By adopting and furthering the categories imposed by dominant legal discourse in an uncritical fashion, lawyers are guilty of 'entrenching the bias'.[42] These critiques form what Koskenniemi describes as the 'negative aspect' of the critical programme.[43] The 'positive aspect' consists of a common engagement to identify social injustice with a view to advancing social transformation.[44] This requires lawyers to challenge existing dogma and start to reconceptualise international law.[45]

International trade law would appear to be fertile ground for critical theorists. A number of contestable notions are essential to the cohesiveness of the WTO project and arguably sanitise what are highly inequitable arrangements.[46] The term 'contracting parties' wrongly signifies a free and comparable input into trade

---

[39] M Koskenniemi, *From Apology to Utopia: The Structure of International Law* (Cambridge, CUP, 2005) 541.

[40] See D Kennedy, 'A New Stream of International Law Scholarship' (1988) 7 *Wisconsin International Law Journal* 1.

[41] Roman, for example, points to positivists' 'failure to question the underpinnings and normative values of their doctrinal formulations [which] renders their laws to be limited, incoherent, anachronistic, and apologistic attempts to be objective in spite of historical occurrences.' E Roman, 'Reconstructing Self-Determination: The Role of Critical Theory in the Positivist International Law Paradigm' (1999) 53 *University of Miami Law Review* 943, 949.

[42] J Ngugi, 'Making New Wine for Old Wineskins: Can the Reform of International Law Emancipate the Third World in the Age of Globalisation?' (2002) 8 *UC Davis Journal of International Law and Policy* 73, 76. See also S Dillon, 'Opportunism and the WTO: Corporations, Academics and "Member States"' in *International Economic Law* (n 20) 57 (underlining how WTO literature dominated by a focus on disputes obscures the social realities of the WTO).

[43] Koskenniemi (n 39) 540–541.

[44] As Koskenniemi notes, this is theoretically speaking inherently difficult for the critical theorist whose own solutions for countering hidden domination, may be, in itself, the imposition of another form of oppression. ibid 541.

[45] Authors who take up this challenge include M Mutua, 'Critical Race Theory and International Law: The View of an Insider-Outsider' (2000) 45 *Villanova Law Review* 841, 851 and CG Gonzalez, 'Deconstructing the Mythology of Free Trade: Critical Reflections on Comparative Advantage' (2006) 17 *Berkeley La Raza Law Journal* 65, 72.

[46] See MH Davis and D Neacsu, 'Legitimacy, Globally: The Incoherence of Free Trade Practice, Global Economics and their Governing Principles of Political Economy' (2001) 69 *University of Missouri, Kansas City Law Review* 733, 737 (showing how 'law legitimises its unstated assumptions ... the underlying economic system').

negotiations,[47] 'globalisation' falsely implies a process of change beyond the control of specific vested interests,[48] and 'trading nations' conceals the role of multinational business in establishing the WTO agenda.[49] For a critical theorist, the SPS Agreement would appear to offer specific scope for scrutiny. One of the driving aims of the Agreement, harmonisation, has been described as 'a benign sounding concept that, in reality, robs nations of the ability to choose legal regimes appropriate to their level of economic development'.[50] Likewise, the neutrality of science, which assumes a prominent place in the operation of the SPS Agreement, is highly contested.[51] Notwithstanding this potential, it has been noted that critical theory's contribution to the study of the WTO in general has been relatively meagre.[52]

As this discussion on alternative fields of enquiry demonstrates, prior assumptions as to what should form the object of study will significantly shape the type of research undertaken. The field of enquiry adopted by the commentator will not in itself determine answers as to the impact of the SPS Agreement. However, the range of elements scrutinised, be they formal texts, domestic practice or social reality will significantly inform the scope of any conclusion.

2.3 Conception of How Law Functions

The analyst who moves beyond the descriptive, that is, who attempts not only to identify what law *is*, but also reflect on its influence on society, must hold certain expectations as to how international law functions. Without a conception of how the legal regime and WTO Members interrelate, it is not possible to posit the impact of the regime upon domestic society.

To sketch out the choices available to the analyst, it is helpful to borrow a conceptualisation of international society more familiar within international-relations theory. If international interaction (or law) is considered 'societal structure' and states are 'agents', the relationship between the two can be conceived in three ways.

---

[47] ibid 743–744.

[48] UU Ewelukwa, 'Centuries of Globalisation; Centuries of Exclusion: African Women, Human Rights, and the "New" International Trade Regime' (2005) 20 *Berkeley Journal of Gender, Law and Justice* 75, 84.

[49] Dillon (n 42) 63.

[50] Davis and Neascu (n 46) 764.

[51] Orford notes that the increasing value placed upon science is

> premised upon a gendered and racialised hierarchy of knowledge, in which Western science is treated as value-free, objective, impartial and rational, while other forms of knowledge are dismissed as emotive, partial, subjective, and irrational.

A Orford, 'Contesting Globalization: A Feminist Perspective on the Future of Human Rights' (1998) 8 *Transnational Law and Contemporary Problems* 172, 188.

[52] Dillon (n 42) 63 (claiming that scholarship on the WTO offers 'scarcely a whiff of critical legal studies, feminism or postmodernism').

The simpler analytical method is to focus on one of the elements, either structure or agents, and proceed on the basis that the one determines the other.[53] We could thus firstly postulate, as realists do, that international law is entirely constituted by the actions and interests of states: states will behave according to their own interests and international law will not have any independent impact on state behaviour.[54] Alternatively, one could presuppose that societal structure dictates the action of agents, in which case law would be expected to 'regulate' state behaviour.[55] However, the relationship can also be treated in a third, more dynamic way, and one that acknowledges that states and international law are 'mutually constituted'.[56] From this perspective, we can understand international law only through the actions and intentions of states, but national interests and the state's very identity are themselves shaped by international law. This 'generative'[57] conception of how law functions opens up the possibilities of studying social interaction between states, and generates more fluid expectations as to the ultimate influence of law. As our interest here is in the impact rather than non-impact of law, this section will sideline the realist perspective to concentrate in turn on the regulative and generative conceptions of how law functions.

2.3.1 Regulative Function

A regulative conception of international law casts the WTO Agreement as 'a set of rules guiding and constraining the behaviour of governments'.[58] However, while the meaning of 'constraining' the state is relatively straightforward, the particular process through which this occurs is less obvious. There are three particular accounts: coercive, strategic and normative.

Coercive Force

'Coercion' may appear an unpromising way to describe the mechanism by virtue of which states comply with the law. In the absence of credible, enforceable sanctions,

---

[53] A Wendt, 'The Agent-Structure Problem in International Relations Theory' (1987) 4 *International Organization* 335, 339.

[54] See J Goldsmith and EA Posner, 'The New International Law Scholarship' (2006) 34 *Georgia Journal of International and Comparative Law* 463.

[55] ATF Lang, 'Some Sociological Perspectives on International Institutions and the Trading System' in *International Economic Law* (n 20) 73.

[56] Wendt (n 53) 339.

[57] The term is used by Brunnée and Toope, drawing on the work of Lon Fuller, to describe an alternative view of law 'not as hierarchical ordering but as an ongoing generative activity, oriented toward the construction of relatively stable patterns of practices'. J Brunnée and SJ Toope, 'The Changing Nile Basin Regime: Does Law Matter?' (2000) 43 *Harvard International Law Journal* 105, 110.

[58] Lang (n 55) 73.

an understanding of international law in these terms has long been disfavoured. The very lack of sovereign control famously led Austin to cast doubt over the legal status of international law.[59] While this challenge to international law has since been rebutted,[60] the empirical validity of the Austinian argument has not been contested. Ultimately, '[t]here is no world policeman to command or coerce obedience to international law rules.'[61] Strictly speaking, the WTO changes nothing in this account.[62] Yet, while no world policeman, the WTO dispute-settlement mechanism enjoys an unparalleled reputation as an effective mechanism for securing changes in behaviour. Leading authors and functionaries have characterised the WTO's dispute settlement as 'very, very powerful',[63] 'robust'[64] and 'impressive',[65] and have celebrated 'its unique enforcement power'.[66] The coercion variant of the regulative conception of law remains a convincing narrative for many.

Strategic Choice

An alternative explanation for the expectation that international law 'regulates' state behaviour is offered by game theory.[67] According to this rationalist account, a legal regime created by states establishes important benefits for cooperation, but also (through monitoring and sanctions such as retaliation) significant costs for non-compliance.[68] Over time, the state's interests become increasingly 'enmeshed' in

---

[59] J Austin, *The Providence of Jurisprudence Determined* (Indianapolis, Hackett, 1998) 142.

[60] See A D'Amato, 'Is International Law Really "Law"?' (1985) 79 *Northwestern University Law Review* 1293 (in particular challenging the idea that enforcement is essential to domestic legal systems at 1293–1297); TM Franck, 'Legitimacy in the International System' (1988) 82 AJIL 705 (criticising the importance placed on this coercive element).

[61] DJ Bederman, 'Counterintuiting Countermeasures' (2002) 96 AJIL 817, 818.

[62] As Matsushita writes: 'Unlike domestic courts, the WTO is not equipped with the power to coerce non-complying parties to comply with its requirements by means of imposing fines or imprisonment.' M Matsushita, 'The Sutherland Report and its Discussion of Dispute Settlement Reforms' (2005) 8 JIEL 623, 624.

[63] JH Jackson, 'The Role of International Law in Trade' (2004) 36 *Georgetown Journal of International Law* 663, 664.

[64] S Charnovitz, 'The World Trade Organization in 2020' (2005) 1 *Journal of International Law and International Relations* 167, 175.

[65] C-D Ehlermann and L Ehring, 'The Authoritative Interpretation under Article IX:2 of the Agreement Establishing the World Trade Organization: Current Law, Practice and Possible Improvements' (2005) 8 JIEL 803, 809.

[66] Comments by P Sutherland, J Sewell, and D Weiner cited in GP Sampson, 'Is There a Need for Restructuring the Collaboration among the WTO and UN Agencies so as to Harness their Complementarities?' (2004) 7 JIEL 717, 724.

[67] See, e.g. AT Guzman 'A Compliance-Based Theory of International Law' (2002) 90 *California Law Review* 1826; ET Swaine, 'Rational Custom' (2002) 52 *Duke Law Journal* 559.

[68] See J Talberg, 'Paths to Compliance: Enforcement, Management, and the European Union' (2002) 56 *International Organization* 609, 612.

the legal regime amplifying the costs of non-compliance.[69] In the case of the SPS Agreement, this would suggest that WTO Members will, for the most part, adhere to the rules, as they have a long-term interest in doing so. From this perspective, the 'power' of the WTO, and expectation of compliance, essentially lies in the extent to which states' interests are locked into the trading regime.

Normative Function

Notwithstanding claims that a 'major generational change' towards a rationalist paradigm for international legal scholarship has occurred,[70] many international lawyers would anticipate a regulative effect of law without any calculation of the specific advantages states may have in compliance.[71] Instead, the expectation is that states pay attention to international rules as a result of a normative obligation, 'a sense that they *ought* to be followed'.[72] This premise is most famously captured in that fundamental norm of international law: '*pacta sunt servanda*'.[73]A satisfactory explanation as to why states feel this normative pull to keep their promises remains elusive.[74] The point here is not to establish or deny this phenomenon. Rather, it is to note that this view of law—that states take obligations seriously[75]—is itself taken seriously, not least by legal scholars.[76] The latter is less puzzling. Whatever disappointments arise about the effectiveness of international law, lawyers remain epistemologically inclined to accept the specificity of law[77] and retain a professional

---

[69] See CR Kelly, 'Enmeshment as a Theory of Compliance' (2005) 37 *New York University Journal of International Law and Politics* 303.

[70] J Goldsmith and EA Posner (n 54) 465.

[71] It is possible to argue that these norm-based approaches 'still predominate in the international legal academy in both the United States and Europe'. K Anderson, 'Remarks by an Idealist on the Realism of the Limits of International Law' (2006) 34 *Georgia Journal of International and Comparative Law* 253, 254–255.

[72] A Chayes and AH Chayes, *The New Sovereignty* (Cambridge, MA, Harvard University Press, 1995) 113 (emphasis in original).

[73] VCLT, Art 26.

[74] See Anderson (n 71) 256 (referring to the 'ghost-in-the-machine character of traditional norm-based law') and Chayes and Chayes (n 72) 116 (noting that international law 'has an enormously complex derivation that stubbornly resists specification').

[75] This view is reflected in Henkin's well-known dictum that 'almost all nations observe almost all principles of international law and almost all of their obligations almost all of the time' L Henkin, *How Nations Behave: Law and Foreign Policy* (London, Pall Mall Press, 1968) 42.

[76] Chayes and Chayes argue that this is 'the practice of states, and of diplomats, international lawyers, political theorists, journalists, and others who think [about state obligations] professionally'. Chayes and Chayes (n 72) 118.

[77] FV Kratochwil, *Rules, Norms, and Decisions* (Cambridge, CUP, 1989) 200–205.

interest in advancing its distinctiveness.[78] Indeed, some have argued it is the duty of lawyers to honour this normative commitment.[79]

Of course, even at a theoretical level, faith in the regulative power of law is not as complete as the above summary may suggest. Rationalists would not predict that international law inevitably leads to compliance, but would rather expect states to defect from international rules 'when the stakes are sufficiently high'.[80] Likewise, scholars who recognise the normative force of law acknowledge that compliance will be conditional on factors such as the legitimacy of the rules[81] and the clarity of meaning and transparency of procedures established by a regime.[82] Yet as Lang has observed, in the context of the WTO, such reflections are less common, due to a perception of the heightened 'salience' of WTO obligations.[83] Whereas in other highly contested regimes the impact of normative obligations remains doubtful, the WTO—'the envy of international lawyers'[84]—appears to inflate expectations of law's regulative force. Whether it is the result of rational calculation, deep-seated professional epistemological commitments, or intuition about the WTO's power, trade lawyers regularly assume that states will comply with their international obligations.

2.3.2 Generative Function

A fundamental criticism of the regulative conception of law is that it offers a very limited perspective on the influence that law exerts. As Finnemore and Toope argue:

> Law in this view is constraint only; it has no creative or generative powers in social life. Yet law working in the world constitutes relationships as much as it limits acceptable behaviour.[85]

[78] M Finnemore, 'Are Legal Norms Distinctive?' (2000) 32 *New York University Journal of International Law and Politics* 699, 704.

[79] See J Klabbers, 'The Relative Autonomy of International Law or the Forgotten Politics of Interdisciplinarity' (2005) 1 *Journal of International Law and International Relations* 35, 42 (recommending that lawyers 'must cherish and preserve the relative autonomy of the law, for a law that has lost its autonomy ceases to be law'); P Allott, 'The International Lawyer in Government Service: Ontology and Deontology' (2005) 23 *Wisconsin International Law Journal* 13, 22 (describing lawyers as belonging to 'a surreptitious priesthood [with] an ideal allegiance, as servants of law').

[80] JO McGinnis and ML Movsesian, 'The World Trade Constitution' (2000) 114 *Harvard Law Review* 511, 569.

[81] See TM Franck, *The Power of Legitimacy Among Nations* (New York, OUP, 1990) Chap. 1.

[82] Chayes and Chayes (n 72) Chap. 6.

[83] A Lang, 'Re-thinking Trade and Human Rights' (2007) 15 *Tulane Journal of International and Comparative Law*335, 349.

[84] J Alvarez, 'How Not to Link: Institutional Conundrums of an Expanded Trade Regime' (2001) 7 *Widener Law Symposium Journal* 1.

[85] M Finnemore and SJ Toope, 'Alternatives to "Legalisation": Richer Views of Law and Politics' (2001) 55 *International Organization* 743, 745.

It is, for instance, international law that establishes a state's identity as a meaningful actor[86] offering, in the case of the WTO, the possibility of participating in a structured framework in which states can manage trade issues. Viewed in this way, law does not directly determine behaviour, but sets in motion a social process of interaction and provides common reference points through which the behaviour of others can be interpreted.[87] It is during this process that a new understanding of law is generated.[88] The agreement of a treaty is therefore considered—contrary to the logic of regulative assumptions about law—as the beginning and not the end of the law-making process. As with the regulative conception of law, there are different explanations of the process that takes place, most prominently socialisation and cognitive change.[89]

Socialisation

In research on the interaction of states, two particular social mechanisms are singled out for attention: persuasion and social influence.[90] 'Persuasion' is the process whereby states within a regime work to change the preferences of others. This can be through illuminating the opportunities associated with adherence to new norms, framing norms in a way that is acceptable to recalcitrant states or highlighting particularly relevant elements of the norm.[91] Through argumentation, even states initially opposed to international norms can become 'entrapped' into a rational review of their behaviour.[92]A common characteristic of this process is that the state consciously reassesses its position.[93] By contrast, 'social influence' refers to the psychological implications of maintaining behaviour that differs from the norm. A state acting under social influence does not re-evaluate its preferences, but rather seeks to alleviate the discomfort generated by non-conformity with international norms. States will accordingly moderate their positions to garner the esteem of others[94]

---

[86] AC Arend, 'Do Legal Rules Matter? International Law and International Politics' (1998) 38 VJIL 107, 130–133.

[87] See Brunnée and Toope (n 85) 68 (describing law as 'a purposive enterprise'); Lang (n 55) 87 (characterising law as 'a venue for the production and exchange of innovative policy learning').

[88] See Berman's discussion of sociolegal scholarship which highlights how 'legal categories become reflected in ordinary discourse and thought.' PS Berman, 'Seeing beyond the Limits of International Law' (2006) 84 *Texas Law Review* 1265, 1281.

[89] To explain these processes, the following sections draw on the work of both international-relations and international-law scholars.

[90] See AI Johnston, 'Treating International Institutions as Social Environments' (2001) 45 *International Studies Quarterly* 487.

[91] ibid 469–498.

[92] T Risse, '"Let's Argue!": Communicative Action in World Politics' (2000) 54 *International Organization* 1, 32.

[93] Goodman and Jinks (n 36) 643.

[94] M Finnemore, 'International Norm Dynamics and Political Change' (1998) 52 *International Organization* 887, 903.

or to escape the shame or notoriety associated with actions viewed as illegal.[95] In the day-to-day management of international regimes, both these sets of processes—persuasion and social influence—are considered to be integral to instigating compliance.[96]

Cognitive Change

While broadening our understanding of how law functions, the socialisation perspective underplays one element of its constructivist foundations, namely intersubjectivity. Constructivists consider that states, through interaction, reform the social structure within which state actions take place. States develop what are variously described as 'collective knowledge',[97] 'intersubjective beliefs'[98] and 'collective understandings',[99] through which they make sense of international society. When applied to legal norms, this insight offers different expectations to those created in relation to socialisation. Whereas the very assumption of the latter is that a state adjusts to established norms,[100] shared understandings are intersubjective and their evolution unpredictable. As a result, research oriented towards cognitive frameworks cannot presume compliance as such. Indeed, as an understanding of law and its meaning change over time, the whole concept of compliance is itself problematic.[101]

As this section has demonstrated, alternative conceptions of how international law functions involve different expectations as to how states will behave in a legal regime. A generative understanding of law can involve more fluid expectations. It anticipates change over time as states are either persuaded into adopting new forms of behaviour or, as a result of interaction with other states, reconceive both international society and their role within it. This is in sharp contrast to a regulative

[95] HH Koh, 'Transnational Legal Process' (1996) 75 *Nebraska Law Review* 181, 204. For a concrete example of the shaming process, see Moravcsik's review of the implementation of human rights in Europe. A Moravcsik, 'Explaining International Human Rights Regimes: Liberal Theory and Western Europe' (1995) 1 *European Journal of International Relations* 157, 161.

[96] Chayes and Chayes consider persuasion to be the more preponderant of these two processes, but note that 'if the party consistently fails to respond, the possibility of diffuse manifestations of disapproval or pressures from other actors in the regime is present in the background.' Chayes and Chayes (n 72) 26.

[97] Wendt (n 53) 399.

[98] JG Ruggie, 'What Makes the World Hang Together? Neo-Utilitarianism and the Social Constructivist Challenge' (1998) 52 *International Organization* 855, 869.

[99] JW Legro, 'Which Norms Matter? Revisiting the "Failure" of Internationalism' (1997) 51 *International Organization* 31, 33.

[100] See A Alkolby, 'Theories of Compliance with International Law and the Challenge of Cultural Difference' (2008) 4 *Journal of International Law and International Relations* 151, 194; Johnston (n 90) 494.

[101] B Kingsbury, 'The Concept of Compliance as a Function of Competing Conceptions of International Law' (1998) 19 *Michigan Journal of International Law* 345, 359.

understanding of law which, be it presented in coercive, strategic or normative terms, maintains high expectations of compliance with WTO law.

2.4 Evaluative Perspective

Combined, the two analytical dimensions already discussed—field of enquiry, and conception of how law functions—generate expectations of how international norms will infiltrate domestic society. But how do we judge this anticipated outcome? What conclusions can be drawn? A judgement could simply reflect the normative views of the author.[102] Yet, what distinguishes lawyers' analysis from non-legal commentary is that the anticipated functioning of law is measured against the purposes and intentions of the lawmakers.[103]

Koskenniemi notes that there are two ways of arguing about international legal obligations. The first is to consider that international rules are superior to and override individual State's interests. The second is to argue that as sovereign states must give their consent to international laws, these laws must reflect state interests. Each is vulnerable to criticism by the other. In the absence of adequate state support for the international norm, the former 'descending' perspective is considered 'utopian'. The latter 'ascending' perspective, in that it disregards norms that do not reflect state behaviour, becomes an 'apology' for state power. In Koskenniemi's view, it is the resulting 'incoherent argument which constantly shifts between the opposing positions [that] provides the dynamics of international legal argument'.[104] A similar incoherence can apply in the evaluation of the impact of the SPS Agreement.[105] WTO Members have given their consent to disciplines which by definition limit their sovereign control. Yet, it is precisely this constraint which many commentators, as

[102] It is possible for the outcome of dispute-settlement decisions to be evaluated simply according to the authors' particular view of the issue at hand. A critic of biotechnology, for example, may lament the panel's decision in *EC—Biotech* on the illegitimacy of EU Member State safeguard measures.

[103] Koskenniemi describes this expectation as 'the persisting intuition that legal argument somehow follows a logic which is external to lawyers' preferences or those of their social group'. Koskenniemi (n 39) 67.

[104] ibid 60.

[105] A good example of this inherent tension can be seen in Croley and Jackson's discussion of the common plea for WTO dispute-settlement bodies to take a more deferential approach towards national policy choices:

> Standing alone, the argument that deferential review is necessary to protect authorities' national sovereignty fails to acknowledge that some balance between authorities' interest in protecting their sovereignty, on the one side, and the broader interest in realising the gains of international coordination, on the other, must be struck. The argument proves too much, in other words, as it unwittingly challenges the very rationale of the GATT/WTO itself.

SP Croley and JH Jackson, 'WTO Dispute Procedures, Standard of Review, and Deference to National Governments' (1996) 90 AJIL 193, 212.

we saw in Chap. 1 find disconcerting. A discussion about the impact of the Agreement is therefore subject to the same argumentative logic identified by Koskenniemi. Either one accepts the premise that SPS norms override state interests and evaluate the achievements of the regime from this descending perspective; or one adopts an ascending perspective that assesses the SPS regime from the standpoint of state interests.

In relation to the SPS Agreement, it is not self-evident where either an ascending or descending perspective would lead. Reflection on the SPS Agreement's performance with reference to its purpose is complicated by the surprising level of ambiguity about precisely what this is. Likewise, viewing the operation of the Agreement from the standpoint of the 'state' will depend very much on how the latter is characterised. Each argumentative perspective therefore permits a diverse range of evaluations. This section explores possible angles of analysis that may emerge within both ascending and descending perspectives, drawing on the wider literature of international economic law.

2.4.1 Ascending Perspective

Koskenniemi identifies as the basic unifying assumption of the ascending perspective that '[i]f State practice, will and interest point in some direction, the law must point in that direction too.'[106] But even among commentators sympathetic to this basic premise, there are likely to be disparate views about what is essential to the state, and therefore where international law should be pointing. Writing on the WTO contains three prominent variants of the ascending perspective, focusing respectively on sovereign power, state values and state will.

Sovereign Power

For some commentators, the state's particular significance lies in its 'sovereignty', or power to make its own policy decisions.[107] The primary interest from this perspective is in the WTO's capacity to enhance or usurp this power. Three challenges are particularly prominent. Firstly, dispute-settlement bodies retain the potential to scrutinise the domestic policy process, considered by some to be an intrusion upon

[106] Koskenniemi (n 39) 59.

[107] While the notion of sovereignty is contested, in the context of work on the WTO the term is widely understood to reflect interest in the 'allocation of power'. See, e.g. JH Jackson, 'The Great 1994 Sovereignty Debate: United States Acceptance and Implementation of the Uruguay Round Results' (1997) 36 *Columbia Journal of Transnational Law* 157; K Raustiala, 'Rethinking the Sovereignty Debate in International Economic Law' (2003) 6 JIEL 841; D Saroshi, 'Sovereignty, Economic Autonomy, United States, and the International Trading System: Representations of the Relationship' (2004) 15 EJIL 651.

sovereignty.[108] The SPS and TBT Agreements in particular (with their discipline of administrative processes) seem to invite the second-guessing and overturning of a state's underlying rationale for regulations.[109] Secondly, as the WTO text leaves gaps that require interpretation, there is an opportunity for Panels to perform a legislative role elaborating new rules,[110] a process that inevitably removes power from the state,[111] although views differ as to the extent to which such judicial activism will occur.[112] The third challenge to national sovereignty concerns the way in which the WTO can empower international bodies which had a previously marginal influence on domestic policy.[113] Enhancing their role can lead to the 'practical devolution of decision-making authority…[,] the essence of the loss of national sovereignty'.[114] The extent to which states still retain sovereign power over these bodies will depend largely on their ability to participate in global governance.[115]

State Values

For others, the significance of the state lies in its role as a guarantor of values considered important to society. While closely linked to the sovereignty critique, this particular focus places emphasis on the substantive implications of WTO law rather than the locus of decision-making. The literature on the relationship between trade and non-trade values is vast and the detail of this debate is not relevant here. In short, there has been a concerted academic backlash to what is seen as the international trade framework's subordination of important state concerns—cultural,

[108] See M Presley, 'Sovereignty and Relegation Issues regarding US Commitment to the World Trade Organisation's Dispute Settlement Process' (1998) 8 *Journal of Transnational Law and Policy* 173, 187–188 (drawing this conclusion from the *US—Gasoline* case).

[109] JP Trachtman, 'Regulatory Jurisdiction and the WTO' (2007a) 10 JIEL 631, 632.

[110] K Raustiala, 'Sovereignty and Multilateralism' (2000) 1 *Chicago Journal of International Law* 401, 410 (referring to this phenomenon, in no way unique to the WTO, as 'generativity').

[111] Barfield considers this activism to be a side-effect of the cumbersome law-making capacities of the WTO. C Barfield, 'Free Trade, Sovereignty, Democracy: The Future of the World Trade Organisation' (2001) 2 *Chicago Journal of International Law* 403, 408. For Trachtman, it is simply an intrinsic and important feature of dispute resolution. JP Trachtman, 'The Domain of WTO Dispute Resolution' (1999) 40 *Harvard International Law Journal*333, 336.

[112] Regardless of the legal limitations on the Appellate Body's power in this respect, politically speaking it remains highly sensitive to the risks in developing potentially divisive jurisprudence. See RH Steinberg, 'Judicial Lawmaking at the WTO: Discursive, Constitutional, and Political Constraints' (2004) 98 AJIL 247, 274.

[113] See J Atik, 'Democratising the WTO' (2001) 33 *George Washington International Law Review* 451, 467 (claiming 'positive law within the WTO emerges indirectly').

[114] R Trimble, 'Globalisation, International Institutions, and the Erosion of National Sovereignty and Democracy' (1997) 95 *Michigan Law Review* 1944, 1944–1945.

[115] HV Morais, 'The Quest for International Standards: Global Governance Versus Sovereignty' (2002) 50 *University of Kansas Law Review* 779, 806.

environmental or social—to free-trade ideology.[116] The relative strength and coherence of WTO law is perceived to dominate the 'anaemic, quasi-voluntary systems allocated to non-trade concerns.'[117] The WTO has therefore become detached from the broad interests of its Members, pursuing narrow economic interests at the expense of other fundamental values.[118] There is also an organisational dimension to this critique of state values, focusing on the insularity of the WTO and the dearth of public input into its processes.[119] Commentators reflect in particular on what practical changes can be made to the body to ensure a better reflection of non-trade values.[120]

State Will-Contractual Obligations

A third variant of the ascending perspective places emphasis on the state's will and seeks to pinpoint exactly to what the state has consented. This approach understands WTO law as a 'contract', one in which '[s]tates have delegated … limited authority to international public bodies … [who can] constrain governments within relatively defined parameters.'[121] It is a view that finds resonance within the organisation as well as among commentators.[122] Many of the key concerns overlap with analyses that focus on sovereignty, namely whether the dispute-settlement bodies are disciplined or instead engage in law-making beyond the remit provided by states. However, the dilemma here is not the inherent appropriateness of greater WTO power,

[116] See, e.g. PN Nichols, 'Trade without Values' (1996) 90 *Northwestern University Law Review*658, 660; P Ala'i, 'A Human Rights Critique of the WTO: Some Preliminary Observations' (2001) 33 *George Washington International Law Review* 537, 540.

[117] S Dillon, 'A Farewell to "Linkage": International Trade Law and Global Sustainability Indicators' (2002) 55 *Rutgers Law Review* 87, 90.

[118] See C Summers, 'The Battle in Seattle: Free Trade, Labour Rights, and Societal Values' (2001) 22 *University of Pennsylvania Journal of International Economic Law* 61, 80; FJ Garcia, 'Building a Just Trade Order for a New Millennium' (2001) 33 *George Washington International Law Review* 1015, 1058.

[119] See Y Bonzon, 'Institutionalizing Public Participation in WTO Decision Making: Some Conceptual Hurdles and Avenues' (2008) 11 JIEL 751, 760 (noting that concerns within the WTO about public participation have been largely oriented towards improving the body's image).

[120] See GR Shell, 'The Trade Stakeholders Model and Participation by Nonstate Parties in the World Trade Organisation' (2004) 25 *University of Pennsylvania Journal of International Economic Law* 703, 721; P Ala'i, 'Free Trade or Sustainable Development? An Analysis of the WTO Appellate Body's Shift to a More Balanced Approach to Trade Liberalisation' (1999) 14 *American University International Law Review* 1129.

[121] JP Kelly, 'The WTO and Global Governance: The Case for Contractual Treaty Regimes' (2001) 7 *Widener Law Symposium Journal* 109, 112–113.

[122] See *Japan—Taxes on Alcoholic Beverages*, Appellate Body Report (adopted 4 October 1996) WT/DS8/AB/R, WT/DS10/AB/R, WT/DS11/AB/R, para 14 (describing the WTO Agreement as 'the international equivalent of a contract'). See also JO Nzelibe, 'Interest Groups, Power Politics, and the Risks of WTO Mission Creep' (2004) 28 *Harvard Journal of Law and Public Policy* 89; JP Trachtman, 'The WTO Cathedral' (2007b) 43 *Stanford Journal of International Law* 127, 145.

but rather whether this trend is in accordance with the 'negotiated contractual rights of member states'.[123]

The characterisation of the WTO as a contract is in one sense attractive. It reflects the body's underlying economic rationale—the trading of reciprocal trade concessions for mutually beneficial market access[124]—and appropriately captures the nature of the WTO law-making process: effectively a series of painstakingly constructed bilateral deals.[125] However, this conception of the WTO is not universally accepted.[126] A contract may imply a self-standing document, a view that collides with an understanding of the WTO as embedded within the broader framework of international obligations.[127] It is also questionable whether the analogy of contract, though relevant perhaps to the precise scheduling of import tariffs, is adequate to the broad discipline of regulatory measures foreseen in the SPS Agreement.

2.4.2 Descending Perspective

In contrast to the ascending perspectives outlined above, a descending perspective takes as its starting point the common goals underpinning the regime. The precise purpose of the SPS Agreement is, however, more contested than one might first assume. Any evaluation of the impact of the regime will therefore depend on basic presumptions as to its purpose.[128] Some of the alternatives are briefly considered below.

Enhancing Trade

To state that the SPS Agreement aims to enhance trade is uncontroversial. However, identifying the precise expectations of the regime is surprisingly difficult. There are three plausible premises. The first is that the SPS Agreement roots out

[123] Kelly (n 121) 117.

[124] See K Bagwell, PC Mavroidis and RW Staiger, 'It's a Question of Market Access' (2002) 96 AJIL 56; J Pauwelyn, 'New Trade Politics for the 21st Century' (2008) 11 JIEL 559, 599.

[125] J Pauwelyn, 'A Typology of Multilateral Treaty Obligations: Are WTO Obligations Bilateral or Collective in Nature?' (2003) 14 EJIL 907, 931.

[126] See DP Steger, 'The Culture of the WTO: Why it Needs to Change' (2007) 10 JIEL 483, 491 (describing the idea that the WTO is a contract as a 'myth').

[127] See *US—Standards for Reformulated Conventional Gasoline*, Appellate Body Report (adopted 29 April 1996) WT/DS2/AB/R, para 46 (famously holding that WTO law cannot be considered in 'clinical isolation' of public international law).

[128] Charnovitz acknowledges this, and notes that in the analysis of the WTO, such premises often remain unarticulated. He therefore draws up a list of potential alternative 'purposes'—harmonisation, neutralising powerful domestic actors and risk reduction among others—some of which would fall, under the scheme outlined here, under the ascending perspective. S Charnovitz, 'Triangulating The World Trade Organization' (2002) 96 AJIL 28, 48.

unfair discrimination against foreign products as an unacceptable barrier to trade. In this sense, the Agreement extends the principle of non-discrimination established by GATT.[129] This appears to make historical sense, as the SPS Agreement arose from the collective fear that, as tariff protection disappeared, sanitary measures could constitute 'an alternative form of protection'.[130] Moreover, the non-discrimination principles found in GATT provisions are echoed in the text of the Agreement, providing a solid basis for considering the SPS Agreement in these terms.[131]

A second view is that the SPS Agreement seeks to eliminate not simply discriminatory measures, but all burdens that stand in the way of trade, following the principle of *laissez faire*.[132] Certain Agreement provisions and jurisprudence seem indeed to point in this direction.[133] However, it is not clear why Members would advance a trade philosophy through the SPS Agreement so clearly at odds with other parts of the WTO system.[134] Regan argues that the SPS Agreement does not aim to remove all barriers, only those that are 'domestically irrational' and place unnecessary costs on both domestic and foreign actors. From this perspective, the SPS Agreement is an extension rather than a repudiation of the principle of non-discrimination.[135]

A third possibility is to take regulatory harmonisation as a starting point for analysis of the regime. However, although 'harmonisation' is an explicit goal of the Agreement, its precise intentions can be differently construed. For some it represents a step towards 'positive integration'[136] and a shift from 'what governments

---

[129] GATT Arts I and III respectively provide that states must not treat like products from different WTO Members in a different way and not impose burdens on imported products in excess of those on domestic ones. See V Heiskanen, 'The Regulatory Philosophy of International Trade Law' (2004) 38 JWT 1 (describing non-discrimination as GATT's 'underlying regulatory philosophy').

[130] J Croome, *Reshaping the World Trading System: A History of the Uruguay Round* (Geneva, WTO Secretariat, 1995) 236. See also JP Trachtman (n 109) 632.

[131] SPS Agreement Arts 2.3 and 5.5.

[132] See DM Driesen, 'What Is Free-Trade?: The Real Issue Lurking behind the Trade and Environment Debate' (2001) 41 VJIL 279, 291; PM Gerhart, 'Slow Transformations: The WTO as a Distributive Organization' (2002) 17 *American University International Law Review* 1045, 1048 (characterising the WTO as a body primarily striving for economic efficiency).

[133] Under SPS Agreement Art 5.6, WTO Members must ensure that measures are 'not more trade-restrictive than required' to achieve the Member's chosen level of protection, permitting other states to challenge domestic policy on the basis that they are sub-optimal in trading terms. The Appellate Body's finding in the *Hormones* decision that the EU's measures were illegal while not discriminatory, would also seem to suggest the SPS Agreement's pursuit of a more far-reaching free trade agenda. *EC—Measures concerning Meat and Meat Products (Hormones)*, Appellate Body Report (adopted 16 January 1998) WT/DS26/AB/R, WT/DS48/AB/R, para 246.

[134] See Charnovitz (n 128) 34 (pointing to the 'rampant inefficiency' created by permitted maintenance of tariffs, antidumping duties and quotas).

[135] DH Regan, 'What Are Trade Agreements For?—Two Conflicting Stories Told by Economists, with a Lesson for Lawyers' (2006) 9 JIEL 951, 968 (arguing that the SPS regime is a 'natural extension of the protectionism story').

[136] D Kalderimis, 'Problems of WTO Harmonisation and the Virtues of Shields over Swords' (2004) 13 *Minnesota Journal of Global Trade* 305, 320.

must not do, to positive regulations, or what governments must do'.[137] Yet the SPS Agreement's 'harmonisation' project falls considerably short of this level of integration. It accords considerable leeway to WTO Members to deviate from international standards,[138] allowing them to implement more stringent measures, where desired.[139] Rather than a catalyst for positive integration, Codex standards serve simply to 'provide incentives that guide conduct'.[140]

Non-Economic Goals

The competing economic rationales outlined above provide the most obvious perspectives for a descending evaluation of the SPS regime, but this does not preclude reflection on other non-economic ambitions. The WTO has formally embraced other overarching goals such as environmental sustainability and development, and while they have 'not become a part of the theology and culture of the WTO'[141] there could still be a legitimate legal argument for assessing the SPS Agreement in these terms. An evaluation of the SPS Agreement with reference to human rights, for example, would offer one such alternative descending standpoint.[142]

The evaluative perspective chosen by the analyst will bring to the fore different aspects of the SPS Agreement's operation and inevitably colour conclusions about its overall impact. Neither perspective is inextricably linked with either a positive or negative evaluation of the Agreement. Commentators concerned about the effects of trade liberalisation may be inclined to choose an ascending perspective whereas critics of non-trade barriers may naturally tend towards a descending perspective. Yet in each case their findings could either confirm or undermine the preconceptions that led to that choice of perspective.

2.5 Conclusion

This chapter has identified three analytical dimensions that will underpin any evaluation of the impact of SPS law: field of enquiry, conception of how law functions, and evaluative perspective. The choices made in these areas (deliberately or unconsciously) by commentators on the Agreement will establish the parameters of any

---

137 S Ostry cited in Barfield (n 111) 406.

138 Members are only expected to 'base' measures on international standards. SPS Agreement Art 3.1.

139 SPS Agreement Art 3.3.

140 Trachtman (n 109) 649.

141 Steger (n 126) 486.

142 See, e.g. E-U Petersmann, 'Human Rights and International Economic Law in the 21st Century' (2001) 4 JIEL 3, 27 (arguing that protectionist WTO rules may infringe the 'human rights interests of consumers in maximum equal liberty and open markets').

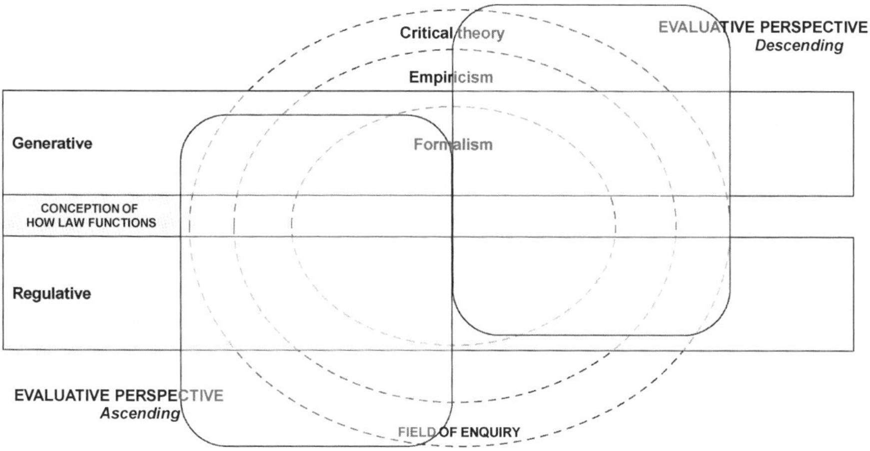

Fig. 2.1 Analytical choices in the assessment of the impact of law

investigations and in large part determine the scope of their outcomes. By exploring the different possible approaches to each dimension, this chapter has proposed a taxonomy of analytical choices.

One might expect certain theoretical assumptions to be aligned. For example, an ascending contractualist evaluative perspective easily co-exists with a formalist field of enquiry. Yet most combinations are theoretically compatible. An empirical evaluation of law could adopt a descending or ascending evaluative perspective, just as a critical theorist could draw on either a regulative or generative conception of how law functions. Different alignments of these dimensions therefore have the capacity to open alternative vistas and angles of research. A diagrammatic representation of these interlocking dimensions can be seen in Fig. 2.1.

This taxonomy permits us to identify the central analytical choices shaping individual studies and build up a clearer picture of the orientation of existing research on the SPS Agreement. With this framework in place, Chap. 3 will turn to a review of that literature.

References

Ala'i P, 'Free Trade or Sustainable Development? An Analysis of the WTO Appellate Body's Shift to a More Balanced Approach to Trade Liberalisation' (1999) 14 *American University International Law Review* 1129.

Alkolby A, 'Theories of Compliance with International Law and the Challenge of Cultural Difference' (2008) 4 *Journal of International Law and International Relations* 151.

Allott P, 'The International Lawyer in Government Service: Ontology and Deontology (2005) 23 *Wisconsin International Law Journal* 13.

Alvarez JE, 'How Not to Link: Institutional Conundrums of an Expanded Trade Regime' (2001) *Widener Law Symposium Journal* 1.

Anaya SJ, 'Divergent Discourses about International Law, Indigenous Peoples, and Rights over Lands and Natural Resources: Toward a Realist Trend' (2005) 16 *Colorado Journal of International Environmental Law and Policy* 237.

Anderson K, 'Remarks by an Idealist on the Realism of the Limits of International Law' (2006) 34 *Georgia Journal of International and Comparative Law* 253.

Arend AC, 'Do Legal Rules Matter? International Law and International Politics' (1998) 38 VJIL 107.

Austin J, *The Providence of Jurisprudence Determined* (Indianapolis, Hackett, 1998).

Bagwell K, Mavroidis PC and Staiger RW, 'It's a Question of Market Access' (2002) 96 AJIL 56.

Barfield C, 'Free Trade, Sovereignty, Democracy: The Future of the World Trade Organisation' (2001) 2 *Chicago Journal of International Law* 403.

Bederman DJ, 'Counterintuiting Countermeasures' (2002) 96 AJIL 817.

Bederman DJ, 'Constructivism, Positivism, and Empiricism in International Law' (2007) 89 *Georgetown Law Journal* 469.

Berman PS, 'From International Law to Law and Globalisation' (2005) 43 *Columbia Journal of Transnational Law* 485.

Berman PS, 'Seeing beyond the Limits of International Law' (2006) 84 *Texas Law Review* 1265.

Bhala R, 'The Precedent Setters: *De Facto Stare Decisis* Fact in WTO Adjudication (Part Two of a Trilogy)' (1999) 9 *Journal of Transnational Law & Policy* 1.

Bonzon Y, 'Institutionalizing Public Participation in WTO Decision Making: Some Conceptual Hurdles and Avenues' (2008) 11 JIEL 751.

Brunnée J and Toope SJ, 'The Changing Nile Basin Regime: Does Law Matter?' (2000) 43 *Harvard International Law Journal* 105.

Charnovitz S, 'Triangulating The World Trade Organization' (2002) 96 AJIL 28.

Charnovitz S, 'The World Trade Organization in 2020' (2005) 1 Journal of International Law and International Relations 167.

Chayes A and Chayes AH, '*The New Sovereignty: Compliance with International Regulatory Norms*' (Cambridge, MA, Harvard University Press, 1995).

Cleveland SH, 'Human Rights Sanctions and International Trade: A Theory of Compatibility' (2002) 5 JIEL 133.

Croley SP and Jackson JH, 'WTO Dispute Procedures, Standard of Review, and Deference to National Governments' (1996) 90 AJIL 193.

Croome J, *Reshaping the World Trading System: A History of the Uruguay Round* (Geneva, WTO Secretariat, 1995).

D'Amato A, 'Is International Law Really "Law"' (1985) 79 *Northwestern University Law Review* 1293.

Davis MH and Neacsu D, 'Legitimacy, Globally: The Incoherence of Free Trade Practice, Global Economics and their Governing Principles of Political Economy' (2001) 69 *University of Missouri, Kansas City Law Review* 733.

Dickinson LA, 'Toward a "New" New Haven School of International Law?' (2007) 32 YJIL 547.

Dillon S, 'Opportunism and the WTO: Corporations, Academics and "Member States"' in C Picker, I Brunn and D Arner (eds), *International Economic Law: The State and Future of the Discipline* (Oxford, Hart Publishing, 2008).

Driesen DM, 'What Is Free-Trade?: The Real Issue Lurking behind the Trade and Environment Debate' (2001) 41VJIL 279.

Dunoff JL, 'The WTO in Transition: Of Constituents, Competence and Coherence' (2001) 33 *George Washington International Law Review* 979.

Ehlermann C-D and Ehring L, 'The Authoritative Interpretation under Article IX:2 of the Agreement Establishing the World Trade Organization: Current Law, Practice and Possible Improvements' (2005) 8 JIEL 803.

Ewelukwa UU, 'Centuries of Globalisation; Centuries of Exclusion: African Women, Human Rights, and the "New" International Trade Regime' (2005) 20 *Berkeley Journal of Gender, Law and Justice* 75.

Finnemore M, 'International Norm Dynamics and Political Change' (1998) 52 *International Organisation* 903.

Finnemore M, 'Are Legal Norms Distinctive?' (2000) 32 *New York University Journal of International Law and Politics* 699.

Finnemore M and Toope SJ, 'Alternatives to "Legalisation": Richer Views of Law and Politics' (2001) 55 *International Organisation* 743.

Franck TM, 'Legitimacy in the International System' (1988) 82 AJIL 705.

Franck TM, '*The Power of Legitimacy Among Nations*' (New York, OUP, 1990).

Franck SD, 'Empiricism and International Law: Insights for Investment Treaty Dispute Resolution' (2008) 48 VJIL 767.

Garcia FJ, 'Building a Just Trade Order for a New Millennium' (2001) 33 *George Washington International Law Review* 1015.

Garth BG, 'Introduction: Taking New Legal Realism to Transnational Issues and Institutions' (2006) 31 *Law and Social Inquiry: Journal of the American Bar Foundation* 939.

Gerhart PM, 'Slow Transformations: The WTO as a Distributive Organization' (2002) 17 *American University International Law Review* 1045.

Goldsmith J and Posner EA, '*The Limits of International Law*' (Oxford, OUP, 2005).

Goldsmith J and Posner EA, 'The New International Law Scholarship' (2006) 34 *Georgia Journal of International and Comparative Law* 463.

Gonzalez CG, 'Deconstructing the Mythology of Free Trade: Critical Reflections on Comparative Advantage' (2006) 17 *Berkeley La Raza Law Journal* 65.

Goodman R and Jinks D, 'How To Influence States: Socialization and International Human Rights Law' (2004) 54 *Duke Law Journal* 621.

Goodman R and Jinks D, 'International Law and State Socialisation: Conceptual, Empirical, and Normative Challenges' (2005) 54 *Duke Law Journal* 983.

Guzman AT, 'A Compliance-Based Theory of International Law' (2002) 90 *California Law Review* 1826.

Hathaway OA, 'The New Empiricism in Human Rights: Insights and Implications' (2004) 98 *American Society of International Law Proceedings* 206.

Heiskanen V, 'The Regulatory Philosophy of International Trade Law' (2004) 38 JWT 1.

Henkin L, '*How Nations Behave: Law and Foreign Policy*' (London, Pall Mall Press, 1968).

Hillgenberg H, 'A Fresh Look at Soft Law' (1999) 10 EJIL 499.

Hoffman M and Topulos K, 'Tyranny of the Available: Under-Represented Topics, Approaches, and Viewpoints' (2008) 35 *Syracuse Journal of International Law and Commerce* 175.

Howse R and Mavroidis PC, 'Europe's Evolving Regulatory Strategy for GMOs—The Issue of Consistency with WTO Law: Of Kine and Brine' (2000) 24 *Fordham International Law Journal* 317.

Jackson JH, 'The Great 1994 Sovereignty Debate: United States Acceptance and Implementation of the Uruguay Round Results' (1997) 36 *Columbia Journal of Transnational Law* 157.

Jackson JH, 'The Role of International Law in Trade' (2004) 36 *Georgetown Journal of International Law* 663.

Johnston AI, 'Treating International Institutions as Social Environments' (2001) 45 *International Studies Quarterly* 487.

Kalderimis D, 'Problems of WTO Harmonisation and the Virtues of Shields over Swords' (2004) 13 *Minnesota Journal of Global* 305.

Kelly JP, 'The WTO and Global Governance: The Case for Contractual Treaty Regimes' (2001) 7 *Widener Law Symposium Journal* 109.

Kelly JP, 'Judicial Activism at the World Trade Organization: Developing Principles of Self-Restraint' (2002) 22 *Northwestern Journal of International Law and Business* 353.

Kelly CR, 'Enmeshment as a Theory of Compliance' (2005) 37 *New York University Journal of International Law and Politics* 303.

Kelly JP, 'Naturalism in International Adjudication' (2008) 18 *Duke Journal of Comparative and International Law* 395.

Kennedy D, 'A New Stream of International Law Scholarship' (1988) 7 *Wisconsin International Law Journal* 1.
Kingsbury B, 'The Concept of Compliance as a Function of Competing Conceptions of International Law' (1998) 19 *Michigan Journal of International Law* 345.
Klabbers J, 'The Relative Autonomy of International Law or the Forgotten Politics of Interdisciplinarity' (2005) 1 *Journal of International Law and International Relations* 35.
Koh HH, 'Transnational Legal Process' (1996) 75 *Nebraska Law Review* 181.
Koskenniemi M, 'What is International Law?' in MD Evans (ed), *International Law* (Oxford, OUP, 2003).
Koskenniemi M, '*From Apology to Utopia: The Structure of International Law*' (Cambridge, CUP, 2005).
Kratochwil FV, '*Rules, Norms, and Decisions*' (Cambridge, CUP, 1989).
Lang A, 'Re-thinking Trade and Human Rights' (2007) 15 *Tulane Journal of International and Comparative Law* 335.
Lang A, 'Some Sociological Perspectives on International Institutions and the Trading System' in C Picker, I Brunn and D Arner (eds), *International Economic Law: The State and Future of The Discipline* (Oxford, Hart Publishing, 2008).
Legro JW, 'Which Norms Matter? Revisiting the "Failure" of Internationalism' (1997) 51 *International Organization* 31.
Levit JK, 'Bottom-Up Lawmaking through a Pluralist Lens: ICC Banking Commission and Transnational Regulation of Letters of Credit' (2008) 57 *Emory Law Journal* 1147.
Lindros A and Mehring M, 'Dispelling the Chimera of Self-Contained Regimes: International Law and the WTO' (2005) 16 EJIL 857.
Matsushita M, 'The Sutherland Report and its Discussion of Dispute Settlement Reforms' (2005) 8 JIEL 623.
McGinnis JO and Movsesian ML, 'The World Trade Constitution' (2000) 114 *Harvard Law Review* 511.
Moravcsik A, 'Explaining International Human Rights Regimes: Liberal Theory and Western Europe' (1995) 1 *European Journal of International Relations* 157.
Mutua M, 'Critical Race Theory and International Law: The View of an Insider-Outsider' (2000) 45 *Villanova Law Review* 841.
Ngugi J, 'Making New Wine for Old Wineskins: Can the Reform of International Law Emancipate the Third World in the Age of Globalisation?' (2002) 8 *UC Davis Journal of International Law and Policy* 73.
Nichols PN, 'Trade without Values' (1996) 90 *Northwestern University Law Review* 658.
Nzelibe JO, 'Interest Groups, Power Politics, and the Risks of WTO Mission Creep' (2004) 28 *Harvard Journal of Law and Public Policy* 89.
Orford A, 'Contesting Globalization: A Feminist Perspective on the Future of Human Rights' (1998) 8 *Transnational Law and Contemporary Problems* 172.
Palmeter D and Mavroidis PC, 'The WTO Legal System: Sources of Law' (1998) 92 AJIL 398.
Pauwelyn J, 'The Role of Public International Law in the WTO: How Far Can We Go?' (2001) 95 AJIL 535.
Pauwelyn J, 'A Typology of Multilateral Treaty Obligations: Are WTO Obligations Bilateral or Collective in Nature?' (2003) 14 EJIL 907.
Pauwelyn J, 'New Trade Politics for the 21st Century' (2008) 11 JIEL 559.
Petersmann E-U, 'Human Rights and International Economic Law in the 21st Century' (2001) 4 JIEL 3.
Presley M, 'Sovereignty and Relegation Issues regarding US Commitment to the World Trade Organisation's Dispute Settlement Process' (1998) 8 *Journal of Transnational Law and Policy* 173.
Raustiala K, 'Sovereignty and Multilateralism' (2000) 1 *Chicago Journal of International Law* 401.
Raustiala K, 'Rethinking the Sovereignty Debate in International Economic Law' (2003) 6 JIEL 841.

Regan DH, 'What Are Trade Agreements for?—Two Conflicting Stories Told by Economists, with a Lesson for Lawyers' (2006) 9 JIEL 951.

Risse T, '"Let's Argue!": 'Communicative Action in World Politics' (2000) 54 *International Organisation* 1.

Roman E, 'Reconstructing Self-Determination: The Role of Critical Theory in the Positivist International Law Paradigm' (1999) 53 *University of Miami Law Review* 943.

Ruggie JG, 'What Makes the World Hang Together? Neo-Utilitarianism and the Social Constructivist Challenge' (1998) 52 *International Organization* 855.

Sampson GP, 'Is There a Need for Restructuring the Collaboration among the WTO and UN Agencies so as to Harness their Complementarities?' (2004) 7 JIEL 717.

Saroshi D, 'Sovereignty, Economic Autonomy, United States, and the International Trading System: Representations of the Relationship' (2004) 15 EJIL 651.

Scott J, '*The WTO Agreement on Sanitary and Phytosanitary Measures. A Commentary*' (Oxford, OUP, 2007).

Shaffer GC, 'The World Trade Organization Under Challenge: Democracy and the Law and Politics of the WTO's Treatment of Trade and Environment Matters' (2001) 25 *Harvard Environmental Law Review* 1.

Shaffer GC, 'A New Legal Realism: Method in International Economic Law Scholarship' in C Picker, I Brunn and D Arner (eds), *International Economic Law: The State and Future of The Discipline* (Oxford, Hart Publishing, 2008).

Shaffer GC and Pollack MA, 'Hard Versus Soft Law: Alternatives, Complements and Antagonists in International Governance' (2010) 94 *Minnesota Law Review* 706.

Shell GR, 'The Trade Stakeholders Model and Participation by Nonstate Parties in the World Trade Organisation' (2004) 25 *University of Pennsylvania Journal of International Economic Law* 703.

Steger DP, 'The Culture of the WTO: Why it Needs to Change' (2007) 10 JIEL 483.

Steinberg RH, 'Judicial Lawmaking at the WTO: Discursive, Constitutional, and Political Constraints' (2004) 98 AJIL 247.

Summers C, 'The Battle In Seattle: Free Trade, Labor Rights, and Societal Values' (2001) 22 *University of Pennsylvania Journal of International Economic Law* 61.

Talberg J, 'Paths to Compliance: Enforcement, Management, and the European Union' (2002) 56 *International Organization* 609.

Trachtman JP, 'The Domain of WTO Dispute Resolution' (1999) 40 *Harvard International Law Journal* 333.

Trachtman JP, 'Regulatory Jurisdiction and the WTO' (2007a) 10 JIEL 631.

Trachtman JP, 'The WTO Cathedral' (2007b) 43 *Stanford Journal of International Law* 127.

Trachtman JP, 'International Economic Law Research: A Taxonomy' in C Picker, I Brunn and D Arner (eds), *International Economic Law: The State and Future of the Discipline* (Oxford, Hart Publishing, 2008).

Trimble PR, 'Globalisation, International Institutions, and the Erosion of National Sovereignty and Democracy' (1997) 95 *Michigan Law Review* 1944.

Verdirame G, '"The Divided West": International Lawyers in Europe and America' (2007) 18 EJIL 553.

Wendt A, 'The Agent-Structure Problem in International Relations Theory' (1987) 4 *International Organization* 335.

Yackee JW, 'Conceptual Difficulties in the Empirical Study of Bilateral Investment Treaties' (2008) 33 *Brooklyn Journal of International Law* 405.

Young MA, 'The WTO's Use of Relevant Rules of International Law: An Analysis of the Biotech Case' (2007) 56 ICLQ 907.

Chapter 3
The Standard View of the SPS Agreement: A Literature Review

Abstract This chapter reviews legal commentary on the SPS Agreement using the taxonomy developed in Chap. 2 to characterise the literature and reflect on the analytical perspectives adopted. This review identifies an orientation towards analysis with three principal characteristics. Firstly, study of the SPS Agreement is mostly confined to its text and to jurisprudence, with commentators rarely developing empirical or critical theoretical accounts of the regime. Secondly, the majority of studies assume that states follow international law, be it under duress or for strategic or normative reasons. Only a few studies explore the generative effects of SPS rules, identifying the processes through which national regulators reflect on and respond to international norms. Finally, the overriding tendency is to evaluate the SPS regime from the ascending perspective of the State, and the possible encroachment on national sovereignty and values. Commentators have only exceptionally assessed the operation of the regime from the perspective of its trade and nontrade goals. In the absence of any empirical demonstration of the commonly presumed constraint of SPS law, this chapter suggests that the conclusions drawn are largely the product of the analytical choices made. While entirely valid as an approach, alternative analytical choices could deepen our understanding of the impact of SPS rules.

3.1 Introduction

This chapter undertakes a review of scholarly commentary on the World Trade Organisation (WTO) Agreement on the Application of Sanitary and Phytosanitary Measures (SPS Agreement) which is structured according to the taxonomy of analytical choices developed in Chap. 2. It makes no claim to give a comprehensive account of all that has been written about the Agreement. Given the quantity of writing that has appeared within a short period, an exhaustive survey would probably not be feasible and would in any case be of limited interest. The review therefore focuses on the most influential studies of the regime over the first decade or so of its functioning.[1] It aims to capture the overall orientation of academic work on the

[1] As was acknowledged in Chap. 1—see n 6 and related text—while one of the aims of this book was initially to understand the predominantly critical views of the SPS Agreement in this period,

C. Downes, *The Impact of WTO SPS Law on EU Food Regulations,* Studies in European Economic Law and Regulation 2, DOI 10.1007/978-3-319-04373-9_3,

Agreement and in particular to identify the analytical approaches underpinning the view that the Agreement constrains national regulators. It treats each dimension of the taxonomy in turn: field of enquiry (Sect. 3.2), conception of how law functions (Sect. 3.3), and evaluative perspective (Sect. 3.4).

3.2 The Field of Enquiry: What Are Commentators Studying?

Chapter 2 discussed three possible fields of enquiry relevant to the study of the SPS Agreement: formalism, empiricism and critical theory. Not all studies fit neatly into one of these categories. For example, some contain elements of empirical analysis, while not necessarily drawing their understanding of SPS law from this empirical contribution. Equally, any study of the regime is likely to refer in some manner to the Agreement's formal provisions, without hereby being predominantly formalist. With these provisos in mind, this section seeks to identify the dominant field of enquiry used in evaluation of the SPS Agreement.

3.2.1 Formalism

Many studies of the SPS Agreement centre on the text itself, and in particular the meaning that has been brought to its provisions through the interpretation of World Trade Organisation (WTO) dispute-settlement bodies.[2] This is neither surprising

---

the *US—Continued Suspension* dispute has somewhat softened this criticism. In order to identify the relevant articles, a preliminary selection was made, via Westlaw, of studies including five references to both the SPS Agreement and 'food'. A further selection was made, again with the aid of Westlaw, according to the frequency with which the selected articles had been cited, with the inclusion for review of those that had been cited at least ten times. As this would potentially give a bias towards older literature, all articles from the preliminary selection published between 2005 and 2008 were also included in this second selection. Those studies that focused purely on the environmental rather than the food aspects of the SPS Agreement were eliminated. Around 80 articles and frequently cited books remained from this process. Of these, 30 articles did not address the impact of SPS rules on domestic policy-making; see Chap. 1 (n 52) and related text. While this method offers no guarantees of producing a representative selection, there are no particular reasons to believe that the chosen articles do not adequately reflect academic understanding of the regime during this period.

[2] By way of illustration, see S Charnovitz, 'The Supervision of Health and Biosafety Regulation by World Trade Rules' (2000) 13 *Tulane Environmental Law Journal* 271; T Christoforou, 'Settlement of Science-Based Trade Disputes in the WTO: A Critical Review of the Developing Case Law in the Face of Scientific Uncertainty' (2000) 8 *New York University Environmental Law Journal* 622; CE Foster, 'Public Opinion and the Interpretation of the World Trade Organisation's Agreement on Sanitary and Phytosanitary Measures' (2008) 11 JIEL 427; M Trebilcock and J Soloway, 'International Trade Policy and Domestic Food Safety Regulation: The Case for Substantial Deference by the WTO Dispute Settlement Body under the SPS Agreement' in DLM

nor problematic as a starting point for research. The SPS provisions are far from self-explanatory and the detailed reports into the Agreement's most controversial elements offer copious and accessible material for study. They therefore provide the most obvious reference point for legal commentators grappling with the significance of the regime.[3] Nevertheless, it is striking that scholars rarely extend their focus beyond these disputes.[4] How can formalist accounts that do not study actual state behaviour draw conclusions about the Agreement's significance in a domestic context? They do so through three types of analysis: comparative, explorative and expansive.

Comparative

Some formalist analyses infer the influence of the SPS Agreement by measuring it against an external reference point. In some cases, this can be another legal framework. Kalderimis and Shapiro both assess the significance of the SPS Agreement by comparing its provisions with those of the GATT. The identified divergences—failing to include GATT Article XX-style public interest exceptions (Shapiro) or extending international scrutiny to measures that are not discriminatory (Kalderimis)—are treated as evidence of significant new restrictions on WTO Members. Others draw comparisons between the SPS regime and domestic legal frameworks. Peel contrasts the deference paid by US and European Union (EU) judicial organs to regulatory bodies in risk regulation with WTO jurisprudence and identifies the heavy reliance in the latter on a notion of universal and objective science.[5] Slotboom pinpoints restrictive elements of the SPS Agreement through comparison of EU jurisprudence and the findings of the Appellate Body (AB) in *Hormones*.[6] Likewise, Alemanno weighs up EU and WTO food safety risk-analysis schemes and highlights

---

Kennedy and JD Southwick (eds), *The Political Economy of International Trade Law: Essays in Honour of Robert E. Hudec* (Cambridge, CUP, 2002) (*Political Economy*) 537; VR Walker, 'Keeping the WTO from Becoming the "World Trans-Science Organisation": Scientific Uncertainty, Science Policy, and Fact-Finding in the Growth Hormones Dispute' (1998) 31 *Cornell International Law Journal* 251, 319.

[3] This reliance on jurisprudence is such that some writers contend that we must await disputes to understand the implications of the SPS Agreement. See LA Gruszczynski, 'Risk Management Policies under the WTO Agreement on the Application of Sanitary and Phytosanitary Measures' (2008) 3 *Asian Journal of WTO and International Health Law and Policy* 261, 303 (claiming that 'the overall assessment of the SPS Agreement as far as risk management is concerned will only be possible after they are addressed in case law').

[4] Often, as Scott notes, the work of the dispute body is 'presented as entirely occupying the field of WTO law'. J Scott, *The WTO Agreement on Sanitary and Phytosanitary Measures. A Commentary* (Oxford, OUP, 2007) 74.

[5] J Peel, 'Risk Regulation under the WTO SPS Agreement: Science as an International Normative Yardstick?' (Jean Monnet Working Paper 02/04 95) centers.law.nyu.edu/jeanmonnet/papers/04/040201.pdf.

[6] MM Slotboom, 'The Hormones Case: An Increased Risk of Illegality of Sanitary and Phytosanitary Measures' (1999) 36 CML Rev 471, 489–490.

the notable lack of attention to risk management in the latter.[7] For others, the point of comparison is a more abstract conception of what constitutes good policy-making. Trebilcock and Soloway appraise the SPS Agreement against an 'idealized domestic risk regulation regime' and find it to lack a coherent vision as to the appropriate level of supranational interference in domestic risk regulation.[8] Walker explores the complex place of scientific fact-finding in policy-making and warns of the danger of the WTO imposing a uniform approach to science policy.[9] Winickoff et al measure the functioning of the SPS Agreement against 'state-of-the-art social science scholarship' on risk analysis and point to the inadequate incorporation of public values in the WTO model.[10] These comparative analyses identify the outstanding characteristics of the SPS Agreement, strongly suggesting its implications for domestic governments without explicitly claiming that such impacts actually occur.

Explorative

A second method of elaborating on the influence of SPS rules is to explore the legality of measures not yet before the WTO. While clearly remaining conjectural, such analysis effectively identifies the broader implications of the regime. The labelling of genetically modified food (GM labelling) has proved a popular topic for studies of this kind. Both Keane and Schramm point to the likely illegality of GM labelling were the measure to pass before the WTO, while Fredland draws similar conclusions from a more specific study of EU GM labelling requirements.[11] Other areas of international food policy that have been treated in this way include the US ban of tetrahydrocannabinol and the US Bioterrorism Act.[12] Some authors use such

[7] A Alemanno, Trade in Food: Regulatory and Judicial Approaches in the EC and the WTO (London, Cameron May, 2007) pt IV, Chap. I.

[8] Trebilcock and Soloway (n 2) ss III and V.

[9] Walker (n 2).

[10] D Winickoff et al., 'Adjudicating the GM Food Wars: Science, Risk, and Democracy in World Trade Law' (2005) 30 YJIL 81, 94. By contrast, Epps analyses the role of public participation in the SPS regime with reference to a range of sources from social scientific work and domestic practice and finds the WTO to be adequately sensitive to distinct national interests. T Epps, 'Reconciling Public Opinion and WTO Rules under the SPS Agreement' (2008) 7 *World Trade Review* 359.

[11] See S Keane , 'Can the Consumers Right to Know Survive the WTO?: The Case of Food Labeling' (2006) 16 Transnational Law and Contemporary Problems 291; D Schramm, 'The Race to Geneva: Resisting the Gravitational Pull of the WTO in the GM Labelling Controversy' (2007) 9 Vermont Journal of Environmental Law 93; JS Fredland, 'Unlabel Their Frankenstein Foods: Evaluating a US Challenge to the European Commission's Labeling Requirements for Food Products Containing Genetically-Modified Organisms' (2000) 33 *Vanderbilt Journal of Transnational Law* 183, 218 (arguing that these provisions 'would not survive a US challenge').

[12] See HS Shapiro, 'The Rules That Swallowed the Exceptions: The WTO SPS Agreement and Its Relationship to GATT Articles XX and XXI' (2007) 24 *Arizona Journal of International and Comparative Law*199; CS Boisen, 'Title III of the Bioterrorism Act: Sacrificing US Trade Relations in the Name of Food Security' (2007) 56 *American University Law Review* 667.

explorations of a single issue to draw more sweeping conclusions on the operation of the SPS regime. Keane's findings on food labelling lead him to question 'the legitimacy of the system'[13] while Schramm considers that a critical WTO ruling on GM labelling 'would be a blow to… American political values as much as it would be a blow to Europe's millennia-old agricultural traditions'.[14] This example demonstrates the dangers of projecting the impact of the SPS Agreement from an individual case study. An alternative formalist reading of the Agreement could plausibly conclude that GM labelling rules, in that they engage non-scientific issues, fall entirely outside the scope of the SPS Agreement.[15] A formalist analysis of a single case may provide a fragile basis on which to draw more far-reaching assertions about the SPS framework. Perhaps because of these limitations, or because many issues would not find their way to litigation, there remain relatively few explorative studies despite the wide range of food policies affected by the Agreement.

Expansive

A comparative or explorative analysis may leave the broader ramifications of SPS law on domestic policy-making implicit rather than explicit. By contrast, the third style of formalist analysis identified here takes a more expansive approach, extrapolating directly from textual analysis or jurisprudence to assert that a particular change in state behaviour *is* occurring or *will* inevitably ensue. In such studies, WTO decisions are perceived to have dramatic implications. For example, the AB's interpretation of article 3.1 in *Hormones* is said to have 'severely constrained the ability of states to choose the level of sanitary advice and protection'[16] and 'represents a shackle on the government's ability to regulate'.[17] Article 5.1, likewise, has been narrowly construed by WTO courts, 'thus limiting Members' ability to consider non-scientific factors within their management procedures'.[18] The *EC—Biotech* Panel's reading of article 5.7 'severely restricts the ability of WTO Members to impose provisional SPS measures in the face of new scientific evidence of risk to

[13] Keane (n 11) 331.

[14] Schramm (n 11) 129.

[15] See J Scott, 'European Regulation of GMOs and the WTO' (2003) 9 *Columbia Journal of European Law* 213; R Howse and PC Mavroidis, 'Europe's Evolving Regulatory Strategy for GMOs—The Issue of Consistency with WTO Law: Of Kine and Brine' (2000) 24 *Fordham International Law Journal* 317. Equally, Appleton anticipates that if GM labelling were to come before the Appellate Body (AB) a 'reasonable solution' reflecting political sensitivities would be found. AE Appleton, 'The Labelling of GM Products Pursuant to International Trade Rules' (2000) 8 *New York University Environmental Law Journal* 566, 578.

[16] D Livshiz, 'Updating American Administrative Law: WTO, International Standards, Domestic Implementation and Public Participation' (2007) 24 *Wisconsin International Law Journal* 961, 979.

[17] Livshiz, ibid 980.

[18] Alemanno (n 7) 447.

human health and the environment'.[19] Put simply, the outcomes of WTO dispute settlement demonstrate 'a serious threat to the democratic system of government of WTO Members'.[20] The assumptions about the functioning of international law that lie behind these interpretations will be discussed below (Sect. 3.3). Here we may simply observe that the formalist nature of the analysis seems not to inhibit commentators from making strong assertions about the actual impact of the SPS regime.

3.2.2 Empiricism

None of the analyses of the SPS Agreement reviewed may be described as a systematic empirical account of the impact of law on policy-making. Where empirical evaluations are undertaken, the focus tends to be on the Agreement's more tangible effect (or lack of effect) on trade rather than its meaning for policy-makers. For example, Mayeda reports on the costs incurred by developing countries through raising food-processing conditions to meet international standards,[21] and Gatthi assesses the impact of allegedly non-compliant EU domestic SPS measures on Kenya's export markets.[22] The most elaborate review of this sort is Das's account of the problems caused to Indian agricultural exports by other WTO Members' non-adherence to SPS rules.[23]

Nevertheless, empirical analysis is used by some writers to posit a specific concrete impact of the SPS Agreement on domestic policy-making; such writers are generally among the most virulent critics of the regime. Wallach, for example, points to a number of regulatory changes that suggest to her the influence of the international regime. These include US government recognition of the equivalence of Australia's meat-processing inspection system, the Codex Committee on Food Additives and Contaminants' endorsement of a proposal to remove dose limits for irradiation, and the undermining of US standards for organic food by acceptance of 'foreign systems'.[24] Closer scrutiny reveals that all the claimed effects are merely anticipated, rather than actually having occurred. In a similar vein, Silverglade

[19] CG Gonzalez, 'Genetically Modified Organisms and Justice: The International Environmental Justice Implications of Biotechnology' (2007) 19 *Georgetown International Environmental Law Review* 583.

[20] Christoforou (n 2) 622–623.

[21] G Mayeda, 'Developing Disharmony? The SPS and TBT Agreements and the Impact of Harmonisation in Developing Countries' (2004) 7 JIEL 737, 753.

[22] J Gatthi, 'A Critical Appraisal of the NEPAD Agenda in Light of Africa's Place in the World Trade Regime in an Era of Market-Centred Development' (2003) 13 *Transnational Law and Contemporary Problems* 179, 204–207.

[23] K Das, 'Coping with SPS Challenges in India: WTO and Beyond' (2008) 11 JIEL 971.

[24] LM Wallach, 'Accountable Governance in the Era of Globalization: The WTO, NAFTA, and International Harmonization of Standards' (2002) 50 *University of Kansas Law Review* 823, 846.

asserts that concerns about lowering standards 'are more than theoretical'.[25] He focuses in particular on the adoption by Codex of a number of standards at odds with US policy, including permitting lower levels of minerals in bottled water, non-mandatory pasteurisation of dairy products, and allowing non-authorised food additives. Once again, however, the analysis fails to demonstrate that actual domestic policy changes have occurred as a result of meeting international requirements.[26] These studies may be more accurately considered as quasi-empirical, making selective use of regulatory examples to support underlying normative concerns.

More recent work has sought to investigate the relationship between international law and domestic regulation in greater depth. Livshiz has studied both developments in the setting of standards and the willingness of the US Administration to enter into Mutual Recognition Agreements (MRA) following the establishment of the SPS Agreement. With regard to the former, he notes how US regulatory agencies have increasingly used international standards to justify their own domestic proposals.[27] However, the Agreement's significance in creating recognition of the equivalence of other state standards is found to be less marked. Although the US has been willing to negotiate MRAs, it has rarely been successful.[28] Masson-Matthee's study of the Codex Alimentarius considers the extent to which European legislation has been shaped by Codex standards, offering several examples of where the analytical techniques and methods of sampling used in secondary legislation originate from the international body.[29] Her careful examination of EU food law demonstrates how WTO recognition of Codex standards has led to their 'increased status' and hence greater attention from Community institutions.[30] However, she also indicates that the recognition given to these standards falls short of that foreseen by the Agreement.[31]

---

[25] BA Silverglade, 'The Impact of International Trade Agreements on US Food Safety and Labelling Standards' (1998) 53 *Food and Drug Law Journal* 537, 539.

[26] ibid 539. Indeed, while the author anticipates that international standards will lead to a 'levelling down' of consumer protection, his examples demonstrate that the US actually maintains standards. However, he contends that it is 'just a matter of time' until international standards prevail. See also L Sikes, 'FDA's Consideration of Codex Alimentarius Standards in Light of International Trade Agreements' (1998) 53 *Food and Drug Law Journal* 327, 333 (pointing to the dangers associated with the imposition of inferior Codex standards, but acknowledging that this was not yet taking place).

[27] Livshiz (n 16) 976–977.

[28] ibid 988.

[29] MD Masson-Matthee, *The Codex Alimentarius Commission and its Standards* (The Hague, TMC Asser Press, 2007) 123.

[30] ibid 120.

[31] Masson-Matthee specifically argues that EU general food law (Regulation 178/2002) foresees under Art 5(3) that Codex standards be 'taken into consideration', a procedural obligation that she considers to be less far-reaching than the substantive requirement—'Members shall base their sanitary or phytosanitary measures on international standards'—provided for in SPS Agreement Art 3.1. ibid 122.

A different dimension of the SPS Agreement is revealed in Scott's analysis of the SPS Committee.[32] Contrary to the impression created in formalist analyses, within the SPS Committee, regulatory measures 'are not merely condemned or saved, as lawful or not, but are frequently mitigated or adjusted to reflect the concerns of both importing and exporting states'.[33] Scott's work provides a number of concrete examples of how careful negotiation between WTO Members can lead them to rethink regulatory measures, taking into account their impact on the trade of others.[34] For example, she illustrates how a regulatory demand from the Philippines for a third-party audit of hygiene procedures of all meat and milk plants was postponed and ultimately dropped, following discussion within the Committee.[35] Her detailed study of the body's work provides a more nuanced and less hostile characterisation of the regime.

Given the amount written on the SPS Agreement and the strength of the claims about its impact, the relative lack of empirical forays into domestic food policy may seem puzzling. Outside the specific studies discussed above, empirical demonstrations of the SPS's influence remain fleeting.[36] Certainly, the specific influence of international obligations may not always be easy to determine.[37] Yet it is notable that those authors who choose a more thorough empirical approach are rewarded with a different understanding of the Agreement's operation. Livshiz, Masson-Matthee and Scott all identify areas where the Agreement affects national regulatory practice, but do little to sustain the contention that it dramatically constrains WTO Members.

---

[32] Scott (n 4) Chap. 2.

[33] ibid 45.

[34] ibid 54–60.

[35] ibid 54–55.

[36] See L Biukovic, 'Selective Adaptation of WTO Transparency Norms and Local Practices in China and Japan' (2008) 11 JIEL 803 (discussed further in s 3.3.2 below) and DS Johanson and WL Bryant, 'Eliminating Phytosanitary Trade Barriers: The Effects of the Uruguay Round Agreements on California Agricultural Exports' (1996) 6 *San Joaquin Agricultural Law Review* 1, 23. Johanson and Bryant suggest that the SPS framework has influenced the manner in which bilateral negotiations on sanitary issues are discussed by creating a framework for exchanging scientific data and ensuring Japan's domestic measures were WTO-compatible. In the same vein, Roberts documents a number of changes to sanitary measures in New Zealand and Australia which she argues have been encouraged by SPS disciplines. D Roberts, 'Preliminary Assessment of the Effects of the WTO Agreement on Sanitary and Phytosanitary Trade Regulations' (1998) 1 JIEL 377, 397.

[37] One particular challenge in this respect is adequate access to information. For example, Livshiz explains how federal registers do not always publicly report where equivalency determinations have been established. Livshiz (n 16) fn 137. See also comments by Biukovic identifying opaque rules as a barrier to evaluating China's implementation of SPS law. ibid 823.

3.2.3 Critical Theory

Very few of the studies reviewed contain a critical-theoretical element. The work of Gonzalez is a prominent exception. She critically exposes the origins of the GM food controversy, tracing developing countries' dependence on developed countries from colonial roots, through the Green Revolution, to the 'double standards' of the WTO Agreement on Agriculture.[38] This process has 'transformed self-reliant subsistence economies into economic satellites of the developed world'.[39] Gonzalez argues that by removing developing countries' rights to restrict genetically modified organisms (GMOs) for reasons of food security, cultural integrity or environmental protection, the SPS Agreement effectively perpetuates historical injustices. Science-based SPS disputes serve to obscure rather than expose these injustices.[40] The author then calls for an interpretation of the regulatory framework for GMOs which invokes the principle of 'environmental justice', based upon the primacy of human rights, such as the rights to food, life, health and self-determination.[41] Gonzalez's concern with the structural inequities underlying the SPS regime is shared by a few other authors. Gatthi demonstrates how inadequate resources and expertise for managing SPS measures prevents African countries from benefiting from the trade regime. Concurring, Mayeda argues that the SPS and TBT Agreements need to be infused with a 'procedural conception of justice' which involves empowering developing countries as equal partners in the trade regime.[42]

This section has demonstrated the scarcity of empirical and critical-theoretical accounts of the impact of the SPS Agreement and the dominance of the formalist approach. Why, when formalism is generally considered to be on the wane in international legal studies,[43] have commentators concentrated so steadfastly on the text of the Agreement and a handful of disputes? There are a number of possible explanations. One could be a latent tendency in all lawyers to veer towards a formalist

---

[38] Gonzalez (n 19) 595–602.

[39] ibid 598.

[40] ibid 625.

[41] ibid 626–628. A limited number of other authors also seek an interpretation of the SPS Agreement that incorporates human rights. Donat proposes that a human-rights test, most notably the right to food, be applied to biotechnology policies, but with a view, unlike Gonzalez, to ensuring easy access among the world's poorest to potentially beneficial food technology. KJ Donat, 'Engineering Akerlof Lemons: Information Asymmetry, Externalities, and Market Intervention in the Genetically Modified Food Market' (2003) 12 *Minnesota Journal of Global Trade* 417.Elsewhere the 'right to participate in public affairs' is invoked to support a call for greater attention to public opinion in the assessment of SPS measures and a 'consumer's right to know' as a defence of GM labelling. See respectively Foster (n 2) 453 and Keane (n 11).

[42] Mayeda (n 21) 762–763. See also O Aginam, 'Trade Health or Politics? Protectionism, Risk Assessment and the Globalisation of Food Safety' (2008) 63 *Food and Drug Law Journal* 665.

[43] See M Koskenniemi, 'What is International Law?' in MD Evans (ed), *International Law* (Oxford, OUP, 2003)100–103.

approach.[44] Mastery of jurisprudence singles out the legal scholar from other academics who may provide competing analysis on issues of public importance.[45] Another influential factor could be the notorious ambiguity of the SPS provisions, which perhaps accentuates the value of the additional guidance provided by jurisprudence. This tendency is no doubt reinforced by the perceived strength of the dispute-settlement system. An arguably misplaced confidence in the significance of dispute settlement[46] magnifies the importance of rulings and therefore academic interest in them.[47] Moreover, disputes, by definition, accentuate the regime's most problematic and controversial areas, therefore appearing to offer the most promising opportunity to identify the SPS Agreement's significance and potential influence. Finally, wider public and media interest in the results of disputes emphasise their relevance and appeal as an object of study.

A formalist focus alone does not necessarily sustain the dramatic predictions of the Agreement's influence described in Chap. 1. Other analytical choices, to be discussed below, are instrumental in this respect. Nevertheless, heavy reliance on the outcome of WTO reports for an understanding of the regime does entail certain dangers. Myopic focus on dispute settlement can encourage a disturbingly introverted understanding of the SPS Agreement.[48] It can stimulate expansive interpretations that, because they conflate expectations arising from formal legal analysis of law with actual impact, may be disconcertingly removed from social reality. In addition, it can vastly exaggerate the importance of the results of disputes.[49]

These comments are not intended to imply that formalism should be altogether abandoned. Comparative and explorative analyses are important in teasing out the meaning and implications of SPS provisions. However, in order to ascertain the

---

44 Even among US lawyers who are sceptical about international rules, Jouannet has noted, there remains a 'residual formalism… the simple necessity of argument at the international level about rules and institutions [tied to]… a profoundly legalist and procedural domestic tradition'. E Jouannet, 'French and American Perspectives on International Law: Legal Cultures and International Law' (2006) 58 *Maine Law Review* 292, 305.

45 As Cho has pointed out, 'WTO jurisprudence is full of esoteric semantics and codes, which very few would actually venture to read, let alone comprehend.' S Cho, 'The WTO Gemeinschaft' (2004) 56 *Alabama Law Review* 483, 539.

46 For a more sceptical view of the importance of dispute settlement, see DA Faber, 'The Case Against Clarity' in *Political Economy* (n 2) 583 (suggesting that 'if the WTO is to open markets, it will not be primarily through the direct effects of litigation. Rather, it will be through voluntary compliance or negotiation—the same ways that most of international law functions').

47 Scott (n 4) 74 (arguing that the strengthening of the dispute settlement system 'has allowed international lawyers to emulate their domestic counterparts in their fixation on case law').

48 S Dillon, 'Opportunism and the WTO: Corporations, Academics and "Member States"' in C Picker, I Brunn and D Arner (eds), *International Economic Law: The State and Future of The Discipline* (Oxford, Hart Publishing, 2008) 57 (discussing how the 'unseemly technical focus on dispute-generated jurisprudence' has inhibited scholars from critically appraising the purpose of the WTO).

49 See Winickoff et al. (n 10) 84 (boldly proclaiming that '[t]he outcome of *Biotech Products* carries profound implications for the balance between state and global power and the relationship of science to democracy').

overall repercussions of law in this context, it is necessary to acknowledge the limitations of such evaluations and be wary of any claims made. When Foster promises to 'examine experience to date'[50] or Victor proposes an 'analysis of the system at work', we must be alert to the overriding dominance of jurisprudence in these assessments and the limitations that this implies.[51] As a minority of researchers have demonstrated, moving beyond formalist accounts of the SPS Agreement delivers contrasting insights into its functioning.

3.3 Conception of How Law Functions: What Are the Expectations of SPS Law?

As discussed in Chap. 2, the claim that the SPS Agreement has an influence on domestic policy-makers does not *per se* reflect any particular view of international law. Both a regulative understanding of international law (that law constrains the actions of states) and a generative conception (that law generates interaction which reshapes the interests of states and the way they perceive the world) may support that conclusion. However, the former generally assumes a causal relationship between law and state behaviour, and thus a direct correlation between the two. A generative understanding of law, by contrast, anticipates the impact to be more gradual and indirect. This section considers which concept of how law functions is the most prevalent in research into the Agreement. It should first be emphasised that writers do not in general explicitly elaborate on the mechanisms through which states are swayed by international rules. A claim, for example, that the *Hormones* case has 'great implications'[52] for health regulations is not necessarily accompanied by an exposition of precisely how law exerts an influence on national policy-makers. Reaching an understanding of the conceptual underpinnings of SPS Agreement research therefore remains in great measure a process of inference.

---

[50] Foster (n 2) 427.

[51] DG Victor, 'The Sanitary and Phytosanitary Agreement of the World Trade Organisation: An Assessment After Five Years' (2000) 32 *New York University Journal of International Law and Politics*865, 913. Victor is sensitive to this point, drawing attention to possible harmonisation effects not captured through analysis of dispute resolution. He acknowledges (at 927) that 'systematic research on the possible effect is needed'.

[52] MD Carter, 'Selling Science under the SPS Agreement: Accommodating Consumer Preference in the Growth Hormones Controversy' (1997) 6 *Minnesota Journal of Global Trade* 625, 655.

3.3.1 A Regulative Understanding of SPS Law

Coercive Force

The first variant of the regulative account of law described in Chap. 2, coercive force, appears to be the least favoured characterisation of the SPS regime. Nevertheless, some writers do advance a conception of the WTO as a powerful enforcer. The body is presented as one that can 'compel' Members into compliance or impose financial damage,[53] its 'control' emanating from the 'WTO's wide membership, sophisticated dispute resolution system, and effective sanctions'.[54] Developing-country Members are particularly vulnerable to coercive force, potentially allowing more powerful countries to export their preferred food policies.[55] In some instances, the most WTO Members can do is 'ready their societies to accept defeat and implement reform'.[56]

Strategic Calculation

More commonly, work on the SPS Agreement assumes that WTO Members will anticipate and seek to avoid potential conflicts that may arise with the development of non-compliant SPS measures. States are not forced to adhere to SPS rules, but do so as a long-term strategic necessity.[57] From this perspective, the legal regime is a decisive element in the calculations of policy-makers who 'take defensive measures to foreclose the WTO attack'.[58] A number of commentators allude to this process with specific reference to European policy. Masson-Matthee suggests that the EU has made several substantive changes to secondary legislation which can best be understood as an attempt to 'anticipate and avoid complications' that might arise in the WTO context.[59] Likewise, Keane predicts that future labelling laws will be constructed to avoid references to food safety and thus escape the remit of the

[53] BA Silverglade 'The WTO Agreement on Sanitary and Phytosanitary Measures: Weakening Food Safety Regulations to Facilitate Trade?' (2000) 55 *Food and Drug Law Journal* 517.

[54] D Kalderimis, 'Problems of WTO Harmonisation and the Virtues of Shields over Swords' (2004) 13 *Minnesota Journal of Global Trade* 305, 310. See also Aginam (n 42) 667 (attributing the legal significance of the SPS Agreement to the dispute-settlement system).

[55] See DM Strauss, 'Feast or Famine: The Impact of the WTO Decision Favouring the US Biotechnology Industry in the EU Ban on Genetically Modified Foods' (2008) 45 *American Business Law Journal* 775, 824 (predicting that the WTO will drive through a regulatory approach worldwide which is favourable to biotechnology).

[56] Victor (n 51) 922.

[57] See IAR Sien, 'Beefing up the Hormones Dispute: Problems in Compliance and Viable Alternatives' (2007) 95 *Georgetown Law Journal* 565, 589 (arguing that WTO Members are 'ultimately constrained by their own investment in the system').

[58] See, e.g. J Atik, 'Science and International Regulatory Convergence' (1996) 17 *Northwestern Journal of International Law and Business* 736, 745.

[59] Masson-Matthee (n 29) 126.

SPS Agreement.[60] Bronckers and Soopramanien concur, recounting that 'institutions tend to listen carefully when considering draft legislation in the event private parties point out to them that such draft text [*sic*] are problematic from a WTO law perspective'.[61] Peel also explains that pre-emption of international legal complications is becoming increasingly routine in domestic policy practice.[62]

Of course, a rationalist would also expect states not to comply where the benefits outweigh the costs of doing so. In the light of what is widely considered to be the EU's non-application of the AB's ruling in *Hormones*,[63] it should be evident that the long-term benefits of compliance do not always predominate over immediate policy goals. One might have therefore anticipated scepticism about the extent to which states will strive to accommodate WTO law. Yet Guzman is one of the few authors to voice this doubt clearly,[64] challenging the notion that WTO Members will comply with SPS rules where there is a significant national interest in maintaining them. In such a situation, he argues, 'a state might prefer the costs of any "withdrawal of concessions" to exposing itself to products that it considers harmful.'[65]

Normative Obligation

As noted in the above discussion on the expansive analysis characteristic of formalist writing, much work on the SPS Agreement tends to infer the impact of law from the identification of legal obligations. What assumptions about international law are engaged in this practice? Take for example a statement (reflecting on the *Hormones* AB report) that 'the Appellate Body makes it virtually impossible for a Member to set a higher level of protection'?[66] Such a comment conceals a significant intellectual leap from legal analysis (identifying that the SPS Agreement says *x*) to a projection on social reality (WTO Member behaviour conforms to *x*). It tacitly assumes that WTO Members adhere to international law in accordance with AB interpretations. Contrary to the rationalist logic, this outcome is not contingent. Rather, the assumption that WTO law is a normative force taken seriously by the regime's Members is the starting point of the analysis. The expectation is that a Member

[60] Keane (n 11) 320.

[61] M Bronckers and R Soopramanien, 'The Impact of WTO Law on European Food Regulation' (2008) 6 *European Food and Feed Law Review* 361, 394.

[62] J Peel, 'A GMO by Any Other Name.... Might be an SPS Risk!: Implications of Expanding the Scope of the WTO Sanitary and Phytosanitary Measures Agreement' (2006) 17 EJIL 1009, 1028.

[63] For a discussion of the EU's compliance with *Hormones*, see D Wüger, 'The Never-Ending Story: The Implementation Phase in the Dispute between the EC and the United States on Hormone-Treated Beef' (2002) 33 *Law and Policy in International Business* 777.

[64] See also Keane (n 11) 332 (who points to the possibility of 'widespread non-compliance … or an era of highly local and harmonised trade rules').

[65] AT Guzman, 'Food Fears: Health and Safety at the WTO' (2004) 45 VJIL 20, 25.

[66] RA Pereira, 'Why Would International Administrative Activity Be Any Less Legitimate? A Study of the Codex Alimentarius Commission' (2008) 9 *German Law Journal* 1693, 1704.

complies (the SPS Agreement 'will have to be taken into account by the EC'[67]) and the consequences are therefore self-evidently that the Agreement poses an 'obstacle to the right of governments to establish their own levels of protection'.[68]

Let us try to expand on what the normative obligation—'Members will obey the law'—actually means in the domestic context. Policy-making in the food domain involves developing rules to respond to a specific issue, taking into account the interests of all stakeholders, including consumers, producers, industry and agricultural traders.[69] An assumption of conformity with normative obligation implies that policy-makers are cognisant of and will apply international rules, even in the face of contrary social and political interests. Are these really the expectations of authors who posit that WTO Members adhere to SPS law?

There is no clear answer to this. Often the normative obligation is articulated in the broadest of terms. WTO Members 'must follow SPS rules',[70] and 'whenever any Member seeks to implement a health regulation, it must do so consistently, on the basis of scientific evidence.'[71] However, where studies are more explicit about the national policy-making process, they indicate a direct influence on national regulators. SPS Agreement provisions are deemed to 'affect …the procedures by which member countries' domestic standards are set, the ability of countries to set their own policy priorities and preferences',[72] and Codex standards adjudged to 'strip national regulators of their discretion'.[73] Likewise, the AB's apparent rejection of the precautionary principle translates into 'a shackle on the government's ability to regulate'.[74] Trebilcock and Soloway also call for a clarification of the deference to be paid by WTO dispute settlement bodies to domestic regulatory processes in order to avoid 'unduly constraining the autonomy of Member states'.[75] In short, many authors argue that national regulators' attention to SPS Agreement provisions may fundamentally alter their behaviour. The consequence foreseen is a reorientation in policy away from real domestic

[67] Slotboom (n 6) 490.

[68] JM Wagner, 'The WTO's Interpretation of the SPS Agreement has Undermined the Right of Governments to Establish Appropriate Levels of Protection against Risk' (2000) 31 *Law and Policy in International Business* 855, 858.

[69] In the European context, this is further complicated by the fact that these interests may diverge considerably between Member States.

[70] Charnovitz (n 2) 271.

[71] Carter (n 52) 656.

[72] Wallach (n 24) 823.

[73] Pereira (n 66) 1693.

[74] Livshiz (n 16) 980.

[75] Trebilcock and Soloway (n 2) 551.

interests and concerns,[76] and a reluctance to develop stringent health measures in the future.[77]

For writers with a strategic understanding of law, changing existing international rules may not be viewed as a priority. If Members can successfully opt out of rules at will, amending them may be superfluous. The frequency of calls for the reform of the SPS Agreement therefore underlines the dominance of the normative understanding of law.[78] If the assumption is that laws are *per se* followed, laws judged to be poor *will* lead to unacceptable consequences and therefore *must* be changed. The real impact law may be having is not considered. For instance, a rule demanding a scientific approach to domestic policy is believed unacceptably to exclude non-scientific public concerns, and therefore has to be amended to include an 'escape clause'.[79] Similarly, a view that Article 5.7 unreasonably precludes Members from a long-term precautionary approach on food issues leads to demands for the reform of the Agreement.[80]

Theoretically, coercive, strategic and normative accounts of the regulative conception of international law could produce differentiated expectations, the first two more dependent on the power of the state concerned or the specific costs and benefits of maintaining national preferences. However, this review demonstrates that whether expressed in coercive, strategic or normative terms, expectations largely converge: WTO Members *will* comply with international rules. In one sense, such assumptions are a convenient and unobjectionable shorthand. It would hardly be reasonable (or desirable) to expect each evaluation of WTO law to be prefaced by the author's thesis on the operation of international law. Yet the food-related disputes that have arisen under the SPS Agreement directly challenge this regulative assumption. European policies on biotechnology and hormones in meat are widely viewed as at odds with SPS provisions, yet WTO criticisms have had little effect on them. Elsewhere, disputes have been resolved, but the conformity of domestic rules

[76] See Charnovitz (n 2) 271 (anticipating that the SPS Agreement 'can affect the ability of governments to provide health and achieve biosafety'). See also Gonzalez's anticipation of the impact of the *EC—Biotech* Panel Report on biotechnology policy in developing countries. Gonzalez (n 19) 617–618.

[77] See Wallach (n 24) 831 (anticipating a 'regulatory chill') and Peel, 'A GMO by Any Other Name' (n 62) 1028 (foreseeing a 'dampening effect on national regulatory practices' as policy-makers fear the implications of a WTO challenge).

[78] For a few proposals of this nature, see Kalderimis (n 54) 347; Wallach (n 24) 862; Walker (n 2) 319; Christoforou (n 2) 648; Sien (n 57) 585; KC Kennedy, 'Resolving International Sanitary and Phytosanitary Disputes in the WTO: Lessons and Future Directions' (2000) 55 *Food and Drug Law Journal* 81, 102–103. For a contrary view that the SPS can be reorganised to operate more efficiently without major reform see R Neugebauer, 'Fine-Tuning WTO Jurisprudence and the SPS Agreement: Lessons from the Beef Hormone Case' (2000) 31 *Law and Policy in International Business* 1255.

[79] J Bohanes, 'Risk Regulation in WTO Law: A Procedure-Based Approach to the Precautionary Principle' (2002) 40 *Columbia Journal of Transnational Law* 323, 387.

[80] Silverglade (n 53) 523–524.

with the Agreement remains suspect.[81] If anything, ineffective rulings perversely appear to heighten expectations that the WTO will intrude on national regulatory power. What these disputes appear to demand, but fail to provoke, is reflection on the basic premise that underpins much current analysis: that WTO law directly regulates state behaviour.

3.3.2 Generative Function

The studies cited above portray national policy-makers as passive recipients of international law. There is little sense that international law may affect state behaviour in less immediate ways, as foreseen by a generative understanding of law.

Two studies, however, offer a glimpse of alternative conceptions of how the SPS Agreement functions. They point to elements of both the socialisation and cognitive mechanisms discussed in Chap. 2. Both aspects are therefore dealt with together here. Biukovic's work on the adoption of WTO transparency norms in China and Japan offers useful insights into the socialisation process. In neither country is domestic policy 'in compliance' with SPS requirements: many WTO complaints remain in both cases.[82] However, Biukovic illustrates how participation in the WTO has triggered 'far-reaching political and legal reforms that have affected Japan's internal legal processes'.[83] To enhance its status as a trading partner, the country has undertaken institutional, regulatory and educational reforms through 'selective adaptation': that is, applying international rules in a manner consistent with local norms. A similar process is under way in China, though to a lesser extent.[84] The conformity of Chinese regulatory measures with international standards remains questionable, but engagement with WTO partners on SPS issues has 'caused a major shift in perspective by state elites' which is gradually leading to changes in regulatory structures.[85]

Whereas Biukovic's study reveals conscious adaptation to the demands of international law, Scott's commentary on the SPS Committee illustrates the more subtle cognitive changes that the regime provokes. She explains how the Committee offers a venue for negotiation and interaction between Members, which can gradually reform participants' understanding of the Agreement's provisions. Law is represented here as far more fluid, subject to constant review and open to challenge

[81] Whitlock, for example, questions in his study of *Japan—Varietals* whether Japan did actually comply with DSB recommendations, although their action was enough to resolve the dispute at hand. JP Whitlock, '*Japan-Measures Affecting Agricultural Products*: Lessons for Future SPS and Agricultural Trade Disputes (2002) 33 *Law and Policy in International Business* 741, 776.

[82] Biukovic (n 36) comments respectively on outstanding problems in relation to Japanese agricultural goods (at 815–816) and Chinese non-compliance with international standards (at 824).

[83] ibid 813–814.

[84] As Biukovic notes, the norm-internalisation process may not yet have extended to Chinese local authorities where much policy-making takes place. ibid 821.

[85] ibid 824.

and reinterpretation. The SPS Committee helps to generate '(provisionally) settled understandings' and a 'mutual adjustment of regulatory expectations and regulatory performance'.[86] Law is certainly influencing state behaviour, but not in the direct way implied by a regulative understanding: compliance occurs in part because the discursive process 'serves also to elucidate what it is that compliance demands'.[87]

A number of other studies, albeit less extensively, also identify non-regulative ways in which SPS law is shaping domestic practice. Bronckers and Soopramanien argue that although the European Court of Justice has not directly cited WTO rulings in its own decisions, international cases are swaying European practice as a result of a 'muted' dialogue between judicial bodies.[88] In another study, Scott speculates on the more indirect influence that the SPS Agreement may have had on the establishment of the European Food Safety Authority given the need to strengthen the scientific basis of EU measures facing international scrutiny.[89] Others point to the impact of international norms in changing expectations in bilateral negotiations.[90]

Despite the exceptions noted in this section, this review suggests that commentators overwhelmingly favour a regulative conception of how law functions. The limitation of this perspective is that its basic assumptions effectively bury important questions. Where policy-makers resist changes to domestic regulation (as we know they do), does international law prove entirely irrelevant? If states do not simply follow international rules, what particular role, if any, do the latter play? Without answering these questions, can we believe the frequent claims that the Agreement needs reform? The few commentaries that have moved beyond the regulative conception of law, starting to explore some of these issues, are particularly useful in lifting the veil on the microprocesses through which national regulators reflect on and respond to international norms. As Scott suggests, such accounts are 'descriptively more accurate than the dominant court-centric approach, and normatively richer and more challenging'.[91]

3.4 Evaluative Perspective: On What Do Commentators Focus?

As indicated in Chap. 2, commentators will typically evaluate the impact of an international treaty from one of two perspectives: either ascending (ascertaining its effect on state interests or behaviour) or descending (focusing on the goals of

[86] Scott (n 4) 47.

[87] ibid 75.

[88] Bronckers and Soopramanien (n 61) 372–373.

[89] Scott (n 15) 233.

[90] See n 36.

[91] Scott (n 4) 75.

the regime).[92] This section reviews which type of evaluation is most favoured in analysis of the Agreement.

3.4.1 Ascending Perspective

Given the considerable public attention paid to the outcome of controversial WTO disputes, it is perhaps unsurprising that the standpoint of the state has been a popular one for evaluating the Agreement. This section will consider this analytical preference with reference to the variants—sovereign power, values, and state will as contracted—identified in Chap. 2.

Sovereignty Critique

A sovereignty critique of the SPS Agreement, examining the impact of the regime on where decisions are made and the residual power retained by WTO Members, is much favoured among analysts. Infringement of sovereignty may be deemed to occur where national regulatory practices are unduly hampered by SPS rules, or more obviously, where a regulatory measure is overturned during dispute settlement. Walker focuses primarily on the former scenario in his extensive work on the *Hormones* dispute. While WTO Members formally retain the right to set their own protection, he argues that the SPS Agreement is propelling states towards science policy which elevates the role of risk in shaping regulatory measures to the detriment of a normal balance between competing economic and social concerns. As Walker asks,

> if benefits could not be weighed in the balance, or consumer anxieties could not be respected, or domestic politics could not be taken into account, what would remain of the sovereignty inherent in these management decisions?[93]

For others, the central concern is the discretion permitted to an international tribunal to judge the legitimacy of a national health or safety measure: if review panels try to 'second-guess' the motivations underlying a particular measure, this could pose a significant threat to the integrity of national decision-making.[94] While early evaluations of the SPS Agreement were relatively sanguine about this possibility,[95]

[92] It is of course possible for analysts to combine both perspectives. However, perhaps as this type of account is less argumentatively compelling, commentators do not generally shift perspective in this way. One exception is Mayeda (n 21) in his balanced account of the advantages and dangers for developing countries associated with harmonisation. Charnovitz also reflects on both the overall aims of the regime and potential impact on states, an approach that leads to the conclusion that the SPS Agreement 'has worked reasonably well'. Charnovitz (n 2) 301.

[93] Walker (n 2) 306–307.

[94] See discussion in Trebilcock and Soloway (n 2) 541.

[95] DA Wirth, 'The Role of Science in the Uruguay Round and NAFTA Trade Disciplines' (1994) 27 *Cornell International Law Journal* 817.

the *Hormones* dispute provoked a number of writers to question the nation state's long-term control over SPS decision-making.[96]

The arguments presented against ceding decision-making power to the WTO are twofold. The first is that the dispute settlement bodies have no democratic legitimacy to make judgements on sensitive policy issues. In doing so, the WTO 'is making decisions in the context of a trade dispute between a few parties on the future of the food supply for all'.[97] Some consider this to be particularly indefensible in the culturally sensitive context of food policy, 'implicat[ing] deeply held notions of sovereignty and autonomy'.[98] A second reservation about a shift in decision-making towards the WTO is a more technical one of expertise. Trade lawyers are considered to be 'patently unqualified'[99] to draw conclusions on questions involving the interpretation of complex data, which could lead to 'serious mistakes in evaluating and weighing scientific evidence'.[100]

However, research focused upon the sovereignty implications of the SPS Agreement does not inevitably lead to a negative view of the Agreement's impact on decision-making. Responding to fears that domestic policy-making will be constrained, a few authors have argued that the SPS provisions provide WTO Members with considerable leeway for national discretion.[101] Atik goes further, contending that relatively modest obligations concerning scientific evidence provide Members with an opportunity to reinforce domestic policies previously vulnerable to attack under GATT.[102] Even with regard to dispute settlement, commentators are not uniformly pessimistic: Wüger believes that a 'satisfactory balance between internationalization of standards and national interests might still be discovered'.[103] Nevertheless, the dominant view remains that the WTO rulings are 'a step in the wrong direction,'[104] and have 'handle[d] the clash between international regulation and domestic authority poorly'.[105] In short, what we are witnessing is 'a slow motion *coup d'etat* against accountable, democratic governments'.[106]

---

[96] See, e.g. Slotboom (n 6) 489–491; Silverglade (n 53) 522; Livshiz (n 16) 979–980.

[97] Strauss (n 55) 824.

[98] Guzman (n 65) 4.

[99] Wagner (n 68) 857.

[100] T Christoforou (n 2) 645.

[101] Epps (n 10) 387–388; Howse and Mavroidis (n 15) (arguing that EU GMO legislation is compatible with the SPS Agreement).

[102] Atik (n 58) 745.

[103] Wüger (n 63) 825. For a counter-argument that in most cases no such balance is possible between national policy preferences and objective scientific standards, see AO Sykes, 'Domestic Regulation, Sovereignty, and Scientific Evidence Requirements: A Pessimistic View' (2002) 3 *Chicago Journal of International Law* 353.

[104] Wagner (n 68) 859.

[105] Guzman (n 65) 38.

[106] Wallach (n 24) 826.

Values Critique

For other analysts, the primary interest is the substantive outcome of policy developed according to SPS Agreement principles rather than the locus of decision-making. The starting point of this critique is that citizens share certain values in the context of food policy which international rules threaten to undermine. This occurs in three ways. Firstly, the WTO is perceived to be advancing values other than those most important to the general public. The organisation thus stands accused of trying 'to regulate health and environment policies from a purely trade-oriented perspective'[107] and of 'elevat[ing] free trade in food and foodstuffs over a host of other concerns'.[108] As a result, 'social order, public confidence, trust, community, rights, democracy and deliberation has no role.'[109] By ignoring cultural concerns, the WTO 'threatens the way of life that people have an interest in protecting'.[110] Secondly, not only the ethos of the organisation, but the processes the WTO establishes through the SPS Agreement act to marginalise public values. A notable target for this criticism is the SPS's treatment of science: it is feared that a dispute-settlement panel will attempt to treat scientific evidence in an artificially objective way, disregarding the social issues integral to effective risk assessment.[111] This approach to risk is inconsistent with trends to integrate public participation in policy-making.[112] Thirdly, the public is institutionally sidelined by inadequate access to the decision-making processes. Standard-setting bodies such as Codex Alimentarius create prohibitive thresholds for participation by many stakeholders,[113] resulting in a bias towards industrial interests.[114] More intense reliance on international rather than domestic standard-setting therefore risks further marginalising public interests.

State Will

The third common ascending critique identified in Chap. 2 concerns the will of the state as expressed in the SPS text. This line of evaluation is less popular in the study of the SPS Agreement than more normative arguments related to sover-

[107] Foster (n 2) 456.

[108] Shapiro (n 12) 339–340.

[109] J Scott, 'On Kith and Kine (and Crustaceans): Trade and Environment in the EU and WTO' in JHH Weiler (ed), *The EU, the WTO and the NAFTA: Towards a Common Law of International Trade*, 125 (Oxford, OUP, 2000) 157.

[110] L Zurek, 'The European Communities Biotech Dispute: How the WTO Fails to Consider Cultural Factors in the Genetically Modified Food Debate' (2007) 42 *Texas International Law Journal* 345, 363.

[111] Winickoff et al. (n 10) 93–94. See also Sien (n 57) 577. For an extensive discussion on the relative roles played by scientific and non-scientific concerns in food measures, see Chap. 4 below.

[112] Epps (n 10) 367–369.

[113] Livshiz (n 16) 1007–1008.

[114] MA Livermore, 'Authority and Legitimacy in Global Governance: Deliberation, Institutional Differentiation, and the Codex Alimentarius' (2006) 81 *New York University Law Review* 766, 786.

eignty and democracy. While criticism of the WTO's interpretation of the provisions abound,[115] the argument that the WTO may be guilty of judicial activism (as opposed to the SPS Agreement itself being flawed in some way) is most pertinent to the *EC—Biotech* dispute. Here the Panel undertook a rather idiosyncratic interpretation of what constitutes an SPS measure with reference to the Agreement's Annex A.[116] As a result, the Panel 'upset conventional understandings regarding its scope of operation',[117] leading to the criticism that in so doing it had dramatically expanded the scope of the regime.[118] Beyond these instances, a contractual view of the SPS Agreement is not forthcoming. The attractiveness of this type of critique is perhaps limited, due to the Agreement's 'general and enigmatic language',[119] which makes it difficult to establish whether dispute settlement has indeed taken SPS law beyond the limits intended by WTO Members.

3.4.2 Descending Perspective

The alternative to an ascending evaluation of the SPS Agreement is to consider its impact in terms of the regime's regulatory goals. The number of authors within the reviewed literature who choose this approach is relatively limited. Of those who do, a distinction can be made between those that consider the Agreement's trade-oriented aims and those focused on non-economic aspects.

Enhancing Trade

A few commentators evaluate the SPS Agreement with reference to its free-trade goals. Das's account of India's trading experiences finds that the Agreement has been 'ineffective' in restricting non-trade barriers. He notes in particular how trading partners have been able to escape discipline largely due to the 'ample space [left] for Member governments to use these measures for protectionist purposes under the guise of addressing their "legitimate" concerns'.[120] Gatthi's study of African economic policy, albeit less focused on SPS obligations, also appraises the regime from the point of view of free trade. He shows that in multiple respects, European pesticide regulations are failing to adhere to SPS disciplines, thereby

[115] See, e.g. Walker (n 2) 305 (criticising the AB's inattention to the question of science policy).

[116] See discussion in MA Young, 'The WTO's Use of Relevant Rules of International Law: An Analysis of the *Biotech* Case' (2007) 56 ICLQ 907.

[117] Peel, 'A GMO by Any Other Name' (n 62) 1031.

[118] See also A Thomison, 'A New and Controversial Mandate of the SPS Agreement: The WTO Panel's Interim Report on the *EC—Biotech* Dispute' (2007) 32 *Columbia Journal Environmental Law* 287.

[119] Gruszczynski (n 3) 302.

[120] Das (n 23) 1016.

inhibiting African development.[121] Horton examines whether developing countries are complying with the expectations of international rules and thus facilitating trade in food products. Her study, although undertaken shortly after the adoption of the Agreement, finds that the legal framework alone is not enough to drive developing countries towards compliance. Inadequate regulatory means for enforcing standards and limited technical expertise restrict the extent to which the SPS regime's ambitions can be met.[122] Mayeda also explores the potential benefits of harmonisation for developing countries and finds that they are failing to be realised, in part due to inadequate assistance from developed countries.[123] Finally, Marc Victor assesses how the application of the 'precautionary principle' in GM regulatory measures can be reconciled with the trade-enhancing principles of the WTO. He concludes that the principle encourages 'a vague system of regulation that may inevitably lead to protectionism'.[124]

Non-Trade Goals

Howse is one of a few authors to develop a descending critique of the SPS Agreement, analysing the regime from the perspective of 'deliberative democracy'. He recounts how the Agreement strives to instil 'a range of disciplines on how governments engage in deliberation and justification'.[125] While clearly advocating greater inter-governmental transparency in policy-making, Howse's supposition that the SPS obligations drive states internally towards more deliberative democracy is not entirely convincing.[126] The particular interest of his study here is that by approaching the SPS regime from a descending perspective, the author opens up new lines of analysis, effectively turning on their head the arguments of critics of the Agreement and demanding that readers rethink the operation of the regime.

As can be seen from this review, while some commentators reflect on the trade achievements of the SPS regime, the ascending perspective is the favoured

---

[121] Gatthi (n 22) 206–209.

[122] LR Horton, 'Food from Developing Countries: Steps to Improve Compliance' (1998) 53 *Food and Drug Law Journal* 139.

[123] Mayeda (n 21) 761–762 (proposing a variation on harmonisation where developing countries harmonise working practices according to their institutional ability to do so).

[124] M Victor, 'Precaution or Protectionism? The Precautionary Principle, Genetically Modified Organisms, and Allowing Unfounded Fear to Undermine Free Trade' (2001) 14 *Transnational Lawyer* 295, 320.

[125] R Howse, 'Democracy, Science, and Free Trade: Risk Regulation on Trial at the World Trade Organisation' (2000) 98 *Michigan Law Review* 2329, 2336.

[126] Howse's examples—allowing governments to set up their own level of protection, permitting 'nonmainstream' science and taking into account risk in the real world—appear to grant WTO Members policy flexibility without necessarily instilling democratic decision-making as such. It is questionable whether the purpose of enhancing deliberative democracy can really be ascribed to the Agreement. Howse partially acknowledges this, noting that 'to address the critics, it would then be necessary to amend the actual text of the SPS agreement to make it explicitly reflect the democratic values in question'. ibid 2338.

analytical choice. Why has a descending evaluation of the SPS Agreement proved unattractive? One reason may be the ambiguity surrounding its precise purpose. A researcher may be wary of undertaking an extensive evaluation of the Agreement's harmonisation effects, for example, if its intentions in this respect cannot be easily discerned. Alternatively, the lawyer may consider that if the impact implied in a descending evaluation is largely of an economic nature, such study is best pursued by non-lawyers.[127] Perhaps a free-trade perspective on the SPS Agreement is considered to be an ignoble topic for study, unlike a descending critique of, say, a human-rights regime. Or perhaps the affinity of the ascending critique with popular public discourse on the WTO simply makes this type of analysis appear more relevant.

Whatever the reasons for the dominance of ascending perspective, it could be detrimental to our overall understanding of the SPS regime's operation. This is not to question the validity of the ascending critiques, which raise entirely pertinent concerns about the potential impact of the WTO rules on democratic governance and society as a whole. However, the imbalance between the two approaches, evident from this review, has two possible negative effects. The first is that by focusing on the state and evaluating the Agreement from a purely domestic standpoint, we fail to observe other important elements of the Agreement's influence. State-oriented critiques of the SPS Agreement bring the inherent danger not only of overlooking some of the potential social gains of an enhanced trade regime, but of failing to acknowledge the implications of national regulations on other countries and their citizens. As Scott reminds us, regulation is not a purely domestic affair and can have significant, even devastating effects on other communities.[128] The second problem is the potentially distorted picture of the regime's impact provided by a preponderantly ascending perspective. Ascending critiques often suggest that policy-makers are heavily constrained by the international legal framework. Descending critiques, by contrast, depict an international regime that is failing to make its mark, with national regulatory practice still a considerable barrier to trade for both importers and exporters. However, these studies, relatively small in number, remain isolated voices amid the prevailing scholarly clamour about the SPS Agreement's restrictive effects.

3.5 Conclusion

Although a great deal has been written about the SPS Agreement, the analytical focus of these numerous studies is relatively homogenous, as this review has shown. Section 3.2 demonstrated the predominance of formalist assessments of the regime, typified by the study of WTO disputes, with a small minority of studies adopting al-

[127] Indeed, economists have evaluated some of the socioeconomic impacts of SPS measures. See, e.g. T Otsuki, JS Wilson and M Sewadeh, 'Saving Two in a Billion: Quantifying the Trade Effect of European Food Safety Standards in African Exports' (2001) 26 *Food Policy* 495.

[128] See Scott (n 4) 41–43.

ternative interpretive approaches. Section 3.3 established that most studies assume that law directly regulates state behaviour, with only a handful investigating the generative possibilities of SPS law. Section 3.4 discovered only a peripheral interest in the extent to which regulatory goals of the SPS Agreement have been achieved, with the vast majority of scholars adopting an evaluative perspective centred entirely on the implications of the Agreement for state interests. Not all studies necessarily share the same theoretical assumptions in all three dimensions. However, as Fig. 3.1 illustrates, when the reviewed studies are categorised according to the taxonomy developed in Chap. 2, a clear analytical paradigm—formalist, regulative and ascending—emerges.

The aim of Part I of this book was to understand the scholarly disquiet surrounding the SPS Agreement. Contrary to what one might expect, given the extensive criticism of the regime in early writing on the Agreement, fears of a far-reaching curtailment of domestic policy powers have no real empirical grounding: there is scant evidence in the research of this type of impact. Rather, this review suggests that the study of the SPS Agreement has been dominated by an analytical paradigm that potentially exaggerates expectations of legal influence. If WTO disputes are the principal source for understanding the SPS Agreement and the findings of these disputes are critical of national measures, if law is assumed to act as a direct constraint on state behaviour, and if the perspective chosen from which to assess this effect is that of the sovereign state, then the most likely outcome of any analysis is that the SPS Agreement infringes significantly on national powers.

The lack of concrete proof of the Agreement's influence in academic literature does not necessarily mean that the associated characterisation presented and concerns expressed are without foundation. This review simply suggests that in spite of the wealth of articles on the SPS regime, our appreciation of its importance to domestic regulators remains relatively superficial. While analysis within the dominant paradigm is entirely valid, an overly narrow analytical approach could be problematic in three ways.

Firstly, the analytical homogeneity identified in this chapter threatens to close off for study large areas of the SPS Agreement's potential reach. WTO disputes have focused (and will likely focus in the future[129]) on a limited number of the Agreement's articles, leaving a dispute-oriented literature that underplays the importance of significant SPS Agreement provisions. A predominantly formalist and ascending (state-oriented) approach to research therefore risks ignoring the potentially important monitoring, co-ordination and cooperative elements of the Agreement. Secondly, if commentators continue to conflate supposition of influence with real social impact, there may be little incentive to advance beyond our current incomplete understanding of the role played by the Agreement. If the chosen paradigm is already considered to explain the impact of international law, commentators may not feel the need to embark on tiresome verification of the proclaimed effects. Moreover, given the dominance of this particular paradigm, there is an additional danger that it becomes considered as the *only* appropriate mode for analysing the SPS system.

[129] For example, it seems improbable that a WTO Member would seek consultations on, for example, alleged non-conformity with SPS Agreement Art 7 transparency obligations.

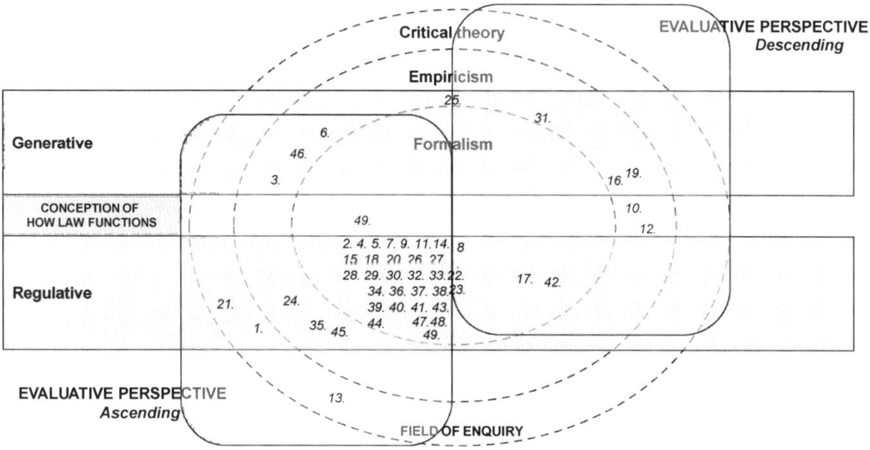

Fig. 3.1 The dominant paradigm in analysis of the SPS. (This figure categorises, inevitably in an impressionistic fashion, the majority of the articles discussed in this chapter in the framework developed in Chap. 1. In some instances, categorisation is not possible due to the size and scope of the work, e.g. Scott (n 4) or Masson-Matthee (n 29))

Key: Authors (Footnote)			
1)	Aginam (42)	26)	Peel (5)
2)	Alemanno (7)	27)	Peel (62)
3)	Biukovic (36)	28)	Pereira (66)
4)	Bohanes (79)	29)	Schramm (11)
5)	Boisen (12)	30)	Scott (9)
6)	Bronckers/Soopramanien (61)	31)	Scott (15)
7)	Carter (52)	32)	Shapiro (12)
8)	Charnovitz (2)	33)	Sien (57)
9)	Christoforou (2)	34)	Sikes (26)
10)	Das (23)	35)	Silverglade (25)
11)	Foster (2)	36)	Silverglade (53)
12)	Gatthi (22)	37)	Slotboom (6)
13)	Gonzalez (19)	38)	Strauss (55)
14)	Gruszczynski (3)	39)	Thomison (117)
15)	Guzman (65)	40)	Trebilcock/Soloway (2)
16)	Horton (122)	41)	Victor DG (51)
17)	Howse (125)	42)	Victor M (124)
18)	Howse/Mavroidis (15)	43)	Wagner (68)
19)	Johanson/Bryant (36)	44)	Walker (2)
20)	Kalderimis (54)	45)	Wallach (24)
21)	Keane (11)	46)	Whitlock (81)
22)	Kennedy (78)	47)	Winickoff et al. (10)
23)	Livermore (113)	48)	Wirth (94)
24)	Livshiz (16)	49)	Zurek (109)
25)	Mayeda (21)		

If so, the trends and biases specified in this chapter could be perpetuated and further entrenched. Thirdly, in the absence of any empirical verification of the Agreement's influence, there is a risk that legal commentary will remain detached from the realities of domestic experience. If lawyers wish to deepen their understanding of the real significance of the Agreement or facilitate its future reform, they may need to look beyond the analytical paradigm that has thusfar prevailed in the literature.

As has been seen in this chapter, when commentators have explored outside the dominant analytical paradigm, a different picture has started to emerge. Empirical studies point to a more ambiguous role for the SPS Agreement in policy-making. Appreciation of the generative function of the Agreement exposes the essential interactive aspects of the regime, while descending critiques demonstrate how the regime has *not* delivered free trade, not least for those countries for which it is most required. In short, a shift in analytical paradigm reveals an SPS Agreement that may be less predictable and far more complex than we are sometimes led to believe.

References

Aginam O, 'Trade Health or Politics? Protectionism, Risk Assessment and the Globalisation of Food Safety' (2008) 63 *Food and Drug Law Journal* 665.

Alemanno A, 'Trade in Food: Regulatory and Judicial Approaches in the EC and the WTO' (London, Cameron May, 2007).

Appleton AE, 'The Labelling of GM Products Pursuant to International Trade Rules' (2000) 8 NYU *New York University Environmental Law Journal* 566.

Atik J, 'Science and International Regulatory Convergence' (1996) 17 *Northwestern Journal of International Law and Business* 736.

Biukovic L, 'Selective Adaptation of WTO Transparency Norms and Local Practices in China and Japan' (2008) 11 JIEL 803.

Bohanes J, 'Risk Regulation in WTO Law: A Procedure-Based Approach to the Precautionary Principle' (2002) 40 *Columbia Journal of Transnational Law* 323.

Bronckers M and Soopramanien R, 'The Impact of WTO Law on European Food Regulation' (2008) 6 *European Food and Feed Law Review* 361.

Carter MD, 'Selling Science under the SPS Agreement: Accommodating Consumer Preference in the Growth Hormones Controversy' (1997) 6 *Minnesota Journal of Global Trade* 625.

Charnovitz S, 'The Supervision of Health and Biosafety of Regulation by World Trade Rules' (2000) 13 *Tulane Environmental Law Journal* 271.

Christoforou T, 'Settlement of Science-Based Trade Disputes in the WTO: A Critical Review of the Developing Case Law in the Face of Scientific Uncertainty' (2000) 8 *New York University Environmental Law Journal* 622.

Das K, 'Coping with SPS Challenges in India: WTO and Beyond' (2008) 11 JIEL 971.

Donat KJ, 'Engineering Akerlof Lemons: Information Asymmetry, Externalities, and Market Intervention in the Genetically Modified Food Market' (2003) 12 *Minnesota Journal of Global Trade* 417.

Epps T, 'Reconciling Public Opinion and WTO Rules under the SPS Agreement' (2008) 7 *World Trade Review* 359.

Faber DA, 'The Case Against Clarity' in DL Kennedy and JD Southwick (eds), *The Political Economy of International Trade Law: Essays in Honour of Robert E Hudec* (Cambridge, CUP, 2002).

Foster CE, 'Prior Approval Systems and the Substance—Procedure Dichotomy under the WTO SPS Agreement' (2008) 42 JWT 1203.

Fredland JS, 'Unlabel Their Frankenstein Foods: Evaluating a U.S. Challenge to the European Commission's Labeling Requirements for Food Products Containing Genetically-Modified Organisms' (2000) 33 *Vanderbilt Journal of Transnational Law* 183.

Gatthi J, 'A Critical Appraisal of the NEPAD Agenda in Light of Africa's Place in the World Trade Regime in an Era of Market-Centred Development' (2003) 13 *Transnational Law and Contemporary Problems* 179, 204.

Gonzalez CG, 'Genetically Modified Organisms and Justice: The International Environmental Justice Implications of Biotechnology' (2007) 19 *Georgetown International Environmental Law Review* 583.

Gruszczynski L, 'Risk Management Policies under the WTO Agreement on the Application of Sanitary and Phytosanitary Measures' (2008) 3 *Asian Journal of WTO and International Health Law and Policy* 261.

Horton LR, 'Food from Developing Countries: Steps to Improve Compliance' (1998) 53 *Food and Drug Law* 139.

Howse R, 'Democracy, Science, and Free Trade: Risk Regulation on Trial at the World Trade Organisation' (2000) 98 *Michigan Law Review* 2329.

Howse R and Mavroidis PC, 'Europe's Evolving Regulatory Strategy for GMOs—The Issue of Consistency with WTO Law: Of Kine and Brine' (2000) 24 *Fordham International Law Journal* 317.

Johanson DS and Bryant WL, 'Eliminating Phytosanitary Trade Barriers: The Effects of the Uruguay Round Agreements on California Agricultural Exports' (1996) 6 *San Joaquin Agricultural Law Review* 1.

Jouannet E, 'French and American Perspectives on International Law: Legal Cultures and International Law' (2006) 58 *Maine Law Review* 292.

Kalderimis D, 'Problems of WTO Harmonisation and the Virtues of Shields over Swords' (2004) 13 *Minnesota Journal of Global* 305.

Keane S, 'Can the Consumers Right to Know Survive the WTO?: The Case of Food Labeling' (2006) 16 *Transnational Law and Contemporary Problems* 291.

Kennedy KC, 'Resolving International Sanitary and Phytosanitary Disputes in the WTO: Lessons and Future Directions' (2000) 55 *Food and Drug Law Journal* 81.

Koskenniemi M, 'What is International Law?' in MD Evans (ed), *International Law* (Oxford, OUP, 2003).

Livermore MA, 'Authority and Legitimacy in Global Governance: Deliberation, Institutional Differentiation, and the Codex Alimentarius' (2006) 81 *New York University Law Review* 766.

Livshiz D, 'Updating American Administrative Law: WTO, International Standards, Domestic Implementation and Public Participation' (2007) 24 *Wisconsin International Law Journal* 961.

Masson-Matthee MD, *The Codex Alimentarius Commission and its Standards* (The Hague, TMC Asser Press, 2007).

Mayeda G, 'Developing Disharmony? The SPS and TBT Agreements and the Impact of Harmonisation in Developing Countries' (2004) 7 JIEL 737.

Neugebauer R, 'Fine-Tuning WTO Jurisprudence and the SPS Agreement: Lessons from the Beef Hormone Case' (2000) 31 *Law and Policy in International Business* 1255.

Otsuki T, Wilson JS and Sewadeh M, 'Saving Two in a Billion: Quantifying the Trade Effect of European Food Safety Standards in African Exports' (2001) 26 *Food Policy* 495.

Peel J, 'A GMO by Any Other Name… Might be an SPS Risk!: Implications of Expanding the Scope of the WTO Sanitary and Phytosanitary Measures Agreement' (2006) 17 EJIL 1009.

Pereira RA, 'Why would International Administrative Activity Be Any Less Legitimate?—A Study of the Codex Alimentarius Commission' (2008) 9 *German Law Journal* 1693.

Roberts D, 'Preliminary Assessment of the Effects of the WTO Agreement on Sanitary and Phytosanitary Trade Regulations' (1998) 1 JIEL 377.

Schramm D, 'The Race to Geneva: Resisting the Gravitational Pull of the WTO in the GMO Labelling Controversy' (2007) 9 *Vermont Journal of Environmental Law* 93.

Scott J, 'On Kith and Kine (and Crustaceans): Trade and Environment in the EU and WTO' in JHH Weiler (ed), *The EU, the WTO and the NAFTA: Towards a Common Law of International Trade* (Oxford, OUP, 2000).

Scott J, 'European Regulation of GMOs and the WTO' (2003) 9 *Columbia Journal of European Law* 213.

Scott J, 'The WTO Agreement on Sanitary and Phytosanitary Measures. A Commentary' (Oxford, OUP, 2007).

Shapiro HS, 'The Rules That Swallowed the Exceptions: The WTO SPS Agreement and Its Relationship to GATT Articles XX and XXI' (2007) 24 *Arizona Journal of International and Comparative Law* 199.

Sien IAR, 'Beefing up the Hormones Dispute: Problems in Compliance and Viable Alternatives' (2007) 95 *Georgetown Law Journal* 565.

Sikes L, 'FDA's Consideration of Codex Alimentarius Standards in Light of International Trade Agreements' (1998) 53 *Food and Drug Law Journal* 327.

Silverglade BA, 'The Impact of International Trade Agreements on US Food Safety and Labelling Standards' (1998) 53 *Food and Drug Law Journal* 537.

Silverglade BA, 'The WTO Agreement on Sanitary and Phytosanitary Measures: Weakening Food Safety Regulations to Facilitate Trade?' (2000) 55 *Food and Drug Law Journal* 517.

Slotboom MM, 'The Hormones Case: An Increased Risk of Illegality of Sanitary and Phytosanitary Measures' (1999) 36 CML Rev 471.

Strauss DM, 'Feast or Famine: The Impact of the WTO Decision Favouring the US Biotechnology Industry in the EU Ban on Genetically Modified Foods' (2008) *American Business Law Journal* 775.

Sykes AO, 'Domestic Regulation, Sovereignty, and Scientific Evidence Requirements: A Pessimistic View' (2002) 3 *Chicago Journal of International Law* 353.

Thomison A, 'A New and Controversial Mandate of the SPS Agreement: The WTO Panel's Interim Report on the *EC—Biotech* Dispute' (2007) 32 Colum *Journal of Environmental Law* 287.

Trebilcock M and Soloway J, 'International Trade Policy and Domestic Food Safety Regulation: The Case for Substantial Deference by the WTO Dispute Settlement Body under the SPS Agreement' in DL Kennedy and JD Southwick (eds), *The Political Economy of International Trade Law: Essays in Honour of Robert E Hudec*' (Cambridge, CUP, 2002).

Victor DG, 'The Sanitary and Phytosanitary Agreement of the World Trade Organisation: An Assessment After Five Years' (2000) 32 *New York University Journal of International Law and Politics* 865.

Victor M, 'Precaution or Protectionism? The Precautionary Principle, Genetically Modified Organisms, and Allowing Unfounded Fear to Undermine Free Trade' (2001) 14 *Transnational Lawyer* 295.

Wagner JM, 'The WTO's Interpretation of the SPS Agreement has Undermined the Right of Governments to Establish Appropriate Levels of Protection against Risk' (2000) 31 *Law and Policy in International Business* 855.

Walker VR, 'Keeping the WTO from Becoming the "World Trans-Science Organisation": Scientific Uncertainty, Science Policy, and Fact-Finding in the Growth Hormones Dispute' (1998) 31 *Cornell International Law Journal* 251.

Wallach LM, 'Accountable Governance in the Era of Globalization: The WTO, NAFTA, and International Harmonization of Standards' (2002) 50 *University of Kansas Law Review* 823.

Whitlock JP, '*Japan-Measures Affecting Agricultural Products*: Lessons for Future SPS and Agricultural Trade Disputes' (2002) 33 *Law and Policy in International Business* 741.

Winickoff D, Jasanoff S, Busch L, Grove-White R and Wynne B, 'Adjudicating the GM Food Wars: Science, Risk, and Democracy in World Trade Law' (2005) 30 YJIL 81.

Wirth D, 'The Role of Science in the Uruguay Round and NAFTA Trade Disciplines' (1994) 27 *Cornell International Law Journal* 817.

Wüger D, 'The Never-Ending Story: The Implementation Phase in the Dispute between the EC and the United States on Hormone-Treated Beef' (2002) 33 *Law and Policy in International Business* 777.

Young MA, 'The WTO's Use of Relevant Rules of International Law: An Analysis of the Biotech Case' (2007) 56 ICLQ 907.

Zurek L, 'The European Communities Biotech Dispute: How the WTO Fails to Consider Cultural Factors in the Genetically Modified Food Debate' (2007) 42 *Texas International Law Journal* 345.

Part II
Reviewing Expectations of SPS Constraint on Domestic Food Regulations in the European Context

Chapter 4
Is Science Really the Only Thing that Counts? An Evaluation of the SPS Agreement's Expectations of Science in the Context of EU Food Policy

Abstract A recurrent criticism of the SPS Agreement and related jurisprudence has been the importance accorded to scientific evidence in determining the compliance of sanitary measures with WTO rules. A reliance on technical risk assessments to determine the necessity of a Member's SPS measure could prohibit policies that respond to legitimate public concerns over certain types of food. This chapter evaluates whether the Agreement proffers an approach to science which excludes social value judgements in setting SPS measures and assesses the extent to which this may constrain domestic regulators. It first analyses whether the Agreement necessitates a particular approach—technical or socio-cultural—to food risk. It suggests that the Agreement's demands in this respect are more ambiguous than sometimes contended, but acknowledges notable limitations in the permitted interpretation of scientific evidence. The chapter then explains, using a diagrammatic characterisation of risk management scenarios, why the tensions identified may have limited implications for domestic regulators. It anticipates SPS rules to be strained only where international consensus on the technical safety of a given food coincides with a sharp divergence on social-value judgements. The chapter finally scrutinises this sensitive area of policy making with reference to a range of EU policies. It finds that, in practice, the EU has adopted measures that reflect citizens' concerns in spite of potential challenge under the SPS Agreement. The chapter concludes that criticism of the SPS approach to science and proposed remedies should be rethought in light of this assessment.

4.1 Introduction

In recent decades, innovation in food technology has challenged policy-makers worldwide. The rising voices of media and public confronted with food cloned from animals[1] and nanotechnology[2] have lately added to the cacophony generated by the unresolved controversies on growth hormones in meat and GM foods. The

[1] E Pilkington, 'If this Meat was from a Cloned Animal, Would You Eat It?' *The Guardian* (21 April 2008) www.guardian.co.uk/science/2008/apr/21/genetics.gmcrops.

[2] F Macrae, '"Grey Goo" Food Laced with Nanoparticles Could Swamp Britain' *Daily Mail* (8 January 2010) www.dailymail.co.uk/news/article-1241506/Britain-maybe-swamped-nanoparticle-grey-food.html 2011.

C. Downes, *The Impact of WTO SPS Law on EU Food Regulations,* Studies in European Economic Law and Regulation 2, DOI 10.1007/978-3-319-04373-9_4,

risk to consumers is a central preoccupation. But enmeshed in this debate are far-reaching concerns about the production of food, its impact on the environment and local people, and ethical questions about the food we eat and the society we desire. The nature of the dialogue between public and regulators on such issues diverges within and across continents, leaving a complex and uneven international regulatory landscape.

To bring some order to the management of food safety and phytosanitary measures, World Trade Organisation (WTO) Members negotiated a pivotal place in the Agreement on the Application of Sanitary and Phytosanitary Measures (SPS Agreement) for scientific knowledge and principles. Yet, in so doing, in the eyes of many, the Agreement has threatened to marginalise important social debate, rendering illegal entirely legitimate outlooks on what constitutes an acceptable risk in the domestic food chain. A more 'mediative style' of food policy[3] sensitive to public needs is 'under threat from the supremely technocratic world view endorsed by the SPS Agreement'.[4] The Agreement has over time become 'notorious for its emphasis on the universalising force of science'.[5] But is science really the only thing that can count under the SPS regime and just how serious is the threat to democratically grounded domestic food policy? This chapter considers these questions. Section 4.2 outlines the principal elements of risk analysis and their treatment in the Agreement and related jurisprudence, finding that the limitations upon the incorporation of non-scientific interests into sanitary measures may be less extensive than generally claimed, but are nonetheless significant. Section 4.3 assesses what these legal constraints may mean for policy-makers, providing an abstract characterisation of EU food-risk management that seeks to pinpoint the specific risk situations in which measures will most readily come into conflict with SPS law. Finally, Sect. 4.4 considers empirical examples of EU measures that typify this risk situation and assesses how far the concerns of European citizens have been sidelined, in the way anticipated in Sect. 4.2. The analysis suggests that in the EU at least, science is not the only thing that counts in defining policy.

Before turning to the Agreement, a brief explanation of the terminology used in this chapter may be helpful. In European legislation, the non-scientific factors relevant to risk management are known as 'other legitimate factors' including 'societal, economic, traditional, ethical and environmental factors',[6] a category broad enough

---

[3] G Skogstad, 'The WTO and Food Safety Regulatory Policy Innovation in the European Union' (2002) 39 JCMS 484, 488. The term reflects well the delicate balancing act both between institutions and stakeholders required in the EU.

[4] J Scott, 'On Kith and Kine (and Crustaceans): Trade and Environment in the EU and WTO' in JHH Weiler (ed), *The EU, the WTO and the NAFTA: Towards a Common Law of International Trade* (Oxford, OUP, 2000) 158. For comparable views by other commentators, see discussion in s 4.2.2 below.

[5] E Stokes, 'Book Review: *EU Regulation of GMOs: Law and Decision Making for a New Technology*. By Maria Lee' (2010) 22 *Journal of Environmental Law* 163, 165.

[6] Regulation (EC) 178/2002 of the European Parliament and of the Council laying down the general principles and requirements of food law, establishing the European Food Safety Authority and laying down procedures in matters of food safety [2002] OJ L31/1 (GFL).

to encompass the genuine social concerns that commonly emerge in the food-policy debate. However, the present chapter avoids this expression, for two reasons. Firstly, in an EU context, 'other legitimate factors' are deemed relevant only to the process of selecting regulatory measures and not in the production of science, a narrow conceptualisation which has proved controversial.[7] Secondly, the phrase 'other legitimate factors' has a different and more limited meaning in international food-safety discussions,[8] and could therefore be confusing. Since what is 'legitimate' to the task of managing risk is contested, the term 'social value judgements',[9] capturing both the ethical and subjective nature of national perspectives, will be favoured throughout this chapter.

4.2 The SPS Agreement's Constraint of Social Value Judgements

Nowadays, it is commonplace both in Europe and internationally to break down the process of food-risk analysis into its component parts: risk assessment, risk management, and risk communication.[10] Put simply, risk assessment is the scientific process of identifying risk, while risk management entails finding appropriate responses to this risk.[11] Risk communication, less relevant to our discussion here, relates to the way in which information is effectively passed between assessors and managers.[12] Although the SPS Agreement refers explicitly only to risk assessment,[13]

---

[7] See discussion in s 2.2 below.

[8] In Codex Alimentarius, following a debate on the role of science in the body's work, it was agreed in 1995 to limit other legitimate factors to those 'relevant for the health protection of consumers and for the promotion of fair practices in food trade'. See Joint FAO/WHO Food Standards Programme, *Codex Alimentarius Commission Procedural Manual* (Rome, FAO/WHO, 19th edn, 2010) (*Codex Manual*) 180. The EU objected to this definition and requested (in vain) for the words 'health protection of' to be removed. Codex Alimentarius Document ALINORM 95/37, para 24–25.

[9] This was the expression chosen by the parties in the *Hormones* dispute. See *EC—Measures concerning Meat and Meat Products (Hormones)*, Panel Report (adopted 18 August 1997) WT/DS26/R/USA, WT/DS48/R/CAN, para 8.94.

[10] See respectively EU GFL (n 6) Art 3 and the *Codex Manual* (n 8) 86–91.

[11] In European law, risk assessment is defined as 'a scientifically based process consisting of four steps: hazard identification, hazard characterisation, exposure assessment, and risk characterisation'. Risk management is a process 'of weighing policy alternatives in consultation with interested parties considering risk assessment and other legitimate factors, and, if need be, selecting appropriate prevention and control options.' EU GFL, Arts 3(11) and 3(12) respectively.

[12] In the European context, risk communication also comprises how risk is conveyed to other parties e.g. industry and consumers. EU GFL, Art 3(13).

[13] The Appellate Body rejected attempts by the Panels in both the *Hormones* and *US—Continued Suspension* disputes to argue that factors pertinent to risk management and not risk assessment should be excluded on the basis that only risk assessment is mentioned. See respectively *EC—Measures concerning Meat and Meat Products (Hormones)*, Appellate Body Report (adopted

to facilitate understanding of the implications of the Agreement for policy-makers, this section treats risk assessment and risk management in turn.

4.2.1 Risk Assessment

What Is Risk?

Scientific risk assessment is widely considered as the cornerstone of the SPS Agreement.[14] But what precisely is the risk that is assessed, and how does it relate to public concerns about food? Underlying this question is a philosophical debate that has raged for many decades.[15]

One view is that risk is 'out there', and that it can be discovered and quantified by systematic assessment, using models based largely upon the physical sciences.[16] This perception of risk has been characterised as 'naive positivism', sustained by a belief that facts can be separated from values.[17] It embraces the view that 'risk is a natural product of science, devoid of bias, ethics, sociological shaping'.[18] The 'technical' approach to risk, as it is commonly referred to,[19] marginalises all elements felt potentially to interfere with objective evaluation of a particular phenomenon.

By contrast, social constructivists argue that risk is essentially 'a cultural phenomenon, not a physical one'.[20] In simple terms, something is only a risk if there is a cultural understanding that it is one. Taken to the extreme, this subjective view

16 January 1998) WT/DS26/AB/R, WT/DS48/AB/R, para 181 and *United States/Canada—Continued Suspension of Obligations in the EC—Hormones Dispute (US—Continued Suspension)*, Appellate Body Report (adopted 31 March 2008) WT/DS320/R, WT/DS321/R, paras 538–542.

[14] See, e.g. J Atik, 'Science and International Regulatory Convergence' (1996) 17 *Northwestern Journal of International Law and Business* 736, 740; WH Maruyama, 'A New Pillar of the WTO: Sound Science' (1998) 32 *The International Lawyer* 651.

[15] For an early exposition that very much captures the essence of contemporary debate, see AM Weinberg, 'Science and Trans-Science' (1972) 10 *Minerva* 209 (noting that problems arising from the relationship between society and technology 'are unanswerable by science; they transcend science'). For a helpful summary of the different schools of thought, see A Arcuri, 'Food Safety at the WTO after Continued Suspension: A Paradigm Shift?' in A Antoniadis, R Schütze and E Spaventa (eds), *The European Union and Global Emergencies–A Law and Policy Analysis* (Oxford, Hart Publishing, 2011) 209–212.

[16] JF Short, 'The Social Fabric at Risk: Toward the Social Transformation of Risk Analysis' (1984) 49 *American Sociological Review* 711.

[17] KS Shrader-Frachette, *Risk and Rationality—Philosophical Foundations for Populist Reforms* (Berkeley, University of California Press, 1991) 39–41.

[18] EA Rosa, 'Metatheoretical Foundations for Post-Normal Risk' (1998) 1 *Journal of Risk Research* 15, 54.

[19] See D Lupton, *Risk* (London, Routledge, 1999) 17–20; O Renn, 'Three Decades of Risk Research: Accomplishments and New Challenges' (1998) 1 *Journal of Risk Research* 49, 52.

[20] Rosa (n 18) 21. The term 'social constructivist' in fact brings together a diverse range of orientations towards risk. For an accessible overview, see also Lupton (n 19) 28.

could question the utility of any physical assessment of risk. However, in practice, the insights of social constructivism have served to challenge positivist pretensions towards risk assessment, and exposed the process to greater scrutiny.[21] Such insights challenge the notion of objectivity in assessment, highlighting the mediating factors in any physical analysis, such as the personal epistemology of the scientist concerned or the particular techniques and conventions he has inherited from the scientific establishment.[22] For example, the basic terms through which the risk assessor defines the parameters of assessment—'risk', 'adverse effect', 'damage'—reflect prior understandings that will shape the assessor's ultimate evaluation and thus characterisation of risk.[23] Moreover, the insinuation of values into risk assessment does not start at the moment of physical analysis. The very decision to undertake risk research represents a choice coloured by social values as to what merits scientific attention.[24] From a socio-cultural perspective, a technocratic approach to policy-making is simply inadequate.[25]

The aim here is not to debate the merits of alternative standpoints for food policy-making, but rather to evaluate whether the SPS Agreement clearly embraces either the technical or socio-cultural perspectives outlined above. If it is the former, this would indicate a first area in which the policy-maker's sensitivity to social-value judgements may be curtailed by SPS provisions.

---

[21] Most critics of technical risk assessments nevertheless acknowledge their valid place in risk analysis. As Renn notes, they 'help decision makers to estimate physical harm [and] provide the best knowledge about actual damage that is logically and empirically linked with each possibility of action.' Renn (n 19) 54.

[22] Shrader-Frechette (n 17) 39–41; D Winickoff et al., 'Adjudicating the GM Food Wars: Science, Risk, and Democracy in World Trade Law' (2005) 30 YJIL 81, 94 (giving the example of the zero value placed in risk assessment on protecting non-humans). In the specific case of European food policy, Chalmers claims that European Food Safety Authority (EFSA) 'is presenting a particular ideological model of politics'. D Chalmers, '"Food for Thought": Reconciling European Risks and Traditional Ways of Life' (2003) 66 MLR 532, 543. However, one must wonder how this could be the case, given the wide cultural and disciplinary diversity of scientists engaged in EFSA's work.

[23] See VR Walker, 'The Myth of Science as a "Neutral Arbiter" for Triggering Precautions' (2003) 26 *Boston College International and Comparative Law Review* 197, 201; A Scherzberg, 'EU-US Trade Disputes about Risk Regulation: The Case of Genetically Modified Organisms' (2006) 19 *Cambridge Review of International Affairs* 121, 125; O Wolf, D Ibarreta and P Sørup (eds), 'Science in Trade Disputes Related to Potential Risks: Comparative Case Studies' (IPTS Technical Report Series EUR 21301 EN 2004) Chap. 4, ipts.jrc.ec.europa.eu/publications/pub.cfm?prs=1203.

[24] L Levidow and S Carr, 'How Biotechnology Regulation Sets a Risk/Ethics Boundary' (1997) 14 *Agriculture and Human Values* 29, 30. The Food and Agriculture Organization of the United Nations (FAO) has described 'the triggering of a risk analysis [as] one of the most deeply value-lead dimensions of risk management'. FAO, 'FAO Expert Consultation on Food Safety: Science and Ethics' (September 2002) 21, www.fao.org/docrep/006/j0776e/j0776e00.htm.

[25] Stirling's view, for example, is that '[i]t is better to be roughly accurate in [the] task of mapping the social and methodological context-dependencies, than it is to be precisely wrong in spurious aspirations to a one-dimensional quantitative expression of technological risk'. Andrew Stirling, 'On Science and Precaution in the Management of Technological Risk. An ESTO Project Report' (Report to the EU Forward Studies Unit, IPTS, EUR 19056 EN May 1999) 16, ftp.jrc.es/EURdoc/eur19056en.pdf.

The SPS Agreement—A Purely Technical Approach to Risk Assessment?

Many commentators, albeit to differing degrees, concur that the SPS legal framework advocates a technical view of risk. For some, the prominence of science in the Agreement in itself reflects a common (but flawed) belief in the discipline's capacity to provide definitive and objective answers.[26] The WTO's turn to 'sound science'[27] thus expresses a confidence in the determinism of science at odds with more cultural approaches to risk. Winickoff et al. outline the deleterious effects of adopting a technical view of risk in advance of the WTO Panel review of the EU's GM foods policy. However, they fall short of arguing that this is what the SPS Agreement necessitates.[28] Other authors are less equivocal. The regime is accused of 'ignoring'[29] both public attitudes to risk and the role values play in denoting the effects of food on humans as 'adverse'.[30] Scott's early work encapsulates these views, presenting the SPS realm as a 'world in which the contingency of scientific knowledge is denied, and in which the values which enter law through science remain obscured'.[31]

Seen in the context of general international trends in food policy, this reading of the SPS Agreement is entirely plausible. The strict separation of the two elements of risk analysis—scientific risk assessment and political risk management—has become a leitmotif of food policy-making over the last decade, although largely anomalous to the treatment of risk in all other areas of society.[32] The reasons for this particular evolution differ on both sides of the Atlantic. In

---

[26] J Peel, 'Risk Regulation Under the WTO SPS Agreement: Science as an International Normative Yardstick' (Jean Monnet Working Paper 02/04) 54, www.jeanmonnetprogram.org/archive/papers/04/040201.pdf. See also Walker (n 23).

[27] A number of authors construe the SPS Agreement to advocate 'sound science' although the term does not appear in the text of the Agreement. See G Goh, 'Tipping the Apple Cart: The Limits of Science and Law in the SPS Agreement after *Japan—Apples*' (2006) 40 JWT 655, 677; Maruyama (n 14).

[28] Rather, they suggest that in interpreting the SPS Agreement '[t]he *temptation* will be to invoke a singular conception of sound science in order to achieve harmonisation' (emphasis added). Winickoff et al. (n 22) 106. Indeed, their analysis of *Hormones* rather reveals the AB's 'sympathetic view towards value-infused scientific policy making' (at 96).

[29] Scherzberg (n 23) 133.

[30] J Bohanes, 'Risk Regulation in WTO Law: A Procedure-Based Approach to the Precautionary Principle' (2002) 40 *Columbia Journal of Transnational Law* 323, 367. Similarly, Foster describes this as 'an implicit systemic determination to view the [risk assessment as] excluding considerations relating to public opinion.' CE Foster, 'Public Opinion and the Interpretation of the World Trade Organization's Agreement on Sanitary and Phytosanitary Measures' (2008) 11 JIEL 427, 431.

[31] Scott (n 4) 157.

[32] An extensive review of risk-management frameworks for human health and environmental risks singles out food standards for their categorical approach on this issue. CJ Jardine et al., 'Risk Management Frameworks for Human Health and Environmental Risks' (2003) 6 *Journal of Toxicology and Environmental Health* 569, 590.

the US, reinforced independence of scientific bodies was a response in the 1980s to perceived interference by policy-makers in the operation of scientific assessment.[33] A parallel development occurred much later in Europe, but here largely to correct the perceived interference of agricultural interests in both British and European risk-assessment work, considered a catalyst in the inadequate response to the BSE threat.[34] It finally resulted in the creation of the European Food Safety Authority (EFSA), both a physical and symbolic reinforcement of the independence of science.[35] Although in reality, the practical interaction between risk assessors and managers blurs this dividing line,[36] European policy-makers hold tenaciously to the principle.[37] Trans-Atlantic developments in this respect have been mirrored, at least until lately, by international organisations.[38] In that the latter are an established reference point in SPS provisions,[39] it would seem logical to conclude that the predominantly technical 'politics-free' approach to assessment is that envisaged by the regime.

The SPS Agreement's Neutral View of Risk

One can legitimately observe that both in Europe and internationally, policy-makers have, as a matter of practice, tended towards a technical view of risk.[40] The

---

[33] EL Anderson, 'The Contrast Between Risk Assessment and Rules of Evidence in the Context of International Trade Disputes: Can the US Experience Inform the Process?' (2004) 24 *Risk Analysis* 449, 452.

[34] P van Zwanenberg and E Millstone, 'BSE: A Paradigm of Policy Failure' (2003) 74 *The Political Quarterly* 27, 34.

[35] For an insight into the rationale behind the creation of EFSA, see P James, F Kemper and G Pascal, 'A European Food and Public Health Authority: The Future of Scientific Advice in the EU' (Report commissioned by the European Commission 1999) 10, ec.europa.eu/food/fs/sc/future_food_en.pdf.

[36] For example, Commission officials do attend the EFSA Committee, Panel and Working Group meetings in order to 'clarify the mandate and sometimes change the terms of reference'. E Vos and F Wendler, 'Food Safety Regulation at the EU Level' in E Vos and F Wendler (eds), *Food Safety Regulation in Europe* (Antwerp, Intersentia, 2006) 120.

[37] As the European Commission's then Director General for Health and Consumer Protection reaffirmed in May 2007: 'This principle provides an important safeguard for the independence of the scientific advice by ensuring that it is not influenced by the policy preferences of the operational departments'. R Madelin, 'How Can We Make Food Safety Governance In Europe More Inclusive?' (Keynote speech, Safe Foods Conference, Brussels, 11 May 2007).

[38] More recently, Codex Alimentarius has emphasised the need for a 'risk assessment policy' implying a more self-conscious framing of the work of risk assessors. For a discussion of this 'remarkable' development, see T Hüller and ML Maier, 'Fixing the Codex? Global Food-Safety Governance under Review' in C Joerges and E-U Petersmann (eds), *Constitutionalism, Multilevel Trade Governance and Social Regulation* (Oxford, Hart Publishing, 2006) 281–286, and especially 284.

[39] Under SPS Agreement Art 5.1, WTO Members' assessment shall 'tak[e] into account risk assessment techniques developed by the relevant international organizations'.

[40] Peel (n 26) 54.

argument that the SPS Agreement demands this view of risk or excludes a more socio-cultural oriented variation is more problematic. In part, it evokes an improbable picture of trade lawyers in the early days of the Uruguay Round negotiations embracing a naive faith in science. Indeed, some commentators maintain it was only realised after the negotiations that 'science was "not as certain" as had been envisaged and did not give "black-and-white" answers'.[41] Such explanations are not convincing. It is difficult to comprehend why SPS negotiators would not have been alert to the pitfalls of science. The use of science to assess the validity of trade measures has a history dating back to the League of Nations[42] and controversies about science and expertise were a prominent feature in the political backdrop to SPS negotiations.[43] In this context, it is implausible that negotiators had high expectations that technical risk assessment would provide definitive answers to controversies about risk.

A review of the SPS negotiating history also provides little support for the contention that negotiators embraced a uniform concept of 'sound science', or in fact any particular view of risk assessment. Confusion about terminology used to describe risk assessment was certainly noted,[44] but negotiators appear to have been fully aware of the limitations of science as a method of resolving trade disputes. Although the conception of sound scientific evidence was promoted at an early stage in negotiations,[45] this was a notion that was later challenged by participants in the discussions who argued that 'risk assessment was based in part on ethical and political factors'.[46] In addition, negotiators were sensitive to the limited capacities

---

[41] Wolf, Ibarreta and Sørup (n 23) 32. The quote comes from an interview with a WTO official who goes on to comment: '[A]ll of this is very new to us, and we are struggling to deal with it… Understanding the nature of science is a key issue at WTO.' This is a naivety that is deemed to extend in a general way to the majority of international trade lawyers. See SD Harlow, 'Science–Based Trade Disputes: A New Challenge in Harmonizing the Evidentiary Systems of Law and Science' (2004) 24 *Risk Analysis* 443, 444–445 (arguing that insights into science garnered from lawyers engaged in civil and tort law are not widely understood in the international trade arena).

[42] S Charnovitz, 'The Supervision of Health and Biosafety of Regulation by World Trade Rules' (2000) 13 *Tulane Environmental Law Journal* 271, 272.

[43] The role of scientific expertise lay at the heart of a controversial GATT dispute settlement panel in a case relating to salmon fishing between US and Canada in 1989 at the time the SPS drafts were under negotiation. See DA Wirth, 'The Role of Science in the Uruguay Round and NAFTA Trade Disciplines' (1994) 27 *Cornell International Law Journal* 817, 845–847. Moreover, heated exchanges on the scientific evidence behind the use of growth hormones had already formed a major element of attempts to resolve the EU–US dispute under the GATT Standards Code. See AR Halpern, 'The US–EC Hormone Beef Controversy and the Standards Code: Implications for the Application of Health Regulations to Agricultural Trade' (1989) 14 *North Carolina Journal of International Law and Commercial Regulation* 136, 149–150.

[44] GATT Doc MTN.GNG/NG5/WGSP/W/22 (31 May 1990) 3 (reporting that '[c]oncerns about misunderstanding of the term of risk assessment and a preference for using 'acceptable level of protection' were again raised').

[45] See MTN.GNG/NG5/WGSP/W/24 (2 July 1990) 2.

[46] MTN.GNG/NG5/WGSP/W/6 (17 October 1989) 3.

of many developing countries to undertake risk assessment at all, and therefore cautious in their demands in this respect.[47] Science was clearly not perceived as a panacea.[48]

However, is it possible that through the subsequent application and interpretation of SPS rules, a narrower, technical understanding of risk has emerged? Would the efforts of those who advocate a more social constructivist understanding of risk assessment be thwarted by the Agreement?[49] There is little evidence that they would. Article 5.1 establishes that sanitary measures shall be 'based on an assessment, as appropriate to the circumstances, of the risks to human … health, taking into account risk-assessment techniques developed by the relevant international organizations.' Paragraph 4 of Annex A defines what constitutes a risk assessment according to its purpose, ie, evaluating potential adverse effects, and not the methodology to be used. The Appellate Body (AB) has presented the scientific element of this process in the broadest terms, namely as one 'characterised by systematic, disciplined and objective enquiry',[50] which must constitute 'legitimate science according to the rationale of the relevant scientific community.'[51] Beyond this, the Agreement places no constraints on the scientific approach taken in risk assessments. Assessments need not necessarily take account only those factors explicitly listed in the provisions.[52] Neither must they be performed according to the same methods used by international bodies developing related standards.[53] Nor, moreover, could socially sensitive risk-assessment findings that fulfil demands of legitimacy and objectivity be outweighed by technical risk assessments. As was ruled in *Hormones* (and confirmed in *US—Continued Suspension*), a minority scientific opinion that diverges from mainstream opinion can be an adequate basis for the SPS measure.[54] Most significantly in *US—Continued Suspension*, the AB acknowledged that a Member's level of protection (invariably reflecting social-value judgements[55]) can legitimately

---

[47] See MTN.GNG/NG5/WGSP/W/2 (14 November 1988) 3.

[48] Even the US, later vigorous proponents of 'sound science' arguments, did not have illusions about the definitive role science could play. The US Uruguay Round Statement of Administrative Action argued that the SPS Agreement 'recognises … that scientific certainty is rare and many scientific determinations require judgments between differing scientific views'. Cited in Maruyama (n 14) 663.

[49] For examples of the type of methods that can be employed, see A Ely and A Sterling, 'The Process of Assessment' in M Dreyer and O Renn (eds), *Food Safety Governance: Integrating Science, Precaution and Public Involvement* (Berlin, Springer, 2009) (*Food Safety Governance*).

[50] *Hormones*, Appellate Body Report, para 187.

[51] *US—Continued Suspension,* Appellate Body Report, para 591.

[52] *Hormones*, Appellate Body Report, para 187 (establishing that SPS Agreement Art 5.2—referring to the 'available scientific evidence; relevant processes and production methods; relevant inspection, sampling and testing methods; prevalence of specific diseases or less; existence of free areas; relevant ecological and environmental conditions'—is not a 'closed list').

[53] *US—Continued Suspension,* Appellate Body Report, para 685.

[54] See respectively *Hormones*, Appellate Body Report, paras 187 and 194.

[55] See s 4.2.2 below.

shape the framing of the risk assessment.[56] All these elements point towards a 'pragmatic approach' to risk assessment,[57] rather than a rigid adherence to a technical understanding. Certainly, advocates of a method to risk analysis that integrates values are confident that the SPS regime poses no fundamental barriers to the methods they propose.[58] Neither the intentions of negotiators, the text of the Agreement, nor jurisprudence, therefore, sustain the argument that the WTO aspires to a purely technical approach to SPS risk. At the level of risk assessment at least, social-value judgements may play a role in the framing of risk assumptions and contribute to a scientific basis for WTO-legal sanitary measures.

4.2.2 Risk Management

The great academic attention paid to risk assessment belies the often limited input that it may bring to the final sanitary measure chosen. At best, risk assessment provides adequate raw material with which to define the contours of the potential risk options facing the policy-maker. Which measure is finally taken will depend heavily on the social and political context in which the risk manager operates.[59] It is therefore culture, not risk assessment, that dictates that peanuts with a 'life-threatening character'[60] may be placed on the market, yet Para Red dye that is 'only' 'potentially genotoxic and possibly carcinogenic'[61] must be removed.[62] Social factors—customary eating patterns, public attitudes about the value and merits of the food concerned—provide a mould within which the raw scientific findings of risk

[56] *US—Continued Suspension,* Appellate Body Report, para 534. Arcuri cautiously points to this decision as a possible 'paradigm shift' in the AB's treatment of science away from a more technical understanding of risk. Arcuri (n 15) 219.

[57] Goh (n 27) 669.

[58] E Vos and F Wendler, 'Legal and Institutional Aspects of the General Framework' in *Food Safety Governance* (n 49) 108–109.

[59] The actual impact of science in this process is viewed by many to be minimal. Wirth contends that the public-health goal of legislation 'reflects societal values as to which science may provide little, if any, guidance'. Wirth (n 43) 833. Trebilcock and Soloway concur that '[s]cientists in scientific risk assessment have little or nothing to offer on the appropriate regulatory response to a given risk, which entails risk management decisions involving socio-political judgements.' M Trebilcock and J Soloway, 'International Trade Policy and Domestic Food Safety Regulation: The Case for Substantial Deference by the WTO Dispute Settlement Body under the SPS Agreement' in DLM Kennedy and JD Southwick (eds), *The Political Economy of International Trade Law: Essays in Honour of Robert E. Hudec* (Cambridge, CUP, 2002) 562.

[60] EFSA, 'Opinion of the Scientific Panel on Dietetic products, nutrition and allergies [NDA] related to a notification from FEDIOL and IMACE on fully refined peanut oil and fat pursuant to Art 6 paragraph 11 of Directive 2000/13/EC' (2004) 133 *EFSA Journal* 1.

[61] EFSA, 'Opinion of the Scientific Panel on food additives, flavourings, processing aids and materials in contact with food (AFC) to review the toxicology of a number of dyes illegally present in food in the EU' (2005) 263 *EFSA Journal* 1.

[62] In the UK, for example, products containing Para Red were withdrawn from sale, see UK Food Standards Agency website: www.food.gov.uk/news/newsarchive/2005/may/parared.

assessment evolve into a final regulatory form. If these elements were excluded by international legal obligations, then, regardless of the limited constraint of the SPS Agreement on the use of risk assessment noted above, its impact on social-value judgements could be significant.

The Changing Perception of the SPS Agreement

Early assessments of the SPS regime raised the spectre of dispute bodies encroaching upon national values by scrutinising domestic determination of scientific findings.[63] Nevertheless, for some time, commentators were relatively sanguine about any potential restrictions. Scientific justification of the sort demanded by the Agreement in some ways liberated WTO Members from the horizontal constraints that might otherwise arise under basic GATT provisions. The turn to science therefore constituted a 'pendulum-swing back towards greater national discretion' in the field of health regulation.[64] Far from being a constraint, the leeway permitted to WTO Members was 'so large that nearly all *bona fide* attempts to protect food safety will be consistent with the SPS Agreement'.[65]

In the light of the first SPS disputes, this earlier insouciance gave way to criticism. The trade body's condemnation in *Hormones* of measures recognised to be non-protectionist and genuine efforts to protect citizens from the risk of cancer[66] provoked commentators to decry the SPS Agreement's scientific focus. The legal framework has since been judged to 'not yet accommodate value-based perspectives'[67] and cast aside social considerations, 'no matter how "thick" and enlightened these national preferences are'.[68] Though this development is welcome for some,[69]

---

[63] Wirth (n 43) 858.

[64] Atik (n 14) 740.

[65] DG Victor, 'The Sanitary and Phytosanitary Agreement of the World Trade Organization: An Assessment After Five Years' (2000) 32 *New York University Journal of International Law and Politics* 865, 872. This is a view shared by Barceló who claims that '[i]t is difficult to see how any good faith [sanitary and phytosanitary] measure could fail to meet this test'. JJ Barceló, 'Product Standards to Protect the Local Environment—The GATT and the Uruguay Round Sanitary and Phytosanitary Agreement' (1994) 27 *Cornell International Law Journal* 755, 765.

[66] See *Hormones*, Appellate Body Report, para 245.

[67] J Tait and A Bruce, 'Globalisation and Transboundary Risk Regulation: Pesticides and Genetically Modified Crops' (2001) 3 *Health, Risk and Society* 99, 105.

[68] Hüller and Maier (n 38) 28. See also A Alemanno, *Trade in Food: Regulatory and Judicial Approaches in the EC and the WTO* (London, Cameron May, 2007) 396 (asserting that by 'exalting the role of science, the SPS Agreement tends to rule out all non-scientific factors from standard setting'); Peel (n 26) 85 (concurring that 'legitimate policy or social concerns … tend to be screened out').

[69] Quick and Blüthner support the scientific focus, warning that 'it will be extremely difficult to replace the "scientific" route chosen by the SPS Agreement with a new approach taking socio-economic considerations into account without opening Pandora's box and allowing WTO Members to introduce protectionist measures'. R Quick and A Blüthner, 'Has the Appellate Body Erred? An Appraisal and Criticism of the Ruling in the WTO Hormones Case' (1999) 2 JIEL 603, 639.

for most it is sinister, ensuring that 'context, as well as culture, is silenced in [a] unidimensional world of scientific rationality'.[70] In short, the SPS regime has turned science into the 'ultimate arbiter, placed above the democratic decision-making capacity of a society'.[71] Let us review these claims.

Openings for Social Value Judgements

During the risk-management process, policy-makers have to weigh up different policy measures, aiming to select the one that best responds to the risk identified. As already noted, 'risk management', the moment at which social elements are customarily assumed to be pertinent, does not explicitly appear in the SPS text. The practice of weighing and selecting suitable measures associated with risk management is, however, conceptually captured by the term 'appropriate level of protection' (ALOP). A Member has an 'autonomous right'[72] to establish the ALOP it sees fit, which can, if so desired, be as high as 'zero risk'.[73] The risk manager can assert this right even in the context of a situation covered by international standards. The measure he chooses may result in a higher ALOP than that implied by the standard.[74] Both this, and the opportunity, previously alluded to, for Members to shape risk assessment according to their ALOP,[75] demonstrate how the level of protection is dictated by factors other than scientific ones. It is thus the WTO Member's judgement, not science, that determines whether 'a risk of one in 1 million of kidney failure from a particular activity [is] acceptable'.[76] There appears to be little dispute that social-value judgements play a central and legitimate role in defining the ALOP.[77] For example, the EU's uncontested level of protection in *US—Continued Suspension*—namely, 'no (avoidable) risk, [a level that] does not allow any *unnecessary* addition from exposure to genotoxic chemical substances'[78]—clearly reflects a particular judgement of the broader value of the substances concerned.

Of course, the role of the ALOP in protecting social-value judgements would be meaningless if SPS provisions demanded measures that simply mirrored risk assessments. This is not the case. A measure must, in accordance with Article 5.1, be 'based on' a risk assessment. In *Hormones*, the Panel assessed whether the EU's measure complied in this respect by evaluating the scientific conclusion implicit in

---

[70] Scott (n 4) 157.

[71] Bohanes (n 30) 363.

[72] *Hormones*, Appellate Body Report, para 172.

[73] *Australia—Measures Affecting Importation of Salmon (Australia—Salmon)*, Appellate Body Report (adopted 20 October 1998) WT/DS18/AB/R, para 125.

[74] SPS Agreement Art 3.3.

[75] See s 4.2.1. above.

[76] This example was put forward by the US in *Hormones, Panel* Report, para IV.51.

[77] In the *Hormones* dispute, the US, EU and Australia all appeared to concur on this point. See *Hormones*, Panel Report, respectively paras IV.51, IV.90 and V.9.

[78] *US—Continued Suspension,* Appellate Body Report, para 536 (emphasis added).

its hormones prohibition against risk assessment conclusions. While accepting the approach taken, the AB clarified that this was not the only relevant measure 'to the exclusion of anything else'.[79] Rather, to meet the requirement of Article 5.1, the assessment must 'reasonably support' the measure and a 'rational'[80] and 'objective'[81] relationship between the two. In that a wide range of actions by risk managers may constitute a 'rational' response to scientific data presented, Article 5.1 appears to offer ample scope to Members to interpret assessments in a way that accommodates social-value judgements.

The Limits of Defending Social Value Judgements

So far so good. Both the concept of ALOP and the relationship between risk assessment and measure permit space for incorporating social-value judgements in the establishment of measures. However, the interpretation of these provisions by the AB, most notably in *Hormones*, has exposed significant limits upon risk managers. In two particular risk situations, guaranteeing that a Member's ALOP is met is particularly problematic: these are cases of theoretical risk or general, unspecified risk.

Theoretical Risk

Scientists cannot know everything: it is therefore a truism to say that they cannot demonstrate with certainty that a food presents no risk at all. In *Hormones*, the EU argued that this 'inherent limit of science' was one of six categories it was seeking to address, in its measures to limit the use of hormones.[82] The Panel responded that a Member could not invoke this type of risk as a justification for a measure, as it is not one that can be subjected to risk assessment of the type foreseen under Article 5.1.[83] The AB concurred, describing this as 'theoretical uncertainty',[84] a risk it contrasted in a later case to 'ascertainable risk', for which risk assessors must 'ask whether … adverse effects could ever occur.'[85] That testing theoretical uncertainty lies beyond risk assessment is not in itself contentious, but the ramifications for risk managers are significant. As a failure to comply with Article 5.1 is also considered to signal a breach of Article 2.2,[86] a risk manager, fully cognisant of the limitations of science, and wishing to reflect this in a high ALOP, will not

[79] *Hormones*, Appellate Body Report, para 193.

[80] ibid.

[81] *Hormones*, Appellate Body Report, para 189.

[82] *Hormones,* Panel Report, para 8.139.

[83] *Hormones*, Panel Report, para 8.153.

[84] *Hormones*, Appellate Body Report, para 186.

[85] *US—Continued Suspension,* Appellate Body Report, para 572 (emphasis in original).

[86] *Australia—Salmon,* Appellate Body Report, para 138.

be able to do so. One could not, one might argue, judge otherwise. If a Member could call upon the 'uncertainty of science' at will to justify restrictive measures, the disciplines imposed by the SPS framework would quickly be undermined. However, in choosing the appropriate measure the risk manager must weigh this theoretical uncertainty against other factors beyond the immediate substance-risk assessment. In other words, to choose to permit naturally occurring hormones in food on the basis that they have been consumed safely for centuries, but to prohibit synthetic hormones, is not to *base* a measure on 'theoretical uncertainty' but to favour relative certainty over uncertainty.[87] It is not clear why such a course of action would be irrational on the part of the risk manager, or in general terms not demonstrate an 'adequate relationship'[88] with the total state of scientific knowledge or ignorance. Yet, the relationship between Articles 5.1 and 2.2 as construed by the AB appears to preclude such a choice.[89]

General Science

In addition to looking unfavourably upon theoretical risk, the AB has also ruled against measures where scientific evidence of risk exists, but where that evidence is not adequately specific to justify the contended measure. In *Hormones*, the EU referred to monographs pointing to 'the carcinogenic potential of entire *categories* of hormones, or of the hormones at issue *in general*' rather than the 'carcinogenic potential of those hormones where used specifically for growth promotion purposes'.[90] As the EU selected (reflecting consumer antipathy to hormone treatment) an ALOP that did not permit 'any unnecessary addition from exposure', its action on the basis only of general evidence of risk would seem rational. The AB's finding to the contrary therefore indirectly places limits upon the scope of the ALOP and potentially the capacity of Members adequately to defend social-value judgements. The right to establish an ALOP would appear to be a hollow one, if, in order to maintain a selected level of protection, a Member is then required to generate additional specific scientific evidence by way of justification.

---

[87] In this instance, the absence of a risk assessment under Art 5.1 to underpin the 'relative certainty' is not significant. The AB has argued that a regulatory intervention concerning natural hormones in meat would be an 'absurdity'. One can assume that a risk assessment of natural hormones would be equally so. See *Hormones*, Appellate Body Report, para 221.

[88] This is the definition of 'sufficient science' in Art 2.2 provided by the Appellate Body in *Japan—Measures Affecting Agricultural Products (Japan—Varietals)*; Appellate Body Report (adopted 22 February 1999) WT/DS76/AB/R, para 73.

[89] Scott therefore justifiably describes the AB's presumption that a breach of Art 5.1 implies inconsistency with Art 2.2 as 'surprising'. J Scott, *The WTO Agreement on Sanitary and Phytosanitary Measures. A Commentary* (Oxford, OUP, 2007) (*SPS Commentary*) 83. Perhaps future dispute-settlement bodies may rule that while the implication was correct in the given circumstances of the *Australia—Salmon* case, it may not always be so.

[90] *Hormones*, Appellate Body Report, para 199 (emphasis added).

4.2.3 *Are There Other Legal Defences Under the WTO?*

If recourse to arguments relating to theoretical or general risk prove incompatible with SPS obligations, can risk managers faced with a strong public expression of social-value judgements not simply put the scientific arguments to one side? Where the chosen measures respond to fundamental ethical or social unease as much as scientifically demonstrable risk,[91] does the broader WTO legal framework not provide them with more appropriate shelter? Two further WTO treaties the General Agreement on Tariffs and Trade (GATT)[92] and the Technical Barriers to Trade Agreement (TBT)[93]—are particularly relevant in this respect. A domestic measure which treats foreign products unfavourably could, for example, nevertheless be considered legal if captured by one of the policy exceptions under GATT Article XX. The most relevant in the case of sensitive food issues (and given that public health issues under XX(b) are momentarily sidelined) is Article XX(a), on the protection of 'public morals'.[94] For example, rules identifying non-kosher foods, or beef- or pork-related products which may be offensive for religious reasons, fall squarely within this definition.[95] Likewise, Pauwelyn has suggested that policy-makers wishing to defend the EU's cautious biotechnology policy could do so with recourse to Article XX.[96]

[91] Concerns about pesticides, for example, may manifest themselves in terms of public-health issues, but at their roots reflect anxiety about 'intensive farming systems and the sustainability or otherwise of such systems'. Tait and Bruce (n 67) 105. Likewise, fears about biotechnology could be considered not so much a food-safety issue, but an underlying unease about the cavalier and profit-driven exploitation of nature. See e.g. Levidow and Carr (n 24) 33.

[92] General Agreement on Tariffs and Trade, opened for signature 15 April 1994, 55 UNTS 194, 1867 UNTS 187 (entered into force 1 January 1995) (GATT).

[93] Agreement on Technical Barriers to Trade, opened for signature 15 April 1994, 1868 UNTS 120 (entered into force 1 January 1995) (TBT Agreement).

[94] In a dispute relating to gambling, the dictionary definition of 'public morals' adopted was 'standards of right and wrong conduct maintained by or on behalf of the whole community or nation'. *United States Measures Affecting the Cross-Border Supply of Gambling and Betting Services (US—Gambling)*, Panel Report (adopted 10 November 2004) WT/DS285/R, para 6.465.

[95] Indeed, Art XX(a) was invoked by Saudi Arabia during accession to the WTO with a view to prohibiting foodstuffs containing animal blood. See H Gao, 'The Mighty Pen, the Almighty Dollar, and the Holy Hammer and Sickle: An Examination of the Conflict between Trade Liberalisation and Domestic Cultural Policy with Special Regard to the Recent Dispute between the United States and China on Restrictions on Certain Cultural Products' (2007) 2 *Asian Journal of WTO and International Health Law and Policy* 313, 325. A non-religious example is provided by Kysar, pointing to the requirements of vegetarians to know whether food may have been inserted with animal genes. DA Kysar, 'Preferences for Processes: The Process/Product Distinction and the Regulation of Consumer Choice' (2004) 118 *Harvard Law Review* 525, 616.

[96] J Pauwelyn, 'The GMO Debate Under the Rules of the World Trade Organization' (GMOs in European Agriculture and Food Production conference, The Hague, November 2009). Switzerland would be particularly well placed to make such a claim, having amended its Constitution to reinforce the 'dignity of creation' in response to GM regulation. See FX Perrez, 'Taking Consumers Seriously: The Swiss Regulatory Approach to Genetically Modified Food' (2000) 8 *New York University Environmental Law Journal* 585, 591–592. For a counter view, see P Bentley, 'A Reassessment of Article XX, Paragraphs (b) and (g) of GATT 1994 in the Light of Growing Consumer

The TBT Agreement also provides legal avenues for defending socially inspired measures that 'fulfil a legitimate objective' under Article 2.2. Unlike under GATT Article XX, the list of acceptable public-policy rationales is not a closed one, and the general view is therefore that Article 2.2 offers Members 'wide discretion' in defining what constitutes a legitimate objective.[97] As no scientific substantiation is necessarily required, defending a measure under the TBT Agreement is arguably more achievable than under SPS rules.[98]

The openings provided by GATT and TBT have been treated only fleetingly, for regardless of the legal arguments that can be constructed outside the SPS Agreement, the interrelationship between these treaties severely limits their relevance. If a measure is considered to contain a food safety-related element, SPS rules are inevitably the first point of legal analysis.[99] Moreover, there is a cumulative obligation to be in compliance with all agreements.[100] Consistency with the TBT or GATT Agreements therefore cannot 'save' a measure that does not comply with SPS rules. In many cases, scientific and social-value judgements are inextricably linked, meaning that a measure which involves some element of risk management will most appropriately be considered under the SPS Agreement with the constraints already identified.

The hierarchical relationship between the SPS regime and other legal texts creates a situation where *bona fide* social-value judgements may be sidelined. There appear to be only two possible ways in which social concerns at play in food policy measures can gain a sure legal footing in WTO law. The first would be a narrow interpretation of the scope of the Agreement and self-restraint on the part of Members and dispute bodies in subjecting evidently resonant social concerns to science-based disciplines.[101] However, the *EC—Biotech* case would suggest a trend

---

and Environmental Concern about Biotechnology' (2000) 24 *Fordham International Law Journal* 107, 128 (claiming that GM foods do not incite 'moral depravity', which the author believes to be the objective of Art XX (a)). For more detailed examination of these issues, see discussion on the compatibility of animal cloning technology with Art XX in Chap. 5 below, s 5.4.4.

[97] D Morgan and G Goh, 'Genetically Modified Food Labelling and the WTO Agreements' (2004) 13 *Review of European Community and International Environmental Law* 306, 317. TBT-related jurisprudence is limited, but in *Sardines* at least, there appeared to be no questioning of the legitimacy of the EU's chosen objectives, namely market transparency, consumer protection, and fair competition. See *European Communities—Trade Description of Sardines,* Appellate Body (adopted 26 September 2002), WT/DS231/AB/R, para 263.

[98] See A Alemanno (n 68) 312.

[99] Art 1.5 of the TBT Agreement explicitly excludes sanitary or phytosanitary measures, therefore limiting parallel SPS analysis of the measures. SPS Agreement Art 2.4 establishes that measures conforming to the Agreement are presumed to be compliant with GATT.

[100] See G Marceau and JP Trachtman, 'The Technical Barriers to Trade Agreement, the Sanitary and Phytosanitary Measures Agreement, and the General Agreement Tariffs and Trade—A Map of the World Trade Organisation Law of Domestic Regulation of Goods' (2002) 36 JWT 811, 816.

[101] For example, imagine a dispute were to arise in relation to imported food containing pesticide residues in excess of EU pesticide limits. The SPS focus would be confined to the immediate scientific evidence relating to the individual limit and would not question the policy framework—

in the opposite direction. In this instance, the Panel contrived to stretch the meaning of SPS provisions to encompass environmental risks arguably better scrutinised under other legal frameworks.[102] Alternatively, in the absence of restraint, WTO Members could themselves seek to separate the political and scientific elements of a given policy into more distinct TBT and SPS measures. However, not only are some issues not amenable to such a contrived approach, overlapping or disjointed regulations would do little to enhance either public understanding or confidence in the governance of food. The reality of the constellation of WTO treaties and the nature of sanitary measures is that, in practice, the SPS regime is the correct venue for judging the vast majority of food-related regulations.

To a certain extent, the above analysis runs counter to some of the common criticisms of the SPS Agreement's treatment of science. In particular, it finds that there is little substantiation for the argument that it imposes a strictly technical view of risk, to the detriment of social factors. Nevertheless, it recognises that while the Agreement's provisions appear to permit considerable scope to social-value judgements, this has been significantly constrained by the interpretation of dispute-settlement bodies. Where the implications of new technology are unknown or evidence of risk insufficiently precise, the ability of WTO Members to act upon genuine public concern would appear to be impaired. In the light of this analysis, Sect. 4.3 reflects on the implications of the legal constraints identified.

4.3 How Relevant Are Fears of a 'Science Only' Constraint on Policy-Making?

What is the significance for policy-makers of the legal limitations placed by the SPS Agreement on social-value judgements? As noted in Part I of this book, where legal commentators draw conclusions about the impact of SPS law, there is often a tacit assumption that the social effect of law will mirror the content of its provisions. It is little wonder then that the conclusions of the above analysis—that SPS law may discount legitimate concerns about risk in the absence of convincing scientific data—cause commentators such disquiet.[103] Rigidly science-based demands

---

socially and environmentally driven EU preference for a reduction in pesticides—that gave rise to these limits. This would involve a dispute body artificially dissecting regulation into manageable pieces.

[102] See discussion by J Peel, 'A GMO by Any Other Name … Might be an SPS Risk!: Implications of Expanding the Scope of the WTO Sanitary and Phytosanitary Measures Agreement' (2006) 17 EJIL 1009, 1021–1024.

[103] Among the more worried are AT Guzman, 'Food Fears: Health and Safety at the WTO' (2004) 45 VJIL 20; D Kalderimis, 'Problems of WTO Harmonisation and the Virtue of Shields over Swords' (2004) 13 *Minnesota Journal of Global Trade* 305; HS Shapiro, 'The Rules that Swallowed the Exceptions: The WTO SPS Agreement and its Relationship to GATT Articles XX and XXI: The Threat of the EU—GMO Dispute' (2007) 24 *Arizona Journal of International and Comparative Law* 199; Winickoff et al. (n 22); Walker (n 23).

for food policy can appear authoritarian, given the deep-rooted cultural sensitivities generally associated with food choices. The implications therefore stretch far beyond the technical realm to potentially 'redefine the balance between state and global power in legal, political terms'.[104] As a result, many writers propose that the WTO actively take steps to redress the perceived imbalance by reconnecting with domestic preferences.[105] In the light of the fears expressed, this section assesses in greater detail the possible disruption that SPS Agreement constraints could impose on EU policy-making.

4.3.1 How Relevant Are Fears of the 'Science Only' Approach to of EU Policy?

In the light of the *Hormones* case, legitimate questions have been raised about the EU's future capacity to maintain its policy preferences.[106] Yet, without disputing the overall validity of this concern, as we turn from treaty interpretation to evaluation of policy impact, certain factors must be borne in mind that may mitigate the anticipated effects.

The Limitations of Extrapolating from WTO Disputes We should be wary of extrapolating from the findings of what is, after all, rather limited SPS jurisprudence, for a number of reasons. Firstly, given the factual specificity of each case, the relevance of conditions scrutinised in one dispute settlement to the development of other sanitary measures is doubtful.[107] Secondly, one may question whether findings in, for example, *Hormones* reflect inherent constraints imposed by the SPS Agreement or rather the particular legal strategy chosen by the EU. In *US—Continued Suspension* the EU elected to change strategy and defend its prohibition of five hormones as a provisional measure under Article 5.7. Although the AB was unable, due to flaws in the Panel's approach,[108] to complete the legal analysis, the

---

[104] Winickoff et al. (n 22) 93.

[105] In particular, there is a growing consensus on the need for greater sensitivity by panels to public opinion, for example, by taking into account scientifically-based analysis of public perceptions or limiting the standard of review in cases where social value judgements are contested. See A Alemanno, 'Public Perception of Food Safety Risks Under WTO Law: A Normative Perspective' in G van Calster and D Prévost (eds), *Research Handbook on Environment, Health and the WTO* (Cheltenham, Edward Elgar, 2012); J Peel, 'Of Apples and Oranges (and Hormones in Beef): Science and the Standard of Review in WTO Disputes under the SPS Agreement' (2012) 61 ICLQ 47; Foster (n 30).

[106] MM Slotboom, 'The Hormones Case: An Increased Risk of Illegality of Sanitary and Phytosanitary Measures' (1999) 36 CML Rev 471, 490.

[107] After all, it is necessary to take into account 'the particular circumstances of the case, including the characteristics of the major issue in quality and quantity of the scientific evidence'. *Japan—Varietals*, Appellate Body Report, para 84. See also *Hormones*, Appellate Body Report, para 79.

[108] *US—Continued Suspension,* Appellate Body Report, para 735.

Panel's major findings of SPS inconsistency were rejected.[109] In other words, the right legal defence may allow greater accommodation of social-value judgements than is immediately apparent from *Hormones*. Thirdly, there is an element in the relationship between science and measure as yet underexplored in jurisprudence. In *Japan—Varietals*, the AB characterised 'sufficient science' as a relational concept, one that requires weighing scientific evidence against the particular measure chosen, and therefore indirectly the ALOP and social-value judgements reflected herein.[110] While the criteria to be used in such a proportionality test remain unclear, subjecting measures to this type of scrutiny could potentially allow dispute panels to take valid social-value judgements into account.[111] Finally, in the interest of balance, it is worth noting that in other cases, the SPS Agreement is deemed to have effectively managed the balance between trade obligations and domestic social values.[112] Indeed, in the case of *Japan—Apples,* the AB has been praised for its 'masterly exercise in balancing the political, legal and scientific complexities of the dispute'.[113]

Socially Contentious Food Policy Is the Exception Not the Rule Using highly sensitive cases as the prism through which to view the Agreement may also risk exaggerating the overall policy implications of WTO constraint. Guzman, for example, claims that food-related decisions 'are central to a state's sense of sovereignty and authority'.[114] Certainly, much EU food legislation will reflect specific European consumer preferences. However, for many sanitary measures, social-value judgements may be marginal: cadmium levels in squid and brown rot in potatoes are examples of EU sanitary measures that have elicited international scrutiny, but hardly threaten the essence of European society.[115] Moreover, some measures that

---

[109] In particular, the AB rejected the Panel's claim that the EU could not require a different level of scientific evidence due to the higher ALOP adopted, and dismissed the notion that the EU required a 'critical mass' of new scientific evidence in order to call into question the sufficiency of previous evidence. See respectively, *US—Continued Suspension,* Appellate Body Report ss V.I.E.1 and V.I.E.3.

[110] *Japan—Varietals*, Appellate Body Report, para 73. In the case in question, the measure was found to be disproportionate to the 'negligible risks' demonstrated. See s V.II.B of the AB report.

[111] Admittedly, this view may be overly benevolent. Scott suggests the contrary, that '[a]s the dispute settlement bodies move further down the road towards substantive assessments of right and wrong in risk regulation, they curtail the range of acceptable regulatory outcomes.' Scott, *SPS Commentary* (n 89) 79.

[112] The lower-profile SPS cases involving Japan involved a lack of deference paid to Japan's judgment of risk comparable to that of the more sensitive cases of *Hormones* and *Australia—Salmon*. Yet, the appraisal of the Appellate Body's judgment of these cases has generally been positive. See ML Miller, 'Does the WTO Substantially Limit the Ability of Countries to Regulate Harmful Nonindigenous Species? (2003) 17 Emory *International Law Review*, 1059, 1085; JP Whitlock, '*Japan-Measures Affecting Agricultural Products*: Lessons for Future SPS and Agricultural Trade Disputes' (2002) 33 *Law and Policy in International Business* 741, 776.

[113] Goh (n 27) 671.

[114] Guzman (n 103) 20.

[115] For information on all trade concerns raised by WTO Members, see the SPS Information Management System: spsims.wto.org.

have proved extremely sensitive in the European policy process, such as those concerning vitamin and mineral supplements and additives, have passed without comment from trading partners.[116] While not underestimating the genuine concerns surrounding more celebrated WTO cases, we should note that direct international intervention into the sensitive core of European food policy remains relatively infrequent.

Conforming to SPS Law Does Not Necessarily Mean Abandoning Favoured Policy A third element that mitigates the impact of the SPS regime is that a pertinent challenge of a domestic measure does not by definition necessitate significant compromise in the policy goals of the Member concerned. Either additional scientific assessment or slight modification of the measures concerned may satisfy a dispute body. For example, following Canada's successful SPS challenge of Australia's import ban on salmon, Australia introduced strict import guidelines which, although rechallenged by Canada, were found to be largely consistent with the Agreement. Far from radically compromising Australian policy, the new import guidelines met and even reinforced Australia's policy goals.[117] The impact of WTO compliance upon national preferences is therefore not necessarily dramatic.

Restraint Has Been the Favoured Approach of Other WTO Members Finally, whereas complaints about EU measures are numerous, the limited number of cases coming before dispute settlement demonstrates 'considerable restraint' by WTO Members.[118] This can be explained in a number of ways. Firstly, even where trade disruption occurs, it may not be significant enough to warrant the considerable efforts and resources required to launch a WTO case,[119] particularly for developing countries with limited means and technical expertise.[120] Secondly, fomenting a culture of litigation within the SPS context may be a high price to pay for resolving a single issue. Over-zealous pursuit of non-conforming domestic policy may encourage reciprocation, thus reducing any leeway states currently have to address

[116] For the EU's notification of measures related to vitamin and mineral supplements and additives respectively, see WTO Docs G/SPS/N/EEC/87 (16 June 2000) and G/SPS/N/EEC/291 (10 August 2006).

[117] Only one requirement within the guidelines, that salmonid products are 'consumer-ready' before being released from quarantine, was found to violate the SPS Agreement. In other respects, the new guidelines enhanced consumer protection by introducing more stringent rules for non-salmonid products and have been rendered WTO-compliant by removing previous discrepancies in treatment of the different fish. See *Australia—Measures Affecting Importation of Salmon*, Article 21.5 Panel Report (adopted 18 February 2000) WT/DS18/RW, paras 7.144–53. For a review, see MD Taylor, 'The WTO Panel Decision on Australia's Salmon Import Guidelines: Evidence that the SPS Agreement Can Effectively Protect Human Health Interests' (2000) 9 Pacific Rim Law and Policy Journal 473.

[118] Goh (n 27) 678.

[119] Victor (n 65) 918 (explaining that 'there must be a strong and apparent trade effect for a complaining country to justify the cost of raising and prosecuting a dispute').

[120] KC Kennedy, 'Resolving International Sanitary and Phytosanitary Disputes in the WTO: Lessons and Future Directions' (2000) 55 *Food and Drug Law Journal* 81, 103.

particular national concerns. Thirdly, legal clarification of the SPS text arising from a dispute, even if helpful in the short term, may inhibit the future legal defence of domestic food policy.[121]

Each of the above observations demonstrates the need to place dispute settlements in the broader context of the SPS regime, and to treat some of the more pessimistic accounts of its effect with caution. Nevertheless, the question remains of whether SPS disciplines sometimes undermine EU social-value judgements.

4.3.2 *Recharacterising the SPS Agreement's Challenge to Sanitary Measures*

To aid understanding of the anticipated impact of SPS rules, let us characterise the EU risk-management domain. Winickoff et al. suggest that risk situations can be conceptualised according to the *certainty* of the scientific knowledge base and the level of *consensus* surrounding the public values that need to be protected.[122] For these authors, there exists a continuum with *high certainty* and *high consensus* at one end, and *low certainty* and *low consensus* at the other. This taxonomy is consistent with arguments about the inseparability of science and values. However, it also implies, more questionably, a necessary relationship between knowledge and values. One should recognise that international consensus around public values on a given food technology may be low and public scepticism unwavering in some states, even where scientific data amasses and uncertainty (as expressed through technical risk assessment) dwindles. This low value consensus and high certainty scenario (and its high value consensus/low certainty counterpart) is not catered for by the one-dimensional conceptualisation proposed by Winickoff and colleagues. In the characterisation offered here, *consensus* on policy values again forms one dimension. But international scientific *certainty* is treated as a second independent dimension ranging from *high certainty of safety* to *high certainty of risk*. In simple terms, this two-dimensional framework characterises food risk management into six areas (as illustrated in Fig. 4.1).[123]

The first risk management situation (both areas A and C in Fig. 4.1) occurs where there is a high level of certainty about risk or safety, and consensus (or limited controversy) about the social-value judgements at stake. With its access to scientific expertise, the EU may be more likely than most WTO Members to question international scientific consensus and therefore tend to fall more frequently outside

[121] It is this type of calculation and the risk of provoking clarification of GATT Arts III and XX that led the EU to retreat from a prohibition of animal-tested cosmetic products. See G de Búrca and J Scott, 'The Impact of the WTO on EU Decision-Making', in G de Búrca and J Scott (eds), *The EU and the WTO, Legal and Constitutional Issues* (Oxford, Hart Publishing, 2001) 10–11.

[122] Winickoff et al. (n 22) 104–105.

[123] A similar response to the work of Winickoff et al. also led Jaqueline Peel to seek a more refined understanding of risk situations, although resulting in four rather than six scenarios. Peel (n 105) 47.

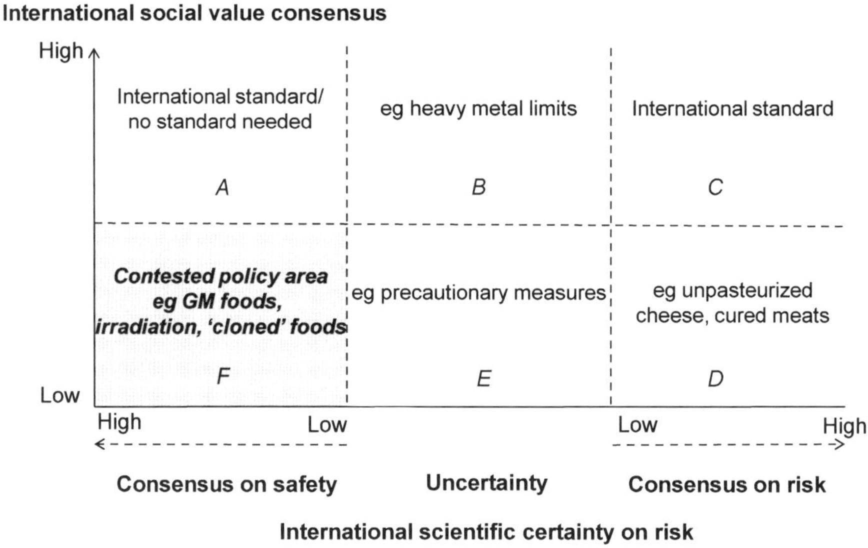

Fig. 4.1 Characterisation of risk management situations in food policy

these areas. Nevertheless, as Masson-Matthee notes, the EU has in a number of instances either deferred to Codex standards (e.g. using methods for testing honey approved by Codex[124]) or explicitly adopted internationally agreed methodology (e.g. pesticide control[125]). One example is the EU's adoption of a new plan developed by Codex for sampling nuts.[126] It is worth noting that in such instances, rather than threatening social value judgements, international standards can legitimise and reinforce practices welcomed by the EU.[127]

Secondly, it is possible that while scientific uncertainty remains at an international level, there is a basic consensus that the risk is legitimate and must be managed. In such situations (area B), a WTO Member has some leeway to shape the final form of a measure to reflect local dietary habits or domestic preferences, without significant risk of legal challenge. For example, the introduction in Europe of

[124] MD Masson-Matthee, *The Codex Alimentarius Commission and its Standards* (The Hague, TMC Asser Press, 2007) 107.

[125] ibid 124.

[126] Commission Regulation 178/2010 amending Regulation (EC) No 401/2006 as regards groundnuts (peanuts), other oilseeds, tree nuts, apricot kernels, liquorice and vegetable oil [2010] OJ L52/32.

[127] For example, in the case of pesticides mentioned above (in text to n 125) Codex's recommended methods were ones that 'the Community supported and endorsed'. Commission Directive 2002/63/EEC repealing Directive 79/700/EC [2002] OJ L187/30, rec 4. Indeed, the EU is perceived to be particularly successful in enforcing national preferences at an international level. See 'EU Rebuffs US Claims of Standards "Internationalisation"' EU Food Law (23 April 2010).

limits for lead in kale, spinach and mushrooms or cadmium in fish, even where they are not set specifically as an international level, may be presumed safe from third-party challenge.[128] Generally not the focus of public attention, a large proportion of European food-safety measures would most likely fall within this area of risk management.

A third risk situation (area D) is characterised by a relatively high certainty of risk, but divergent social preferences. For example, the danger of *listeria monocytogenes* associated with raw milk products is well known. Yet, while the US demands the pasteurisation of milk, producers of French soft cheeses have resisted any hygiene-related rules that could impair the taste of traditional products.[129] A further illustration is the EU's decision not to impose, although scientifically justifiable, the strictest levels of nitrites in meat which would have meant the elimination of certain meat products produced in a traditional manner.[130] Such culturally led risk-taking by food regulators is not limited to Europe. Japan, unlike the EU, has not imposed rules on freezing procedures for raw fish, due to their unacceptable impact upon taste, in spite of the known risks of herring worm disease.[131] Where WTO Members wish, in spite of established risk, to permit the consumption of food in accordance with cultural preferences, such socially tinted risk management will not face international scrutiny.[132]

A fourth situation arises where there is only limited probability or extent of risk, and measures may be socially contentious (area E). In this context, WTO Members enjoy considerable leeway in choice of measure. Initially, this can take the form of a provisional measure in accordance with Article 5.7. Yet, even in the longer term, the onus is on the exporting country to first establish a *prima facie* case against the scientific basis of the importing Member's measure. To do so in a situation of clear scientific controversy, and without reference to an international standard or consensus, will be difficult. Therefore, counter-intuitively perhaps, it is not primarily in

[128] T Berg and D Licht, 'International Legislation on Trace Elements as Contaminants in Food: A Review' (2002) 19 *Food Additives and Contaminants* 916, 923.

[129] For a review of EU and US policy approaches to this issue, see M Ingram, 'Raw Deal: Trade Implications of the US Food and Drug Administration's Pending Review of Unpasteurised Cheeses' (2003) 12 *Minnesota Journal of Global Trade* 461. A further example is the European approach to cured meats, such as Italian and Spanish hams and sausages, permitted in the EU but temporarily prohibited in the US, albeit in this instance to prevent the spread of animal diseases rather than for food-safety purposes. See MA Echols, 'Food Safety Regulation in the European Union and the United States: Different Cultures, Different Laws' (1998) 4 *Columbia Journal of European Law* 525, 531.

[130] For a discussion of these rules and Denmark's maintenance of derogations in the interests of consumer health, see A Szajkowska, *Regulating Food Law: Risk Analysis and the Precautionary Principle as General Principles of EU Food Law* (Wageningen, Wageningen Academic Publishers, 2012) 123–127.

[131] M De Rosa et al., 'Risk Analysis-Based Food Safety Policy: Scientific Factors Versus Socio-Cultural Factors' (2008) 133 *Tijdschrift voor Diregeneeskunde* 746, 746–748.

[132] This is of course not the case where a WTO Member attempts to export products governed by this policy.

cases of genuine scientific uncertainty, typified by emerging and largely undocumented risks, that Members are most vulnerable to a WTO challenge.

In practice, a threat to domestic social-value judgements is only likely to occur in a relatively confined area of policy-making (area F), at one extreme of the science–politics relationship, where a relatively high international technical consensus on scientific certainty of safety coincides with a low level of international social value consensus. Measures taken under such conditions may constitute a rational response to public anxiety: regardless of the scientific basis, a measure that directly addresses and mitigates public concerns may fulfil a valuable social role.[133] Nevertheless, within the context of the SPS agreement, the dissonance between the international assertion of safety and the proposed measure places the latter in jeopardy. In such situations, SPS-compliant alternatives which could adequately reflect scientific knowledge may not meet the social value expectations of a Member's citizens.[134]

As this simplified characterisation of EU food-risk management illustrates, fears that SPS disciplines work to the detriment of social-value judgements should not be exaggerated. In some situations, international standards may help to reinforce domestic preferences, and in others, social-value judgements leading to measures seemingly at odds with international scientific assessments may remain unchallenged. However, in one particular type of risk-management situation, characterised by a significant level of scientific certainty (at least according to international risk assessment bodies) and a low level of value consensus, the tension between domestic measures and SPS provisions is clear. Section 4.4 will take a closer look at a number of EU policies that fall within the contours of this risk situation to assess whether the EU's social value preferences have been compromised in practice.

4.4 The Status of 'Social Value Judgements' in EU Policy-Making

Before turning to specific policies, let us first consider the general claim that social-value judgements are excluded from EU risk management, notwithstanding their formal standing in general food law.[135] Instinctively, many involved in the European policy process may concur that the 'predominating science' paradigm commonly

[133] As Howse explains, the 'psychological security' gained by seeing governmental action on an issue is valuable regardless of any real risk reduction that may occur. R Howse, 'Democracy, Science, and Free Trade: Risk Regulation on Trial at the World Trade Organisation' (2000) 98 *Michigan Law Review* 2329, 2350. For a counter-view, see CR Sunstein, 'Probability Neglect: Emotions, Worst Cases, and Law' (2002) 112 *Yale Law Journal* 61, 70 (arguing that responding to irrational fears produces wasteful, ineffective regulations).

[134] Thus, for example, the US's offer to label hormone-treated meat was not considered sufficient to alleviate EU citizens' fears. See MD Carter, 'Selling Science under the SPS Agreement: Accommodating the Consumer Preference in the Growth Hormones Controversy' (1997) 6 *Minnesota Journal of Global Trade* 625, 654.

[135] See n 6.

associated with the SPS Agreement is an equally apt characterisation of EU food law. Most obviously, EFSA has gained a dominant role in the EU decision-making process and is frequently the foundation for EU measures.[136] The emphasis upon science is reinforced by Commission rhetoric. In advocating EFSA's expertise, the Commission's enthusiasm for science can appear to depreciate the value of other socio-economic factors. For example, on his arrival as the new EU Health Commissioner in early 2010, John Dalli promptly authorised the cultivation of the first GM potato and commended the 'science-based Union authorisation system',[137] thereby perpetuating the pro-science discourse of his predecessors.[138] The Commission's role in GMO policy in particular[139] is widely considered a paradigm of the relationship between science and socio-economic factors in food-safety measures:[140] in spite of persistent public concern about GMOs, the Commission has continued to authorise new GM events based on its 'extreme confidence'[141] in EFSA's scientific guidance. Inevitably, the Commission stands accused of 'looking exclusively at the science without taking into account other factors'.[142] The EU's GM legislation may pay lip service to 'other legitimate factors',[143] but the consensus is that these factors

---

[136] EFSA has provided over 2000 scientific opinions since its establishment in 2002. See 'Commissioner Dalli speech to EFSA' (Parma, 12 March 2010) ec.europa.eu/commission_2010–2014/dalli/headlines/speeches/docs/100312_efsa.pdf.

[137] Cited in L Phillips, 'EU Commission Approves Cultivation of First GM Crop in 12 Years' euobserver.com (3 March 2010).

[138] See, e.g. Commissioner A Vassiliou, 'Introductory Speech for the 1st International Conference on Risk Assessment: A Global Risk Assessment Dialogue' (Brussels, 13 November 2008) (stating: 'The EU is fully committed to science-based risk management. Scientific risk assessment provides the necessary basis for effective and efficient risk management measures') ec.europa.eu/health/archive/ph_risk/documents/s08_riskassessment.pdf.

[139] The Commission's room for manoeuvre is probably overstated. Lee, for example, claims there is 'considerable power in the hands of the Commission', while it can alternatively be argued that the institution is simply proceeding in accordance with adopted EU legislation. See M Lee, *EU Regulation GMOs: Law and Decision-Making for a New Technology* (Cheltenham, Edward Elgar, 2008) 71.

[140] A broad civil society project conducted under the EU's Sixth Framework Programme concluded that 'GMOs may be unique in terms of mobilisation of public opinion, but exactly for that reason it is a good case study for probing into possible avenues for enhancing participation in science.' PSx2, 'Participatory Science and Scientific Participation: The Role of Civil Society Organizations in Decision-Making about Novel Developments in Biotechnologies' (2010) 6, cordis.europa.eu/publication/rcn/13368_es.html.

[141] Lee (n 139) 103.

[142] Euro Coop, 'Position Paper, Euro Coop Statement Labelling: Making the Non-GM Alternative Possible' (December 2007) www.eurocoop.org/index.php?option=com_content&view=article&id=200%3Aeuro-coop-statement-labelling-making-the-non-gm-alternative-possible&catid=42%3Afood-policy&Itemid=189&lang=en. See also Friends of the Earth and Greenpeace, 'Briefing Note on The EU's GMO Reform Debate' (August 2008) (calling for independent expertise evaluating the socio-economic impact of GM as an integral part of the assessment process) www.foeeurope.org/sites/default/files/press_releases/GP_FoEE_200808_Briefing_Adhoc_GMO_workinggroup_FINAL%5B1%5D.pdf.

[143] 'Other legitimate factors' may be taken into account in the authorisation process under Art 7.7 of Regulation (EC) 1829/2003 of the European Parliament and of the Council on genetically modified food and feed [2003] OJ L268/1.

are currently peripheral to decision-making.[144] Given that the drive to biotechnology emanates from outside the EU, at first glance, the predictions of international lawyers that EU social values would be marginalised appear well founded.

However, far from being emblematic of the EU approach to social-value judgements, the case of GM policy is arguably misleading. Casting one's eye across the broader policy landscape immediately throws up contradictions to the 'science-based' claims of the Commissioners. Firstly, as van der Meulen has pointed out, many of the major recent proposals of food-safety legislation (such as hygiene or the food additives package) have themselves not been subject to scientific scrutiny.[145] EFSA is instead principally required for decisions relating to specific substances or technologies. In other words, it is EU institutions, sensitive to underlying social-value judgements about certain foods or materials, that have dictated in which circumstances scientific evidence must come to the fore. Thus, certain categories of food—food supplements, food additives, foods for particular nutritional use and novel foods among others—have been singled out as requiring particular attention by risk analysts. It is social-value judgements, not anything intrinsic to these foods, which define the necessity of their pre-market approval. Secondly, many of the guiding principles in the management of foods are blatantly not science-based. Whether an additive is permitted in food, for instance, is not determined by risk assessment alone. As a response to societal decisions to limit overall use of additives, a manufacturer must demonstrate not only the safety of the substance but that 'there is a reasonable technological need' for its use in food.[146] Likewise, contaminants in foods are subject to risk assessment, but the levels established by risk managers must be 'as low as can be reasonably achieved', an approach taking into account both scientific and social considerations.[147] Such examples warn against any crude generalisations about the role played by science in EU policy. However, pre-market authorisation procedures and a cautious treatment of contaminants and additives are measures broadly accepted beyond the EU,[148] and thus arguably fall outside the most contentious risk-management situation (area F of Fig. 4.1) identified in

[144] Consider, for example, the questionnaire prepared by an external consultancy for the Commission sent to Member States with the purpose of evaluating current GM legislation. Respondents were asked to give their views (in the autumn of 2009) on the preferable operation of risk assessment and management. The option 'socio-economic criteria should not be considered' was inaccurately, but tellingly, described as the '*status quo*'. See 'Evaluation of GM food and feed legislation. Survey of Competent Authorities by the Food Chain Evaluation Consortium', ec.europa.eu/food/food/biotechnology/evaluation/docs/gmo_evaluation_survey_competent_authorities.doc.

[145] BMJ van der Meulen, 'Science Based Food Law' (2009) 4 *European Food and Feed Law* 58, 60. See also A Szajkowska (n 130) 77 (contrasting the limited demands on the EU legislator to produce risk-assessment based measures compared to the EU Treaty constraints on Member States).

[146] Regulation (EC) 1333/2008 of the European Parliament and of the Council on food additives [2008] OJ L354/16, Art 6.1(b) (EU Food Additive Regulation).

[147] Council Regulation (EEC) 315/93 of 8 February 1993 laying down Community procedures for contaminants in food [1993] OJ L37/1, Art 2.2.

[148] For a discussion of the WTO-compatibility of pre-market authorisation procedures, see ns 60–67 in Chap. 5 below and related text.

Sect. 4.3. The crucial question in assessing the penetration of the science-based paradigm is whether, in situations where measures most strain SPS provisions, social-value judgements have been preserved.

4.4.1 Social Value Judgements Versus Science in EU Policy

The best-known case of the EU grappling with the tension between scientific evidence and social values, that of hormone-treated beef, has been extensively discussed elsewhere.[149] It is sufficient to mention here that the EU maintained its policy preferences in spite of the US's imposition of retaliatory tariffs on European products to the value of € 130 million.[150] The debate about the scientific adequacy of the measures remains unresolved, but the antipathy generated towards the technology by a powerful coalition of consumers, agricultural interests and the European Parliament[151] is such that, even if the scientific consensus alters, a policy change currently remains unthinkable. Is the hormones issue an isolated incident of values transcending pure science? This sub-section introduces other lesser-known EU policy areas where scientific rationality has come under strain.

Antimicrobial Treatment of Poultry

In the US, there is a well-established practice of treating poultry with antimicrobial substances which can reduce pathogens. In the EU, this treatment has been banned since 1997.[152] In general terms, there is a well-documented threat to public health associated with passing on to humans antimicrobial resistance built up in animals.[153] However, in the context of intense technical cooperation created by the EC–US

---

[149] See, e.g. D Roberts, 'Preliminary Assessment of the Effects of the WTO Agreement on Sanitary and Phytosanitary Trade Regulation' (1998) 1 JIEL 377; WA Kerr and JE Hobbs, 'The North American-European Union Dispute Over Beef Produced Using Growth Hormones A Major Test for the New International Trade Regime' (2002) 25 *The World Economy* 283–296; G Skogstad, 'The WTO and Food Safety Regulatory Policy Innovation in the European Union' (2001b) 39 JCMS 485; Slotboom (n 106).

[150] A solution to the dispute and phasing out of sanctions was negotiated in May, 2009. See European Commission, 'Memorandum on Beef Hormones Dispute Signed with the United States', MEMO/09/239 (13 May 2009).

[151] For an overview of how this movement grew, see L Caduff, 'Growth Hormones and Beyond' (Centre for International Studies, Working Paper 2–2002) www.ib.ethz.ch/docs/working_papers/wp_2002_08.pdf.

[152] Regulation (EC) 853/2004 of the European Parliament and of the Council laying down specific hygiene rules for food of animal origin [2004] OJ L139/55. For a comprehensive review of the measures taken by the EU with regard to pathogens in poultry, see US Department of Agriculture Foreign Agricultural Service, 'GAIN Report' (E48148, 19 December 2008) www.fas.usda.gov/gainfiles/200812/146306944.pdf.

[153] For an overview, see DP Fidler, 'Legal Challenges Posed by the Use of Antimicrobials in Food Animal Production' (1999) 1 *Microbes and Infection* 29.

Veterinary Agreement,[154] the US submitted dossiers on four specific antimicrobial substances for assessment. EFSA subsequently analysed different aspects—public health, antimicrobial resistance and environmental impact—of the four substances. The risk assessors were hampered by limited data, but nevertheless did not establish a notable food-safety or environmental risk associated with the specific treatments proposed.[155] The Commission therefore submitted a proposal in June 2008 to permit the use of the four substances 'according to very strict conditions and requirements'.[156] It did not deny the possibility of risk, but noted that 'it is impossible … to consider the complete elimination of any risk as a realistic objective for the risk management decision in the present matter.'[157]

European concerns about this form of meat treatment were manifest. Consumer groups baulked at the perceived attempt to introduce short cuts into hygiene processes, which would ultimately provide an inferior product.[158] The European Parliament rallied against a treatment of poultry at odds with the 'total food chain approach' favoured in Europe.[159] Under public pressure, the Commission's proposal was rejected first by the Standing Committee on the Food Chain and Animal Health and subsequently in Council by all Member States except the abstaining UK. The US subsequently initiated proceedings on the issue before the WTO.[160] The Council invoked insufficient knowledge and the precautionary principle as the basis for its decision. If the complaint proceeds to dispute settlement, the case is likely to turn on whether there is 'insufficient evidence' under Article 5.7 to justify recourse to a provisional measure, in the light of the Council's chosen ALOP. EFSA's opinions and the Commission's own risk-management proposal will not facilitate the EU's defence in this respect. By introducing stringent conditions to the use of antimicrobial

---

[154] Council Decision 98/258/EC on the conclusion of the Agreement between the European Community and the United States of America on sanitary measures to protect public and animal health in trade in live animals and animal products [1998] OJ L118/1.

[155] See EFSA, 'Scientific Opinion of the Panel on Biological Hazards, Assessment of the possible effect of the four antimicrobial treatment substances on the emergence of antimicrobial resistance' (2008) 659 *EFSA Journal* 1; EFSA Scientific Committee on Health and Environmental Risks and Scientific Committee on Emerging and Newly Identified Health Risks, 'Environmental impact and effect on antimicrobial resistance of four substances used for the removal of microbial surface contamination of poultry carcasses' (adopted on 12 March and 2 April 2008 by the respective Committees) ec.europa.eu/health/archive/ph_risk/committees/04_scenihr/docs/scenihr_o_015.pdf.

[156] European Commission, 'Proposal for a Council Regulation implementing Regulation (EC) No 853/2004 as regards the use of antimicrobial substances to remove surface contamination from poultry carcasses' (COM(2008) 430 final). ('Commission Proposal on poultry contamination').

[157] ibid rec 8.

[158] S Poulter, '"Dirty" US Chicken Washed with Chlorine Heading for British Shops as EC Seeks to Improve Relations with America' Daily Mail (29 May 2008) www.dailymail.co.uk/news/article-1022821/Dirty-US-chicken-washed-chlorine-heading-British-shops-E-C-seeks-improve-relations-America.html.

[159] European Parliament, 'Resolution on Authorisation of Chlorinated Chicken' (B6–0309/2008, 19 June 2008) point 4.

[160] 'US Requests WTO Panel in Poultry Processing Dispute With EU' *Inside US Trade* (9 October 2009).

substances, the Commission attempted to put forward a measure that would balance scientific and social-value judgements, but the latter ultimately prevailed.

Food Irradiation

Food irradiation is a process of exposing living cells in food to ionising radiation, in order to prevent these cells from reproduction: this slows the food's decaying process, allowing longer periods of preservation and shelf life.[161] International bodies praise food irradiation's potential to reduce the microbiological risk to the consumer, whilst adversely affecting neither human health nor human nutritional status.[162] Global commercialisation has been slowed by persistent consumer concerns and industrial unwillingness to provoke consumer backlash.[163] In 1999, the European Parliament and Council adopted a framework Directive concerning the authorising and labelling of irradiated foods.[164] It subsequently established a list of food and ingredients authorised for treatment with ionising radiation.[165] However, as yet, irradiation of only 'dried aromatic herbs, spices and vegetable seasonings' is permitted in the EU.[166] Following a consultation process, the European Commission reported in 2001 that completing the positive list of products would be highly controversial, and no further additions have been made.[167]

The unequivocal scientific view is that 'food irradiation is safe for the health of the consumers'.[168] However, this does not necessarily place the EU in conflict

---

[161] J Farkas, 'Irradiation for Better Foods' (2006) 17 *Trends in Food Science and Technology* 148.

[162] SE Pickett and T Suzuki, 'Regulation of Food Safety Risks: The Case of Food Irradiation in Japan' (2000) 1 *Journal of Risk Research* 95 (summarising the conclusions of the WHO, FAO and IAEA on food irradiation). One of the major concerns is that irradiation may mislead the consumer about the freshness of the product.

[163] See C Hunter, 'Changing Attitudes to Irradiation Throughout the Food Chain' (2000) 57 *Radiation Physics and Chemistry* 239 (recounting deep-seated industry and consumer doubts about irradiation).

[164] European legislation sets out four basic conditions for the use of the food irradiation. Irradiation is permitted where there is a 'reasonable technological need', when it presents no health hazard, if it is 'of benefit to the consumer', and finally, provided that it is not used as a substitute for good hygiene and manufacturing practices. Directive 1999/2/EC of the European Parliament and of the Council on the approximation of the laws of the Member States concerning foods and food ingredients treated with ionising radiation [1999] OJ L66/1 (EU Irradiation Directive), Annex I.

[165] Directive 1999/3/EC of the European Parliament and of the Council on the establishment of a Community list of foods and food ingredients treated with ionising radiation [1999] OJ L66/24.

[166] Seven Member States have maintained national authorisations, as they are permitted under Directive 1999/2/EC, for certain food and food ingredients. In general, irradiation remains limited to specific sectors, primarily frog's legs, herbs and spices and poultry. European Commission, 'Report from the Commission on food irradiation for the year 2007' [2009] OJ C242/02, para 1.2.

[167] European Commission, 'Communication from the Commission on foods and food ingredients authorised for treatment with ionising radiation in the Community' [2001] OJ C241/6 ('Commission Irradiation Communication') Conclusions.

[168] ibid.

with SPS disciplines. The non-scientific criteria—technological need and consumer benefit[169]—for approving irradiation in the European Directive are also explicitly included in the Codex Standard on irradiated food.[170] The rejection of an individual product on the basis of these criteria would therefore not in itself contradict international standards. Yet, a third country that can demonstrate the consumer benefits for irradiating a specific food has good grounds to challenge the EU's approach.[171] The refusal of the EU specifically to evaluate the merits of a single product, in spite of positive scientific opinions,[172] sustains the suspicion that it is maintaining a *de facto* moratorium on most irradiated foods, at odds with both SPS scientific disciplines and the demands of the Codex standard. Nevertheless, in spite of complaints made to the WTO by the US in 2001,[173] the EU has thus far managed to withstand pressure to resolve the issue. In this instance, domestic social value preferences have been maintained.

Azo Dyes

In 2004, the UK Food Standards Agency (UK FSA) commissioned research into the relationship between mixtures of artificial food colours and hyperactivity in children. The results of this study, undertaken by the University of Southampton, were reviewed by the FSA's Committee on Toxicity in September 2007,[174] provoking the Agency to advise the removal of these substances from the diets of children showing signs of hyperactivity.[175] The study was reviewed by EFSA, which identified a number of weaknesses and concluded that 'it is not possible to ascribe the observed effects to any of the individual compounds'.[176] However, notwithstanding the flimsiness of the scientific evidence, the UK FSA maintained pressure on the UK government to take regulatory action.[177] These developments coincided with the passage of a proposed revision to EU additives legislation through the Euro-

[169] EU Irradiation Directive, Annex I.

[170] Codex Alimentarius, General Standard for Irradiated Foods, Codex Stan 106–1983, Rev1-2003, point 4.1.

[171] See Farkas (n 161) 150 (outlining the positive effects of the process for US beef).

[172] Favourable SCF opinions have been provided on a number of foodstuffs including fruit, vegetables, cereals, fish, shellfish, egg white and rice flour. 'Commission Irradiation Communication' (n 167) para 3.

[173] G/SPS/GEN/265 (10 July 2001).

[174] UK FSA, 'Committee on Toxicity of Chemical in Food, Consumer Products and the Environment, Statement 2007/04' (September 2007) cot.food.gov.uk/pdfs/colpreschil.pdf.

[175] UK FSA, 'Agency Revises Advice on Certain Artificial Colours' (11 September 2007) www.food.gov.uk/news/newsarchive/2007/sep/foodcolours.

[176] EFSA, 'Assessment of the Results of the Study by McCann et. al. (2007) on the Effect of Some Colours and Sodium Benzoate on Children's Behaviour' (2008) 660 *EFSA Journal* 1.

[177] For a detailed account of the UK FSA's management of azo dyes risk, see R *Lofstedt*, 'Risk Communication and the FSA: The Food Colourings Case' (2009) 12 *Journal of Risk Research* 537.

pean Parliament led by the UK,[178] the Parliament embraced the azo dye issue and introduced amendments proposing warning labels for these colours.[179] The final Regulation, published in December 2008, introduced mandatory labelling for six food colours, on the basis that they 'may have an adverse effect on activity and attention in children'.[180] The EU's response is unprecedented and, given the negative market impact on the substances concerned, lays it open to criticism from trading partners.[181] The response to social concerns in this instance, amplified by media interest,[182] is particularly striking in view of the limited risk rationale for the measure provided by EFSA.

Thrombin

Thrombin—unaffectionately known as 'meat glue'—is a food additive whose function is to bind together small pieces of meat into a single meat product. In February 2010, the Standing Committee adopted a draft Commission Directive to amend the list of permitted additives to include 20 new substances, including thrombin.[183] The proposal then passed to the European Parliament for scrutiny under comitology rules. Consumer groups reacted with hostility to the proposal, arguing in particular that the consumer may be misled as to the quality of the product.[184] In response, the European Parliament adopted a Resolution which condemned various aspects of the product: the higher risk of infection by pathogenic bacteria as a result of the increased surface area created by attaching small pieces of meat, the potential to mislead consumers that they were buying a single-meat product, and the failure to demonstrate the product's benefits for consumers.[185] The Commission defended the proposal on the basis of the positive safety assessment provided by EFSA and the reduced consumer costs of the meat products resulting from use of thrombin.

---

[178] UK FSA Chair Deidre Hutton called for 'mandatory action by the EU' to phase out the use of food colours. Comments cited in 'Europe-wide Colour Ban Call', BBC News (10 April 2008) news.bbc.co.uk/2/hi/7340426.stm.

[179] 'Azo Dyes: MEPs Take a Strong Line', *EU Food Law* (9 May 2008).

[180] Commission Regulation (EU) No 238/2010 of 22 March 2010 amending Annex V to Regulation (EC) No 1333/2008 of the European Parliament and of the Council with regard to the labelling requirement for beverages with more than 1, 2 % by volume of alcohol and containing certain food colours [2008] OJ L75/17.

[181] At the time of writing, the issue has not been formally raised in a WTO context.

[182] See Lofstedt (n 177) 549–550.

[183] European Commission, 'Draft Commission Directive amending Directive 2008/84/EC laying down specific purity criteria on food additives other than colours and sweeteners' (SANCO/2010/10035).

[184] 'SANCO Challenged over Glue Meat Additive Authorisation', *EU Food Law* (11 February 2010).

[185] European Parliament, 'Resolution on the draft Commission directive amending the Annexes to European Parliament and Council Directive 95/2/EC on food additives other than colours and sweeteners and repealing Decision 2004/374/EC' (RSP/2010/2679).

However, Members of the European Parliament (MEPs), who found the process 'disgusting' and 'repulsive', finally vetoed the Commission Directive, obliging the Commission to table a new proposal.[186] Once more, in this case, risk (hygiene) issues and social-value judgements are interlinked, although the latter were undoubtedly instrumental to the fate of this proposal.[187]

As explained above, in many areas policy-makers have significant scope to incorporate social-value judgements into risk-management measures without fear of third-country retaliation. The cases presented here suggest that even where scientific rationale tends towards trade-liberalising measures, social value preferences may push EU regulators to choose more restrictive options. In each, the scientific basis for EU measures is vulnerable to an SPS challenge. There are certainly concerns related to antimicrobial treatment, but the Commission's own willingness to propose alternative measures to a prohibition suggests vulnerability for the EU if the WTO dispute were pursued. Restrictive measures for irradiated foods, azo dyes or thrombin have even more limited scientific support. The point here is not whether the EU would be able successfully to defend each policy in a dispute: argumentation and legal strategy would likely be decisive in this respect. Rather, the striking feature is that far from being excluded from the legislative process, as some legal commentators fear, social-value judgements continue to play a decisive role in shaping EU food policy. As public preferences find their voice, the scientific framework provided by the SPS Agreement starts to buckle. No amount of risk assessment would reverse the public rejection of growth hormones. A groundswell of public scepticism towards artificial colours, not a study by Southampton University, propelled the Union towards the effective removal of these products from the food chain. Public perception of risk, encompassing both scientific and non-scientific concerns, remains an integral element of EU sanitary measures. Nor is this likely to change. As De Rosa and colleagues put it: 'No European government can manage a global trade system that would force consumers against their explicit wishes and against the policies of the government to accept certain food products.'[188]

4.5 Conclusion

This chapter has argued that, while perhaps less stark than sometimes claimed, the SPS Agreement, or rather how it has been interpreted in dispute settlement, does create a conflict for policymakers bound to provide scientific evidence for policies inevitably determined by social-value judgements. Nevertheless, a review of EU food safety measures would suggest that the impact of SPS obligations has not and probably will not be as profound as many commentators have feared. Cer-

---

[186] 'MEPs Vote to Block Meat Glue Approval', *EU Food Law* (30 April 2010).

[187] The example is of particular interest because of the Parliament's explicit invocation of ethical concerns making it something of a 'test case' in the eyes of Green MEP Carl Schlyter. ibid.

[188] De Rosa et al. (n 131) 751.

tainly, in the case of growth hormones, the EU's failure adequately to adhere to the rules came at a price. Yet, far from being cowed into a hyper-scientific approach to food policy, EU policy-makers remain strongly influenced by citizens' social-value judgements. If the WTO is influencing EU policy-making, it would not appear to be having the systemic impact on the balance between science and social-value judgements that many assume. To understand how the EU's participation in the WTO shapes domestic food policy, a more detailed analysis is required of the type that will be undertaken in Chap. 5 on another controversial area of EU food policy: The Novel Foods Regulation.

The observations made in this chapter are important for our overall appreciation of the impact of WTO law in practice. They may also somewhat allay the fears of those lawyers who perceive the SPS Agreement to be undermining domestic policy-making. The assessment of EU policy undertaken here does not discount the existence of the underlying tensions between a more scientific and socio-cultural approach to risk. Simply, if scientific disciplines do have some capacity to deter protectionism and if WTO members, such as the EU, can in practice continue to adequately accommodate their citizens' preferences, it may be worthwhile to reflect again both on the inappropriateness of the SPS Agreement's current relationship with science, and the urgency and need for a fundamentally new approach.

References

Alemanno A, *Trade in Food: Regulatory and Judicial Approaches in the EC and the WTO* (London, Cameron May, 2007).

Alemanno A, 'Public Perception of Food Safety Risks Under WTO Law: A Normative Perspective' in G van Calster and D Prévost (eds), *Research Handbook on Environment, Health and the WTO* (Cheltenham, Edward Elgar, 2012).

Arcuri A, 'Food Safety at the WTO after Continued Suspension: A Paradigm Shift?' in A Antoniadis, R Schütze and E Spaventa (eds), *The European Union and Global Emergencies—A Law and Policy Analysis* (Oxford, Hart Publishing, 2011).

Atik J, 'Science and International Regulatory Convergence' (1996) 17 *Northwestern Journal of International Law and Business* 736.

Barceló JJ, 'Product Standards to Protect the Local Environment—The GATT and the Uruguay Round Sanitary and Phytosanitary Agreement' (1994) 27 *Cornell International Law Journal* 755.

Bentley P, 'A Re-assessment of Article XX, Paragraphs (b) and (g) of GATT 1994 in the Light of Growing Consumer and Environmental Concern about Biotechnology' (2000) 24 *Fordham International Law Journal* 107.

Berg T and Licht D, 'International Legislation on Trace Elements as Contaminants in Food: A Review' (2002) 19 *Food Additives and Contaminants* 916.

Bohanes J, 'Risk Regulation in WTO Law: A Procedure-Based Approach to the Precautionary Principle' (2002) 40 *Columbia Journal of Transnational Law* 323.

Caduff L, 'Growth Hormones and Beyond' (Centre for International Studies, Working Paper 2–2002).

Carter MD, 'Selling Science under the SPS Agreement: Accommodating Consumer Preference in the Growth Hormones Controversy' (1997) 6 *Minnesota Journal of Global Trade* 625.

Chalmers D, '"Food for Thought": Reconciling European Risks and Traditional Ways of Life' (2003) 66 MLR 532.

Charnovitz S, 'The Supervision of Health and Biosafety of Regulation by World Trade Rules' (2000) 13 *Tulane Environmental Law Journal* 271.

de Búrca G and Scott J, 'The Impact of the WTO on EU Decision-Making', in G de Búrca and J Scott (eds), *The EU and the WTO, Legal and Constitutional Issues* (Oxford, Hart Publishing, 2001).

De Rosa M, van Knapen F and Brom FWA, 'Risk Analysis-Based Food Safety Policy: Scientific Factors Versus Socio-Cultural Factors' (2008) 133 *Tijdschrift voor Diregeneeskunde* 746.

Echols MA, 'Food Safety Regulation in the European Union and the United States: Different Cultures, Different Laws' (1998) 4 *Columbia Journal of European Law* 525.

Ely A and Sterling A, 'The Process of Assessment' in M Dreyer and O Renn (eds), *Food Safety Governance: Integrating Science, Precaution and Public Involvement* (Berlin, Springer, 2009).

Farkas J, 'Irradiation for Better Foods' (2006) 17 *Trends in Food Science and Technology* 148.

Fidler DP, 'Legal Challenges Posed by the Use of Antimicrobials in Food Animal Production' (1999) 1 *Microbes and Infection* 29.

Foster CE 'Public Opinion and the Interpretation of the World Trade Organisation's Agreement on Sanitary and Phytosanitary Measures' (2008) 11 JIEL 427.

Gao H, 'The Mighty Pen, the Almighty Dollar, and the Holy Hammer and Sickle: An Examination of the Conflict between Trade Liberalisation and Domestic Cultural Policy with Special Regard to the Recent Dispute between the United States and China on Restrictions on Certain Cultural Products' (2007) 2 *Asian Journal of WTO and International Health Law and Policy* 313.

Goh G, 'Tipping the Apple Cart: The Limits of Science and Law in the SPS Agreement after *Japan—Apples*' (2006) 40 JWT 655.

Guzman AT 'Food Fears: Health and Safety at the WTO' (2004) 45 VJIL 1.

Halpern AR, 'The US—EC Hormone Beef Controversy and the Standards Code: Implications for the Application of Health Regulations to Agricultural Trade' (1989) 14 *North Carolina Journal of International Law and Commercial Regulation* 136.

Harlow SD, 'Science—Based Trade Disputes: A New Challenge in Harmonizing the Evidentiary Systems of Law and Science' (2004) 24 *Risk Analysis* 443.

Howse R, 'Democracy, Science, and Free Trade: Risk Regulation on Trial at the World Trade Organisation' (2000) 98 *Michigan Law Review* 2329.

Hüller T and Maier ML, 'Fixing the Codex? Global Food-Safety Governance under Review' in C Joerges and E-U Petersmann (eds), *Constitutionalism, Multilevel Trade Governance and Social Regulation* (Oxford, Hart Publishing, 2006).

Hunter C, 'Changing Attitudes to Irradiation Throughout the Food Chain' (2000) 57 *Radiation Physics and Chemistry* 239.

Ingram M, 'Raw Deal: Trade Implications of the US Food and Drug Administration's Pending Review of Unpasteurised Cheeses' (2003) 12 *Minnesota Journal of Global Trade* 461.

James P, Kemper F and Pascal G, 'A European Food and Public Health Authority: The Future of Scientific Advice in the EU' (Report commissioned by the European Commission, 1999).

Jardine C, Hrudey S, Shortreed J, Craig L, Krewski D, Furgal C and McColl S, 'Risk Management Frameworks for Human Health and Environmental Risks' (2003) 6 *Journal of Toxicology and Environmental Health* 569.

Kalderimis D, 'Problems of WTO Harmonisation and the Virtues of Shields over Swords' (2004) 13 *Minnesota Journal of Global* 305.

Kennedy KC, 'Resolving International Sanitary and Phytosanitary Disputes in the WTO: Lessons and Future Directions' (2000) 55 *Food and Drug Law Journal* 81.

Kerr WA and Hobbs JE, 'The North American-European Union Dispute Over Beef Produced Using Growth Hormones: A Major Test for the New International Trade Regime' (2002) 25 *The World Economy* 283.

Kysar DA, 'Preferences for Processes: The Process/Product Distinction and the Regulation of Consumer Choice' (2004) 118 *Harvard Law Review* 525.

Lee M, *EU Regulation GMOs: Law and Decision-Making for a New Technology'* (Cheltenham, Edward Elgar, 2008).
Levidow L and Carr S, 'How Biotechnology Regulation Sets A Risk/Ethics Boundary' (1997) 14 *Agriculture and Human Values* 29.
Lofstedt R, 'Risk Communication and the FSA: The Food Colourings Case' (2009) 12 *Journal of Risk Research* 537.
Lupton D, *Risk* (London, Routledge, 1999).
Marceau G and Trachtman JP, 'The Technical Barriers to Trade Agreement, the Sanitary and Phytosanitary Measures Agreement, and the General Agreement Tariffs and Trade—A Map of the World Trade Organisation Law of Domestic Regulation of Goods' (2002) 36 JWT 811.
Maruyama WH, 'A New Pillar of the WTO: Sound Science' (1998) 32 *The International Lawyer* 651.
Masson-Matthee MD, *The Codex Alimentarius Commission and its Standards* (The Hague, TMC Asser Press, 2007).
Miller ML, 'Does the WTO Substantially Limit the Ability of Countries to Regulate Harmful Nonindigenous Species? (2003) 17 *Emory International Law Review* 1059.
Morgan D and Goh G, 'Genetically Modified Food Labelling and the WTO Agreements' (2004) 13 *Review of European Community and International Environmental Law* 306.
Pauwelyn J, 'The GMO Debate Under the Rules of the World Trade Organization' (GMOs in European Agriculture and Food Production conference, The Hague, November 2009).
Peel J, 'Risk Regulation under the WTO SPS Agreement: Science as an International Normative Yardstick?' (Jean Monnet Working Paper 02/04, 1995).
Peel J, 'A GMO by Any Other Name… Might be an SPS Risk!: Implications of Expanding the Scope of the WTO Sanitary and Phytosanitary Measures Agreement' (2006) 17 EJIL 1009.
Peel J 'Of Apples and Oranges (and Hormones in Beef): Science and the Standard of Review in WTO Disputes under the SPS Agreement' (2012) 61 ICLQ 47.
Perrez PFX, 'Taking Consumers Seriously: The Swiss Regulatory Approach to Genetically Modified Food' (2000) 8 NYU *Environmental Lawyer* Journal 585.
Pickett SE and Suzuki T, 'Regulation of Food Safety Risks: The Case of Food Irradiation in Japan' (2000) 1 *Journal of Risk Research* 95.
Quick R and Blüthner A, 'Has the Appellate Body Erred? An Appraisal and Criticism of the Ruling in the WTO Hormones Case' (1999) 2 JIEL 4, 603.
Renn O, 'Three Decades of Risk Research: Accomplishments and New Challenges' (1998) 1 *Journal of Risk Research* 49.
Roberts D, 'Preliminary Assessment of the Effects of the WTO Agreement on Sanitary and Phytosanitary Trade Regulations' (1998) 1 JIEL 377.
Rosa EA, 'Metatheoretical Foundations for Post-Normal Risk' (1998) 1 *Journal of Risk Research* 15.
Scherzberg A, 'EU-US Trade Disputes about Risk Regulation: The Case of Genetically Modified Organisms' (2006) 19 *Cambridge Review of International Affairs* 121.
Scott J, 'On Kith and Kine (and Crustaceans): Trade and Environment in the EU and WTO' in JHH Weiler (ed), *The EU, the WTO and the NAFTA: Towards a Common Law of International Trade* (Oxford, OUP, 2000).
Scott J, *The WTO Agreement on Sanitary and Phytosanitary Measures. A Commentary* (Oxford, OUP, 2007).
Shapiro HS, 'The Rules That Swallowed the Exceptions: The WTO SPS Agreement and Its Relationship to GATT Articles XX and XXI' (2007) 24 *Arizona Journal of International and Comparative Law* 199.
Short JF, 'The Social Fabric at Risk: Toward the Social Transformation of Risk Analysis' (1984) 49 *American Sociological Review* 711.
Shrader-Frachette KS, *Risk and Rationality–Philosophical Foundations for Populist Reforms* (Berkeley, University of California Press, 1991).
Skogstad G, 'Internationalization, Democracy, and Food Safety Measures: The (Il)Legitimacy of Consumer Preferences' (2001a) 7 *Global Governance* 293.

Skogstad G, 'The WTO and Food Safety Regulatory Policy Innovation in the European Union' (2001b) 39 JCMS 485.

Slotboom MM, 'The Hormones Case: An Increased Risk of Illegality of Sanitary and Phytosanitary Measures' (1999) 36 CML Rev 471.

Stirling A, 'On Science and Precaution in the Management of Technological Risk. An ESTO Project Report' (Report to the EU Forward Studies Unit, IPTS, EUR 19056 EN May 1999).

Stokes E, 'Book Review: *EU Regulation of GMOs: Law and Decision Making for a New Technology*. By Maria Lee' (2010) 22 *Journal of Environmental Law* 165.

Sunstein CR, 'Probability Neglect: Emotions, Worst Cases, and Law' (2002) 112 *Yale Law Journal* 61.

Szajkowska A, *Regulating Food Law: Risk Analysis and the Precautionary Principle as General Principles of EU Food Law* (Wageningen, Wageningen Academic Publishers, 2012).

Tait J and Bruce A, 'Globalisation and Transboundary Risk Regulation: Pesticides and Genetically Modified Crops' (2001) 3 *Health, Risk and Society* 99.

Taylor MD, 'The WTO Panel Decision on Australia's Salmon Import Guidelines: Evidence that the SPS Agreement Can Effectively Protect Human Health Interests' (2000) 9 *Pacific Rim Law and Policy Journal* 473.

Trebilcock M and Soloway J, 'International Trade Policy and Domestic Food Safety Regulation: The Case for Substantial Deference by the WTO Dispute Settlement Body under the SPS Agreement' in DL Kennedy and JD Southwick (eds), *The Political Economy of International Trade Law: Essays in Honour of Robert E Hudec*' (Cambridge, CUP, 2002).

van der Meulen BMJ, 'Science Based Food Law' (2009) 1 *European Food and Feed Law* 58.

van Zwanenberg P and Millstone E, 'BSE: A Paradigm of Policy Failure' (2003) 74 *The Political Quarterly* 27.

Victor DG, 'The Sanitary and Phytosanitary Agreement of the World Trade Organisation: An Assessment After Five Years' (2000) 32 *New York University Journal of International Law and Politics* 865.

Vos E and Wendler F, 'Food Safety Regulation at the EU Level' in E Vos and F Wendler (eds), *Food Safety Regulation in Europe* (Antwerp, Intersentia, 2006).

Walker VR 'The Myth of Science as a "Neutral Arbiter" for Triggering Precautions' (2003) 26 *Boston College International and Comparative Law Review* 197.

Weinberg AM, 'Science and Trans-Science' (1972) 10 *Minerva* 209.

Whitlock JP, '*Japan-Measures Affecting Agricultural Products*: Lessons for Future SPS and Agricultural Trade Disputes' (2002) 33 *Law and Policy in International Business* 741.

Winickoff D, Jasanoff S, Busch L, Grove-White R and Wynne B, 'Adjudicating the GM Food Wars: Science, Risk, and Democracy in World Trade Law' (2005) 30 YJIL 81.

Wirth D, 'The Role of Science in the Uruguay Round and NAFTA Trade Disciplines' (1994) 27 *Cornell International Law Journal* 817.

Wolf O, Ibarreta D and Sørup P (eds), 'Science in Trade Disputes Related to Potential Risks: Comparative Case Studies' (IPTS Technical Report Series EUR 21301 EN 2004).

Chapter 5
Bringing in the Old and the New: The Influence of the SPS Agreement on the EU Novel Food Saga

Abstract This chapter undertakes a detailed analysis of the EU's controversial policy on 'novel foods' to reveal the potential and limits of the WTO's influence on the domestic decision-making process. As EU institutions were forced in 2011 to abandon a proposal for a new Novel Food Regulation (NNFR), WTO commitments were cited as a key cause for the inter-institutional failure to find legislative compromises. Two elements of this sanitary measure—the regulation of traditional exotic products from outside the EU and the treatment of food from cloned animals—proved particularly problematic, illustrating the difficulties of reconciling international trade obligations and domestic policy preferences. This chapter first recounts the development of the NNFR, and then traces the influence of SPS and other WTO disciplines in the EU's proposed regulation of traditional and 'cloned' food. This account finds that SPS obligations do have a role in shaping EU food policy, but in a far more subtle and complex way than is commonly assumed.

5.1 Introduction

In March 2011, the European Union (EU) institutions were forced to admit that after 3 years of negotiations, their efforts to write new legislation governing foods not traditionally widely consumed in Europe, known as 'novel foods',[1] had come to nothing.[2] The so-called conciliation procedure, designed to align the views of the European Parliament (EP) and Council, had failed. The EP's compromise proposal of mandatory labelling for all food produced using the controversial technique of

This chapter was first published as 'The Rise and Fall of the New EU Novel Food Regulation: The Complex Influence of the WTO SPS Agreement' (2013) 8 *Asian Journal of WTO and International Health Law and Policy* 249.

[1] For a discussion of the definition of novel foods, see s 5.2.1 below.

[2] J Dalli, 'Statement by Commissioner Dalli on the Lack of Agreement in the Conciliation Procedure on the Novel Food Regulation', *Europa Press Releases RAPID* (29 March 2011) europa.eu/rapid/press-release_MEMO-11-202_en.htm.

C. Downes, *The Impact of WTO SPS Law on EU Food Regulations,* Studies in European Economic Law and Regulation 2, DOI 10.1007/978-3-319-04373-9_5,

animal cloning was rejected by the Council.[3] The latter claimed this policy would breach World Trade Organisation (WTO) law and propel the EU into a trade war.[4] As the inquest into this breakdown got under way at an EP plenary meeting in Strasbourg, the parliamentary rapporteur Kartika Liotard angrily brandished a leaked legal paper prepared by the Council's Legal Service. In it, she argued, was proof that claims by the Council and Commission that international law stood in the way of the EP's demands were demonstrably false.[5] This moment of theatre[6] laid bare the fundamental tensions between domestic policy preferences and international obligations.

Looking beyond the institutional grandstanding, to what extent did legal considerations govern the rise and fall of the NNFR? This chapter offers a detailed analysis of EU novel foods policy, a case study which provides both greater insight into the potential constraints faced by decision-makers and an opportunity to assess the real influence of the Agreement on the Application of Sanitary and Phytosanitary Measures (SPS Agreement) and other WTO obligations.[7] This chapter focuses in particular on the two types of foodstuffs covered by the proposed Regulation which are most relevant to international trade and therefore SPS rules: traditional exotic products (treated in Sect. 5.3) and foods derived from cloned animals (Sect. 5.4).[8] Each of these sections explores how current and proposed EU measures designed to manage the placement of these products on the European market strain SPS obligations and the expectations of trading partners. First, Sect. 5.2 examines the origins and functioning of the current Novel Food Regulation (CNFR).

---

[3] See European Parliament, 'Q&A on the Novel Foods Regulation' (29 March 2011) www.europarl.europa.eu/en/pressroom/content/20101019BKG88150/html/QA-on-the-novel-foods-regulation.

[4] Statement of the Hungarian Presidency, 'Cloned Foods Unleashed', HunPR/22/2011 (29 March 2011) www.eu2011.hu/files/bveu/documents/HunPR_22__-_29_03_2011_-_Cloned_foods_unleashed.pdf.

[5] See 'Members of the EP Refute Claims of "Trade War" If EU Regulates Clone Offspring', *AGRA FACTS* (11 May 2011) and the transcript of the EP plenary debate of 11 May 2011, Statement by the President of the European Parliament's delegation to the Conciliation Committee–Novel foods (continuation of debate), agenda point 11 (May 2011 EP debate) www.europarl.europa.eu/sides/getDoc.do?pubRef=-//EP//TEXT+CRE+20110511+ITEM-009+DOC+XML+V0//EN.

[6] The Council's Legal Service subsequently (justifiably) dismissed Mrs Liotard's presentation of their arguments as 'not correct because it is neither precise nor complete'. Council of the European Union, 'Novel Foods–Statement of the Council's Legal Service', 10332/11, PRESSE 140 (17 May 2011) www.consilium.europa.eu/uedocs/cms_data/docs/pressdata/en/lsa/122071.pdf.

[7] While our primary interest is in the influence of SPS rules, the fate of this EU sanitary measure cannot be understood in isolation from GATT and TBT obligations.

[8] A further controversial issue, the regulation of foods produced using nanotechnology, which was prominent in institutional discussions is not discussed here, as the impact of regulating these foods is not expected to be disproportionately burdensome for imported foods and therefore less relevant to the international trade implications which are the focus of this chapter.

5.2 The CNFR: Origins and Functioning

Novel foods are nothing new: the past 50 years have seen various waves of food innovation. A fear in the 1960s and 1970s that the world faced food shortages drove scientists to seek alternative sources of protein from plant and microbial sources.[9] In the 1990s, researchers turned their attention to biotechnology, developing crops resistant to disease and tolerant to herbicides which they claimed would bring greater security to the food supply. Over the decade, food technologists increasingly focused on 'functional' food ingredients, developed to offer specific beneficial health effects.[10] The search for new ingredients in turn stimulated investigation into new food processes. Amongst these, nanotechnology has been singled out for particular scrutiny by authorities[11] and the media.[12] While these innovations vary considerably in technical terms, the products that result from them have all, at some stage, fallen under the regulatory category of 'novel foods'.

Novel foods posed a dilemma for regulators. The risk-assessment methods customarily used to evaluate, for example, food additives—feeding doses considerably beyond normal human intake to animals—were not appropriate for analysis of novel foods.[13] Food regulators therefore started to develop new procedures for case-by-case evaluation.[14] A guiding principle was to ensure that new technology 'does not result in food which is inherently less safe than that produced by conventional means'.[15] This comparative approach—or 'substantial equivalence', as this principle is commonly known—became a central feature of regulatory frameworks worldwide.[16] In Europe, the prospect of different national policy responses to the

---

[9] D Jones, 'Safety Evaluation of Novel Foods: A European and International Perspective' (EUFIC Review 04/2000) www.eufic.org/article/en/expid/review-novel-foods. See also D Wilson, 'Marketing Mycoprotein, The Quorn Foods Story' (2001) 55 *Food Technology Magazine* 48–50 (discussing the development of one of the first novel foods nurtured from a species of fungi).

[10] For an overview, see N Binns and J Howlett, 'Functional Foods in Europe: International Developments in Science and Health Claims' (2009) 48 (Supp 1) *European Journal of Nutrition* S3.

[11] See generally European Food Safety Authority (EFSA), 'Scientific Opinion of the Scientific Committee, The Potential Risks Arising from Nanoscience and Nanotechnologies on Food and Feed Safety' (2009) 958 *EFSA Journal* 1.

[12] F Macrae, '"Grey Goo" Food Laced with Nanoparticles Could Swamp Britain' *Daily Mail* (8 January 2010) www.dailymail.co.uk/news/article-1241506/Britain-maybe-swamped-nanoparticle-grey-food.html.

[13] J Maryanski, 'Special Challenges of Novel Foods (Biotechnology)' (1990) 45 *Food, Drug, Cosmetic Law Journal* 545, 549 (explaining how the bulk of many novel foods meant that the hundredfold increase normally applied in animal studies would entirely disrupt the diet of the animal).

[14] An early definition of a novel food—those not previously eaten by a human population—was established by the United Nations Protein Advisory Committee (PAC). 'PAG/UNU Guideline No. 6: Preclinical Testing of Novel Sources of Food' (1983) 5 *Food and Nutrition Bulletin* 94, 60–63.

[15] World Health Organization, 'Strategies For Assessing The Safety of Foods Produced by Biotechnology: Report of a Joint FAO/WHO Consultation' (1991) 24.

[16] Jones (n 9).

challenges posed by novel foods[17] threatened the operation of the European Single Market and provided the impetus for EU legislation.

A first proposal for a European novel food regulation was published in July 1992.[18] Its adoption was a particularly protracted process, described at the time as 'one of the longest and most difficult in the whole area of European food law'.[19] From the outset, the EP expressed fundamental doubts about the common regulatory approach proposed for both genetically modified (GM) food and other types of novel products.[20] In addition, the simple notification procedure foreseen for some novel foods was deemed inadequate for protecting consumers, and there were fears (a foretaste of today's discussions on food from clones) that novel foods would be placed on the market without specific labelling.[21] To respond to these concerns, the final text of the CNFR tightened both procedural and labelling provisions and brought consumer-safety issues to the fore.[22] One significant amendment to the CNFR occurred in 2003 with the removal of GM foods from its scope, following the elaboration of a specific legal framework for these products.[23]

5.2.1 The Operation of the CNFR

To be considered 'novel' in the EU, food has to fulfil two criteria. Firstly, it must have 'not been used for human consumption to a significant degree within the Community' before 15 May 1997.[24] Secondly, it must fall within one of four categories:[25] food with modified primary molecular structure; food isolated from microorganisms; foods isolated from plants, food ingredients and animals; foods produced by novel processes. A company wishing to place a novel food on the market is required to submit an application, together with information substantiating the safety of the product, to the Member State where it will first be sold. The competent authority

[17] See S Waters, 'The Regulation of Herbicide Resistant Crops in Europe' in S Duke (ed), *Herbicide Resistant Crops: Agricultural, Economic, Environmental, Regulatory, & Technological Aspects* (Cleveland, CRC Press, 1995) 347, 356 (recounting the case of the Netherland's introduction of a novel food Regulation in 1993).

[18] European Commission, Proposal for a Council Regulation (EEC) on Novel Foods and Novel Food Ingredients [1992] OJ C190/4.

[19] P Berry Ottaway, 'New European Controls on Novel Foods and Ingredients' *Nutraceuticals International* (March 1997).

[20] See 'MEPs Vote to Amend Novel Foods Proposal' *Europe Environment* (9 November 1993).

[21] C Kirkham, 'Legislative Developments. Novel Foods and Food Ingredients' (1997) 3 *Columbia Journal of European Law* 317, 318–19.

[22] Regulation (EC) 258/97 of the European Parliament and of the Council Concerning Novel Foods and Novel Food Ingredients [1997] OJ L43/1 (CNFR). The consumer protection element, entirely absent in the original proposal, was included in Recital 2 of the CNFR.

[23] Regulation (EC) 1829/2003 of the European Parliament and of the Council on Genetically Modified Food and Feed [2003] OJ L268/1.

[24] CNFR (n 22) Art 1.2. May 15, 1997 signifies the date of entry into force of the Regulation.

[25] These are the categories that remained following the removal of GM foods.

in that country undertakes an initial assessment and decides whether the food may be placed on the market or whether a further assessment is required. The Commission or a Member State can raise a reasoned objection to the application. In the latter case, or where a further assessment by European Food Safety Authority (EFSA) is needed, the opinion of the Standing Committee on Foods (comprising Member State experts) is sought. The resulting Commission authorisation[26] sets out the specifications of the product and establishes, where appropriate, the conditions of use and relevant labelling. The novel food can only be commercialised by the company to whom the Commission Decision is addressed. A simplified notification procedure exists for products demonstrated to be 'substantially equivalent' to an existing food on the EU market.[27]

5.3 Traditional Foods from Third Countries

5.3.1 The Troubled Existence of Traditional Foods under the CNFR

Since the CNFR was aimed primarily at regulating novel technologies, traditional foods, such as exotic fruit and vegetables, were not a prominent concern in its drafting. For some time, third countries maintained that such traditional foods were not captured by the EU's definition of a novel food.[28] Instead, they were considered to fall under a derogation (Article 1(e)) for foods 'obtained by traditional propagating … and *having a history of safe use*' (emphasis added).[29] From an ordinary reading of this provision, this position seems justified. If a certain category of products were to be spared the evidentiary burden of authorisation due to their extensive use, traditional exotic products, some consumed for centuries, are logical candidates. However, without formally articulating the legal basis for their actions,[30] the Commission and Member States have tended to treat these products as falling within the Regulation. One explanation is that the 'history of safe use' refers to use *within* the

[26] Where the Commission envisages measures that do not have the support of the Standing Committee, it has the option of presenting the measures to Council for adoption. CNFR (n 22) Art 13.

[27] CNFR (n 22) Art 5.

[28] 'Comments on Regulation (EC) N° 258/97 of the European Parliament and of the Council of 27 January 1997 concerning novel foods and novel food ingredients', Working Party on Novel Foods—Peru, ec.europa.eu/food/food/biotechnology/novelfood/peru_en.pdf.

[29] CNFR (n 22) Art 1(e).

[30] The Commission's own evaluation of the CNFR points to 'confusion over the intention of the legislation concerning "exotic plants"'. European Commission, 'Evaluation Report on the Novel Food Regulation 258/97 Concerning Novel Foods and Novel Food Ingredients' (22/1/2004) Commission CNFR Evaluation) 5, ec.europa.eu/food/food/biotechnology/novelfood/evaluation_report_en.pdf.

Community market.[31] Yet, a product with such a history would not be considered a novel food under the first condition of Article 1.2 (non-presence on the European market), rendering recourse to the article 1(e) derogation irrelevant. Notwithstanding this uncertain legal grounding, the EU's treatment of traditional foods as novel foods is unwavering.[32] This practice reflects wariness about the possible impact of traditional foods on the EU population, undoubtedly reinforced by unfavourable early experiences of handling exotic products.[33]

Given the EU's inclusive interpretation of the novel food definition and the considerable procedural implications that this designation carries, demonstrating the 'non-novel' food status has become the most viable marketing strategy for many traditional foods.[34] This is far from simple, exporters must be able to prove 'human consumption to a significant degree in the Community', a concept that still awaits clear definition.[35] Striving to meet (or second-guess) the regulator's expectations in this respect is a particular burden for exporters of traditional foods. These products are often destined for a particular immigrant community and may not be accurately pinpointed by customs nomenclature, leaving unrecorded any import that has occurred.[36] Moreover, the data must predate May 1997, making any Member State

[31] For an elaboration of this view, see UK Foods Standards Agency (UK FSA), 'Goji Berries' (2007) 9, www.food.gov.uk/multimedia/pdfs/gojiberriesrep.pdf.

[32] Thus, the EU's Impact Assessment of the NNFR confidently proclaims: 'At present traditional food which was not on the EU market before 1997, but for which there is information on safe use outside the EU, is subject to the same rigorous safety assessment procedure as any newly developed innovative food'. European Commission, 'Draft report on Impact Assessment for a Regulation Replacing Regulation (EC) No 258/97 on Novel Foods and Novel Food Ingredients', COM (2007) 872 final (Commission NNFR Impact Assessment) 3.

[33] In 2000, Nangai nuts and *Stevia rebaudiana* Bertoni were both rejected due to the inadequacy of the data submitted for assessment. Commission Decision 2001/17/EC on refusing the placing on the market of 'Nangai nuts' as a novel food or novel food ingredient under Regulation (EC) No 258/97 of the European Parliament and of the Council [2001] OJ L4/35; Commission Decision 2000/196/EC refusing the placing on the market of *Stevia rebaudiana* Bertoni: plants and dried leaves as a novel food or novel food ingredient under Regulation (EC) No 258/97 of the European Parliament and of the Council [2000] OJ L61/14.

[34] In the absence of extensive available data, the '[c]hances of EU market authorization for the majority of exotic food species are currently nil'. M Hermann, 'The Impact of the European Novel Food Regulation on Trade and Food Innovation Based on Traditional Plant Foods from Developing Countries' (2009) 34 *Food Policy* 499, 505.

[35] A procedure for defining criteria for clarifying the concept was foreseen in the Commission's proposal. See European Commission, Proposal for a Regulation of the European Parliament and of the Council on novel foods and amending Regulation (EU) No XXX/XXXX COM(2007) 872 final (NNFR), Art 3.2(a).i. The EU's understanding of significant use must currently be inferred from its categorisation of foods in its Novel Foods Catalogue, available at ec.europa.eu/food/food/biotechnology/novelfood/nfnetweb/index.cfm.

[36] See N Craddock, 'The EU Novel Food Regulation, Impact on the Potential Export of Exotic Traditional Foods to the EU: Suggestions for revision' (Discussion paper prepared for UNCTAD and CBI, in cooperation with GTZ, GFU and IPGRI, November 2005) 6, www.underutilized-species.org/Documents/PUBlICATIONS/cbi_unctad_paper_on_eu_nfr.pdf; EM Cumming Smith, *The European Novel Foods Regulation: The Case of Exotic Foods* (Wageningen University, June 2009) 66–67, www.underutilized-species.org/documents/publications/ecsmith_nfr_thesis_09.pdf.

challenge of a food's non-NF status increasingly difficult to counter over time. As exporters are forced to cast the net widely for evidence of use in the EU, the fate of any individual product is unpredictable, and Member State judgments can appear arbitrary.[37] As a result, some exporters opt deliberately to limit the quantities sold to the EU, in order to avoid regulatory scrutiny.[38]

Exporting countries are confident of the economic potential of exotic traditional products. This assessment is based on the tremendous success of other similar non-novel products such as paprika,[39] their estimated value,[40] the extensive variety of products available,[41] and the number of people involved in their production.[42] Yet these countries consider that the CNFR creates a largely insurmountable barrier to the European market, due to the prohibitively expensive data-collection requirements involved in the authorisation procedure.[43] Third-country frustration is exacerbated by the irreconcilability of the EU's CNFR approach with other European and international social initiatives, such as those aimed at conserving biodiversity[44] or discouraging narcotic crop production.[45] As a result, many countries have vociferously challenged the compatibility of EU policy with SPS rules.[46]

---

[37] For instance, the case (accepted by the UK authorities) for the significant use of Goji berries relied on a mixture of information ranging from signed statements by Chinese food outlets to recipes in health magazines appearing before 1997. See UK FSA (n 31) 4–8.

[38] See Cumming Smith (n 36) 52.

[39] The export value of paprika to the European market in 2005 was reported to be US$ 42 million. WTO Document, G/SPS/GEN/713 (12 July 2006) para 8.

[40] A report undertaken by the Central Bank of Ecuador identified the market value of novel foods in their country to be between 67 and 68 million US$. G/SPS/GEN/714 (12 July 2006) para 2.

[41] In one of its submissions to the SPS Committee, Colombia produces a list of around 50 products deemed to be novel foods (although some of those listed would probably not be considered novel by the EU). G/SPS/GEN/735 (18 October 2006) Annex.

[42] Ecuador estimates that exporting only five primary products—manila hemp, Quito orange, tree tomato, Andean lupin and cocoyam—could potentially have a social impact on 154,000 people. G/SPS/GEN/714 (n 40) para 5.

[43] For example, Phytotrade, a well-organised consortium of interests, is reported to have invested £ 150,000 in its successful NF application. Hermann (n 34) 505.

[44] The UN Conference on Trade and Development (UNCTAD) that runs the BioTrade Facilitation Programme (BFTP) aimed at supporting minor crops, views the CNFR to indiscriminately hinder imports of natural products, for some of which market interest is growing steadily. See O Mück, 'Trade Barrier NFR? Underutilised Species under the European Union's Novel Food Regulation' (Paper commissioned by Deutsche Gesellschaft für Technische Zusammenarbeit, 2003) 7, www.underutilized-species.org/Documents/PUBlICATIONS/trade_ barrier_nfr.pdf. For the Dutch governmental partner involved in the BTFP, the contradiction became particularly painful when the Maca root it had been promoting was confiscated by Dutch authorities on import due to its novel-food status. See Cumming Smith (n 36) 49.

[45] The EU has funded the growth of exotic foods to this end in Bolivia and Colombia, but does not allow the resulting novel foods to enter the EU. G/SPS/R/42 (25 September 2006) para 36.

[46] See ns 118 and 119 below and related text on the discussion within the WTO SPS Committee.

5.3.2 The CNFR and Compatibility with the SPS Agreement

In spite of the considerable international criticism levelled at the CNFR, in the absence of dispute-settlement proceedings a thorough examination of the EU measure's compatibility with the SPS Agreement has not been undertaken. This Section assesses the merits of complaints about the CNFR, and the resulting legal compulsion upon the Commission to amend its measures. It first considers whether the SPS Agreement is the relevant WTO text by which to measure the legality of the CNFR.

Does the SPS Agreement Apply to the CNFR?

The EU has tenaciously held to the position that the compatibility of the CNFR with WTO law should be assessed with reference not to SPS rules, but rather to the Technical Barriers to Trade (TBT) Agreement.[47] The CNFR, as indeed the NNFR 11 years later, was therefore notified as a TBT measure.[48] The EU advances two arguments for this judgement. It firstly contends that the CNFR's aim is not food safety, but 'clear product identification and labelling'. Looking to the provisions of the CNFR, this statement is puzzling. The CNFR establishes no general obligation to identify the novel nature of novel foods,[49] only requiring labelling in specific cases.[50] Consequently, European consumers purchasing a novel food will in many cases be entirely unaware of its specific legal identification.[51] The second argument is that the CNFR 'deals with *registration requirements* and *not prohibitions*'.[52] The implication, one might construe, is that measures removing *existing* products from

---

[47] Agreement on Technical Barriers to Trade, 15 April 1994, 1868 UNTS 120 (1 January 1995) (TBT Agreement). A rationale for this position was first expounded in G/SPS/GEN/699 (8 June 2006) para 6. When challenged, the EU has declined to elaborate its standpoint, preferring to reference the initial explanation. See, e.g. the EU's responses to the WTO Trade Policy Review, WTO Document, WT/TPR/M/214/Add.1 (2 July 2009) 219, 407.

[48] See generally respectively WTO Documents: G/TBT/N/EEC/188 (14 March 2008); G/TBT/Notif.97.151 (21 April 1997). The one inconsistency in the EU's practice in this respect was its communication of a pubic consultation on the EU CNFR which was transmitted to the SPS rather than TBT Committee. See G/SPS/GEN/700 (8 June 2006).

[49] The labelling requirements (Art 8) originally provided a basis for identifying GM foods. However, following the introduction of specific GM legislation and at the time of the EU's comments with regard to the TBT Agreement, the significance of labelling provisions was much reduced.

[50] See, e.g. Commission Decision 2003/867/EC authorising the placing on the market of salatrims as novel food ingredients under Regulation (EC) No 258/97 of the European Parliament and of the Council [2003] OJ L326/32, Art 2 (requiring labelling indicating potential risk of gastrointestinal disturbance).

[51] The EU's argument is all the more peculiar, as elsewhere in the same communication, the EU emphasises that 'one of the essential pillars in this [novel food] application is the provision of a safety assessment'. G/SPS/GEN/699 (n 47) para 13.

[52] ibid para 7 (emphasis in original).

the market for safety reasons (which the CNFR does not seek to do) would constitute an SPS measure, whereas the act of introducing a novel food on the market does not. This rationale is flawed. It would implausibly follow that all pre-market approval procedures should fall outside the scope of the SPS Agreement, whereas such measures are explicitly included.[53] Moreover, given that the food-safety purpose of the CNFR is clearly stated in the Regulation,[54] there can be little doubt as to the applicability of SPS rules.[55] In the end, if the CNFR is accepted to have multiple purposes, a parallel notification under the SPS and TBT Agreements would be expected.

Does the CNFR Meet SPS Requirements?

Of the EU's trading partners, Peru has been the most specific in identifying SPS obligations considered breached.[56] These are both substantive (Articles 2.2, 5.1, 5.5 and 5.6) and procedural (annex C).[57] A cursory examination of the trade impacts outlined above and the basic structure of the CNFR appears to lend sustenance to these claims. Can an arbitrary date (15 May 1997) and a judgement on the significance of EU consumption for defining novel food be science-based as required? Is there really no alternative to obliging exotic fruits to undergo the same risk assessment required for new food molecules? In other words, the idiosyncrasies of the CNFR and the inequities they produce would appear to indicate nonconformity with the SPS Agreement. The analysis below tests these assumptions, which begins with the examination of the CNFR's compliance with substantive SPS requirements.

---

[53] See SPS Agreement Art 8 and Annex C.

[54] Recital 2 of the CNFR explains that 'in order to protect public health, it is necessary to ensure that novel foods and novel food ingredients are subject to a single safety assessment through a Community procedure before they are placed on the market within the Community'. See CNFR (n 22).

[55] The elaborate, if rather unconvincing, efforts on the part of the EU to circumvent the SPS regime are all the more striking if, as Bronckers and Soopramanien claim, the TBT Agreement imposes equally strict disciplines as the SPS Agreement. M Bronckers and R Soopramanien,'The Impact of WTO Law and European Food Regulation' (2008) 3 *European Food and Feed Law Review* 361, 366–67. Their account differs, however, from the predominant view that the SPS Agreement places a higher burden on health as opposed to other types of risk. See, e.g. A Alemanno, *Trade in Food: Regulatory and Judicial Approaches in the EC and the WTO* (London, Cameron May, 2007) 312.

[56] G/SPS/GEN/681 (5 April 2006) para 8. In its contributions to the SPS Committee, Colombia has emphasised Arts 2.2 and 5.6.

[57] See CE Foster, 'Prior Approval Systems and the Substance–Procedure Dichotomy under the WTO SPS Agreement' (2008) 42 JWT 1203, 1205 (drawing this distinction between substantive and procedural measures in her analysis of the *EC—Biotech* case).

Substantive Provisions

Scientific Basis (Articles 5.1 and 2.2) Does the CNFR have the adequate scientific grounding required by SPS Agreement Articles 2.2 and 5.1? The key question[58] is whether the scope of the CNFR, that is the criteria for defining whether products should be subject to authorisation, adheres to science-based requirements. The absence of a foodstuff on the European market before 15 May 1997 triggers the need for a risk assessment, a measure that is clearly not 'based on' risk assessment within the meaning of Article 5.1. However, while the criteria determining the requirement of novel food approval are perhaps more blatantly non-scientific, the Regulation is not, in essence, different to other EU (and international) pre-market approval systems. For example, scientific evidence does not demonstrate that all substances intended for use as additives are inherently dangerous and thus require pre-market approval. Rather, many WTO Members, including the EU, consider that the nature and purpose of additives justifies a case-by-case pre-approval assessment. We know from the SPS negotiating history that WTO Members were determined that such systems should not be rendered illegal under the new Agreement.[59] The CNFR is therefore simply illustrative of an inherent tension between pre-market approval as a regulatory measure and substantive SPS provisions.

In order not to become ensnared by the apparent incompatibility of a regulatory measure that is both overtly permitted and seemingly prohibited, two possible arguments could be pursued.[60] The first, and one raised by Peru, is that as the basic premise for a pre-market approval is the insufficient nature of the scientific knowledge available, the measure should be considered a provisional one under Article 5.7.[61] In this case, the onus is upon the EU to obtain additional information in order to justify the prohibition.[62] Given the blanket nature of the exclusion of non-authorised novel foods, Peru's contention would rather implausibly place an obligation upon the EU to obtain information (in a 'reasonable period of time',

[58] It cannot be excluded that third countries would contest the EU's use of risk assessment in rejecting a particular authorisation. However, given the limited number of traditional products considered, it is clear that the thrust of third-country discontent is the need for authorisation in the first place.

[59] See Foster (n 57) 1213. See also T Epps, 'Pre-market Approval Systems and the SPS Agreement' in G Van Calster and D Prévost (eds), *Research Handbook on Environment, Health and the WTO* (Cheltenham, Edward Elgar, 2013) (discussing the applicability of both substantive and procedural SPS disciplines to pre-market approval systems).

[60] Foster alternatively suggests that approval procedures should only be considered a measure where they have inhibited international trade. ibid 1215. This appears to be an unduly narrow interpretation of the scope of the SPS Agreement Art 1, which includes 'measures which *may*, directly or indirectly, affect international trade' (emphasis added).

[61] WTO, Sanitary and Phytosanitary Measures, European Communities Regulation 258/97 Concerning Novel Foods, Statement by Peru at the Meeting of the Committee Held on 8 and 9 October 2008, G/SPS/GEN/884 (21 October 2008) para 5.

[62] SPS Agreement Art 5.7 provides that 'Members, where implementing provisional measures, shall seek to obtain the additional information necessary for a more objective assessment of risk and review… within a reasonable period of time'.

to boot) of *all* foods falling within the scope of the CNFR, that is, those not currently consumed in the EU. Had negotiators really intended pre-market approval to be a provisional measure which required WTO Members proactively to seek information, there was adequate opportunity—under Annex C, paragraph 1(i) which specifically treats such procedures—explicitly to include this requirement. On the contrary, with regard to approval systems, Annex C demands only that 'the importing Member shall consider the use of a relevant international standard as the basis for access until a final determination is made'. The characterisation of pre-market approval as a provisional measure is therefore difficult to sustain.

A second explanation of the CNFR's compatibility with the Agreement's scientific requirements draws on the explicit recognition of systems that deny market access in 'the absence of approval'.[63] As the Appellate Body (AB) determined in *Japan—Varietals*, sufficient scientific evidence under Article 2.2 requires a 'rational or objective relationship between the SPS measure and the scientific evidence'.[64] By expressly permitting pre-market approval as an acceptable measure for achieving a Member's chosen level of protection, the Agreement could be argued to have established a general presumption of rationality of a measure aimed at the *procurement of* scientific evidence which will facilitate the fulfilment of Article 5.1 obligations. This does not imply that all pre-market approval systems would necessarily be in conformity with SPS rules, but rather that the threshold to be met for justifying this form of measure in a specific case would be relatively low.[65] In this context, it may not be difficult for the EU, through known cases of risks associated with food not consumed in EU, to justify the overall application of pre-market approvals for novel foods.

Notwithstanding the evident strain between pre-market approvals and Articles 2.2 and 5.1,[66] a concerted challenge of the legality of this form of regulatory measure seems unlikely. Given the use of comparable measures in other areas of food law by most WTO Members worldwide, such a challenge would have far-reaching and untenable consequences.[67]

---

[63] SPS Agreement Annex C, 1(i).

[64] *Japan—Measures Affecting Agricultural Products*, Appellate Body Report (adopted 22 February, 1999) WT/DS76/AB/R, para 84.

[65] The difficulty for a complainant in this context is that it would have to demonstrate that the CNFR is irrational in its demand for evidence. However, this would require establishing the eminent safety of a product, and presumably precisely the type of detailed risk assessment the complainant views to be unnecessary.

[66] The second explanation remains difficult to reconcile with the presumption emerging from jurisprudence that a measure is not consistent with Art 2.2 where not based on risk assessment. For a detailed analysis of the relationship between Art 2.2 and Art 5.1, see J Scott, *The WTO Agreement on Sanitary and Phytosanitary Measures: A Commentary* (Oxford, OUP, 2007) 82–84.

[67] Foster suggests that a challenge on prior approvals 'would potentially expose the SPS Agreement and the WTO itself to ridicule'. Foster (n 57) 1213. This may particularly be the case for novel foods, given the existence of comparable novel-food pre-market approval systems in place in Canada, Australia and New Zealand. For a summary of these measures, see Mück (n 44) 9–10. However, some commentators do anticipate a WTO challenge of the EU's prior authorisation scheme. See A Szajkowska, *Regulating Food Law Risk Analysis and the Precautionary Principle As General Principles of EU Food Law* (Wageningen, Wageningen Academic Publishers, 2012) 79.

Article 5.5 Arbitrary Distinctions Between Levels of Protection Article 5.5 strives to 'avoid arbitrary or unjustifiable distinctions' in the level of protection applied by a Member in different situations. Given that the CNFR's stringent approval requirements for novel products do not apply to very similar non-novel products, Article 5.5 would appear to be a potential area of incompatibility[68] Consider, for example, two food products originating in the Andes. Lucuma is a bronze-yellow fruit with the flavour of maple syrup which has traditionally been central to the diet of poorer communities and is a flavour in milkshakes and ice cream.[69] Yacon is another Andean crop whose roots are described as having the taste of apple or watermelon: 'in some areas, almost everyone has a few plants in the family garden plot.'[70] The former is considered by the EU not to require novel food authorisation,[71] while the latter is judged a novel food[72] and will be detained if discovered entering the EU market.[73] However justifiable in terms of the CNFR's specific criteria, such distinct treatment of basic crops will inevitably raise suspicions of discrimination.[74]

Whatever the perceptions of arbitrary treatment of similar products, the validity of a challenge under Article 5.5 is questionable, given the three elements that must be fulfilled to determine a violation.[75] Firstly, the Member must establish different levels of protection in different situations. Those differences must, secondly, be 'arbitrary or unjustifiable', and ultimately, the measure must be applied in a way that 'result[s] in discrimination or a disguised restriction in international trade'. In broad terms, the different level of protection adopted for non-novel and novel foods is undeniable. Novelty confers a need for the highest level of scientific scrutiny, whereas non-novel foods, regardless of public knowledge of their safety, can circulate through the EU unchecked. But are novel and non-novel foods sufficiently similar

[68] Peru presents this argument with regard to the disparate treatment of Nangai and other varieties of nuts. G/SPS/GEN/884 (n 61) para 7.

[69] US National Research Council *Lost Crops of the Incas: Little-Known Plants of the Andes with Promise for Worldwide Cultivation* (Washington, D. C, National Academy Press, 1989) 263.

[70] ibid 115.

[71] See EU Novel Foods Catalogue (n 35) reference 'lucuma obovata'; No Rojas, 'La Lúcuma Dejó de ser Novelfood en Francia y ya Tiene Ingreso Libre a Europa', *Agro Negocios Perú* [*Agricultural Business Peru*] (27 April 2009) www.agronegociosperu.org/noticias/270409_n2.htm.

[72] See EU Novel Foods Catalogue (n 35) reference 'smallanthus sonchifolius'.

[73] See European Rapid Alert System for Food and Feed (RASFF), Alert 2009/20 reporting the finding of unauthorised yacon syrup from Peru, ec.europa.eu/food/food/rapidalert/reports/week20-2009_en.pdf.

[74] This is particularly so if one accepts the view of the Panel in *US-Poultry* that the justification for this different treatment needs to be a demonstration of differing risk using scientific evidience. *United States Certain Measures Affecting Imports of Poultry from China, Panel Report* (adopted 29 September 2010) WT/DS392/R, para 7.263.

[75] The cumulative nature of the three elements was established in *Hormones. European Communities—EC Measures Concerning Meat and Meat Products* (*Hormones*) Appellate Body Report, (adopted 16 January 1998) WT/DS26/AB/R and WT/DS48/AB/R, para 214.

to be comparable?[76] In many instances, it would seem not, given the genuinely novel nature of many of the foods that apply for approval. However, in cases such as the Andean example above, the first element could seemingly be met. Equally, the second criterion is fulfilled as the different requirements for products on the market before and after 15 May 1997 are undoubtedly arbitrary. Demonstrating discrimination or a disguised restriction would be more difficult. In *Hormones*, the AB clarified that while the arbitrary nature of a measure may be an effective 'warning signal' of discrimination, ultimately, 'the measure itself needs to be examined and appraised' in order to demonstrate a violation.[77] However arbitrary the different levels of protection in the case of the EU's treatment of various exotic products, few would claim that the obstacles created reflect a particular economic agenda. Indeed, the very arbitrariness of the scope of the CNFR in this instance serves not so much as a warning signal, but rather as evidence of the benevolent intentions of the Regulation in market terms. Even the most vehement critics of the negative consequences of the CNFR acknowledge the 'unintended' nature of the barrier that has been created.[78] Thus, while the CNFR may arbitrarily establish higher levels of protection, the EU would likely rebuff a claim of illegality under Article 5.5.

Article 5.6 The final substantive claim proposed by Peru was a breach of Article 5.6, which provides that Members must not develop measures that are 'more trade-restrictive than required'. A footnote to Article 5.6 sets out criteria that have been judged in *Australia—Salmon* to constitute a 'three-pronged test', namely whether there is another measure which (a) is 'reasonably available taking into account technical and economic feasibility'; (b) achieves the 'appropriate level of sanitary… protection'; (c) is 'significantly less restrictive to trade'.[79] Peru has provisionally suggested two alternative measures: the outright exclusion of traditional products from the scope of the CNFR, and 'certification, where applicable, of the history of safe consumption'.[80] Both these proposals comfortably meet two of the three prongs of the Article 5.6 test, being technically and economically feasible and significantly facilitating trade. But do they meet the EU's appropriate level of protection? Were traditional products to be excluded from the CNFR, they would be subject to general food law. While the EU is not explicit about the level of protection appropriate to novel foods, we can infer[81] that the appropriate level of protection (ALOP) sought by the CNFR is above and beyond this general level of protection. The EU's ALOP reflects a fundamental concern about the effect of food to which

---

[76] ibid para 217 (arguing that situations cannot be compared 'unless they present some common elements or elements sufficient to render them comparable').

[77] ibid para 215.

[78] Hermann (n 34) 506.

[79] *Australia—Measures Affecting Importation of Salmon (Australia—Salmon),* Appellate Body Report (adopted 20 October 1998) WT/DS18/AB/R, para 194.

[80] See G/SPS/GEN/681 (n 56) points 11(a) and (b) respectively.

[81] Such inference is deemed to be permissible in cases where a Member insufficiently clarifies the level of protection sought. See Australia—Salmon, Appellate Body Report, para 207.

European consumers have previously been unexposed,[82] a precaution, moreover, that is manifestly legitimate.[83] Simply excluding traditional foods from the CNFR would not therefore meet the EU's ALOP. In practice, Peru's alternative proposal—certification of the history of safe use—seems a reasonable approach to consider for allaying concerns about traditional foods. However, in the same way, it would be extremely difficult to demonstrate under Article 5.6 that certification can meet the same ALOP achieved by a mandatory safety assessment. Once again, a clear breach of the substantive SPS provisions would be difficult to sustain.

The Operation of the CNFR Procedure

Peru also pointed to the incompatibility of the CNFR with Annex C (covering Control, Inspection and Approval Procedures), but did not specify in which ways the CNFR contravenes the Annex. Two aspects appear particularly relevant: timing and information requirements.

Timing One of the predominant criticisms of the CNFR has been the time taken to complete applications. The average novel-food approval takes 35 months to complete,[84] and a similar time-frame has applied for the few traditional products that have sought authorisation.[85] While this may intuitively appear to be an unjustifiably long procedure for a traditional product,[86] this claim could only be assessed on a case-by-case basis. A more generic claim of the incompatibility of CNFR procedures with Annex C relates to the inefficient nature of the risk-assessment process. In the vast majority of cases,[87] an application is subject to considerable

---

[82] See European Commission, Commission Recommendation 97/618/EC concerning the scientific aspects and the presentation of information necessary to support applications for the placing on the market of novel foods and novel food ingredients and the preparation of initial assessment reports under Regulation (EC) No 258/97 of the European Parliament and of the Council [1997] OJ L253/1 (Commission NF Application Recommendations) 4 (stating that '[w]henever changes are made to the way in which a food is put on the market… the implications for consumer safety and nutritional value will require consideration').

[83] Before the SPS Committee, the EU has reiterated its view that traditional foods cannot be deemed to be safe *per se*, as 'products marketed as "products of biodiversity" had in the past turned out to be unsafe and harmed the users'. G/SPS/R/40 (26 May 2006) para 29. The risk emanates either from the plant constituents which can be toxic or the lack of knowledge among the population of the importing country as how they must be used. See I Knudsen et al., 'Risk Management and Risk Assessment of Novel Plant Foods: Concepts and Principles' (2008) 46 *Food and Chemical Toxicology* 1681, 1682.

[84] See G Brookes, 'Economic Impact Assessment of the way in which the EU Novel Foods Regulatory Approval Procedures Affect the EU Food Sector' (July 2007) 4, www.pgeconomics.co.uk/pdf/novelfoods.pdf.

[85] Hermann reports that the average time for the adoption of traditional foods is 39 months. Hermann (n 34) 505.

[86] This argument is among those raised by third countries. See, e.g. G/SPS/GEN/713 (n 39) para 5.

[87] In its 2008 overview, the Commission reported only one case in which a novel food authorisation had been finalised and approved at the Member-State level. Commission NNFR Impact Assessment (n 32) Annex 1.

scrutiny by various Member States' scientific bodies and subsequent European review. For example, in the course of an NF application for noni juice, the UK disputed Belgian demands for further toxicological tests and the Dutch pointed to insufficient information about consumption.[88] However scientifically valid such concerns, the multiple assessments permitted by the CNFR strain the provisions of Annex C that seek procedural efficiency. In particular, the obligation that the 'competent body transmits as soon as possible the results of the procedure in a precise and complete manner'[89] is almost inconceivable where approval draws, in succession, on disparate sources of scientific expertise.

Information A further common criticism of the CNFR is that informational demands form an outright barrier to traditional foods.[90] Informational requirements clearly do not prove to be a barrier *per se* for traditional products.[91] But Annex C provides that 'information requirements must be limited to what is *necessary* for ... approval procedures'.[92] In the case of the novel foods, these demands are set out in Commission Recommendation 97/618/EC.[93] Given the wide range of foods falling under the CNFR, the Recommendations assign novel foods into six classes, each of which require different supporting information. The relevance of data demands for traditional foods is dubious, as they fall within the broader category of 'complex NF from non-GM sources'. For instance, experience in assessing traditional products suggests they may not require toxicological assessment as prescribed by the Recommendations.[94]

Can the EU defend itself against accusations of excessive informational requirements? It may argue that guidance presented in Recommendation 97/618/EC is simply that, and should not be construed to constitute 'requirements' within the meaning of Annex C(c). Moreover, the fact that exotic products have been authorised on the basis of reduced evidence underlines the non-mandatory nature of the guidance recommendations. These arguments have their limitations. Unlike Annex C(a),

---

[88] See, e.g. UK FSA, 'Letter to the European Commission Concerning Tahitian Noni Juice (Morinda citrifolia)' (NFU 146, 10 December 2001) 1, www.food.gov.uk/multimedia/pdfs/uknoniopin.pdf; Health Council of the Netherlands, 'Noni Juice: Second Opinion Regarding Consumer Safety, in Accordance with European Regulation 258/97 Concerning Novel Foods and Novel Food Ingredients' (No. 2001/03VNV, 13 December 2001) www.cbg-meb.nl/NR/rdonlyres/96B16752-9CA3-43F8-AF79-5592E200C693/0/nonisap.pdf.

[89] SPS Agreement Annex C, para 1(b).

[90] Craddock (n 36) 7–8; Cumming Smith (n 36); WTO, Committee on Sanitary and Phytosanitary Measures, G/SPS/GEN/713 (n 39) para 5.

[91] For example, traditional products such as noni juice, baobab pulp and chia seed have met with success.

[92] SPS Agreement Annex C(c) (emphasis added).

[93] Commission NF Application Recommendations (n 82).

[94] See, e.g. the UK FSA's assessment of baobab pulp. The determinant opinion found that 'the absence of extensive toxicological analyses did not give cause for concern because baobab fruit was a staple part of the diet throughout Africa and a retrospective toxicological assessment would have limited value'. UK FSA, 'Initial Opinion: Baobab Dried Fruit Pulp' (12 July 2007) 9, www.food.gov.uk/multimedia/pdfs/baobabinitialopinion.pdf.

which considers how procedures are 'undertaken and completed', point (c) refers to the design of the requirements rather than their implementation. Notwithstanding potential flexibility in interpretation by individual Member States, trading partners are inhibited by the very existence of data demands 'hang[ing] over them like the sword of Damocles'.[95]

In summary, aspects of the CNFR's operation may be found to fall short of the procedural disciplines envisaged by Annex C. Yet more fundamental complaints, raised by third countries challenging the overall subjection of traditional food to pre-market novel food approval, find little textual support.

5.3.3 The EU's Regulatory Response and the Influence of the SPS Agreement

A regulatory proposal for a revised EU Novel Food Regulation (NNFR) was presented in January 2008.[96] This included a solution for traditional foods in the form of a simplified notification procedure. Innovatively, the Commission sought to establish a legal basis for demonstrating food safety that moved away from the classic risk-assessment methodology previously applied to novel foods. Exporters of 'traditional food'[97] would henceforth not be asked to present toxicological data, but rather provide 'compositional data' and 'evidence of use'.[98] Having collected the requisite evidence, an operator would notify the product to the Commission, and EFSA or a Member State would then have 4 months to make a science-based reasoned safety objection to the food. If this were to occur, the operator would have to undergo a full novel foods authorisation procedure before placing the products on the market.[99]

The Commission's proposal devised a regulatory solution which, in theory at least, would facilitate access to the EU for traditional products and respond to the concerns of third countries. To what extent were legal considerations influential in this policy change? It is always complicated to surmise the specific weight of the various factors that buffer the policy-maker. Nevertheless, by virtue of the public consultations undertaken by the Commission in 2003, it is possible to ascertain the level of domestic support for a new approach to traditional foods and therefore deduce the influence of external factors. Let us consider the key constituents: domestic actors and Member States.

---

[95] G/SPS/GEN/884para 10.

[96] See (n 35).

[97] The Commission's definition of traditional food established four criteria. Firstly, the food cannot merely have been used at one point in time, but must 'continue… to be part of the diet'. Secondly, it must be 'part of the normal diet' and not say a plant that has been used say for medicinal or cosmetic purposes. Thirdly, experience of the use of the product must be extensive, equivalent to that of 'at least one generation'. Finally, use of the product cannot simply be local, but have been consumed by 'a large part of the population of the country'. NNFR (n 35) Art 3.2(b).

[98] NNFR (n 35) Art 8.

[99] ibid.

To judge from the consultations, traditional products were of marginal importance for the European food industry. As a summary report of the consultations concluded, those stakeholders supporting a different regulatory approach for traditional products were 'mainly of non-EU origin'.[100] While there was a general interest among European food operators in simpler market access for novel foods, it was emphasised that this should be 'not restricted to exotic traditional foods'.[101] There was also considerable resistance from other domestic constituents, most notably the consumer lobby, to any relaxing of authorisation requirements.[102] Far from being a self-evident policy choice, a simplified procedure was the issue 'most disputed between stakeholders'.[103] In facilitating only trade of third-country traditional products, the Commission clearly gambled with upsetting both domestic industry and consumer interests.

Even if unpopular among domestic groups, an EU legislative change can sometimes respond to the needs and preferences of national authorities. Can this explain the new approach to exotic foods? For Member States, assessing the appropriate treatment of traditional products had clearly been problematic.[104] However, by the time of the publication of the NNFR, a Novel Food Catalogue had been established which provided an adequate mechanism for resolving the administrative difficulties.[105] In responses to the 2003 consultation, Member States were obviously reluctant to accept less stringent rules for traditional products. Ireland noted that '[s] ome developing countries may not have the structures in place to adequately pass judgement on the safety of foods'.[106] The UK and Denmark concurred, noting respectively that 'in each case there would be a need to investigate the supporting evidence ourselves'[107] and 'that we cannot accept that less evidence requirements *(sic)* could apply to exotic traditional food'.[108] Given this evident national reluctance for a simplified procedure, the Commission's proposal risked facing a critically hostile

---

[100] European Commission, 'Evaluation Report on the Novel Food Regulation 258/97 Concerning Novel Foods and Novel Food Ingredients' (2004 22/1/2004, Annex 1) ec.europa.eu/food/food/biotechnology/novelfood/summary_report_annex1_en.pdf.

[101] See Servicio Nacional de Sanidad Agraria del Peru (SENASA)–'Peru, Novel Foods–Responses to the Online Consultation on the revision of Regulation EC 258/97' (Discussion Paper responses) ec.europa.eu/food/food/biotechnology/novelfood/resp_consult_258_97_en.htm. The original discussion paper is European Commission, Implementation of Regulation (EC) No 258/97 of the European Parliament and of the Council of 27 January 1997 Concerning Novel Foods and Novel Foods Ingredients (2002) ec.europa.eu/food/food/biotechnology/novelfood/discussion _en.pdf.

[102] BEUC European Consumers Organisation–EU, Discussion Paper responses (ibid) 3 (warning that 'we reject any notification procedure').

[103] ibid.

[104] In 2004, the Commission had noted the need to 'clarify their intentions as regards plants and products produced naturally in countries outside of the Community'. Commission CNFR Evaluation (n 30) 8.

[105] See (n 32).

[106] Ireland, Discussion Paper responses (n 101) 1.

[107] UK, Discussion Paper responses (n 101) 2.

[108] Denmark, Discussion Paper responses (n 101) 3.

reception in Council. Indeed, this proved to be the case in 2008. In part, there were objections to the ambiguity surrounding the concept of traditional foods, such as the uncertain time criterion of 'one generation'.[109] More fundamentally, some Member States questioned lowering the standard of demonstrated safety for what potentially could be a large quantity and diversity of plants.[110] Serious doubts were also voiced by EFSA, due to the perception that the evidentiary burden was being placed upon the safety body to demonstrate risk, rather than on the applicant to demonstrate safety.[111] As a result of such controversies, first-reading discussions in Council on the traditional food procedure were prolonged[112] and ultimately led to a substantial revision of the Commission's plans for a simplified notification. Rather than a notification, the Council imposed an accelerated authorisation procedure, thereby reinstating stricter levels of control (returning the burden for demonstrating safety back to the applicant), but allowing traditional products quicker market access.[113]

In the absence of obvious domestic stakeholder or governmental support for relaxing rules on traditional foods, a plausible explanation for the Commission's innovative approach is that it primarily intended to respond to the claims raised by WTO trading partners. Yet, the SPS regime's role in this case does not conform to the customary regulative understanding of international law. As the detailed analysis of Sect. 5.3.2 indicates, the legal arguments put forward by third countries against the current novel-food authorisation procedure are far from compelling. The EU had no real reason to anticipate possible dispute-settlement initiatives, and little to fear from them. The Commission could not therefore use the threat of a trade war to justify its new approach. Moreover, those aspects of the CNFR's functioning identified to be problematic with regard to Annex C did not require the introduction

[109] The Council shared concerns expressed by the EP in first reading and agreed to replace the criterion 'one generation' with 'at least 25 years'. Position (EU) No 6/2010 of the Council at first reading with a view to the adoption of a Regulation of the European Parliament and of the Council on novel foods, amending Regulation (EC) No 1331/2008 and repealing Regulation (EC) No 258/97 and Commission Regulation (EC) No 1852/2001, [2010] OJ C122/3, Art 3.2(d) (NNFR Common Position).

[110] To respond to these concerns, the Council toyed with the idea of limiting the scope of traditional foods to cover only fruits and vegetables. See Council of the European Union, 'Employment, Social Policy, Health and Consumer Affairs Council Meeting of 9 and 10 June 2008' (9689/08) II.B.1.

[111] See comments by EFSA official J Kleiner, EP workshop on novel foods in Brussels, European Parliament Report IP/A/EMVI/WS/2008–15 (2008) 25, www.europarl.europa.eu/RegData/etudes/divers/join/2008/408556/IPOL-ENVI_DV(2008)408556_EN.pdf.

[112] Art 8 of the NNFR providing for the procedural requirements for traditional foods was reported to have been rewritten around ten times. 'Nano, Cloning, Third Countries Threaten Novel Foods Deal' *EU Food Law* (13 February 2009).

[113] The advantage that this procedure offers to third countries is a reduced risk management period (3 months rather than 9 months) permitted to the Commission to submit a proposal to the Standing Committee. NNFR Common Position (n 109) Art 11.

of a specific approval process for traditional products, of the type proposed by the Commission.[114]

The Commission's behaviour can perhaps best be understood as an illustration of what Scott describes as 'institutionalised cooperation'.[115] Through the platform of the Committee on Sanitary and Phytosanitary Measures (SPS Committee) established by the Agreement, third countries had the opportunity, formally and under the public regard of other Members, to call the EU's policy into question. The immediate impact was that the Commission publicised, notably beyond any WTO transparency requirement,[116] a further public consultation on policy options that it was considering.[117] This in turn elicited further comment, scrutiny and criticism of the CNFR. During the proposal-drafting period and early stages of the legislative procedure between 2006 and 2009, the topic became one of those most frequently raised in the SPS Committee.[118] Notwithstanding the tenuous basis of the legal arguments, the number of countries voicing complaints[119] and the frequency of comments created a dynamic for regulatory change to which the European Commission felt compelled to respond.

In the absence of a tenable legal threat, and in the light of known domestic resistance, the Commission's decision to adopt a new course for traditional products suggests that third countries had significant leverage over EU policy. At the same time, there are clearly limits in an EU context to the institutionalised cooperation inspired by the SPS Agreement. Not engaged directly with third countries, the Council evidently did not feel the same compulsion to indulge trading partners and thus reinforced EU scrutiny of traditional products. In its revised and somewhat diluted form,[120] the procedure (expected to be included in future proposals) nevertheless represents a significant step forward for third-country exporters. In addition to the commitment to expedite applications for traditional foods, the NNFR instates reduced informational requirements for these products. It remains to be seen whether the barriers to the European market experienced by third countries will be effectively eliminated by the new procedure. At the very least, interaction in the context of the

[114] A solution addressing the identified inefficiencies of the risk-assessment process for novel foods was already foreseen in Art 7 of the NNFR (n 35). Likewise, the informational shortcomings identified above could have been overcome through the amendment of the Commission's Recommendations.

[115] Scott (n 66) 75.

[116] The obligation to notify under SPS Agreement, Annex B, para 5 is limited to proposed regulations.

[117] See n 48.

[118] These debates took place in March 2006 (G/SPS/R/40, paras 21–29); June 2006 (G/SPS/R/42, paras 35–37); October 2006 (G/SPS/R/43, paras 140–43); February 2007 (G/SPS/R/44, para 64); April 2008 (G/SPS/R/49, paras 48–52); October 2008 (G/SPS/R/53, paras 19–23); October 2009 (G/SPS/R/56, paras 53–55).

[119] Concerns were raised by Bolivia, Brazil, Chile, Colombia, Costa Rica, Cuba, El Salvador, Honduras, India, Mexico, Paraguay, Philippines, Uruguay and Venezuela.

[120] A compromise was agreed with the EP in conciliation which did not make substantial changes to the Council Common Position. See NNFR Common Position (n 109).

SPS regime will have served to secure these products a specific and preferential access to the EU market over other novel foods.

5.4 The Regulation of 'Cloned Food'

A further issue that emerged during the legislative passage of the NNFR, ultimately sealing its fate, was that of food from animal cloning (cloned food). This section briefly introduces the technology and the controversy surrounding its application. It then recounts the EU's failed attempt to manage 'cloned foods' in the context of the NNFR and subsequently considers whether the legal arguments raised in objection to EP proposals were insurmountable. The section concludes with observations on how the SPS and other WTO obligations have influenced the behaviour of EU institutions.

5.4.1 What is Cloning?

Somatic-cell nuclear transfer (commonly known as 'cloning') is a procedure aiming to produce copies of animals which have desirable traits, for a range of purposes including enhancing breeding, improving the characteristics of food, and developing superior breeds for sport.[121] As is the case for many new technologies, animal cloning has the capacity to divide public opinion. It can alternatively be presented as a simple evolution in existing reproductive technologies,[122] or as food production's final step into the moral abyss.[123] Critics' primary concerns relate to animal welfare: EFSA has reported that a significantly higher proportion of cloned animals die at birth or shortly afterwards than sexually produced animals.[124] In addition, Europe's scientific body pointed to the health problems for surrogate dams of carrying unusually large foetuses.[125] As a result of the suffering associated with animal cloning, the European Group on Ethics, reporting to the European Commission,

[121] J Suk et al., 'Dolly for Dinner? Assessing Commercial Land Regulatory Trends in Cloned Livestock' (2007) 25 *Nature Biotechnology* 47, 48.

[122] See L Rudenko et al., 'Animal Cloning and the FDA–The Risk Assessment Paradigms under Public Scrutiny' (2007) 25 *Nature Biotechnology* 39, 40 (explaining how the US FDA 'considers cloning to fall on the continuum of [assisted reproductive technologies] currently in use in agriculture').

[123] S Poulter, 'Cloning Opens Door to "Farmyard Freaks"' *Daily Mail* (11 January 2007) www.dailymail.co.uk/news/article-427963/Cloning-opens-door-farmyard-freaks.html.

[124] EFSA, 'Food Safety, Animal Health and Welfare and Environmental Impact of Animals derived from Cloning by Somatic Cell Nucleus Transfer (SCNT) and their Offspring and Products Obtained from those Animals' (2008) 767 *EFSA Journal* 1, 19–20 (EFSA Cloning Opinion).

[125] ibid 25.

expressed its 'doubts as to whether cloning ... is ethically justified'.[126] Although this Group pointed to potential benefits from cloning to assist in developing genetic resistance to certain diseases, it did 'not see convincing arguments to justify the production of food from clones and their offspring'.[127] With a production cost for a single animal of around US$20,000, economics alone rules out such animals entering the food chain.[128] For consumers, controversy therefore centres on the fate of the offspring of cloned animals, born and reared in an identical manner to other livestock, but nevertheless the indirect product of (and financial reward for) this contentious technology. In response, policy-makers face a familiar dilemma of whether to regulate the production process or allow the market to determine the uptake of this technology.[129]

5.4.2 The Current Legality of Cloned Food

It was always unlikely that treating cloned food simply as another form of novel food would be adequate. While cloning is clearly a novel technique, the resulting food is identical to conventional food, meaning it fits awkwardly within the novel-food paradigm.[130] In the perceived absence of commercialisation of food from cloned animals, the question of the current legality of such food remained a theoretical one. However, in August 2010, the discovery of the sale of meat in the UK from the offspring of a slaughtered cloned animal found national authorities clearly ill prepared to manage the consequences.[131] The UK Food Standards Agency (FSA) dismissed any question of consumer risk from the commercialised meat, but claimed it was on the market illegally, as it had not submitted for authorisation

---

[126] The European Group on Ethics in Science and New Technologies to the European Commission, 'Ethical aspects of animal cloning for food supply' Opinion No 23, Abstract,16 January 2008) (EGE Cloning Opinion) ec.europa.eu/bepa/european-group-ethics/docs/publications/opinion23_en.pdf.

[127] ibid. The discussion of long-term applications of cloning can be found at 15.

[128] GS Becker and T Cowan, 'Biotechnology in Animal Agriculture: Status and Current Issues' 2009) 32 *Congressional Research Service Reports* 1, 11, digitalcommons.unl.edu/crsdocs/32.

[129] For discussion of this dilemma, see generally DA Kysar, 'Preferences for Processes: The Process/Product Distinction and the Regulation of Consumer Choice' (2004) 118 *Harvard Law Review* 525.

[130] Grahame Bulfield, former director of the Roslin Institute responsible for producing the first cloned sheep (Dolly), described the treatment of cloned food as novel to be 'nonsense': 'There's nothing novel about it, and you might as well say every new type of cereal should be treated with the same caution.' Cited in J Meikle and R Smithers, 'Cloning-Derived Milk Claim Prompts Food Agency Enquiry' *The Guardian* (3 August 2010) www.guardian.co.uk/uk/2010/aug/02/fsa-investigating-gm-milk-claims.

[131] W Surman, 'FSA Admits Meat from Cloned Cow's Calf Entered UK Food Chain' *Farmers Guardian* (4 August 2010) www.farmersguardian.com/home/livestock/fsa-admits-cloned-meat-entered-food-chain/33530.article.

under the CNFR. The Commission publicly rejected the UK's interpretation.[132] Article 1.2(e) of Regulation 258/97 excludes from its scope foods 'obtained by traditional propagating or breeding practices'. Whereas a case could arguably be made for the novelty of meat from a cloned animal, the produce of the offspring of clones, bred through normal sexual reproduction, cannot constitute a novel food. The UK's interpretation had little textual basis, and was subsequently revised by the FSA in line with the Commission's reasoning.[133]

5.4.3 EU Response to Animal Cloning in the NNFR

From the outset, the review of the CNFR was not intended to serve as a platform for debating animal cloning. The issue did arise during pre-proposal consultation,[134] but the Commission neither addressed cloning in its impact assessment of the proposal,[135] nor referred to the technology as such in the initial legislative text. Developments across the Atlantic were catalytic in focusing public attention on cloning. Having previously requested breeders not to place cloned animals on the market,[136] the US Department of Agriculture published an assessment on the safety of food from cloned animals in January 2008, which effectively gave the green light to their commercialisation.[137] In spite of rumblings of discontent in the European Parliament,[138] the Council was slow to grasp the significance of the cloning issue as an obstacle to completing the NNFR.[139] The mood changed in the autumn, following overwhelming cross-party support for a EP resolution calling for an outright ban on animal cloning.[140] In the context of the NNFR, this translated into

---

[132] H Mahony, 'Milk From Cloned Cow Offspring Exposes Gap In EU Food Law' euobserver.com (3 August 2010) (citing European Commission spokesman's confirmation of the legal position) euobserver.com/9/30578.

[133] 'UK Changes Stance on Food from Cloned Offspring' *EU Food Policy* (10 December 2010).

[134] In response to the Commission Discussion Paper in 2002, cloning was already flagged up as an issue by consumer organisations. See, e.g. comments from the Danish Consumer Agency, Discussion Paper responses (n 101).

[135] See n 32.

[136] FDA News Release, 'Agency Continues to Ask Producers and Breeders Not to Introduce Food from Clones into Food Supply' (20 December 2006) www.fda.gov/NewsEvents/Newsroom/PressAnnouncements/2006/ucm108819.htm.

[137] See generally US Food And Drug Administration, Centre For Veterinary Medicine, Animal Cloning: A Risk Assessment (2008) www.fda.gov/downloads/AnimalVeterinary/SafetyHealth/AnimalCloning/UCM124756.pdf.

[138] 'Rapporteur Calls for Cloning to be Excluded from Novel Foods' *EU Food Law* (20 June 2008) (reporting on the first discussions of the non-leading EP Agriculture Committee).

[139] In July 2008, one participant reported on the non-controversial nature of the NNFR discussions in Council, noting that 'Member State officials have not been getting excited over cloning'. Cited in 'Slow Council Progress on Novel Foods' *EU Food Law* (25 July 2008).

[140] See generally European Parliament, Resolution of 3 September 2008 on the Cloning of Animals for Food Supply (P6_TA(2008)0400). 622 MEPs voted in favour with just 32 against, and 25 abstentions.

Parliamentary demands for the total exclusion of cloning from the scope of the Proposal and development of specific animal cloning legislation.[141] The (French) Council Presidency initially followed this lead,[142] but Member States feared that such a strategy would create a 'legal vacuum' in which 'cloned food' would not be subject to any regulatory scrutiny.[143] The Council therefore adopted a different approach. It agreed to future legislation on cloning, but in order to prevent 'legislative gaps', also to the inclusion of food both from animal clones *and* their offspring in the scope of the NNFR.[144] The Council's Common Position was reached with considerable difficulty, not least as the Commission, fearing trade reprisals, rejected the proposal, thereby requiring the Council to act unanimously.[145] In second reading, the EP maintained its call for an outright ban of cloned foods, thereby forcing the institutions into a 4-month conciliation period.[146]

As the irreconcilability of Council and Parliament positions became clear, a series of additional measures were developed in order to try and address concerns about cloning, and smooth the way towards a final agreement. Firstly, temporary bans were proposed,[147] with a view to preventing the use of cloning in Europe. Secondly, with the deadline approaching, the Council offered to introduce labelling requirements for fresh meat from offspring of cloned cattle, and promised a Commission report on the feasibility of extending this labelling to other food from cloned animals.[148] The EP compromised by withdrawing its proposal for an outright ban of food from offspring, but demanded immediate comprehensive labelling of all these foods. This proposal was unacceptable to the Council and stalemate was reached.

---

[141] European Parliament legislative resolution of 25 March 2009 on the proposal for a regulation of the European Parliament and of the Council on novel foods and amending Regulation (EC) No XXX/XXXX [2010] OJ C117 E/236.

[142] 'Presidency Amendments Put Cloning outside Novel Food Regulation' *EU Food Law* (17 October 2008).

[143] Council of the European Union, Preparation for the Informal Trialogue, 6414/09 DENLEG 12 CODEC 162 (February 18, 2009).

[144] Council of the European Union, Proposal for a Regulation of the European Parliament and of the Council on novel foods and amending Regulation (EC) No XXX/XXXX, Political Agreement, Addendum to the A Item Note, 10754/09 (17 June 2009) (Council PA) 2.

[145] In accordance with: The Treaty of Amsterdam amending the Treaty on European Union, the Treaties establishing the European Communities and certain related acts—Consolidated version of the Treaty establishing the European Community, Art 251, [2002] OJ C325/33. Ultimately, unanimity was contrived through the abstention of UK and Greece, having allowed these countries to make specific statements. ibid. Addendum, 3–4.

[146] European Parliament, Legislative Resolution of 7 July 2010 on the Council Position at First Reading for Adopting a Regulation of the European Parliament and of the Council on Novel Foods, amending Regulation (EC) No 1331/2008 and repealing Regulation (EC) No 258/97 and Commission Regulation (EC) No 1852/2001 (P7_TA(2010)0266), Art 2.c.

[147] These consisted of a ban on animal cloning in the EU for food production, all food from cloned animals and any supply of clones for food production. This position was confirmed in a Council of the European Union, Press Release 8308/11 (29 March 2011) 1, www.consilium.europa.eu/uedocs/cms_data/docs/pressdata/en/lsa/120351.pdf (Council NNFR PR).

[148] ibid.

In essence, there was little disagreement between institutions about the need for a specific and restrictive approach to animal cloning. Why then did the institutions fail to reach agreement in conciliation, for only the second time in their history?[149] The Hungarian Presidency laid the blame with the EP, who 'risked dragging [the EU] into a full-blown trade war'.[150] The Commission and Council shared this view and rebuked the Parliament for its wilful disregard of international trade agreements which, as the Council rather pointedly recalled, 'the EU, with the European Parliament's consent, has signed'.[151] In response, Members of the European Parliament (MEPs) accused the Council of fabricating the legal arguments and creating 'phoney excuses' for not accepting EP proposals.[152] The next section examines in more detail the weight of legal considerations in the positions taken by EU institutions.

5.4.4 The Constraint of WTO Law on Animal Cloning Measures

As the institutions sought explanations for the breakdown in NNFR negotiations, one particular recrimination came to the fore. From the EP's perspective, the Commission and Council were needlessly in thrall to the demands of international trade and the WTO. This section considers the merits of this criticism. Was the policy course favoured by the Parliament really vulnerable to WTO challenge? Did WTO obligations therefore dictate policy positions? To answer this question, this section first considers the potential compatibility of EP proposals for labelling all clone-derived food. It then considers to what extent Commission and Council positions were determined by international legal requirements.

Does the WTO Allow the EU to Label Cloned Foods?

As they were rejected outright by the other institutions, the EP's precise intentions with regard to labelling provisions never became entirely clear. The analysis below is therefore somewhat speculative, confined to identifying the general legal obstacles for the EU in defending cloned food labelling. Both the General Agreement on Tariffs and Trade (GATT)[153] and the TBT Agreement could be relevant to the assessment of cloned food labelling, with the latter normally forming the starting

[149] The only previous conciliation procedure failure involved a proposal for a working time directive. See n 3.

[150] See 'Cloned Foods Unleashed' (n 4).

[151] Council NNFR PR (n 147).

[152] 'MEPs Refute Claims of "Trade War" if EU Regulates Clone Offspring' (n 5).

[153] General Agreement on Tariffs and Trade, opened for signature 15 April 1994, 55 UNTS 194, 1867 UNTS 187 (1 January 1995).

point of analysis as *lex specialis*.[154] However, it is not entirely certain that measures aimed at restricting cloning technology would constitute technical regulations as covered by the TBT Agreement. TBT Annex 1, paragraph 1 defines a regulation in its first sentence, as a 'document which lays down product characteristics or their related processes…'. One view is that as Process and Production Methods (PPMs) have no impact on, and therefore are not 'related' to, the final product's characteristics, they fall outside the scope of the TBT Agreement.[155] For this reason, and to avoid repetition, the primary challenges to any EU labelling measure of relevance to an analysis under either the TBT or GATT are considered together.

Like Products

One possible line of EU defence for different labelling of cloned and conventional meat is that these products are not 'like'.[156] Dispute-settlement bodies have consistently considered four criteria to assess 'likeness' under GATT Article III.[157] For three of these criteria—physical properties, the use of the products and their tariff classification—clones are undisputedly 'like' products. For the remaining criterion, consumers' tastes and habits, the AB in *Asbestos* placed a particular emphasis on public perception of the products concerned, namely 'the extent to which consumers are… willing to choose one product instead of another to perform those end-uses'.[158] In the light of the publicly expressed rejection of cloned foods, an EU claim for non-likeness on this basis cannot be dismissed. However, in that the Panel is obliged to look at '*each* of those four criteria and, then, weigh … *all* of that

[154] For a discussion of the interrelationship of the GATT and the TBT Agreement, see G Marceau and JP Trachtman, 'The Technical Barriers to Trade Agreement, the Sanitary and Phytosanitary Measures Agreement, and the General Agreement on Tariffs and Trade–Map of the World Trade Organization Law of Domestic Regulation of Goods' (2002) 36 JWT 811, 873.

[155] See MM Du, 'Domestic Regulatory Autonomy under the TBT Agreement: From Non-Discrimination to Harmonisation' (2007) 6 *Chinese Journal of International Law* 269, 287–88. This decision finds support from the Appellate Body's (AB) focus on physical factors in its definition of 'characteristics of a product'. See *European Communities—Measures Affecting Asbestos and Asbestos-Containing Products* (*EC—Asbestos*); Appellate Body Report (adopted 12 March 2001) WT/DS135/AB/, para 67. However, the second sentence of the definition in TBT Annex 1, para 1 reads: 'It may also include… labelling requirements as they apply to a product, process or production method.' It is unclear whether PPMs labelling constitutes a subset of the regulations defined in the first sentence (and excluding non-product PPMs) or an independent discipline applicable to non-product PPMs.

[156] For a discussion of the interpretation of 'like product', see S Charnovitz, 'The Law of Environmental "PPMs" in the WTO: Debunking the Myth of Illegality' 27 YJIL 59, 76–77 (2002), and see generally R Howse and DH Regan, 'The Product/Process Distinction—An Illusionary Basis for Disciplining "Unilateralism" in Trade Policy' (2000) 11.

[157] See, e.g. *United States—Standards for Reformulated and Conventional Gasoline*, Appellate Body Report (adopted 29 April 1996) WT/DS2/AB/R, para 6.8.

[158] *EC—Asbestos*, Appellate Body Report, para 117.

evidence'[159] and that the competitive relationship of products on the market place is of preeminent importance,[160] it is doubtful whether this single characteristic of non-likeness would be determinant. Moreover, a Panel is likely to be highly mindful of the broader implications for the trading system of opening up the definition of likeness in this way to considerations of PPMs.[161] A strategy based on the non-likeness of cloned and conventional meat would seem unlikely to fare better under the TBT Agreement. The AB recently dismissed, in *US—Clove Cigarettes,* an approach by the Panel which may have been favourable to the EU in this context, namely the additional consideration of a technical regulation's legitimate objective in a TBT like-product analysis.[162]

'Less Favourable Treatment'

A further consideration in the analysis of EU cloned food labelling for determining a breach of GATT or TBT national treatment rules is that imports are subjected to 'less favourable treatment' than domestic products.[163] Under the GATT, this inquiry would be limited to establishing the existence of a detrimental effect on competitive opportunities for imports.[164] Given the existing use of cloning in third countries, but not in Europe, the asymmetric commercial impact of labelling cloned food is highly probable.[165] By contrast, in the context of the TBT Agreement the complainant would have to additionally demonstrate that any detrimental impact on imports does not 'stem exclusively from legitimate regulatory distinctions'.[166] Theoretically, this could provide the EU with a stronger basis for defending labelling of cloned foods. However, the manifold implications of labelling measures would not be restricted to suppliers of cloned meat.[167] The additional complexities that labelling would also

[159] ibid para 109 (emphasis in original).

[160] ibid para 145.

[161] For discussion of the dangers associated with eliminating the product/process distinction, see generally JH Jackson, 'Comments on Shrimp/Turtle and the Product/Process Distinction' (2000) 11 EJIL 303.

[162] United States—Measures Affecting the Production and Sale of Clove Cigarettes (US—Clove Cigarettes), Appellate Body Report (adopted 4 April 2012) WT/DS406/AB/R, paras 108–12.

[163] See respectively GATT Art III.4 and TBT Art 2.1.

[164] *Korea—Measures Affecting Imports of Fresh, Chilled and Frozen Beef* (*Korea—Beef*), Appellate Body Report (adopted 11 December 2000) WT/DS161/AB/R, WT/DS169/AB/R, paras 135–37.

[165] An asymmetric test (evaluating the impact on domestic cloned *and* non-cloned meat versus imported cloned *and* non-cloned meat) is more stringent than the possible diagonal test (evaluating the treatment of a conventional food versus a clone-derived equivalent). For an explanation of these methods for testing impact, see L Ehring, '*De Facto* Discrimination in World Trade Law' (2002) 36 JWT 921, 924–25.

[166] *US—Clove Cigarettes*, Appellate Body Report, para 174.

[167] See discussion on trade restrictiveness in ns 189–193 below and related text.

create for foreign suppliers of conventional meat would possibly complicate such a defence.[168]

Information on Cloning: a Legitimate Objective or Basis for a General Exception?

Assuming, on the above analysis, that the EU would be hard pressed to deny a breach of GATT national treatment rules, it would have to make recourse to the permitted public-policy exceptions provided for under GATT Article XX. Article XX(a) on public morals offers the most probable legal basis[169] for defending the EU's animal-welfare goals.[170] In the absence of significant jurisprudence on the scope of Article XX(a), its precise meaning and applicability to cloning are not clear.[171] In *US—Gambling*, the Panel argued that '[m]embers should be given some scope to define and apply for themselves the concept of "public morals"',[172] but heavily relied on international expressions of the morality.[173] There is as yet no international reflection on animal cloning which could guide a panel's moral stance, but to dismiss the relevance of cloning on this basis would imply that any newly emerging issue, however offensive to public morality, could not benefit from this exception. Rather, a panel seems likely to cite domestic evidence of the salience of the issue.[174] Given EFSA's clear expression of concern about animal welfare and the

[168] For example, in *US—COOL,* the Appellate Body took exception to the amounts of information required by upstream producers for meat which did not require origin labelling. *United States—Certain Country of Origin Labelling (COOL) Requirements* (*US—COOL*), Appellate Body Report (adopted 29 June 2012) WT/DS384/AB/R, WT/DS386/AB/R,paras 346–49.

[169] Art XX(b) permits WTO-inconsistent policies where necessary to protect human, animal or plant life or health. However, commentators generally consider this provision not to be applicable to a purely welfare-oriented measure where human health is not directly implicated. See P Stevenson, 'The World Trade Organisation Rules: A Legal Analysis of Their Adverse Impact on Animal Welfare' (2007) 8 *Animal Law* 107, 136; EM Thomas, 'Playing Chicken at the WTO: Defending an Animal Welfare-Based Trade Restriction under GATT's Moral Exception' (2007) 34 *Boston College Environmental Affairs Law Review* 605, 618; R Galantucci, 'Compassionate Consumerism within the GATT Regime: Can Belgium's Ban on Seal Product Imports be Justified under Article XX?' (2009) 39 *California Western International Law Journal* 281, 304.

[170] NF Diebold, 'The Morals and Order Exceptions in WTO Law: Balancing the Toothless Tiger and the Undermining Mole' (2008) 11 JIEL 43, 69. However, other commentators consider it unlikely that animal welfare concerns could be included in this way. See A Hobbs, 'Ethics, Domestic Food Policy and Trade Law: Assessing the EU Animal Welfare Proposals to the WTO' (2002) 27 *Food Policy* 437, 450.

[171] MA Gonzalez, 'Trade and Morality: Preserving "Public Morals" without Sacrificing the Global Economy' (2006) 39 *Vanderbilt Journal of Transnational Law* 939, 943–45.

[172] *United States Measures Affecting the Cross-Border Supply of Gambling and Betting Services (US—Gambling)*, Panel Report (adopted 10 November 2004) WT/DS285/R, para 6.461.

[173] ibid para 6.472.

[174] For discussion of the uncertain evidentiary requirements in this respect, see M Wu, 'Free Trade and the Protection of Public Morals: An Analysis of the Newly Emerging Public Morals Clause Doctrine' (2008) 33 YJIL 215, 233–35. The Council's Legal Service has expressed doubts about the applicability of Art XX(a) in the light of the ambivalent response (41 % agreement) of EU

EU's long-standing prohibition of practices causing animal suffering,[175] a reasonable case could be made justifying the policy objective.[176]

A second public-morals consideration is whether, regardless of its welfare impact on animals, cloning is simply 'wrong' or 'unethical'. It is unclear how far this is a moral consideration further to, and independent of, animal-welfare concerns. Although charged with exploring these issues, the European Group on Ethics dealt with them only superficially.[177] The challenge in pursuing an Article XX(a) defence on these grounds would be to demonstrate a categorical difference between cloning and other breeding or farming practices currently tolerated by European consumers.[178] Nonetheless, 61 % of EU citizens are reported to consider animal cloning to be 'morally wrong',[179] and a larger degree of ethical concern has been reported in the US.[180] In such circumstances, it would take some courage on the part of a Panel to dismiss outright a public-morals defence of regulating animal cloning.

Imagining, in spite of the problems identified above, that the EU established the compliance of labelling with TBT Article 2.1, the measure would also likely be challenged under Article 2.2 on the grounds that it is more trade restrictive than necessary. Establishing the 'legitimate objective' fulfilled by labelling is generally less complex than justifying recourse to an Article XX exception. The adequacy of 'the provision of information to consumers' as a legitimate objective was largely resolved in *US—COOL*.[181] Nevertheless, the current ambiguity around the rationale for labelling identified above could prove problematic under the scrutiny of Article 2.2.

---

citizens, when questioned 'whether animal cloning would cause animals unnecessary pain'. Council of the European Union, Opinion of the Legal Service, 7771/11 (15 March 2011) (Council Legal Opinion), para 11 and fn 6. However, the relevance of this finding is questionable as it provides an indication of knowledge rather than moral judgement.

[175] Council Directive 98/58/EC of 20 July 1998 concerning the protection of animals kept for farming purposes [1998] OJ L221/23, Annex, para 20.

[176] Certainly, WTO Members have called upon public morals to justify variety of issues, seemingly more tenuous than the cloning issue, ranging from lottery tickets to automobile radar detectors. See JC Marwell, 'Trade and Morality: WTO Public Morals Exception after Gambling' (2006) 81 *New York University Law Review* 802, 818; See also generally S Charnovitz, 'The Moral Exception in Trade Policy' (1997) 38 VJIL 689.

[177] The discussion is limited to the exposition of a philosophical strand that analogises human and non-human animals as moral entities. EGE Cloning Opinion (n 126) 33–34.

[178] See G Matheny and C Leahy, 'Farmer-Animal Welfare, Legislation, and Trade', 70 *Law and Contemporary Problems* (2007) 325, 325–27 (illustrating the range of farming techniques systematically employed in US agriculture which compromise animal welfare).

[179] Council Legal Opinion (n 174) 5, n 7.

[180] 71 % of US respondents in a FOX News/Opinion Dynamics Poll answered that cloning to reproduce livestock was unacceptable and 65 % of respondents to a Gallup Poll found the practice immoral. See JF Murphy, 'Mandatory Labelling of Food Made from Cloned Animals: Grappling with Moral Objections to the Production of Safe Products' (2008) 63 *Food and Drug Law Journal* 131, 138.

[181] *US—COOL*, Appellate Body Report, para 445.

Could the EU Defend the Necessity of Labelling?

Under GATT Article XX or TBT Article 2.2, the necessity of labelling cloned foods would be subject to a comparable Panel process of 'weighing and balancing'[182] or a 'relational analysis'[183] of four factors: the importance of the interest protected, the impact on trade, the contribution made by the measure to the issue being regulated and the availability of alternative more GATT-consistent measures.[184]

Importance of Objective/Gravity of Consequences Arising from Non-Fulfilment In *Korea—Beef*, the AB ruled that accepting a measure as necessary under Article XX would be easier the 'more vital or important those common interests or values are'.[185] While logical, one wonders to what extent a Panel can meaningfully discern the importance of the objective beyond the essentiality it already needed to determine in order to merit recourse to Article XX.[186] The task of judging relative essentiality would be further complicated, if, as the Panel proposed in *US—Gambling*, WTO Members apply the concept of public morals 'according to their own systems and scales of values'.[187] For some, animal-welfare concerns may be judged of lesser importance than, say, the public-health concerns considered in *EC—Asbestos* to be 'both vital and important in the highest degree'.[188] But in applying such an anthropocentric perspective, a panel would be at risk of encroaching upon the Member's 'scales of values'. Taking into account these difficulties, other factors may be more decisive in determining any panel's judgement of necessity either under Article XX or TBT Article 2.2.

Impact on Trade/Trade Restrictiveness of Measure In *Korea—Beef*, the AB also proposed that a 'measure with a relatively slight impact upon imported products might more easily be considered as "necessary" than a measure with intense or broader restrictive effects'.[189] This element of any necessity analysis is the most

[182] *Korea—Beef*, Appellate Body Report, para 164. This is assuming that paragraph (a) would be interpreted in the same manner as other clauses under Art XX, as suggested by the AB's similar approach to Art XX(b) in *Asbestos*. See *EC—Asbestos*, Appellate Body Report, para 172.

[183] *United States—Measures Concerning the Importation, Marketing and Sale of Tuna and Tuna Products*, Appellate Body Report (adopted 16 May 2012) WT/DS381/AB/R, para 318.

[184] *Korea—Beef*, Appellate Body Report, para 164. The equivalent factors under TBT Art 2.2 are (in the same order) 'the nature of the risks at issue and the gravity of consequences that would arise from non-fulfilment', 'the trade restrictiveness of the measure', 'the degree of contribution made by the measure to the legitimate objective at issue' and 'in most cases, a comparison of the challenged measure and possible alternative measures'. ibid para 322.

[185] *Korea—Beef*, Appellate Body Report, para 162.

[186] See B McGrady, 'Necessity Exceptions in WTO Law: Retreaded Tyres, Regulatory Purpose and Cumulative Regulatory Measures' (2009) 12 JIEL 153, 161–63.

[187] *US—Gambling*, Panel Report, para 6.461.

[188] *EC—Asbestos*, Appellate Body Report, para 172.

[189] *Korea—Beef*, Appellate Body Report, para 163.

problematic one for the EU.[190] Mandatory labelling would require third-country suppliers of food to demonstrate a negative, namely the non-use of cloning, even in countries (including developing ones) where the use of cloning is not foreseen. This would constitute a wholesale, worldwide reform in the management and demonstration of traceability.[191] In addition, unlike in parallel cases such as GM labelling, no analytical techniques are available to determine the cloned or non-cloned origins of foods. This greater dependence on traceability and certification would in turn necessitate new and additional systems of controls. Even in the EU, more accustomed to animal identification in the light of the BSE crisis, the establishment of the necessary registration, audit and testing capabilities are expected to 'create a heavy and costly burden on both industry and officers in Member States tasked with enforcement and prosecution'.[192] With respect to suppliers beyond the EU, regardless even of cost, it is doubtful whether the requisite traceability can effectively be put in place.[193]

Contribution of Measure to Policy and Alternative Policies The extent to which a measure contributes to a Member's policy goal has been judged according to whether 'the means are, in principle, reasonably related to the ends'[194] and whether it makes 'a material contribution to the achievement of this objective'.[195] The current ambiguity, noted above, surrounding the public-morals rationale

---

[190] This assumes that EU bans are not considered indispensable in which case, according to the interpretation of the AB in *Korea—Beef*, they would not be subjected to a necessity analysis. See DH Regan, 'The Meaning of "Necessary" in GATT Article XX and GATS Article XIV: The Myth of Cost-Benefit Balancing' (2007) 6 *World Trade Review* 347, 354.

[191] As the Commission has noted, only 2 % of the calves born in the EU each year results from insemination of imported bovine semen, of which most probably only a tiny proportion would be semen from cloned bulls. Likewise, imports of embryos were limited to 747 consignments. Report from the Commission to the European Parliament and the Council on animal cloning for food productionCOM (2010) 585 final (19 October 2010) (Commission Cloning Report) 9.

[192] J Gunning et al., *Challenges in Regulating Farm Animal Cloning* (Danish Centre for Bioethics and Risk Assessment, 2006) 27, www.curis.ku.dk/ws/files/50665433/CHALLENGES_IN_REGULATING.pdf. See also EGE Cloning Opinion (n 126) 43. However, note that some MEPs were not convinced about the technical constraints associated with labelling. See EP Group Alliance of liberals and Democrats Press Release, 'Cloning: Council Distorts the Debate, ALDE' (12 May 2011) www.alde.eu/press/press-and-release-news/press-release/article/cloning-council-distorts-the-debate-37396/.

[193] See generally European Livestock and Meat Trades Union [UECBV], 'Cloning for food production—UECBV Position', UECBV Ref. 248 (31 January 2011) www.uecbv.eu/doc/UECBV-%20Position%20on%20Cloning%200.13.pdf. The US currently maintains a voluntary tracking system for animal clones, but provides for no traceability at all for the offspring of clones. Commission Cloning Report (n 191) 7.

[194] *United States—Import Prohibition of Certain Shrimp and Shrimp Products*, Appellate Body Report (adopted 12 October 1998) WT/DS58/AB/R, para 141.

[195] *Brazil—Measures Affecting Imports of Retreaded Tyres*, Appellate Body Report (adopted 3 December 2007) WT/DS332/AB/R, para 151. For the purposes of argument (and because the EU would strategically be unwise to claim otherwise), the assumption in this case is that the animal cloning measures are not deliberately aimed at extraterritorial impact, but rather measures foreseen for the EU territory with extraterritorial effects.

under the GATT or TBT Agreement is highly relevant to this stage of the analysis. In broad terms, the EU's 'end' may be that the consumer does not 'benefit from or be associated with what they regard as wickedness even if they are unable to prevent it'.[196] This idea is captured in the concept popularly invoked in the EP of the consumers' 'right to know'.[197] Yet while presented in absolutist terms, the right to know has intrinsic limits.[198] For instance, does the right to know extend to information that gelatine contained in sweets emanates from the bones of cloned offspring?[199] Does it require, as Hungarian Minister Sándor Fazekas sardonically suggested, a family tree accompanying each slice of salami?[200] Where the moral arguments remain as vaguely articulated as is currently the case for the ethics of labelling, it would be difficult for the EU to make a convincing argument for the necessity of such measures.[201] Moreover, even if the EU's ethical objectives can be clarified; there is no guarantee that the Panel would accept its characterisation of these goals.[202]

In the absence of precision on the aims of labelling food clones, it is difficult to speculate on alternative policies that would meet these aims. If the right to know is considered absolute, nothing but comprehensive labelling would appear to meet the EU's ethical objectives. If, however, labelling aims to permit a choice of food to those consumers particularly concerned with the technology, voluntary labelling, common to other animal-welfare issues, would arguably be feasible.[203]

The Precarious WTO Defence of Labelling Food Clones It is possible that faced with such a sensitive issue, a Panel may shy away from 'weighing' against the

[196] This is one characterisation of the motivation for regulating PPMs provided by Howse and Regan (n 156) 275.

[197] For example, lead EP negotiators, Gianni Pittella and Kartika Liotard stated they were 'not willing to betray consumers on their right to know whether food comes from animals bred using clones'. Cited in 'Bid to Ban Cloned Foods In Europe Collapses' *EU Food Policy* (29 March 2011).

[198] See I Cheyne, 'Proportionality, Proximity and Environmental Labelling in WTO Law' (2009) 12 JIEL 927, 939 (arguing that the freedom of consumers is constrained and must be proportionately applied in order not to infringe on the rights of others). In fact, this limit was acknowledged by the EP rapporteur, Liotard, who reassured: 'We are probably not going to go down to the 100th generation'. Cited in 'Deadlock over Cloning Set Scene for Novel Foods "High Noon"' *EU Food Policy* (18 March 2011).

[199] 'Sweets Would Have Been Labelled "Cloned" under Parliament's Proposals' *EU Food Policy* (1 April 2011) (citing comments by Commission officials).

[200] '"No Control" over Cloning, Warns Dalli' *EU Food Policy* (1 April 2011).

[201] The balancing or relational analysis creates a dilemma in this respect. The more comprehensive the labelling of those foods indirectly related to the cloning process, the more convincing the argument that it serves to attain ethical objectives. Yet, at the same time, the more rigorous this measure becomes, the more costly and burdensome the effects on international trade.

[202] See McGrady (n 186) 159–60 (suggesting that the identification of regulatory goals has been treated rather cavalierly in past disputes).

[203] However, on the limitations of voluntary labelling, see S Keane, 'Can the Consumers' Right to Know Survive the WTO: The Case of Food Labelling' (2006) 16 *Transnational Law and Contemporary Problems* 291, 295; Hobbs (n 170) 451.

EU's ethical concerns.[204] However, if the impact on third countries proves to be as significant as anticipated, a Panel may feel compelled to intervene.[205] At the very least, this review indicates that the doubts voiced by the Commission and Council about the legality of labelling proposals are well founded. If, as feared, the traceability and certification implications of labelling do have the capacity to prevent third countries delivering meat and dairy products to the EU, it seems improbable that comprehensive labelling measures as proposed by the EP would be viewed favourably by the WTO.[206]

Commission and Council Proposals: The influence of WTO rules

In the latter stages of the negotiations of the NNFR, the Commission and the Parliament were very explicit about their fears for WTO-based retaliation. Does this indicate, as MEPs were keen to propound, a slavish adherence to international obligations, at the expense of European citizens? A number of elements suggest that the overall aim of appeasing trading partners was more significant than specific SPS and other WTO provisions in shaping the Commission and Council standpoints.

Firstly, the compatibility of the Commission's own proposal with the SPS Agreement is questionable. With the NNFR, the Commission's intention was to 'clarify the legislative status quo rather than change it,'[207] and thus maintain the pre-market approval for food from cloned animals. As indicated in the discussion of traditional foods,[208] the SPS Agreement's threshold for justifying a pre-market approval may be relatively low. Nevertheless, as EFSA has established that there is no difference from a food-safety perspective between conventional food and its equivalent from cloned animals or their offspring, there is no evident reason under Article 5.1 or 2.2

---

[204] As Regan points out, the Appellate Body has yet to say that any specific legitimate regulatory purpose is less valuable than any other. Regan (n 190) 363.

[205] The situation would possibly be analogous to that confronting the AB in *Korea—Beef*, where they dismissed the relevance of idealistic goals, namely the total elimination of fraud on the basis that this 'would probably require a total ban of imports'. *Korea—Beef*, Appellate Body Report, para 178. For a discussion of this quasi-proportionality approach, see P Eeckhout, 'The Scales of Trade–Reflections on the Growth and Functions of the WTO Adjudicative Branch' (2010) 13 JIEL 3, 20.

[206] In this context, the Council Legal Service's reassurance that a 'simple labelling requirement would pass the necessity test' established by Art XX must be viewed sceptically. Its conclusion is drawn on a misinformed characterisation of labelling measures as simple and therefore a failure to engage in the type of balancing exercise that would be required from a Panel. Council Legal Opinion (n 174) para 44. The services noted the relevance of considering the impact of the measure on international commerce (see para 40), but failed to do so.

[207] M Weimer, 'The Regulatory Challenge of Animal Cloning for Food–The Risks of Risk Regulation in the European Union', 1 *European Journal of Risk Regulation* 31, 36 (2010).

[208] See ns 58–60 and related text.

for maintaining pre-market approval for the latter.[209] The Commission effectively confirmed this view, arguing that 'there is no scientific evidence which could justify restrictions on food from clones and food from offspring of clones based on human health concerns'.[210] Rather, it indicated that GATT Article XX would be the appropriate basis for measures on animal cloning.[211] As discussed above, Article XX provides a potential defence for some regulation of animal cloning. It does not, however, provide a credible legal basis for the type of risk-assessment and management procedure foreseen by the NNFR. If animal cloning is morally unacceptable in the EU, this ethical objection applies irrespective of any scientific evaluation of the type required by novel-food authorisations. The Commission's approach therefore seems inadequately grounded either with respect to the SPS provisions or GATT Article XX. In practice, however, the Commission had been made aware by the US that the new Regulation would not be challenged before the WTO, provided its scope was limited to the (economically unviable) food from clones and not extended to their offspring.[212] This suggests that the search for a viable policy solution, rather than compatibility with legal provisions as such, was instrumental in shaping the Commission's position.

Notwithstanding the Council's strident criticism of the Parliament for its neglect of international rules, the second indication of the limited detailed attention paid to SPS requirements was that the Council did not seek to contest Commission claims that the Council's position was 'at variance with EU international commitments'.[213] Ironically, the Council's Common Position—mandatory NF authorisation of food both from clones and their offspring—arguably had stronger legal merit in this respect than the Commission's own proposal. Although having not identified any specific food-safety risks associated with food from cloned animals, EFSA pointed to the inadequacies of the scientific data available, 'the limited number of studies available, the small sample sizes investigated and, in general, the absence of a uniform approach that would allow all the issues relevant to this opinion to be more satisfactorily addressed'.[214] In this context, there is some justification at least for

[209] See EFSA Cloning Opinion (n 124) 28. EFSA's original assessment was not amended by further evaluations in 2009 and 2010. See generally EFSA Statement, 'Further Advice on the Implications of Animal Cloning (SCNT)' (2009) RN 319 *EFSA Journal* 1; See generally EFSA Statement, 'Update on the State of Play of Animal Cloning' (2010) 8 *EFSA Journal* 1784.

[210] Commission Cloning Report (n 191) 10.

[211] ibid.

[212] There is no formal evidence of this position. It reflects conversations held with Commission officials in the summer of 2010, but is certainly entirely consistent with the US's non-criticism of the CNFR. If other trading partners shared the US position, the Commission theoretically also had recourse to the argument that the measure would not 'directly or indirectly, affect international trade' as set out in Art 1 of the SPS Agreement, and therefore falls outside the scope of the Regulation.

[213] European Commission, 'Communication concerning the position of the Council on the adoption of a Regulation of the European Parliament and of the Council on novel foods, amending Commission Regulation (EC) No 1331/2008 and repealing Regulation (EC) No 258/97 and Commission Regulation (EC) No 1852/2001', COM(2010)124 final, 5.

[214] EFSA Cloning Opinion (n 124) 32.

requiring the provision of additional information related to cloned foods, and therefore pre-market approval as a precautionary measure under Article 5.7.[215] Moreover, given that EFSA has noted that no differences exist in terms of food safety between food products from clones and from offspring, there is logic and consistency in applying the same precautionary approach to both.[216] As discussed above, pre-market approval regimes in general are not easily characterised as provisional measures.[217] Yet in that authorisations foreseen under the NNFR are generic, the acceptance of a first application could, in theory, have opened the European market to cloned food. This could potentially support an argument that the pre-market approval requirement is provisional *de facto*. Whatever the merits of this argument, the Commission, and ultimately the Council itself, was clearly not confident that the Common Position would withstand scrutiny, or at least worried that it would not dissuade third countries from initiating WTO action.[218]

The picture that emerges from the animal-cloning debate is of a Council and Commission whose engagement with international obligations is decidedly patchy. On the one hand, there is heightened sensitivity to the potential initiation of legal action before the WTO, a concern which is entirely justified, according to the analysis in this section. On the other hand, pronouncements about meeting international commitments do not appear to be matched by a rigorous, systematic effort to reflect upon and meet WTO requirements. This rather erratic treatment of legal obligations raises the question of the ultimate influence of WTO rules on policy.

5.5 The Influence of WTO Rules on the NNFR

At first sight, the case of the NNFR may appear to be the apotheosis of the regulatory chill that many have feared WTO obligations would bring about.[219] The EU could not put in place legislation that reflected consumer anxiety about animal cloning for fear of provoking a WTO dispute. Here, WTO rules have surely had the direct inhibiting force that international lawyers tend to assume? Some would undoubtedly

[215] Greece, for example, invoked the precautionary principle, claiming that 'potential future dangers arising from the application of animal cloning technique to food production cannot be ruled out'. Council PA (n 144) 4.

[216] It was certainly the view of 'some Member States that food produced from the offspring would share the same problematic (*sic*) as food produced from cloned animals'. Council of the European Union, 'Progress report', 17100/08 DENLEG 159 CODEC 1797, 4 (12 December 2008).

[217] See ns 61–62 and related text.

[218] Arguably, the need for the US to challenge may not have arisen. With the cloned nature of produce from offspring unidentifiable, and with no incentive to place cloned food through the NF authorisation procedure, actual disruption of trade may not have occurred. This was not a risk the Commission was prepared to take.

[219] For an illustration of this type of view, see comments by Ralph Nader cited in JH Jackson, 'Sovereignty-Modern: A New Approach to an Outdated Concept' (2003) 97 AJIL 782, 790.

present it in these terms.[220] However, this conclusion may be premature. The way that animal cloning will be regulated in the EU will undoubtedly differ from the approach taken by trading partners, with the Commission already firmly committed to prohibiting the technology.[221] Some form of product labelling also seems highly probable.[222] If WTO legislation has a substantive impact upon EU policy preferences, it will be at the still rather uncertain and blurred margins of EU consumer sensitivities.[223] The real impact of WTO obligations is arguably less far-reaching, but nevertheless significant from a policy-making perspective.

5.5.1 Inhibiting Negotiations

A particularly striking aspect of the NNFR debate was the manner in which legal constraints inhibited the normal process of negotiation. Political compromises between institutions can generally be found during the conciliation procedure, even on the most sensitive of issues. Throughout the negotiation of the NNFR, the Commission, charged with moderating discussions between EU institutions, was significantly hampered in this role, due to its acute awareness of international repercussions. It was compelled to reject Council proposals for the NNFR, thereby forcing the Council to seek unanimity, considerably complicating the process of reaching a Common Position. Faced with similar constraints in conciliation, the Commission was obliged to remind the institutions of international commitments, and in so doing was fiercely criticised for failing to fulfil its neutral mediating role.[224] The Council was also severely restricted in conciliation, being unable to make the concessions on labelling required to secure an agreement. There were certainly technical concerns about the feasibility of introducing comprehensive labelling. However, without the need to take into account international obligations, it is questionable

[220] Monique Goyens of the European consumer organisation BEUC criticised the Commission for its 'use [of] commercial arguments to endanger the choice of EU consumers'. 'Cloning: de Gucht Warns of Trade War if There is a Ban on Offspring' *EU Food Policy* (11 March 2011) (de Gucht Warns of Trade War).

[221] See comments by Commissioner Dalli, May 2011 EP debate (n 5).

[222] Following the breakdown in negotiations, the Hungarian Presidency confirmed the Council's support for 'the gradual introduction of labelling to provide a basis for informed consumer choice'. Cloned Foods Unleashed (n 4).

[223] In this context, it is worth noting that the complex dilemma associated with establishing the appropriate amount of consumer information to provide is one not caused by WTO considerations as such. For instance, see G Brookes et al., 'The Global GM Market: Implications for the European Food Chain. An Analysis of Labelling Requirements, Market Dynamics and Cost Implications' (2005), Appendix 2 (pointing to the wide range of ingredients currently derived from GMOs, but not known to consumers as not labelled under current EU rules) www.pgeconomics.co.uk/pdf/Global_GM_Market.pdf.

[224] 'Trade War Comments Sour Mood before Crucial Novel Food Talks' *EU Food Policy* (11 March 2011).

whether the Council would have withstood the political pressure to compromise on the principle of labelling.[225]

5.5.2 Limiting Regulatory Flexibility

A further impediment to reaching a compromise on the NNFR was the limited flexibility available to policy-makers to address ethical concerns about cloning. All institutions fundamentally accepted the need to respect and reflect public hostility to animal cloning in legislation. Nonetheless, in that concerns about cloning were ethically rather than scientifically based, any attempt to manage cloning effectively under a sanitary measure, even on a temporary basis, would have brought the EU into direct conflict with SPS rules. This does not exclude, as many have feared, the sensitive treatment of non-scientific concerns in food policy, but does impose certain restrictions on regulatory form. To be confident of conformity with WTO rules, the EU cannot try to accommodate these concerns directly or indirectly under the NNFR or an alternative SPS measure, but should rather develop new and separate legislative proposals.

The impact of WTO obligations in limiting both EU institutions' room for political manoeuvre and regulatory flexibility can be viewed in two ways. On the one hand, they can be conceived as an unnecessary and intrusive complication in an already extremely delicate European decision-making process. Following the frustration of the NNFR's collapse, this view will be shared by many involved in the process. The thwarted attempt to adopt the NNFR has resulted in considerable loss of time and resources. On the other hand, it may be argued that the case of the NNFR illustrates a conception of SPS law 'serving, not frustrating, democracy';[226] that the deliberative process necessitated by reflecting on international obligations may ultimately improve the rationality and quality of the measures concerned. From this perspective, the weight of international legal argument ensured that the European Commission and Council did not capitulate to EP demands and establish rules of dubious technical feasibility and enforceability. Likewise, the ultimate impact of not being able to forge a compromise on cloning within the NNFR could be that new, separate measures will be developed which are more coherent, transparent and effective in addressing public concerns.

5.5.3 The Influence on Policy Debate

While international trade obligations were marginal to the policy debate in first reading, there were latterly indications of these issues not only shaping the stand-

[225] If feasibility alone had been the issue, the institutions could have agreed, as is frequently the case, to the principle and provided for the subsequent development of detailed implementing rules.

[226] R Howse, 'Democracy, Science, and Free Trade: Risk Regulation on Trial at the World Trade Organisation' (2000) 98 *Michigan Law Review* 2329, 2357.

points of the different actors, but becoming a substantive part of the discussions. The NNFR debate certainly saw a number of unusually explicit evocations of legal concerns—the Commission's explanation of the WTO basis required for animal cloning measures,[227] the Trade Commissioner's uninvited intervention before the EP to stress the danger of WTO litigation,[228] the Council's lamenting of the EP's ignorance of WTO rules,[229] and the leaking of the Council's legal advice[230]—that placed legal arguments centre-stage in the policy debate. Yet the discussion of these issues remained generally superficial, unsubstantiated by reference to specific WTO texts, let alone precise provisions within them. There seems to have been little interest in engaging directly and resolving the legal stumbling-blocks that contributed to the institutional impasse.

Given the embarrassment surrounding the failure to finalise the NNFR, could this case mark a turning point in the attention paid to WTO obligations in EU policy-making? One obvious lesson to be learnt from the collapse of the NNFR would be to address potential conflicts with international law more explicitly at a much earlier stage in the decision-making procedure. Lest international lawyers get too excited, however, MEPs do not seem set to embrace WTO considerations. If anything, the performance of Trade Commissioner de Gucht and the mischievous presentation of the Council's legal advice may, in the eyes of many, have discredited rather than enhanced the status of legal arguments. That said, the debate on how to effectively regulate cloning in the EU is not yet over. Squaring the circle on animal cloning seems likely to require more than the political goodwill on which institutional negotiators appeared to have relied in the EU's conciliation process. On the contrary, negotiators may well need to grapple more intensely with the legal issues summarised above in order to be able to shape a compromise resilient to WTO scrutiny. This implies not only a greater prominence for in-depth legal discussion in future negotiations, but a need for more relevant legal expertise.[231]

5.6 Conclusion

This chapter has recounted the specific circumstances surrounding the EU's attempts to regulate novel foods—the mismatch between the salience of ethical issues and limited scientific evidence of risk—that brought unprecedented attention to the difficulties of reconciling international obligations and domestic preferences. Study of the NNFR, indicative of the tensions underlying all food policy, helps refine

[227] Commission Cloning Report (n 191).

[228] See de Gucht Warns of Trade War (n 219).

[229] See Council NNFR PR (n 147).

[230] See n 6 and related text.

[231] This comment is intended not to cast aspersions about the available expertise in the European Parliament, but reflects a simple observation that the only legal expertise seemingly on offer to that institution's rapporteur was a leaked Council document.

our understanding of the ways that the SPS Agreement and related WTO obligations can shape EU food policy. Certainly, their influence is not straightforward; in the policy considerations of EU institutions, the compatibility of sanitary measures with individual SPS obligations has been shown to play a secondary role to a more general sense of the acceptability of those measures to third countries. As seen in the arguments employed by all EU institutions during the legislative process, the claims and counterclaims for the legality of various proposals under consideration are often tenuously grounded. Actors therefore appear to be steered by what may best be described as quasi-legal rather than legal argument. Yet their decisions cannot be understood simply in strategic terms. The underlying threat of WTO litigation, certainly instrumental in the ultimate collapse of negotiations, can only partially explain the traction gained by third-country trade concerns throughout the development of the NNFR. Even where there is a limited threat of legal action, as in the case for traditional products, the scrutiny and discussion of European policy with third countries initiated in the WTO context has the capacity significantly to steer the EU's regulatory choices. This does not imply a simple sacrifice of the EU's food-safety or animal-welfare goals: the high level of protection demanded by the CNFR remains in place, and animal cloning is destined to remain of marginal importance to EU food production. Yet, when the Commission brings forward new proposals for the NNFR (foreseen for early 2014), they will in all likelihood include special procedures for traditional products, and an approach to labelling that acknowledges and accommodate the realities of international trade.

References

Alemanno A, *Trade in Food: Regulatory and Judicial Approaches in the EC and the WTO* (London, Cameron May, 2007).

Becker GS and Cowan T, 'Biotechnology in Animal Agriculture: Status and Current Issues' (Congressional Research Service Reports, 32, 2009).

Binns N and Howlett J, 'Functional Foods in Europe: International Developments in Science and Health Claims' (2009) 48 *European Journal of Nutrition* 48 (Suppl 1): S3–S1.

Bronckers M and Soopramanien R, 'The Impact of WTO Law on European Food Regulation' (2008) 6 *European Food and Feed Law Review* 361.

Brookes G, 'Economic Impact Assessment of the Way in Which the EU Novel Foods Regulatory Approval Procedures Affect the EU Food Sector' (July 2007).

Brookes G, Craddock N and Kneil B, 'The Global GM Market: Implications for the European Food Chain. An Analysis of Labelling Requirements, Market Dynamics and Cost Implications' (2005).

Charnovitz S, 'The Moral Exception in Trade Policy' (1997) 38 VJIL 689.

Charnovitz S, 'The Law of Environmental "PPMs" the WTO: Debunking the Myth of Illegality' (2002) 27 YJIL 59.

Cheyne I, 'Proportionality, Proximity and Environmental Labelling in WTO Law' (2009) 12 JIEL 927.

Craddock N, 'The EU Novel Food Regulation. Impact on the Potential Export of Exotic Traditional Foods to the EU: Suggestions for revision' (Discussion paper prepared for UNCTAD and CBI, in cooperation with GTZ, GFU and IPGRI, 2005).

Cumming Smith EM, 'The European Novel Foods Regulation: The Case of Exotic Foods' (Wageningen University 2009).

Diebold NF, 'The Morals and Order Exceptions in WTO Law: Balancing the Toothless Tiger and the Undermining Mole' (2008) 11 JIEL 43.

Du MM, 'Domestic Regulatory Autonomy under the TBT Agreement: From Non-Discrimination to Harmonisation' (2007) 6 *Chinese Journal of International Law* 269.

Eeckhout P, 'The Scales of Trade—Reflections on the Growth and Functions of the WTO Adjudicative Branch' (2010) 13 JIEL 3.

Ehring L, '*De Facto* Discrimination in World Trade Law' (2002) 36 JWT 921.

Epps T, 'Pre-market Approval Systems and the SPS Agreement' in G Van Calster and D Prévost (eds), *Research Handbook on Environment, Health and the WTO* (Cheltenham, Edward Elgar, 2013).

Foster CE, 'Prior Approval Systems and the Substance—Procedure Dichotomy under the WTO SPS Agreement' (2008) 42 JWT 1203.

Galantucci R, 'Compassionate Consumerism within the GATT Regime: Can Belgium's Ban on Seal Product Imports be Justified under Article XX?' (2009) 39 *California Western International Law Journal* 281.

Gonzalez MA, 'Trade and Morality: Preserving "Public Morals" without Sacrificing the Global Economy' (2006) 39 *Vanderbilt Journal of Transnational Law* 940.

Gunning J, Hartlev M and Gamborg C, 'Challenges in Regulating Farm Animal Cloning' (Danish Centre for Bioethics and Risk Assessment, Project report 13, 2006).

Hermann M, 'The Impact of the European Novel Food Regulation on Trade and Food Innovation Based on Traditional Plant Foods from Developing Countries' (2009) 34 *Food Policy* 499.

Hobbs AL, 'Ethics, Domestic Food Policy and Trade Law: Assessing the EU Animal Welfare Proposals to the WTO' (2002) 27 *Food Policy* 437.

Howse R, 'Democracy, Science, and Free Trade: Risk Regulation on Trial at the World Trade Organisation' (2000) 98 *Michigan Law Review* 2329.

Howse R and Regan D, 'The Product/Process Distinction—An Illusionary Basis for Disciplining "Unilateralism" in Trade Policy' (2000) 11 EJIL 249.

Jackson JH, 'Comments on *Shrimp/Turtle* and the Product/Process Distinction' (2000) 11 EJIL 303.

Jones D, 'Safety Evaluation of Novel Foods: A European and International Perspective' (EUFIC Review 04/2000).

Kirkham C, 'Legislative Developments. Novel Foods and Food Ingredients' (1997) 3 *Columbia Journal of European Law* 317.

Knudsen I, Søborg I, Eriksen F, Pilegaard K and Pedersen J, 'Risk Management and Risk Assessment of Novel Plant Foods: Concepts and Principles' (2008) 46 *Food and Chemical Toxicology* 1681.

Kysar DA, 'Preferences for Processes: The Process/Product Distinction and the Regulation of Consumer Choice' (2004) 118 *Harvard Law Review* 525.

Marceau G and Trachtman JP, 'The Technical Barriers to Trade Agreement, the Sanitary and Phytosanitary Measures Agreement, and the General Agreement Tariffs and Trade—A Map of the World Trade Organisation Law of Domestic Regulation of Goods' (2002) 36 JWT 811.

Marwell JC, 'The Trade and Morality: WTO Public Morals Exception after Gambling' (2006) 81 *New York University Law Review* 802.

Maryanski JH, 'Special Challenges of Novel Foods (Biotechnology)' (1990) 45 *Food, Drug, Cosmetic Law Journal* 549.

Matheny G and Leahy C, 'Farmer-Animal Welfare, Legislation, and Trade' (2007) 70 *Law and Contemporary Problems* 325.

McGrady B, 'Necessity Exceptions in WTO Law: Retreaded Tyres, Regulatory Purpose and Cumulative Regulatory Measures' (2009) 12 JIEL 153.

Mück O, 'Trade Barrier NFR? Underutilised Species under the European Union's Novel Food Regulation' (Paper commissioned by Deutsche Gesellschaft für Technische Zusammenarbeit 2003).

Murphy JF, 'Mandatory Labelling of Food Made from Cloned Animals: Grappling with Moral Objections to the Production of Safe Products' (2008) 63 *Food and Drug Law Journal* 131.

Rudenko L, Mathesen JC and Sundlof SF, 'Animal Cloning and the FDA—The Risk Assessment Paradigms under Public Scrutiny' (2007) 25 *Nature Biotechnology* 39.

Scott J, *The WTO Agreement on Sanitary and Phytosanitary Measures. A Commentary* (Oxford, OUP, 2007).

Stevenson P, 'The World Trade Organisation Rules: A Legal Analysis of Their Adverse Impact on Animal Welfare' (2007) 8 *Animal Law* 107.

Suk J, Bruce A, Gertz R, Warkup C, Whitelaw CBA, Braun A, Oram C, Rodriguez-Cerezo E and Papatryfon I, 'Dolly for Dinner? Assessing Commercial and Regulatory Trends in Cloned Livestock' (2007) 25 *Nature Biotechnology* 47.

Thomas EM, 'Playing Chicken at the WTO: An Animal Welfare-Based Trade Restriction under GATT's Moral Exception' (2007) 34 *Boston College Environmental Affairs Law Review* 605.

US National Research Council, *Lost Crops of the Incas* (Washington, D. C, National Academy Press, 1989).

Waters S, 'The Regulation of Herbicide Resistant Crops in Europe' in SO Duke (ed), *Herbicide-Resistant Crops: Agricultural, Economic, Environmental, Regulatory, and Technological Aspects* (Cleveland, CRC Press, 1995).

Weimer M, 'The Regulatory Challenge of Animal Cloning for Food—The Risks of Risk Regulation in the European Union' (2010) 1 *European Journal of Risk Regulation* 31.

Wu M, 'Free Trade and the Protection of Public Morals: An Analysis of the Newly Emerging Public Morals Clause Doctrine' (2008) 33 YJIL 216.

Part III
The SPS in Action: The Emerging Transnational Governance of Food

Chapter 6
SPS Mechanisms for a Transnational Approach to Food Governance: Transparency and Equivalence

Abstract This chapter investigates how two procedural SPS Agreement commitments—transparency and equivalence—hitherto little discussed by legal commentators have influenced the EU's regulatory practices and their interaction with trading partners on SPS matters. With regard to both sets of disciplines, it details the Agreement's expectations as elaborated upon by the WTO SPS Committee and then reviews the EU's performance. An evaluation of the EU's efforts in 2008 to inform trading partners about upcoming SPS measures demonstrates that while clearly committed to advancing transparency, the EU's application of SPS norms is inconsistent in practice: non-notification of many EU and EU Member State measures and, in cases, failure to notify in a manner that allows third-country input. A review of the EU's application of equivalence reveals widespread adoption of the principle, although little formal notification of this use to the SPS Committee. This study identifies factors that complicate coherent EU implementation of SPS obligations. In spite of the deficiencies identified in EU practices, this chapter emphasises the important role of SPS disciplines in stimulating the emergence of a transnational approach to food governance—information-sharing, dialogue and cooperation—that can significantly contribute to reducing technical obstacles to agricultural trade.

6.1 Introduction

How or when do you check a chicken to see if it is healthy? Not, as one might initially suspect, a joke of the Christmas-cracker genre, but the earnest preoccupation of the European Union (EU) and US officials who spent many months in early 2008 discussing the appropriate procedure for certifying newly born chicks.[1] Such questions are far from exceptional. The wording of health certificates, the number and type of sanitary controls, the level of permitted contaminants form the day-to-day

This chapter incorporates my article 'The Impact of WTO Transparency Rules: Is the 10,000th SPS Notification a Cause for Celebration?—A Case Study of EU Practice' published in (2012) 15 JIEL 503.

[1] See n 87 below and related text.

C. Downes, *The Impact of WTO SPS Law on EU Food Regulations,* Studies in European Economic Law and Regulation 2, DOI 10.1007/978-3-319-04373-9_6,

work of national food administrators the world over. These issues may not immediately appear contentious. Yet confusion or disagreement as to the correct application of sanitary measures can have significant repercussions: consignments blocked at Europe's ports, the rejection or destruction of food, significant costs to operators and mounting political tension. Effective coordination of such issues therefore lies at the heart of the trade-enhancing agenda set by Agreement on the Application of Sanitary and Phytosanitary Measures (SPS Agreement).

To what extent can SPS rules help World Trade Organisation (WTO) Members to prevent and respond to this type of trade disruption? This chapter analyses two disciplines designed to reduce SPS-related conflicts: transparency (Sect. 6.2) and equivalence (Sect. 6.3).[2] With regard to each, it sets out the Agreement's obligations as elaborated by the Committee on Sanitary and Phytosanitary Measures (SPS Committee), before critically reviewing the EU's integration of these principles. Sect. 6.4 reflects on what this review reveals about the impact of the SPS Agreement.

6.2 Transparency

Transparency aims to facilitate international trade in three ways. By providing a comprehensive picture of the regulatory expectations of the importing country, transparency can reduce the danger of agricultural exports being rejected by customs or health authorities on arrival at destination. Such rejections can result in a considerable and often unnecessary cost to trade.[3] Secondly, notification of measures ahead of adoption allows exporters to make the changes in production or manufacturing required to comply with new requirements. Thirdly, the communication of upcoming measures permits interested third countries to anticipate obstacles to trade and to work with the importing country to avoid disruptions.

6.2.1 The Disciplines

To meet these goals, the SPS Agreement establishes obligations which can be grouped into the three constitutive elements of transparency: information, comment and timing. Annex B specifies expectations associated with the principle of

[2] Regionalisation is a third important principle which is not treated here as of greater relevance to animal health than food safety. For a discussion of regionalisation in an SPS context, see generally J Scott, *The WTO Agreement on Sanitary and Phytosanitary Measures. A Commentary* (Oxford, OUP, 2007) 179–190; D Prévost, *Balancing Trade and Health in the SPS Agreement: The Development Dimension* (Nijmegen, Wolf Legal Publishers, 2009) 769–785.

[3] For an indication of the scale of costs associated with the border rejection of agricultural imports, see P-C Athukorala and S Jayasuriya, 'Food Safety Issues, Trade and WTO Rules: A Developing Country Perspective' (2003) 26 *The World Economy* 1395, 1399–1400.

transparency established in Article 7. These 'hard'[4] provisions have been complemented by 'soft' norms contained in Transparency Procedures adopted by the SPS Committee.[5]

Provision of Information

All adopted regulations must be published 'in such a manner as to enable interested Members to become acquainted with them'.[6] Regulatory proposals must be notified through the SPS Committee Secretariat in English, French or Spanish,[7] and developed countries shall provide, on request, the relevant documents or summaries thereof in the same languages.[8] The SPS Committee's Transparency Procedures have elaborated on Annex B obligations by characterizing the different types of information communicated.[9] In accordance with these Recommendations, and in addition to the original notification of the draft measure, Members should transmit changes in the content of, or comment period for, the original notification as Addenda. Substantial redrafts to regulations previously notified are forwarded to the Committee as Revisions and errors in the original notification as Corrigenda. A separate notification format is foreseen where Members have recognized the equivalence of another Member's sanitary or phytosanitary measures.[10]

The obligation to notify applies only when three somewhat nebulous criteria are fulfilled.[11] A Member must notify (i) a 'proposed sanitary or phytosanitary regulation' which is 'generally applicable', where it is (ii) not 'substantially the same as the content of an international standard' and (iii) 'may have a significant effect on trade of other Members'. Given the centrality of notification to the effectiveness of transparency, it is worth reflecting on each of these conditions in more detail.

---

[4] For a discussion of the interaction between hard and soft law, see GC Shaffer and MA Pollack, 'Hard Versus Soft Law: Alternatives, Complements and Antagonists in International Governance' (2010) 94 *Minnesota Law Review* 706.

[5] Their legal status is described as follows: 'These guidelines do not add to nor detract from the existing rights and obligations of Members under the SPS Agreement.' SPS Committee, 'Recommended Procedures for Implementing the Transparency Obligations of the SPS Agreement (Article 7)' ('Transparency Procedures') WTO Document G/SPS/7/Rev.3 (20 June 2008) para 1. Although this most recent version of the procedures was adopted in June 2008, the central obligations, examined below in the study of EU practice in 2008 were already established in 2002. See G/SPS/7/Rev.2 (2 April 2002).

[6] SPS Agreement Annex B, para 1.

[7] SPS Agreement Annex B, para 7.

[8] SPS Agreement Annex B, para 8.

[9] See 'Transparency Procedures' (n 5) Annexes. The latest version of these notification formats took effect from 1 December 2008.

[10] ibid paras 44–47.

[11] SPS Agreement Annex B, para 5. The first criterion is not explicitly included in paragraph 5, but forms part of the definition of 'phytosanitary regulations' provided in the footnote to paragraph 1.

Which Measures Constitute 'Sanitary and Phytosanitary Regulations'?

It is not immediately clear which type of measures WTO Members are expected to notify. The confusion initially lies in the text of the Agreement, with an apparent discrepancy between the obligation under Article 7 to notify 'sanitary and phytosanitary measures' and Annex B, which concerns 'sanitary and phytosanitary regulations'. The WTO Secretariat's own guidance ('Transparency Handbook') is not helpful in understanding the distinction, suggesting that the SPS Agreement uses the terms 'somewhat interchangeably'.[12] While this interpretation may serve the aims of a Secretariat seeking comprehensive transparency, it has little textual merit. 'Regulations' appear to be a subset of measures 'such as laws, decrees or ordinances which are applicable generally'[13] and not extending to 'requirements and procedures' included in the definition of 'measures' in Annex A.[14] While 'laws, decrees or ordinances' are only examples of regulations, the intention was clearly to restrict the scope of transparency obligations. This becomes all the more evident when reading the negotiating history of the SPS Agreement and the concerns expressed about the administrative burden involved.[15]

That only regulations that are 'applicable generally' must be notified further complicates matters. From an ordinary reading, this could be understood to concern measures of general relevance to all WTO Members and therefore those of greatest significance in trade terms. Yet this is evidently not the case. The Transparency Handbook states that a measure implicating 'bilateral and plurilateral trade' should also be notified where these are 'generic'.[16] Indeed, the most recently adopted format for SPS notification includes the possibility of indicating whether measures apply to 'all trading partners' or to 'specific regions or countries'.[17] Greater clarity can be gleaned only by returning to early drafts of the Agreement, which include a note that the definition of a regulation 'excludes individual permits and approvals based on regulation'.[18] Thus, where a company secures pre-market approval for a product, this need not be notified to the WTO.[19]

---

[12] WTO Secretariat, 'How to Apply the Transparency Provisions of the SPS Agreement: A Handbook Prepared by the WTO Secretariat' (September 2002) ('Transparency Handbook') 11, fn 2, www.wto.org/english/tratop_e/sps_e/spshand_e.pdf.

[13] SPS Agreement Annex B, para 1, fn.

[14] See Scott (n 2) 198.

[15] See GATT Document, MTN.GNG/NG5/WGSP/W/24 (n 45) para 13. In these discussions, the 'Nordic Delegations' in particular emphasized that transparency should be 'limited to essential trade issues'. MTN.GNG/NG5/WGSP/W/10 (12 February 1990) 4.

[16] 'Transparency Handbook' (n 12) para 33.

[17] See 'Transparency Procedures' (n 5) Annexes A and B.

[18] MTN.GNG/NG5/WGSP/W/21 (28 May 1990) Annex I, para 2.

[19] This was the approach adopted by the Panel in *Biotech*. See *EC—Measures affecting the Approval and Marketing of Biotech Products*, Panel Report (adopted in November 2006) WT/DS/291–293/R, paras 7.1775–7.1776 (rejecting the US's claim that Annex B is applicable to the EU's failure to consider specific applications for GM events, on the basis that the measures under discussion were product-specific, and therefore not 'generally applicable').

When Are Measures Substantially the Same as International Standards?

Only measures that are not 'substantially the same' as international standards require notification. Commentators acknowledge that this adds another layer of complexity to the already nuanced relationship between international standards and WTO-Member measures in the SPS Agreement.[20] To recap, Members are under an obligation to 'base' their sanitary measures on international standards (Article 3.1), but enjoy a presumption of compliance with the Agreement where the measures 'conform to' international standards (Article 3.2). Scott adjudges the meaning of 'substantially the same' to lie somewhere in between, perhaps falling short of the complete conversion implied by conformity,[21] whereas Prévost considers it as essentially equivalent to conformity.[22] Given the original intentions of negotiators, noted above, of restricting the burden of notification, the former interpretation seems more probable.[23] This distinction is of less importance today due to a concerted push by Canada and the EU for notification even of those regulations that do conform to international standards, provided they have a significant effect on trade.[24] As a result, the SPS Committee's Transparency Procedures now actively encourage this inclusive practice.[25]

When Is an Effect on Trade Significant?

The final consideration in whether or not to notify is whether a proposed regulation will have a 'significant effect on trade'. This concept remains vague in spite of the clarifications provided by a WTO Panel and the SPS Committee's Transparency Procedures. The latter has interpreted the term broadly, dismissing various arguments that could be used by Members to minimize an effect on trade, such as the limited number of Members implicated by the measure.[26] In *Japan—Apples*, the Panel was asked to judge whether Japan had erred in failing to notify changes to its regulation. It argued that the 'most important factor in this regard is whether … the exported product[s]… [would] still be permitted to enter Japan if they comply with the prescription contained in the previous regulations'.[27] In this respect, the Panel's

---

[20] See Scott (n 2) 199 and Prévost (n 2) 794.

[21] Scott (n 2) 199.

[22] Prévost (n 2) 794.

[23] However (and illustrating the potential for confusion), in a questionnaire to WTO Members on the operation of SPS Enquiry Points and National Notification Authorities in 2006, the WTO Secretariat implied yet another more restrictive interpretation: 'Annex B of the SPS Agreement requires notification of new or changed sanitary and phytosanitary regulations that *are not based on* an international standard.' G/SPS/W/103/Rev.2 (8 December 2006) 4 (emphasis added).

[24] See G/SPS/GEN/778 (Canada, 7 June 2007) and G/SPS/W/159 (EU, 14 October 2004).

[25] 'Transparency Procedures' (n 5) para 8.

[26] A significant effect on trade can refer to trade 'between two or more Members'. ibid para 9.

[27] *Japan—Measures Affecting the Importation of Apples (Japan—Apples),* Panel Report (adopted 15 July 2003) WT/DS/245/R, para 8.314.

approach is not aligned with the Transparency Procedures. If, as suggested in the latter, 'both import-enhancing and import-reducing effects' on trade can constitute 'significant effect',[28] establishing whether the product can still enter a market cannot be 'the most important factor'. Rather, it is the scale of the effect on trade, positive or negative, that should trigger the decision to notify. To this end, the Transparency Procedures point to a range of relevant market factors, including the value of imports and the potential effects on producer interests.[29]

Even with regard to procedural aspects, confusion arises between the approach of the Transparency Procedures and that of the Panel in *Japan—Apples*. The Secretariat proposes that Members evaluate 'information which is available'. Yet the WTO Panel suggested that measuring 'significant effect' should include costs such as 'production, packaging and sales',[30] elements that are not generally readily available to the regulating country. In practice, if a key consideration in the decision as to whether to notify or not is one of administrative burden, the process of investigating 'significant effect' may well prove more time-consuming than simply notifying the regulation.

Interaction with WTO Members

A second key element—and one which sets SPS notification practices apart from other WTO agreements[31]—is the dialogue initiated with other WTO Members who have the right to comment on the notified proposals. As the global implications of adopting new regulations will not always be clear, this is the logical corollary of the obligation established in SPS Agreement Article 5.6 to 'ensure that such measures are not more trade-restrictive than required'. Given the political sensitivity of opening up national decision-making procedures to external scrutiny and contestation, the elaboration of the principle in Annex B is relatively modest. Paragraph 5(d) provides that Members shall 'allow a reasonable time for other Members to make comments in writing, discuss these comments upon request, and take comments and the results of the discussions into account'. The Transparency Procedures have fleshed out the procedural aspects of managing third-country comments by specifying who should handle the information (the National Notification Authority) and appropriate responses (acknowledging receipt of comments, explaining how they will be taken into account and providing adequate follow-up).[32]

[28] 'Transparency Procedures' (n 5) para 10.

[29] ibid.

[30] *Japan—Apples*, Panel Report, para 8.314.

[31] T Collins-Williams and R Wolfe, 'Transparency as a Trade Policy Tool: The WTO's Cloudy Windows' (2010) 9 *World Trade Review* 9 551, 574.

[32] 'Transparency Procedures' (n 5) para 31.

Timeliness

For non-EU countries to have a meaningful influence on the regulatory process, it is crucial to receive and provide information at the right juncture. Annex B is not explicit about this time-frame. The publication of regulations should occur 'promptly' (paragraph 1), but more importantly, must foresee 'a reasonable interval' before entering into force to allow other Members to make the necessary adaptations. A Ministerial Conference clarified that this interval 'shall be understood to mean normally a period of not less than six months'.[33] Annex B is similarly vague with regard to notifications of draft measures which should be provided 'at an early stage' (paragraph 5b). The SPS Committee agreed to a period of at least 60 days for other Members to comment,[34] with a possible 30-day extension period to be granted on request.[35] With each communication of information, publication or notification, Members may deviate from the standard procedures in order to respond to urgent health risks.[36] In addition, the Transparency Procedures set expectations with regard to the management of information. Copies of proposed regulations requested by other Members should be provided within five working days[37] and Members should reply to comments 'at the earliest possible date before the adoption of the measure'.[38]

Notwithstanding the remaining ambiguities surrounding concepts such as 'significant trade', the above overview demonstrates how, from an initially open-ended text, the SPS Committee has gradually constructed a detailed framework for communicating on SPS issues.

6.2.2 *The EU's Implementation of SPS Transparency Disciplines*

The EU has expressed a strong commitment to transparency,[39] and even a superficial review of EU practice finds much to support that claim. The EU has always been one of the most conscientious of WTO Members in providing notifications.[40]

[33] WT/MIN (01)/17, para 3.2.

[34] 'Transparency Procedures' (n 5) para 13. As from December 2008, an exception to the recommended sixty-day period applies for those measures which 'facilitate trade' or are substantially the same as international standards.

[35] ibid para 33.

[36] SPS Agreement Annex B, paras 2 and 6.

[37] 'Transparency Procedures' (n 5) para 19.

[38] ibid para 31.

[39] The EU Notification Authority & Enquiry Point (EU NA & EP) reports that its 'notifications are very welcomed (*sic*) by the trade partners because it is a strong signal of the importance that the EU give to the transparency in the legislative procedure.' European Commission, 'EU NA & EP Activity Report Year 2007', 3. All EU NA & EP Activity Report reports are available at ec.europa.eu/food/international/organisations/sps/transparency_en.htm. Access to earlier reports can be requested from the EU NA & EP.

[40] In 2007, only the US (410) and Brazil (197) exceeded the 58 notifications submitted by the EU. In 2008, the EU's 49 notifications placed them as the seventh most active notifier. ibid 4.

The publication of European legislation is comprehensive, appears in 23 languages, and is complemented by the availability of texts consolidating the various amendments made over time.[41] The meetings among Member States in preparation for the SPS Committee are minuted and published online.[42] The EU is even transparent about its transparency. Its Notification Authority and Enquiry Point (NA & EP) has in the past provided regular updates on its SPS activity, including information on exchanges with third countries arising from notification,[43] and more recently presented its own experience of managing the new Transparency Guidelines.[44]

In itself, this represents a significant level of notification. A more difficult task in assessing the EU's commitment to transparency is to judge whether it has been systematic in its notification of measures.[45] In order to provide a more comprehensive response to this question, this section undertakes an empirical examination of the EU's development of sanitary regulations with reference to the three elements—provision of information, timeliness and interaction with WTO members—identified above. This analysis is limited (for the sake of feasibility[46]) to the EU's 2008 regulatory activity in the field of food safety.[47]

Provision of Information

Regular Notification of New Measures

In the period reviewed,[48] the EU submitted 71 notifications to the SPS Committee. 26 of these were new measures, 18 of which were related to food-safety issues.[49] The remaining 45 took the form of addenda.

[41] Consolidated texts form one of the search options available at eur-lex.europa.eu/en/index.htm.

[42] See ec.europa.eu/food/international/organisations/sps/agendas_en.htm.

[43] See n 45.

[44] See G/SPS/GEN/1044 (8 October 2010). The EU has itself lauded such candour, being 'the only WTO member which has published such a complete review of its deviations from international standards'. WTO/TPR/M/248/Add.1 (31 August 2011) 418.

[45] The WTO Secretariat has long acknowledged the limited significance in terms of evaluating Members' transparency of the data on notification generally collected. See G/SPS/GEN/804 (11 September 2007) paras 10 and 23.

[46] In spite of the ready access to EU legislation and various search functions available, identifying SPS measures requires a day-by-day review of all legislation appearing in the EU's *Official Journal*. In spite of all efforts to undertake a comprehensive evaluation, given the sheer quantity of EU legislation, some measures may well have been overlooked.

[47] 2008 was chosen as a reference point in order to be able to evaluate subsequent WTO member reaction or possible trade concerns arising from any failure to notify regulatory measures. The author has no reason to believe that EU notification practice was in any way exceptional in this period. The irony should not be overlooked that the ability to take a more critical look at the operation of the EU's transparency practices is itself a product of the considerable information publicly available in Europe.

[48] As WTO Members must notify measures in advance of adopting regulations, in order to assess transparency practice in 2008, the reference period took into account notifications made between 1 August 2007 and 31 December 2008, but for simplicity will be referred to throughout this article as '2008'.

[49] Other notifications covered animal health or plant protection measures.

A detailed analysis of food-related legislation published in the *Official Journal of the European Communities* in 2008 points to 50 food-safety measures—Commission Proposals, Decisions and Regulations—that were not notified to the SPS Committee.[50] The discrepancy between measures published and those notified does not in itself confirm deficiencies in the EU's transparency practices. As indicated in Sect. 2.1.1, the obligation to notify is associated with three criteria. Can these criteria explain the EU's non-notification?

Non-notification of EU regulations cannot easily be justified by virtue of their 'substantial sameness' with Codex standards. As international standards must only be 'taken into consideration'[51] under general European food law, there is a high probability that EU measures generally fall short of the 'substantial sameness' threshold, wherever precisely this is deemed to fall. Moreover, vocal EU support for comprehensive notification of regulations conforming to international standards diminishes the likelihood of not notifying on these grounds.[52]

The remaining two criteria—general applicability and significance of effect on trade—may be more instrumental in an EU decision as to whether to notify. 11 non-notified measures concern novel foods, genetically modified food or feed authorisations addressed to the applicant; as such they are not 'generally applicable' and therefore lie outside the scope of Annex B.[53] A further 16 measures concern initiatives taken against foods originating from specific countries and may possibly not have been notified for this reason. Strictly speaking, such measures should be notified, even where negotiated bilaterally, as they are relevant to all exporters and thus 'generally applicable'.

Whether the non-notification of the 39 generally applicable measures could be justified on the basis of not having 'significant effect on trade' would require an extensive contextual analysis of each measure not possible here. Suffice it to say that, at the very least, there is a puzzling inconsistency in what was and was not notified by the EU in 2008. Special conditions applied to guar gum imported from India[54] and sunflower oil originating from the Ukraine[55] were deemed notifiable, but restrictions on, for example, crustaceans imported from Bangladesh, rice products contaminated with unauthorized GM events from China or bivalve molluscs from Peru were not.[56] Maximum residues established for the feed additive canthaxanin

[50] 13 of these related to permission of countries to export meat or fishery products, 7 concerned the authorisation of novel foods, 6 established maximum residue or contaminant levels, 5 were related to GM food authorisations, 5 more responded to food safety problems associated with specific products from a given country, 4 concerned food hygiene, 4 approved residue monitoring plans, 4 were Common Positions on various additive Regulations and 2 were corrigenda (see Appendix I for details).

[51] Regulation of the European Parliament and of the Council 178/2002 [2002] OJ L31/1, Art 5.3.

[52] See n 24 and related text.

[53] See ns 18–19 and related text.

[54] G/SPS/N/EEC/332 (12 August 2008).

[55] G/SPS/N/EEC/333 (12 August 2008).

[56] See respectively Commission Decision 2008/630/EC [2008] OJL 205/49; Commission Decision 2008/289/EC [2008] OJ L 96/29; Commission Decision 2008/866/EC [2008] OJ L307/9.

are reported,[57] but not for veterinary medicinal products as regards dinoprostone or cyfluthrin and lectin.[58] Similarly, the EU notified a regulation establishing a list of third countries and veterinary certification requirements for the import of wild leporidae,[59] but not for the import of poultry or poultry products.[60] Most oddly, those measures specifically aimed at resolving outstanding disputes with a significant impact on trade were not notified. Neither a draft Council Regulation proposing to permit the use of antimicrobial substances for cleaning poultry carcasses[61] (an issue that had already been the subject of considerable international scrutiny),[62] nor a Decision facilitating the import of US peanuts[63] was brought to the attention of the SPS Committee. The significance on trade of all these non-notified regulations is far from established. However, there would appear at least *prima facie* to be numerous lapses in EU notification.

Notification of EU Member State measures

In addition to its responsibilities with regard to European regulatory proposals, the EU NA & EP is responsible for notifying SPS measures proposed by EU Member States.[64] In 2008, only three food-safety-related SPS proposals were notified under the SPS Agreement.[65] Surprisingly, a number of proposals considered by the EU Member States themselves to be of relevance for SPS notification[66] were not presented for international scrutiny.[67]

---

[57] G/SPS/N/EEC/330 (12 August 2008).

[58] See Commission Regulation 61/2008/EC [2008] OJ L22/8; Commission Regulation 542/2008/EC [2008] OJ L157/43.

[59] G/SPS/N/EEC/335 (13 February 2009).

[60] Commission Regulation 798/2008 [2008] OJ L226/1. However, subsequent changes to the third country lists in Regulation 798/2008 were notified in 2009, under G/SPS/N/EEC/348 (24 July 2009) and G/SPS/N/EEC/349 (29 July 2009).

[61] European Commission, 'Proposal for a Council Regulation implementing Regulation (EC) No 853/2004 of the European Parliament and of the Council as regards the use of antimicrobial substances to remove surface contamination from poultry carcases', COM/2008/0430 final.

[62] See s 4.4.1 in Chap. 4 above.

[63] Commission Decision 2008/47/EC [2008] OJ L11/12.

[64] EU Member States are free to adopt national SPS measures in the absence of pertinent European law. There is an obligation to notify such measures. See Directive 98/34/EC of the European Parliament and of the Council [1998] OJ L204/37. For an explanation of how EU Member States' draft measures are procedurally managed in the WTO SPS context, see G/SPS/GEN/456 (5 December 2003) paras 7–8. For an overview of national notifications received, see the Commission's Technical Regulations Information System available at ec.europa.eu/enterprise/tris/.

[65] All three were related to proposals submitted by the Netherlands, namely G/SPS/N/NLD/66 (28 April 2008), G/SPS/N/NLD/67 (3 July 2008) and G/SPS/N/NLD/68 (17 July 2008).

[66] The notification system provided for under Directive 98/34/EC specifically requires Member States to indicate whether the proposed measures are of relevance to either the TBT or SPS Agreement.

[67] Consider, for example, Italy's ministerial decree concerning beta-carotene supplements, TRIS Notification Number 2008/329/I) and The Netherland's draft regulation concerning eel smoked fresh daily (TRIS Notification Number 2008/268/NL). See n 70.

Notification of Addenda

An addendum is presented to the Secretariat in a number of situations, but most notably when a measure has been adopted or significantly changed.[68] As regards adoption and publication, the EU was relatively consistent in informing WTO Members. However, the Addenda were not always produced promptly[69] and in some instances, the EU failed to inform the WTO of the publication of the regulations.[70] The EU's record is less convincing when it comes to signaling changes in the content of a draft proposal. As many proposals concerning consumer health must pass before the European Parliament and Council during the co-decision process, the content of the original proposal will often change significantly. The SPS Committee was not kept informed of the adoption of Common Positions adopted in the context of the EU review on additives.[71]

Publication of Regulations

As already indicated,[72] the EU has an excellent online system for monitoring published regulations which unquestionably meets SPS transparency provisions (Annex B, paragraph 1). In addition, WTO Members are expected to allow six months between publication of the regulation and its entry into force.[73] This does not apply 'in urgent circumstances' where a food-safety threat may necessitate immediate action. The 2008 regulations under scrutiny here predominantly adhere to these rules, either in allowing periods before the entry into force, sometimes up to 12 months, or alternatively allowing a transitional period in which products conforming to prior rules are permitted on to the market for a period of generally around six months.[74]

---

[68] Addenda are also submitted to indicate that the period for comments has been extended, if a proposal is withdrawn or where the timing or the impact of the regulation was not clear in the original notification. 'Transparency Procedures' (n 5) para 36.

[69] The delay in notifying the publication of regulations varied from three to 119 days.

[70] This was the case for G/SPS/N/EEC/316 (1 August 2007); G/SPS/N/EEC/317 (20 November 2007); G/SPS/N/EEC/321 (22 January 2008); G/SPS/N/EEC/329 (3 April 2008). With regard to the latter, the publication was notified under G/SPS/N/EEC/328/Add1 (10 July 2008), but this will not have been obvious to other Members trying to follow up on the original notification. Lapses regarding publication are notable, given that this failing has been one of the specific complaints raised by the EU in the past. See G/SPS/W/159 (n 24) paras 4–5.

[71] See Appendix I for details. The EU's long-term performance is no better in this respect. In 2007, the EU reported the overall notification of 20 co-decision proposals. See G/SPS/GEN/803 (10 October 2007) para 4 and Annex.

[72] See ns 39–42 and related text.

[73] See n 33 and related text.

[74] See for example Commission Decision 2008/752/EC [2008] OJ L261/1, Art 2 (providing a 6 month period to amend certification for import of ungulate animals).

Timeliness

At first glance, the EU's adherence to the timing established by the Transparency Procedures appears exemplary. Of the 18 food-safety-related notifications forwarded in 2008 by the EU, 11 provided the recommended 60 days for comment[75] and two welcomed comments at any time as the regulations were subject to continual review.[76] Of the remaining five, two were emergency measures (absolving the need to provide a comments period),[77] and two were bilateral measures not requiring comment from unaffected third countries.[78] Only one notification appears to fall short of the expectations of the SPS Committee, providing only 43 days to comment on data requirements established by the European Food Safety Authority (EFSA) relating to the assessment of food-contact materials.[79]

Nevertheless, more detailed examination of these notifications casts some doubt on the EU's commitment to take account of third-country input. The purpose of the sixty-day period is to 'allow reasonable time for other Members to make comments in writing, discuss these comments upon request, and take the comments and the results of the discussions into account'[80] However, in the case of one Regulation establishing limits for various contaminants, the decisive decisions on the proposal took place only eight days and 24 days respectively after the circulation of the relevant notifications.[81] In the case of a Commission Decision on flavoring substances, the text of the regulation had already been adopted by the time the notification arrived at the WTO.[82]

[75] This is the case for G/SPS/N/EEC/316 (n 70); G/SPS/N/EEC/317 (n 70); G/SPS/N/EEC/318 (21 November 2007); G/SPS/N/EEC/319 318 (21 November 2007); G/SPS/N/EEC/328 (18 March 2008); G/SPS/N/EEC/329 (n 70); G/SPS/N/EEC/330 (n 57); G/SPS/N/EEC/331 (14 July 2008); G/SPS/N/EEC/335 (n 59); G/SPS/N/EEC/336 (11 November 2008); G/SPS/N/EEC/338 (24 December 2008).

[76] G/SPS/N/EEC/323 (5 February 2008); G/SPS/N/EEC/326 (3 March 2008).

[77] Annex B, para 6 permits Members to 'omit' some of the standard requirements for notification in cases where 'urgent problems of health protection arise or threaten to rise'. The two emergency notifications presented by the EU in 2008 are G/SPS/N/EEC/324 (27 February 2008); G/SPS/N/EEC/339 (8 January 2008).

[78] G/SPS/N/EEC/332 (12 August 2008) (relating to guar gum from India); G/SPS/N/EEC/333 (n 55) (concerning sunflower oil of Ukrainian origin).

[79] G/SPS/N/EEC/321 (n 70).

[80] SPS Agreement Annex B, para 5(d).

[81] The relevant decisions on contaminants in foodstuffs relating to regulations notified in G/SPS/N/EEC/328 (n 75) and G/SPS/N/EEC/329 (n 75) can be found in European Commission, 'Summary Record of the Standing Committee on the Food Chain and Animal Health, Section Toxicological Safety of the Food Chain' (SANCO–D1 (2008) D/410761, 11 April 2008) 1–2.

[82] G/SPS/N/EEC/328 (n 75) was notified on 24 December 2008, the measure having been adopted by Member States 12 days earlier. See 'Summary Record of the Standing Committee on the Food Chain and Animal Health, Section Toxicological Safety of the Food Chain' (SANCO–D1 (2008) D/412413, 12 December 2008) 1.

Interaction with WTO Members[83]

The significance of transparency lies not only in the original notification made by a WTO Member, but in the interaction between Members that it stimulates. The EU receives around 35 comments annually through the NA & EP.[84] The comments can take the form of a request for further information, a signal of impending trade problems or a more specific proposal for amending the legislative text. In response, the EU may provide additional information about the regulatory measure: for example, relevant scientific opinions or a full version of the proposed text.[85] Replies of this sort permit the EU to elaborate on the sometimes brief information provided in the original notification. Alternatively, where comments question or challenge elements of the EU's proposal and request specific changes, the EU will provide a more lengthy response outlining its views on the comments submitted and any action it has undertaken.

The extent to which the EU can take the comments made into account will vary. For example, in response to Ecuadorian fears about the negative effect on trade of pineapples resulting from the planned reduction of a maximum residue level for the pesticide ethephon, the EU proposed in November 2008 the introduction of a temporary Maximum Residue Level of 0.5 mg/kg for 12 months, subject to submitting additional scientific data.[86] In this way, the EU sought to maximize the flexibility available within the constraints of the scientific advice received. The Commission's capacity to respond to issues raised by third countries is sometimes limited. As EU measures are grounded upon EFSA risk evaluations, the Commission may not be able to take into account the concerns raised by a third country unless they are accompanied by relevant scientific data. Thus, for instance, the response to Japan's complaint in early 2008 about the deletion of six substances from the new EU flavorings register was to invite the country to submit a formal application and adequate safety data. Nor, even if the Commission is inclined to introduce new elements into a proposal at the behest of a third country, will these amendments necessarily get the support of Member States. For example, Commission recommendations for a new wording for poultry certificates to accommodate US exports in early 2008 were subsequently rejected by Member State experts due to a perceived conflict with other aspects of EU law.[87] In other words, commenting does not in itself provide an

[83] The detail of the cases below is provided thanks to the kind help of the EU NA & EP.

[84] In 2008, 36 comments were made in total originating from 10 countries, the majority of which were food safety related. For further information, see European Commission, 'EU NA & EP Activity Report Year 2008' (n 45) 1.

[85] By way of example, the EU responded in July 2008 to US comments on a proposal for setting maximum levels for certain contaminants in foodstuffs (G/SPS/N/EEC/328) (n 75) with a detailed explanation of the scientific basis for each of the new levels and relevant references.

[86] Commission Regulation 1097/2009 [2009] OJ L301/6.

[87] The US comments in response to notification G/SPS/N/EEC/320 (30 November 2007) concerned the incompatibility of EU requirements to issue certificates on the day of inspection of one-day old chicks with the US practice of issuing certificates at the moment of consignment. Member States had already agreed in November 2007 to make compromises on this requirement.

easy short cut for a third country seeking to advance its interests. But it is far from redundant. Comments can set in motion an important process of dialogue aimed at resolving problems. If an amendment to the proposal is not feasible, acceptable alternative solutions (as in the US poultry case), a long-term plan of action or technical assistance can be established.[88]

6.2.3 *Reflections on EU Transparency*

How are we to explain the EU's performance in opening up its decision-making process to external scrutiny and influence? With regard to some regulations, transparency has generated valuable dialogue between the EU and trading partners. Yet many measures appear not to have been put forward, or at times too late, for international scrutiny. There are three factors that help explain the inconsistent implementation of transparency commitments.

The Value of Notification

One dilemma for any WTO Member is whether the notification of a new measure is worthwhile. For example, where regulations are addressed to specific countries and the result of intense bilateral discussions, controls and scientific exchanges, the added value of SPS notification may be questionable.[89] The EU's poor record in notifying, via addenda, changes to legislative proposals that arise during inter-institutional discussions is also understandable. Many amendments to legislation proposed during this process are ultimately discarded as new compromises have to be reached. Seeking intermittent third-country comment during this process could generate considerable and ultimately unnecessary work for administrators.[90] Equally, the lower priority placed by the EU on Member States' notifications is not unreasonable. Many Member State proposals are particularly relevant to local production or culinary habits and may be assumed to have little relevance for trading

However, the US followed up with a request to certify day-old chicks before they were hatched, a demand which was incompatible with Council Directive 96/93/EEC [1997] OJ L13/97. A series of discussions between EU and US representatives finally led the US to revise its internal procedures for consultation in order to meet amended EU requirements.

[88] See European Commission, 'EU NA & EP Activity Report Year 2005' (n 39) 7 (in which the EU's commitment to providing technical assistance in this context is stressed).

[89] This would certainly be the case for the updating of lists of authorized third countries for exporting animal products to the EU or approvals of third country residue monitoring plans.

[90] In the EU context, a single sounding of overall third country interests, in response to the original notification, may be the only efficient manner to incorporate concerns. This is the tenor of EU comments that 'there are advantages in notifying proposals to the European Parliament at early stage (*sic*) because there is still time to introduce changes.' G/SPS/GEN/803 (n 71) para 4.

partners.[91] Indeed, the EU's explanation for the non-notification of Member States' SPS measures points in this direction.[92]

Some WTO Members opt for an extremely comprehensive approach towards notification even where the value, or even SPS relevance, may be highly limited.[93] In this respect, the EU's practice may be viewed as judicious rather than errant, given that WTO Members already struggle to manage the existing level of notifications.[94] A little less notification by some countries may better serve the aims of transparency, or at least ensure a greater focus on measures most important for international trade.

Outstanding Ambiguities

In spite of the notable efforts to clarify transparency provisions through Transparency Procedures, there is a significant level of subjective judgment involved in whether or not to notify a given proposal. SPS, TBT or both? Regular notification, addendum or emergency notification?[95] A seemingly inconsistent approach to notification may therefore, in large part, reflect these ambiguities. Nor, it would seem, is further clarification necessarily the answer. Consider, for example, the new notification format which has provided Members since 1 December 2008 with the option of indicating whether or not a regulation conforms to an international standard.[96] Intended to stimulate more comprehensive notification of regulations, a new dilemma is created for the notifier. A regulation can be in conformity (or not in contradiction) with an international standard, but yet highly disruptive to trade. For example, the EU has introduced additional import controls for products considered to be of particular risk.[97] While arguably 'in conformity' with Codex standards (the

[91] Consider, for example, Slovenian rules on the amendments to certain hygiene-related technical requirements for milk processing factories on high mountains, TRIS 2008/274/SI. See n 70. An indication of the limited impact of national legislation is that only four specific trade concerns have ever been raised in relation to specific EU Member State regulations or practices. See G/SPS/R/17 (24 February 2000) paras 87–88; G/SPS/R/31 (23 December 2003) paras 47–49; R/36/Rev.1 (14 June 2005) paras 32–33; G/SPS/R/37/Rev.1 (18 August 2005) paras 72–73.

[92] In its 2009 Trade Policy Review, the EU claimed that 'as external trade issues are to a large extent harmonized at the EU level, including in the field of SPS, it is very unusual for problems of MS compliance with their WTO/SPS Agreement obligations to arise.' WT/TPR/M/214/Add.1 (2 July 2009) 219.

[93] Brazil, for example, has a reputation for being very thorough, but not particularly selective in its notifications. See, e.g. G/SPS/N/BRA/417 (19 May 2008) (notifying quality standards for fermented beverages seemingly unrelated to public health concerns).

[94] This is an observation made by the EU NA & EP in an interview in November 2009.

[95] The reported practice in the EU is to consider 'secondary' changes, such as changes to Annexes as Addenda, and significant textural changes to a Regulation as meriting notification. Third countries could be excused for not grasping the distinction. Consider the different approaches to revisions to substance limits in pesticides legislations (via addenda under G/SPS/N/EEC/196, 11 April 2004) and contaminants (via regular notification under G/SPS/N/EEC/328, n 85).

[96] See 'Transparency Procedures' (n 5) Annex A–1.

[97] Commission Regulation 669/2009 [2009] OJ L194/11. This regulation was notified as in conformity with international standards under G/SPS/N/EEC/341 (18 March 2008).

products are only targeted when regularly breaching international standards), this designation at the time of notification considerably understates the potential impact on trade. This is not simply a pedantic quibble about the word 'conformity'. In practical terms, the new SPS Information Management System permits WTO Members to filter notifications using criteria such as 'conformity to standards' and thus enhance efficiency in monitoring regulatory developments.[98] In this instance, a potentially trade-disruptive regulation may be overlooked due to the assumption that conformity with international standards implies limited trade impact. Attempts made in good faith to enhance transparency may inadvertently mislead.

Organizational Complexity

In addition to the above dilemmas, the European decision-making process offers its own unique challenges to the administrators responsible for SPS transparency. The decision to notify an SPS measure will typically involve various Commission Directorate Generals (e.g. consumer protection, agriculture, enterprise, and trade), the Standing Committee on the Food Chain and EU Member State contact points.[99] Once notified, tracking the development of policy proposals is further complicated by inter-institutional discussions between the Commission, Council and European Parliament. The SPS NA & EP is therefore to a large extent reliant on the varying attentiveness of individuals in the different units across the European Commission's Directorate General for Health and Consumers (DG Sanco). While such complexities do not exonerate the EU for its sometimes tardy notifications, it may point to inefficiency rather than evasiveness as the cause.

On occasions, one suspects that political motivations shape the EU's transparency decisions.[100] Yet in the vast majority of cases, non-notification of measures in 2008 can be explained by the specific applicability of the measures or their bilateral nature and do not appear in practice to have had significant consequences for trading partners.[101] The delays in timing are more troubling as they potentially subvert the opportunity for dialogue and problem-solving that transparency creates. Initiatives are under way to standardize and improve the efficiency of SPS

---

[98] G/SPS/R/47 (8 January 2008) para 21.

[99] For a detailed explanation of this process, see the flowcharts in G/SPS/GEN/456 (n 64) 10–11.

[100] Non-notification of the proposal relating to microbiological treatment referred to above (n 61) could be one example. Another is the finding of food imported from China adulterated with melamine. The EU was reluctant to bring the matter formally to the attention of the SPS Community and only did so (G/SPS/N/EEC/339, n 77) following interventions by other trading partners.

[101] This conclusion is drawn from analysis of trade concerns raised about EU SPS measures by WTO Members since 2008 (see the SPS Information Management System, spsims.wto.org) and comments made by third countries in 2009 and 2011 EU WTO Trade Policy Reviews, see WT/TPR/M/214/Add.1 (n 92) and WTO/TPR/M/248/Add.1 (31 August 2011) respectively. While there are numerous criticisms of various aspects of EU policy, these do not concern those non-notified measures listed in Appendix I.

notification practices across all units of the European Commission's DG Sanco.[102] Notwithstanding the identified lapses, it should be noted that the EU has also often gone beyond SPS requirements, notifying measures that would not necessarily constitute regulations, including scientific guidance documents and Commission recommendations.[103] Moreover, the EU regularly provides explanatory communications on new legislation or regulatory developments,[104] and requests comments on particular regulatory issues even prior to the preparation of a draft proposal.[105] It has proactively sought an inclusive approach to notification and seeks to share its own experience in managing notifications and comments to the benefit of developing countries.[106] In short, while there is scope for improvement, considerable efforts are made to involve third countries in the EU's regulatory process.

6.3 Equivalence

The general principle underpinning the SPS discipline of equivalence is simple. As states strive to find suitable responses to different climatic, economic and political circumstances, divergence in regulatory practices is inevitable.[107] Equivalence looks to minimise the impact of such differences, by obliging WTO Members to recognise, under certain conditions, the validity of another Member's regulations. While the application of equivalence can facilitate trade between all WTO Members, it is expected, in particular, to help open up developed-country markets to developing countries.[108] This section describes the SPS regime's requirements for equivalence and evaluates the EU's application of SPS obligations.

[102] In October 2011, the Multilateral International Relations Unit in DG Sanco responsible for the EU NA & EP produced a detailed internal Procedural Manual to facilitate a standardised approach by Commission officials to the SPS notification process.

[103] See G/SPS/N/EEC/321 (n 70) (relating to EFSA Guidance on submission of a dossier for safety evaluation of recycling practices for food contact materials); G/SPS/N/EEC/135 (6 August 2001) (Recommendation on the reduction of the presence of dioxins and PCBs in feedingstuffs).

[104] See, for example, G/SPS/GEN/557 (29 March 2005) (on active substances for plant protection); G/SPS/GEN/539 (4 February 2005) (on food traceability); G/SPS/GEN/588 (8 July 2005) (on regionalization).

[105] See G/SPS/GEN/719 (8 August 2006) (calling for 'early comments' on a Commission report on animal by-products not intended for human consumption).

[106] Under the mentoring system first proposed by New Zealand (see G/SPS/W/214, 1 October 2007), the EU currently provides assistance to Senegal and Kenya.

[107] See S Zarrilli, 'WTO Agreement on the Sanitary and Phytosanitary Measures: Issues for Developing Countries' (South Centre 1999) s III.3, www.carib-export.com/obic/documents/WTO_Agreement_On_Sanitary_and_Phytosanitary_Measures.pdf.

[108] Zarrilli sees equivalence as 'a key instrument to enhance market access for [developing countries'] products'. ibid. See also G/L/445 (21 March 2001) para 7.

6.3.1 The SPS Equivalence Disciplines

Article 4 of the SPS Agreement sets out the substantive and procedural elements of equivalence.

Substantive Disciplines

Article 4 establishes an obligation on all Members to accept sanitary measures in place in other countries that provide an equivalent level of sanitary protection. The burden for demonstrating the equivalence of sanitary measures lies with the exporting Member, who must 'objectively demonstrate' that it meets the importing Member's appropriate level of protection (ALOP).[109] The substantive obligations have been described as 'clear and binding',[110] but appear less so on further scrutiny:

Which ALOP Does an Exporting State Have to Meet?

In *Australia—Salmon*, the Appellate Body (AB) set out in some detail the relationship between a regulatory measure and the ALOP established by a WTO Member. It explained that the ALOP is an 'objective' chosen prior to and therefore independent from the measure adopted.[111] The ALOP cannot be inferred from the measure adopted, as a state can put in place a measure that in practice falls short of the objective ALOP foreseen.[112] In the context of equivalence, this would imply that, regardless of the actual measures in place in the country of destination, the exporting country would have to meet (and objectively demonstrate) the consumer-protection aspirations of the importing country. Indeed, the 'Equivalence Decision'—adopted by the SPS Committee with a view to assisting the implementation of Article 4– confirms that the 'importing Member should indicate the appropriate level of protection which its sanitary or phytosanitary measure is designed to achieve'.[113] Nevertheless

---

[109] SPS Agreement Art 4.1.

[110] Prévost (n 2) 759.

[111] To cite in full, the AB found:

The "appropriate level of protection" established by a Member and the "SPS measure" have to be clearly distinguished. They are not one and the same thing. The first is an *objective*, the second is an *instrument* chosen to attain or implement that objective. It can be deduced from the provisions of the *SPS Agreement* that the determination by a Member of the "appropriate level of protection" logically precedes the establishment or decision on maintenance of an "SPS measure".

Australia—Measures Affecting Importation of Salmon (Australia—Salmon), Appellate Body Report (adopted 20 October 1998) WT/DS18/AB/R, paras 200–201 (footnote omitted, emphasis in original).

[112] *Australia—Salmon*, Appellate Body Report, para 203.

[113] SPS Committee, 'Decision on the Implementation of Article 4 of the Agreement in the Application of Sanitary and Phytosanitary Measures'('Equivalence Decision') G/SPS/19/Rev.2 (23 July 2004) para 2. It should be noted that the legal status of this Decision is unclear. The Panel in *US*

the same Decision later blurs the concept.[114] The importing Member is instructed to take into account not its chosen ALOP, but whether the exporting Member's measures 'achieve the level of protection *provided* by its own relevant sanitary or phytosanitary measures'.[115] More confusion ensues when the Equivalence Decision calls on Members to 'consider the risk of the product to which the sanitary and phytosanitary measures are applied, in order to reduce requirements … in cases of low risk'.[116] This would appear to replace the AB's defined process (identify ALOP, analyse risk, then establish measure), with an approach (analyse risk, then establish measure) which does away with the ALOP entirely.[117]

Such inconsistencies are not merely quirks in Committee drafting. They reflect the real difficulty, both conceptually and practically, in maintaining the clear distinction between ALOP and measure in the manner prescribed by the AB.[118] By way of illustration, consider Australia's acceptance of an exception to the mandatory pasteurisation of cheese for certain Swiss raw-milk (non-pasteurised) cheeses. Australia recognised equivalence after Swiss exporters had demonstrated that the hard cheeses 'attained at least the same level of pathogen destruction' as pasteurisation.[119] In this instance, it was the measure, not the ALOP, that served as the practical marker for determining equivalence. In many situations, there may therefore be considerable doubt for exporting countries as to the level of protection to which they must aspire. Nor is it clear that the same ALOP can be applied in practice across all WTO members. As Regan has pointed out, having identified systemic weaknesses in the way certain countries manage food risks, WTO members can hardly be blamed for stringent measures that may exceed that member's customary ALOP.[120]

How is an Objective Demonstration of Equivalence Provided?

Assuming that an ALOP can be clearly determined, how can the exporting state meet the importers' expectations? The burden associated with the 'objective demonstration' of equivalence can vary greatly according to the type of sanitary

Poultry, while considering the Decision to contribute to Members understanding of equivalence, note that it 'is not binding and does not determine the scope of Article 4'. *United States—Certain Measures Affecting Imports of Poultry from China*, Panel Report (adopted 29 September 2010) WT/DS392/R, para 7.136. For a discussion hereof, see Marsha Echols, 'Equivalence and risk regulation under the World Trade Organization's SPS Agreement' in G Van Calster and D Prévost (eds), *Research Handbook on Environment, Health and the WTO* (Cheltenham, Edward Elgar, 2013) 94.

[114] Scott (n 2) 166–167.

[115] 'Equivalence Decision' (n 113) para 7 (emphasis added).

[116] 'Equivalence Decision' (n 113) para 5.

[117] It in fact implies that Members are maintaining measures that are not justified by the risk concerned, which would arguably anyway breach Article 2.2.

[118] Note, in this respect, US comments on equivalence, G/SPS/GEN/212 (7 November 2000) para 15 (bemoaning the 'inherent difficulty in linking numerous and disparate measures to a country's ALOP').

[119] G/SPS/GEN/243 (9 April 2001) para 7.

[120] D Regan, '*United States—Certain Measures Affecting Imports of Poultry from China*: The Fascinating Case that Wasn't' (2012) 11 *World Trade Review* 273, 285.

measure under consideration. For example, a New Zealand ban on a previously permitted fumigant as a disinfestation treatment for fruit fly prevented imports of fruit from South Pacific countries. The objective sought by New Zealand—non-infestation of fruit flies—could be relatively easily demonstrated through appropriate testing of an alternative high-temperature forced-air treatment.[121] However, these are, to use the categorisation terminology provided by Codex Alimentarius, 'specific requirements'.[122] Equivalence of assessments of sanitary measures that are more systemic in nature, relating either to 'infrastructure' or 'programme design, implementation and monitoring', are inevitably more qualitative in nature.[123] The determination of equivalence will rarely, as in the fruit-fly case, be limited to a single process. The EU, for example, in ascertaining the suitability of third countries as an origin for animal products, takes into account a long list of factors, including third-country legislation, quality and competence of inspection services and laboratories, and the results of inspections or audits.[124] A decade of discussions in Codex Alimentarius has brought considerable guidance in establishing a fair equivalence evaluation process.[125] Yet ultimately, as noted by the pertinent Codex Committee, 'the determination of the [ALOP] by a country [is] essentially a value judgement rather than a scientific determination.'[126] In reality, any 'objective demonstration' will therefore be highly dependent on the judgement and goodwill of the importing country.

Procedural Disciplines

The clearest procedural obligation in Article 4 is that WTO Members 'upon request, enter into consultations with the aim of achieving bilateral and multilateral agreements'. Some have expressed disappointment at the vagueness of these commitments.[127] The Equivalence Decision addresses this to a certain extent by establishing elements of good procedural practice. Firstly, WTO Members should respond to requests for consultation 'in a timely manner … normally within a six-month

---

[121] G/SPS/GEN/232 (28 February 2001) para 10.

[122] Codex Alimentarius, 'Guidelines on the Judgement of Equivalence of Sanitary Measures Associated Food Inspection and Certification Systems' ('Codex Equivalence Guidelines') (CACGL 53-2003) para 13.

[123] 'Infrastructure' includes the legal framework and administrative systems, whereas 'programme design, implementation and monitoring' refers to documentation systems, monitoring and laboratory capabilities and certification and audit capacities. ibid para 13.

[124] See European Commission, 'General Guidance on EU import and transit rules for live animals and animal products from third countries' (SANCO/7166/2010) ('Commission General Guidance on EU Imports') 4–6, ec.europa.eu/food/international/trade/index_en.htm.

[125] In addition to the 'Codex Equivalence Guidelines' (n 122), see Codex Alimentarius, 'Guidelines for the Development of Equivalence Agreements regarding Food Inspection and Certification Systems' (CAC/GL 34-1999).

[126] ALINORM 01/30A, para 78.

[127] See Prévost (n 2) 769.

period'.[128] Secondly, where there has historically been experience in food trade, this process should be accelerated.[129] Thirdly, there is a commitment not to use a request for equivalence consultations as a pretext for disrupting trade, a response that would obviously discourage equivalence and undermine its trade-facilitating objective.[130] Fourthly, the Equivalence Decision draws into the operation of Article 4 the commitment under Article 9 to provide technical assistance.[131] Finally, the Decision establishes the importance of regularly informing the SPS Committee of equivalence activities.[132]

6.3.2 The EU's Application of SPS Equivalence Disciplines

From the discussion thus far, it may appear that equivalence is primarily a technical issue. However, the extent to which equivalence is or is not applied by developed countries is the object of sustained criticism on two opposing fronts. On the one hand, exporting countries frequently accuse importing states of being insufficiently sensitive to the conditions faced by their food businesses. Some consider that EU rules are excessively stringent, at best placing an unnecessary strain on developing country operators, at worst deliberately sustaining protectionism.[133] European rules are not always sensitive to the small-scale nature of many developing-country businesses,[134] and in some cases have prevented exports with no evidence of the food in question being unsafe for consumption.[135] Furthermore, there can be an

[128] 'Equivalence Decision' (n 113) para 3.

[129] 'Equivalence Decision', ibid para 5.

[130] 'Equivalence Decision', ibid para 7.

[131] 'Equivalence Decision', ibid para 8.

[132] 'Equivalence Decision', ibid para 12.

[133] The suspicion of deliberate obstruction of agricultural imports is never far away. Mehta and George, for example, claim that 'it has been a strategy of EU countries to introduce newer and stricter residue limits every time a need arises to restrict imports from developing countries.' R Mehta and J George, 'Processed Food Products Exports from India: An Exploration with SPS Regime' (Joint Research Project sponsored by the Australian Centre for International Agricultural Research, 2003) 20, digitalcollections.anu.edu.au/bitstream/1885/41962/1/aciar%20_2003_mehta_george.pdf.

[134] See, for example, M Broberg, 'European Food Safety Regulation and the Developing Countries: Regulatory Problems and Possibilities' (DIIS Working Paper 2009:09) 11–12 (citing the example of the difficulty of monitoring Indian dairy producers reliant on many farmers with a limited number of cows) www.acp-eu-trade.org/library/files/Morten_EN_010109_DIIS_European_Food_Safety_Regulation_web.pdf; O'Connor and Company, 'The EC Traceability and Equivalence Rules in Light of the SPS Agreement: A Review of the Many Legal Issues' (CTA 2003) 17 (explaining the difficulties of applying traceability rules in countries where producers will combine products in order to have adequate exportable quantities) agritrade.cta.int/en/content/view/full/1696.

[135] S Ponte, 'Bands, Tests and Alchemy: Food Safety Standards and the Ugandan Fish Export Industry' (DIIS Working Paper 2005:19) 57 (pointing to the lack of any evidence of unsafe fish in the case of the EU's ban of imports of Ugandan fish) subweb.diis.dk/graphics/Publications/WP2005/19_spo_bans_tests_alchemy.pdf.

imbalance between the real health advantages of stricter regulations and the costs incurred.[136] On the other hand, any efforts to accommodate such criticisms risk inciting the wrath of consumers in importing countries. How, it has been asked in the US, can responsible governments expose their consumers to food imported from countries 'whose regulatory systems are simply not up to the task'?[137] Although concerns about the EU's treatment of imports are raised, the accusation generally levelled at the EU is one of unnecessarily high standards rather than insufficient protection from food imports.[138]

Such doughty criticisms of the EU do not *per se* imply any breach of SPS obligations by the EU. As was the case in the EU's 2009 Trade Policy Review, any general assertion that EU measures are excessively stringent can be met with a simple legal rebuff: the EU has the right under SPS Agreement Article 2(1) to protect consumer health and, under Article 3(3), to maintain a level of protection higher than international standards where supported by scientific justification.[139] However, they are highlighted here to illustrate the treacherous political terrain that regulators and inspectors must negotiate when involved in equivalence assessments and underline the critical eye that must be cast over EU practice. With this in mind, we examine the EU's performance with regard to the substantive and procedural elements identified above.

Substantive Elements

The SPS Committee has established that equivalence can be applied in different ways: (i) formal agreements recognising equivalence; (ii) agreements establishing equivalence for specific products; and (iii) *ad hoc* acceptance of specific elements

---

[136] In a much-cited paper, it was demonstrated that EU aflatoxin standards, stricter than international limits, would decrease African exports by 64 % while reducing health risk by around 1.4 deaths per billion per year. T Otsuki, JS Wilson and M Sewadeh, 'Saving Two in a Billion: Quantifying the Trade Effect of European Food Safety Standards in African Exports' (2001) 26 *Food Policy* 495. For a robust counter to this perspective, see LB Diaz Rios and S Jaffee, 'Barrier, Catalyst or Distraction? Standards, Competitiveness, and Africa's Groundnut Exports to Europe' (World Bank, Agricultural, and Rural Development Discussion Paper 39, 2008) siteresources.worldbank.org/INTARD/Resources/AflatoxinPaperWEBpdf.

[137] 'Public Citizen's Global Trade Watch Director Lori Wallach Testifies before House Appropriations Subcommittee on Culture, Rural Development, FDA and Related Agencies' *Fair Disclosure Wire* (28 July 2009).

[138] While a less prominent consumer concern than in the US, research has demonstrated that, European consumers are more concerned about the safety of imported than EU origin food (54 % and 34 % respectively). Safe Food, *Where does our Food Come from?* (July 2009) www.safefood.eu/Publications/Research-reports/Where-does-our-food-come-from-.aspx.

[139] See WT/TPR/214/Add.1 (2 July 2009) 213–214 (in response to a series of Canadian questions attempting, in vain, to draw the EU into more expansive reflections on its sanitary regime).

of SPS measures.[140] The EU's approach to equivalence embraces each of these various forms.

Equivalence Agreements

The EU has negotiated several SPS-related agreements with third countries, including Canada, Chile, Mexico, New Zealand and the US.[141] Such agreements can be uniquely concerned with sanitary and animal-health issues or form part of a broader free-trade agreement. Until now, the EU's sanitary agreements have primarily been focused on measures applicable to trade in live animals and animal products, but agreements with Chile and Switzerland have also included other agricultural products.[142] These agreements typically foresee a series of working procedures aimed at supporting discussions on equivalence, not dissimilar to those proposed by the SPS Committee's Equivalence Decision. A series of annexes then stipulate in which areas equivalence has been determined or requires further discussion. Equivalence is therefore very much a work in progress, whose status is regularly updated.[143] Oversight of work on equivalence falls to a joint management committee made up of EU and trading-partner representatives. Formal recognition of equivalence is prized as it can reduce the number of physical checks of imported products, thereby enhancing the exporter's position as a trading partner.[144] In addition, it may permit a simplification in certification and greater flexibility in the issuing of documentation.[145]

Notwithstanding some positive experiences with EU equivalence agreements,[146] many countries have raised doubts about the viability of wide-ranging agreements.

[140] G/L/423 (29 November 2000) para 7. See also Regan (n 120) 293–295 (reflecting on the mertis of different types of origin-neutral and origin-specific equivalence regimes given the aims of SPS Agreement Article 4).

[141] For an overview of all existing EU sanitary and phytosanitary agreements, see ec.europa.eu/food/international/trade/agreements_en.htm.

[142] The EU's attempt to negotiate a free trade agreement (FTA) with Canada is also reported to include SPS provisions extending beyond those currently included in the Veterinary Agreement. 'Significant Challenges Remain as Canada, EU Seek FTA Mandates' *Inside US Trade* (10 April 2009).

[143] The EU's agreement with New Zealand, for instance, has been revised on four occasions between 1996 and 2006. For details, see webpage indicated in n 141.

[144] All imports of animal products into the EU are subject to documentary checks, identity checks and where appropriate, physical checks.

[145] In the case of the Agreement between the EU and New Zealand, for example, the necessary certification can be delivered while the consignment is in transit rather than having to accompany the consignment, provided that it is available to border inspectors on arrival in the EU. See H Batho et al. 'The EU Veterinarian: Animal health, welfare and veterinary public health developments in Europe since 1957' (European Commission, August 2007) 435 ('The EU Veterinarian') ec.europa.eu/food/resources/the_eu_veterinarian_080410.pdf.

[146] From the veterinary perspective, the view is that 'the increased information exchange has given a greater understanding of, and confidence in, all parties' veterinary systems and has probably resulted in fewer trade disputes'. ibid 438.

The US, in particular, has voiced its scepticism about the real benefits accruing to equivalence agreements given the considerable time and resources involved.[147]

Agreements Establishing Equivalence for Specific Products

The EU's application of the equivalence principle to specific products, although then not termed as such, dates back to 1972, when the Council established that third countries exporting to the Community had to provide equivalent guarantees of animal and public health.[148] The EU could therefore legitimately use its treatment of animal imports to illustrate to the SPS Committee how equivalence influences 'its day-to-day work'.[149] As noted above, equivalence in this context relates to the capacity of the entire system—legislative structure, inspection competence, staff and infrastructure—to provide the level of protection considered appropriate by the EU. The process of establishing equivalence for animal products can be briefly summarised as follows.[150] The third-country national authority with an exporting interest requests approval from the European Commission, providing a dossier outlining the products, anticipated trade involved and confirming the capacity of its establishments to meet EU requirements. The Commission then sends a questionnaire to the applying authorities, the answers to which form the basis of future dialogue. An inspection by the Commission's Food and Veterinary Office (FVO) generally follows. A satisfactory report leads the Commission to prepare legislation adding the third country to the relevant list of approved exporters. The EU considers equivalence as 'an important trump for developing countries', reporting a doubling of imports in the decade since its introduction.[151]

Ad Hoc Acceptance of Specific Elements of SPS Measures

On occasions, specific issues arise that cannot be treated horizontally, because the problem itself is either specific to, or particular severe within, that country. In such cases, the principle of equivalence can form a basis for *ad hoc* solutions. Two cases involving US imports in 2008 are illustrative. The EU has consistently found high levels of toxins in imports of nuts,[152] and national authorities consequently increase

---

[147] See US comments in G/SPS/GEN/212 (n 118) para 16. For a discussion of the complexities surrounding meat equivalence, see Echols (n 113) 97–99.

[148] Council Directive 72/462/EEC on health and veterinary inspection problems upon importation of bovine animals and swine and fresh meat from third countries [1972] OJ L302/28.

[149] G/SPS/GEN/304 (12 March 2002) para 3. The EU's comments pertained specifically to the import conditions for fishery products, but are equally valid for other animal products.

[150] For more detail of this process and the relevant European legislation, see 'Commission General Guidance on EU Imports' (n 124).

[151] G/SPS/GEN/304 (n 149) paras 11–12.

[152] In 2008, 10 % of all Rapid Alerts notified related to mycotoxin contamination, of which 76 % were related to nuts and nut products. European Commission, *Rapid Alert System for Food and*

routine controls.[153] However, given that occurrences of excessive levels of aflatoxin in US peanuts are relatively limited, the high frequency of controls was disproportionate to the risk. The EU and US therefore worked towards a pre-export system of checks based on sampling and analysis, performed by approved laboratories and the provision of certificates signed by the US Department of Agriculture.[154] On the basis of confidence established in the US control systems in place, the Commission could adopt a Decision which 'significantly reduced' the physical checks undertaken by Member State authorities.[155]

A second example is the case of contamination of US rice by the unauthorised GM event LibertyLink (LL) Rice 601.[156] Discussions between the European and US administrations early after the incident occurred in August 2006 explored the idea of EU recognition of US certificates establishing the absence of GM in rice consignments. However, diverging views as to the appropriate method of sampling led these discussions to falter and mandatory testing of all imports of US long-grain rice ensued.[157] Nevertheless, continued dialogue with US authorities[158] finally resulted in 2008 in a protocol recognising the validity of US official sampling procedures, permitting the cessation of mandatory testing.[159]

The types of activities outlined above demonstrate the EU's evident commitment to engaging with third countries. However, developing countries have specifically criticised developed WTO Members for demanding the introduction of

---

Feed Annual Report 2008 (Office for Official Publications of the European Communities 2008) 20 and 37 respectively.

[153] Regulation (EC) No 882/2004 of the European Parliament and of the Council on official controls performed to ensure the verification of compliance with feed and food law, animal health and animal welfare rules [2004] OJ L165/1, Art 3 (providing that the frequency of official controls should be determined by the level of risk).

[154] Confidence in the US control systems was established through an FVO visit in September 2006 and subsequent follow-up on the recommendations made. See European Commission, 'Final Report of a Mission Carried out in the United States of America from 18 September to 22 September 2006 in Order to Assess Control Systems in Place to Control Aflatoxin Contamination in Peanuts Intended for Export to the European Union' (DG (Sanco)/8117/2006–MR Final). All FVO reports are available at ec.europa.eu/food/fvo/index_en.cfm.

[155] See Commission Decision 2008/47/EC approving the pre-export checks carried out the United States of America on peanuts and derived products thereof as regards the presence of aflatoxins [2008] OJ L11/12, in particular Art 4.

[156] For background to this incident, see D Schramm, 'The Race to Geneva: Resisting the Gravitational Pull of the WTO in the GMO Labelling Controversy' (2007) 9 *Vermont Journal of Environmental Law* 93.

[157] Commission Decision 2006/601/EC on emergency measures regarding the non-authorised genetically modified organism 'LL RICE 601' in rice products [2006] OJ L306/17.

[158] See European Commission, 'Summary Record of the Standing Committee on the Food Chain and Animal Health, Held in Brussels on 10 October 2007'; 'Summary Record of the Standing Committee on the Food Chain and Animal Health, Held in Brussels on 19 and 20 December 2007'. Both are available at ec.europa.eu/food/committees/regulatory/scfcah/modif_genet/index_en.htm.

[159] Commission Decision 2008/162/EC amending decision 2006/601/EEC on emergency measures regarding the non-authorised genetically modified organism 'LL RICE 601' in rice products [2008] OJ L52/25.

the 'same' SPS measures, rather than accepting equivalent ones.[160] If the EU could be demonstrated to insist upon sameness, rather than equivalence, the influence of SPS Agreement Article 4 in European policy would indeed be placed in question. A useful insight into the EU's practice in this respect is offered by the FVO's inspection reports. A number of elements suggest that equivalence, and not sameness, is the EU's goal. Firstly, the EU generally adopts a primarily systems-based approach rather than focusing on specific measures.[161] Assessing the implementation of Hazard Analysis Critical Control Point (HACCP)-based procedures[162] is particularly important for the FVO, establishing principles that are sufficiently broad to permit a range of third-country measures.[163] Secondly, equivalence inspection is not the dogmatic application of European norms, but is rather 'tailor-made' to the particular conditions of the third country.[164] Inspectors take a pragmatic line aimed at eliminating immediate risks (e.g. by demanding delisting of non-conforming establishments) whilst stimulating measures that will permit continued exports (e.g. improvements of staff training and accreditation of laboratories).[165] Thirdly, the EU tolerates a reasonable measure of deviation with regard to the appropriate level of protection. Often, inspections note significant deficiencies in third-country standards, but nevertheless do not initiate measures to prevent food imports. Thus, Mexico's control systems were judged insufficient according to EU standards, but '[n]o immediate risk for animal or human health was identified'.[166] Thai controls of fishery products (FP) and monitoring programmes of bivalve molluscs were found wanting, but the 'system is currently able in general to guarantee the quality of the FP exported to [the] EU'.[167] Likewise, numerous deficiencies are identified in Bangladeshi public-health controls, yet 'on balance the measures taken … can largely

[160] See G/L/423 (n140) para 5.

[161] G/SPS/GEN/304 (n 149) para 4.

[162] More specifically, food business operators are expected to 'put in place, implement and maintain a permanent procedure or procedures based on HACCP principles'. Regulation (EC) No 852/2004 of the European Parliament and of the Council on the hygiene of foodstuffs [2004] OJ L139/1, Art 5.4.

[163] The EU intends its new hygiene regulations to establish rules 'more flexible than the old system, as [they] can be adapted to all situations'. European Commission, 'Guidance Document on certain key questions related to import requirements and the new rules on food hygiene and on official food controls' (January 2006) ec.europa.eu/food/international/trade/interpretation_imports.pdf.

[164] G/SPS/GEN/304 (n 149) para 5.

[165] For an illustration of this approach, see European Commission, 'Final Report of a Mission Carried out in Ghana from 13 October to 18 October 2008 in Order to Evaluate the Control Systems in Place Governing the Production of Fishery Products Intended for Export to the European Union' (DG (SANCO)/2008-7659–MR- FINAL).

[166] European Commission, 'Final Report of a Mission Carried Out in Mexico from 04 September to 11 September 2008 in order to evaluate Public Health Control Systems and Certification Procedures over Production of Horse Meat Intended for Export to the EU' (DG (SANCO)/2008-7979–MR- FINAL).

[167] European Commission, 'Final Report of a Mission Carried Out in Thailand from 09 September to 19 September 2008 in order to evaluate the equivalence with Community Standards of the Con-

be considered as providing the necessary guarantees for exporting shrimps to the EU.'[168] Moreover, inspection controls of third countries are neither comprehensive nor even necessarily representative.[169] This is not to suggest dangerous lapses in the EU's system or the overall inadequacy of third-country practices. The point is rather that there is a demonstrated practice of discretion and flexibility in EU assessment of equivalence. Measures will be taken against third countries where the level of protection is not *acceptable*,[170] but not necessarily where protection falls below the *appropriate* level to which the EU aspires. In other words, equivalence as managed in practice is a far more malleable concept, and a far more attainable goal for third countries, than is often acknowledged.

Procedural Commitments

Even where no formal agreement is envisaged, the equivalence process can be a long and extremely laborious one.[171] In this context, the procedural aspects are both less sensitive and more difficult to assess than in the case of transparency. The EU claims that its procedures go significantly beyond the standards set by the Equivalence Decision. In particular, and 'in contrast to' the Decision, the EU's procedures are characterised as both proactive and flexible, which is 'essential in accelerating the process'.[172] Certainly, the Decision's procedural requirements are not overly demanding for a WTO Member with experience in exporting to third countries. Although not carefully documented, it appears that the EU responds to equivalence requests 'in a timely manner'.[173] The requirement to take into account historic

trol Systems in Place Governing the production of Wild and Farmed Fishery Products and Bivalve Molluscs Intended for Export to the European Union' (DG (SANCO)/2008-7650–MR- FINAL).

[168] European Commission, 'Final Report of a Mission Carried Out in Bangladesh from 12 November to 19 November 2008 in order to evaluate the Control of Residues in Aquaculture Products and the Public Health Conditions for the Production of Fishery and Aquaculture Products Intended for Export to the EU' (DG (SANCO)/2008-7655–MR- FINAL).

[169] Ponte suggests that through non-comprehensive inspection of Uganda's fish chain, the EU is guilty of sustaining 'a well-functioning "indulgence regime" that is cleverly and cooperatively managed by regulators, industry, and perhaps the EU as well (through active negligence)'. Ponte (n 135) 72.

[170] See examples in n 78.

[171] Consider, e.g. the efforts undertaken by the EU and Bolivia to establish a pre-export certification programme to facilitate the export of Brazil nuts. Bilateral discussions were initiated in September 1998 and were only completed—following a series of plan submissions, counter-proposals, inspection and technical negotiations—in 2004. See G/SPS/GEN/204/Rev.9/Add.3 (6 February 2009) 30–32.

[172] G/SPS/GEN/304 (n 149) para 8. Where systemic deficiencies are identified, examples of this flexibility include granting restricted equivalence for specific establishments or a limited range of products, and the possible outsourcing of inspection controls to other third countries. See paras 7–8.

[173] A delay in responding to a third country request exceeding six months would be exceptional. Interview with DG Sanco official, September 2011.

experience in assessing third countries is one of the criteria explicitly used by the EU to judge third countries.[174] Likewise, no evidence could be found of the EU limiting trade as a result of such equivalence requests, and this would not be consistent with the EU's overall approach. The final two practices stipulated by the SPS Committee—technical assistance and notification—merit some elaboration.

Technical Assistance

The Equivalence Decision emphasises the importance of aiding developing countries and giving 'full consideration' to requests for technical assistance.[175] The EU does indeed respond to specific needs raised by other WTO Members.[176] But it arguably goes further by virtue of the help offered to developing countries through a substantial number of workshops and seminars.[177] The Commission's *Better Training for Safe Food* has targeted control authorities across Asia, Africa, the Caribbean and Latin America, bringing officials up to date with EU legislative developments.[178] The EC–Association of South East Asian Nations (ASEAN) Economic Cooperation Programme on Standards likewise provides analytical training for laboratory staff throughout the region.[179] In addition, the EU offers considerable assistance to SPS-related projects through the WTO's Aid for Trade scheme (over 110 million euros in 2007[180]) and is involved in the multi-organisation initiative Standards and Trade Development Facility.[181] Available analyses of technical assistance also suggest that the EU's commitment is considerable relative to other trading partners.[182]

---

[174] See 'Commission General Guidance on EU Imports' (n 124) 5, para 7.

[175] 'Equivalence Decision' (n 113) para 8. This is expressed in slightly stronger terms than the corresponding Article 9 of the SPS Agreement.

[176] See, for example, the fruitful request for technical assistance made by Belize to the EU reported in G/SPS/GEN/912 (16 March 2009). See also Ponte (n 135) 58 (explaining how EU funding helped 14 Ugandan fish processing plants successfully upgrade quality systems to permit export).

[177] See G/SPS/GEN/839 (8 April 2008).

[178] See European Commission, *Better Training for Safer Food, Annual Report 2007* (Luxembourg, Office for Official Publication of the European Communities, 2008).

[179] See ec.europa.eu/food/training_strategy/training/asean_en.htm.

[180] European Commission, *SPS Newsletter* (July 2009) trade.ec.europa.eu/doclib/cfm/doclib_section.cfm?sec=279&langId=en.

[181] Established by the FAO, OIE, the World Bank, WHO and WTO, this cooperation assists developing countries with the development and application of SPS measures. See www.standardsfacility.org/.

[182] In a study of Asian trading partners, Ignacio found the EU and Member States to be the largest donor in value terms. LL Ignacio, 'Overview of SPS-related assistance for Cambodia, Lao People's Democratic Republic and Vietnam' (2001–2006) www.aric.adb.org/pdf/a4t/Draft%20final%20-%20Overview%20of%20assistance%2001-06%20_Ignacio_.pdf. Likewise, Brattinga found that 74% of SPS-related projects in Kenya, Tanzania and Uganda were funded by the EU. P Brattinga, 'Overview of SPS-related assistance for Kenya, Tanzania and Uganda (2001–2006)' (September 2007) www.standardsfacility.org/Files/AidForTrade/Consultation_EA_P.Brattinga.pdf

Notification

In spite of the largely dynamic approach taken by the EU to equivalence, one of the seemingly less demanding commitments is generally not met. With the exception of the Agreement with Switzerland,[183] the SPS Committee has not been notified of any of the equivalence initiatives outlined above. The EU is certainly not alone in its failure to notify. Only two equivalence agreements have formally been notified,[184] and little use has been made of the standing agenda point in SPS Committee meetings to inform other Members of successful initiatives.[185] But the EU's behaviour may seem odd in the light of its commitments to transparency. Various explanations can be offered. Firstly, the precise expectations of WTO Members are not entirely clear. The Transparency Procedures unequivocally state that Members 'shall notify' equivalence measures, but this is 'in accordance with the Decision on Equivalence'. The latter is less forthright, providing that 'Members are encouraged to inform the Committee' of such measures. Secondly, the Decision foresees the notification of agreements that have reached a 'successful conclusion'.[186] In that the EU's agreements generally present a framework for agreeing equivalence and include areas requiring additional negotiation, they could be considered agreements in the making rather than 'successfully concluded'.[187] An alternative explanation is that states may be unwilling to be too overt in their communication of equivalence for fear of potentially undercutting the advantages negotiated.[188] Other third countries may well look to piggy-back on established agreements,[189] but given the EU's publication of all formal agreements, non-notification would not appear to be aimed at limiting this practice. The real explanation may be more mundane. Notification is foreseen for 'significant variations to existing equivalence agreements'.[190] Were this to apply, for example, to the updating of third-country lists, the notification

[183] G/SPS/GEN/896 (29 January 2009).

[184] See G/SPS/N/EQV/DOM/1 (16 June 2008) 19 (in which the Dominican Republic reports the determination of the equivalence of US inspection systems as regards bovine products) and G/SPS/N/EQV/PAN/1 (9 August 2007) 9 (establishing Panama's recognition of US sanitary and phytosanitary systems for meat, poultry and all other processed products).

[185] One isolated exception is Brazil's belated reporting of a Memorandum of Understanding signed with Norway in 2003 establishing recognition of equivalence of fishery inspection and quality control. G/SPS/R/54 (28 April 2009).

[186] 'Equivalence Decision' (n 113) para 12.

[187] WTO Members offer the explanation for the non-notification of bilateral arrangements that these are rarely formally presented in terms of 'equivalence'. G/SPS/W/237 (8 May 2009) para 19.

[188] ibid.

[189] One example is provided by Australia's response to FVO recommendations to submit a plan with regard to 'individual cow's milk check'. The Australians noted that New Zealand had established the equivalence of its systems-based approach and therefore also requested equivalence to be granted by the EU for its own practices. European Commission, 'Table of Responses by the Competent Authority of Australia (AQUIS) to the Recommendation of Mission Report Ref. DG (SANCO) 2008-7897', 2.

[190] 'Transparency Procedures' (n 5) Annex E.

burden would be immense. Given that all the relevant information is publicly available, formal notification may simply not serve any real purpose.[191]

The impact of SPS equivalence disciplines on EU policy-making is less immediately obvious than in the case of transparency. The EU is a natural supporter of equivalence,[192] having practised the principle long before its enshrinement in WTO law.[193] Nevertheless, the EU's application of equivalence has evolved and been consolidated as a result of its international recognition. The SPS Agreement has encouraged the EU to enter into more far-reaching formal agreements, which, where successful, offer greater benefits to traders than more *ad hoc* arrangements. In addition, specific arrangements for resolving SPS trade barriers have become an integral element of bilateral free-trade negotiations. Such arrangements embed equivalence into a procedural system that eliminates much of the ambiguity surrounding Article 4 and provide a more reliable short cut to solutions where SPS divergences emerge.[194] In addition, whereas prior to the SPS Agreement, equivalence was only really relevant to the work of veterinary inspectors in the assessment of animal imports, the principle now has far broader application. It is recognised that the EU 'must ensure that all legislation concerning SPS measures provides for the possibility to recognise equivalence also on a case-by-case basis'.[195] This is no panacea for exporters facing regulatory divergences. The EU has resolutely asserted its right to maintain its chosen level of protection.[196] Yet, as illustrated above, even in the most sensitive areas of trade such as GMOs, pesticides and aflatoxins, the EU has sought to work fruitfully within these constraints to find practicable solutions for exporting countries.

[191] However, the capacity of WTO Members to track down relevant information should not be overestimated. For example, in the 2009 EC Trade Policy Review, Brazil requested information from the EU on equivalency agreements that had been available online for many years. WT/TPR/M/214/Add.1 (n 92) 406.

[192] This was already the case during negotiations of the SPS Agreement. See MTN.GNG/NG5/WGSP/W/13 (19 March 1990) para 8 (in which the EU representative recommends that 'equivalency should be applied as broadly as possible').

[193] See n 148 and related text.

[194] Consider the EU's Free Trade Agreement with Korea which creates a bilateral SPS Committee to provide a forum for discussion of problems arising from the application of certain sanitary or phytosanitary measures with a view to reaching mutually acceptable alternatives. In this connection, the Committee shall be convened as a matter of urgency, at the request of a Party, so as to carry out consultations. 2011/265/EU: Council Decision on the signing, on behalf of the European Union, and provisional application of the Free Trade Agreement between the European Union and its Member States, of the one part, and the Republic of Korea, of the other part [2011] OJ L127/1, Art 5.10(1)(e).

[195] European Commission, 'White Paper on Food Safety' (COM (1999) 719 final) para 113.

[196] As the European Commission's then Deputy Director General of DG Sanco Paola Testori has put it, the EU has asked 'the rest of the world to come up to our level. You cannot ask Europe to be more lenient.' 'EU "Just Controls Imports" Commission Told' *EU Food Law* (24 July 2009).

6.4 The SPS Agreement as a Catalyst in Transnational Food Governance

From the perspective most favoured by academics assessing the SPS regime, that which emphasises its constraint on domestic practice, the evidence gathered in this analysis could be considered to point to the Agreement's limited implications for European policy-making. Many EU SPS measures and equivalence initiatives appear to have evaded the notification process. Third countries have therefore not always been informed of the adoption or significant amendment of regulations. In addition, the EU has sometimes failed to allow sufficient time for third countries to comment on new proposals, thereby limiting their influence on adopted measures. But were the analysis to end here, it would crucially misconstrue the impact of SPS disciplines.

Of far greater significance than the deficiencies identified is the extent of the 'transnational governance' that is gradually taking root. Regardless of whether SPS rules are followed to the letter, by generally embracing the principles of transparency and equivalence, WTO Members create a context for intensified scrutiny and negotiation of appropriate regulatory responses to SPS concerns. Indeed, the above review reveals, above all, a bewildering level of international interaction. The EU annually distributes around 4,000 pages of legislative proposals to trading partners,[197] and in 2008 alone, carried out 60 inspection missions to third countries.[198] Moreover, this review focused only on European policy-making, and therefore offers only the briefest of glimpses into global administrative interaction on SPS issues.[199] The vast majority of this transnational cooperation is set in motion by the SPS Agreement, which anchors the underlying practices of transparency and equivalence and provides a strong foundation for the network of bilateral contacts that it spawns.

For international lawyers, there are a number of interesting aspects in this transnational governance process. Firstly, for administrators active in transnational governance of SPS issues, very little distinction is made between the hard norms enshrined in the SPS Agreement and the softer norms that have evolved in the SPS Committee. The practices, deadlines and notification formats adopted by the latter are widely regarded as the norms to which to comply, regardless of the caveats included in SPS documents aimed at limiting their legal status.[200] As a result, the

[197] This is an estimate included in 'EU NA & EP Reports' (n 39) 2007, 9.

[198] European Commission, *Food and Veterinary Office Annual Report 2008* (European Commission, 2008) 4.

[199] Notably, EU notifications in 2008 represented less than 4 % of all notifications made to the SPS Committee. In total, 1266 notifications were submitted in 2008. 'EU NA & EP Reports' (n 39) 2008, 1–2. The EU itself issued 13 comments in 2008 in response to the transparency initiatives of trading partners.

[200] For example, within the first 12 months of operation of the revised Transparency Procedures proposing the notification of proposals conforming to international standards, in excess of 180 regulatory proposals were submitted emanating from more than 30 countries. See SPS Information Management System (n 101).

normative understanding that has grown within the governance network has evolved substantially and purposefully, realigning the expectations of WTO Members without the need for formal renegotiation of the Agreement. If further changes to transparency norms are required to address the types of practical difficulties identified above, this would appear to be entirely feasible within the existing legal framework.

The extensive elaboration of 'soft' norms highlights a second striking feature of the emerging SPS governance culture, namely the constant process of critical self-reflection it engenders. The implementation of transparency rules forces importing countries, under the spotlight of trading-partner scrutiny, to weigh up the implications on trade of specific policy proposals.[201] The EU experience demonstrates how self-assessment can become institutionalized, with regular reports on SPS activities and consequent initiatives to improve its own performance.[202] This process in turn helps to embed international norms more firmly into the domestic system and encourages the identification of the least useful and practical elements of SPS practices, providing a catalyst for new norm generation.

Thirdly, this review of EU activity suggests the limits of an overly narrow assessment of WTO Members' fulfilment of their obligations. For example, given the dearth of explicit notifications, it is sometimes concluded that equivalence arrangements are 'not common in international trade'.[203] Certainly, the number of interventions by third countries in 2008 that led to changes in EU regulatory measures may be limited. But this should not detract from the arguably greater significance of transparency and equivalence provisions which lies not in their ability to impose rigid discipline upon WTO members, but in their capacity to normalize a process of transnational interaction between regulators on SPS issues.[204] SPS transparency and equivalence practices engage national officials in all sanitary fields in the process of understanding and seeking solutions to international divergences in regulations and infrastructure. The procedural necessities of information provision, comment and counter-comment associated with transparency and equivalence enmesh officials in a problem-solving environment. From these semi-formal contexts, more informal relationships grow that replicate and consolidate emerging governance practices.[205]

[201] This reinforces the general practice encouraged by the SPS Committee for members to constantly reflect on the way in which they engage with trading partners. Within its relatively short existence, the SPS regime has already undergone its third operational review. See G/SPS/53 (3 May 2010). In addition, by including governance practices as a standing point on SPS Committee meeting agendas, WTO Members are compelled to reflect critically on their own experiences of managing the SPS system.

[202] See n 102.

[203] D Roberts, D Orden, and T Josling, *Food Regulation and Trade: Toward a Safe and Open Global Food System* (Washington, Peterson Institute for International Economics, 2004) 49.

[204] This important dynamic, generally drawing little attention in legal commentary, has been highlighted by Andrew Lang and Joanne Scott. A Lang and J Scott, 'The Hidden World of WTO Governance', 20 EJIL 575 (2009).

[205] Inevitably, the evidence for this informal process is largely anecdotal. One example may be instructive. Prior to the SPS Committee meetings, there is extensive exchange between authorities in certain countries in order to establish the need for side meetings outside the main Committee

Transparency therefore considerably enhances the role of third countries as valid stakeholders in EU policy debate.

The number of regulatory solutions that emerge as a result will certainly in part depend on domestic political and institutional flexibility to accommodate a third-country's specific context and concerns. But it equally depends on the organizational capacity of trading partners to be attentive, and respond quickly, to looming trade problems. The monitoring of in excess of 1,000 SPS measures annually poses a far greater administrative challenge and potential obstacle to the effective operation of transparency than the notification dilemmas identified above. The regular comments and replies reported by the EU from a variety of WTO members suggest that this process is at least beginning to function effectively.

Finally, should we be rather underwhelmed by the extremely technical nature of the issues that are addressed as a result of transnational food governance? Increased interaction, information exchanges and the like are all very well, the reader might observe, but does this activity lead to meaningful and significant policy change?[206] The power of transnational SPS governance to overcome fundamental divides in policy preferences should certainly not be overstated. Those deep-seated conflicts such as hormones in beef or genetically modified foods most commonly associated with the SPS Agreement will not be magically reconciled by intensified contacts between technical experts. Yet the persistence of these problems should not blind us either to the crucial contribution that aligning sanitary procedures and practices can make in smoothing the functioning of international trade. Harmonizing certification procedures, negotiating residue limits, granting transition periods is made possible through transparency. Such measures, while not making headlines, can make the difference between trading and not trading. For US peanut exporters, for Ecuadorian pineapple growers, for Ugandan fishermen and many more, improved access to the European market is certainly meaningful.

6.5 Conclusion

High-profile WTO disputes often convey an impression of the SPS arena as a theatre of conflict, dominated by isolated and intractable standpoints. This chapter's analysis of the EU's implementation of SPS transparency and equivalence disciplines uncovers a more mundane tableau of transnational technical exchange and cooperation. In this administrative netherworld, the EU's adherence to SPS norms is sometimes found wanting. The EU's application of SPS transparency norms is inconsistent in practice: non-notification of many EU and EU Member State measures

meeting and to ascertain which relevant experts should attend. These contacts are considered as, or even more, important than the formal discussions. Interview with European Commission's DG Trade official in July 2009.

[206] Such skepticism is voiced, for example, in RH Steinberg, 'The Hidden World of WTO Governance: A Reply to Andrew Lang and Joanne Scott', 20 EJIL 1063 (2009) 1071.

and, in cases, failure to notify in a manner that allows third-country comment. Likewise, in spite of the widespread adoption of the principle of equivalence, the EU's conformity with notification disciplines is questionable.

Yet, such lapses should not distract us from the more significant activity that the SPS Agreement has set in motion, namely a slowly emerging transnational approach to the governance of food: the regular sharing of information, a right to and expectation of dialogue, initiatives, at least, to accommodate third-country concerns and, as a result, greater critical self-reflection by WTO members in their policy-making process. This transformation remains in its infancy and can clearly not prevent tensions on commercially and culturally sensitive food issues. But it may nonetheless come to substantially facilitate a large portion of the international trade in food.

References

Athukorala P-C and Jayasuriya S, 'Food Safety Issues, Trade and WTO Rules: A Developing Country Perspective' (2003) 26 *The World Economy* 1395.

Brattinga P, 'Overview of SPS-related assistance for Kenya, Tanzania and Uganda (2001–2006)' (September 2007).

Broberg M, 'European Food Safety Regulation and the Developing Countries: Regulatory Problems and Possibilities' (DIIS Working Paper 2009:09).

Collins-Williams T and Wolfe R, 'Transparency as a Trade Policy Tool: The WTO's Cloudy Windows' (2010) 9 *World Trade Review* 9 551.

Diaz Rios LB and Jaffee S, 'Barrier, Catalyst or Distraction? Standards, Competitiveness, and Africa's Groundnut Exports to Europe' (The World Bank, Agricultural, and Rural Development Discussion Paper 39 2008).

Echols MA, 'Equivalence and risk regulation under the World Trade Organization's SPS Agreement' in G Van Calster and D Prévost, (eds) *Research Handbook on Environment, Health and the WTO* (Cheltenham: Edward Elgar 2013).

Ignacio LL, 'Overview of SPS-Related Assistance for Cambodia, Lao People's Democratic Republic and Vietnam' (2001–2006).

Lang A and Scott J, 'The Hidden World of WTO Governance' (2009) 20 EJIL 575.

Mehta R and George J, 'Processed Food Products Exports from India: An Exploration with SPS Regime' (Joint Research Project sponsored by the Australian Centre for International Agricultural Research, 2003).

O'Connor and Company, 'The EC Traceability and Equivalence Rules in Light of the SPS Agreement: A Review of the Many Legal Issues' (CTA 2003).

Otsuki T, Wilson JS and Sewadeh M, 'Saving Two in a Billion: Quantifying the Trade Effect of European Food Safety Standards in African Exports' (2001) 26 *Food Policy* 495.

Ponte S, 'Bands, Tests and Alchemy: Food Safety Standards and the Ugandan Fish Export Industry' (DIIS Working Paper 2005:19).

Prévost D, *Balancing Trade and Health in the SPS Agreement: The Development Dimension* (Nijmegen, Wolf Legal Publishers, 2009).

Regan D, '*United States—Certain Measures Affecting Imports of Poultry from China*: The Fascinating Case that Wasn't' (2012) 11 *World Trade Review* 273, 285

Roberts D, Orden D, and Josling T, *Food Regulation and Trade: Toward a Safe and Open Global Food System* (Washington, Peterson Institute for International Economics, 2004).

Safe Food, *Where does our Food Come from?* (July 2009).

Schramm D, 'The Race to Geneva: Resisting the Gravitational Pull of the WTO in the GMO Labelling Controversy' (2007) 9 *Vermont Journal of Environmental Law* 93.

Scott J, *The WTO Agreement on Sanitary and Phytosanitary Measures. A Commentary* (Oxford, OUP, 2007).

Shaffer GC and Pollack MA, 'Hard Versus Soft Law: Alternatives, Complements and Antagonists in International Governance' (2010) 94 *Minnesota Law Review* 706.

Steinberg RH, 'The Hidden World of WTO Governance: A Reply to Andrew Lang and Joanne Scott' (2009) 20 EJIL 1063.

Zarrilli S, 'WTO Agreement on the Sanitary and Phytosanitary Measures: Issues for Developing Countries' (South Centre, 1999).

Chapter 7
Is Codex Alimentarius All Talk? The Importance of Standards in Transnational Food Governance

Abstract The SPS Agreement has formally elevated the importance of Codex Alimentarius as a reference point for domestic food regulations. However, the actual influence of this standard-setting body on national policy-making has not been closely examined. This chapter seeks to enrich understanding of the substantive impact of transnational food governance by tracing the uptake of international standards across domestic legislation worldwide. It first draws on the work of international relations scholars to develop a conceptual framework for analysing transnational norm dissemination. It then analyses Codex's standard-setting in two contested areas of food policy: food additives, and vitamin and mineral supplements. After explaining the history and controversies of Codex's work in each area, it uses the framework developed to characterise national regulatory responses to international standards. A complex picture emerges: the levels of attention paid to international norms are shown to vary widely across both countries and issues. The study confirms that substantive standards can contribute importantly to domestic regulations, but their influence is neither automatic nor uniform.

7.1 Introduction

Codex Alimentarius (Codex), once perceived to be of marginal importance, is now taken seriously by most international lawyers. The legal recognition conferred on Codex by the Agreement on the Application of Sanitary and Phytosanitary Measures (SPS Agreement) and its relevance to high-profile disputes have heightened scholarly interest in the body's operation.[1] Conforming to Codex norms creates a valuable presumption of compliance with international law. Given the threat and potential costs of litigation before the World Trade Organisation (WTO), its Members have 'very real incentives to adopt Codex standards'.[2] As a result, Codex

[1] See DE Winickoff and DM Bushey, 'Science and Power in Global Food Regulation: The Rise of the Codex Alimentarius' (2010) 35 *Science, Technology and Human Values* 356 and MD Masson-Matthee, *The Codex Alimentarius Commission and its Standards* (The Hague, TMC Asser Press, 2007), in particular Chap. IV.

[2] MA Livermore, 'Authority and Legitimacy in Global Governance: Deliberation, Institutional Differentiation, and the Codex Alimentarius' (2006) 81 *New York University Law Review* 766, 776.

C. Downes, *The Impact of WTO SPS Law on EU Food Regulations,* Studies in European Economic Law and Regulation 2, DOI 10.1007/978-3-319-04373-9_7,

norms have 'become authoritative, in the sense of having the power to determine outcomes and to compel obedience',[3] and are considered to 'strip national regulators of their discretion'.[4] But what precisely is meant by 'adoption' or 'obedience' in the context of developing domestic food regulations? Will the outcome of this process be the same worldwide? Are national regulators as passive in this process as is often implied? While some aspects of Codex's empowerment have been closely scrutinised,[5] basic assertions about its influence have remained largely unchallenged by legal commentators.[6] The aim of this chapter is to complement the analysis in Chap. 6 on how states interact in the SPS arena with a review of the substantive contribution made by international norms across domestic regulatory regimes. It does so through the examination of Codex's work in two controversial areas: the General Standard on Food Additives (GSFA)[7] and the Guidelines on Vitamin and Mineral Food Supplements.[8]

One would expect the uptake of international standards to be irregular across national regulatory systems for a number of reasons. Most obviously, the substantial discrepancies in scientific and administrative capacity determine a country's ability to build its own regulatory framework independent of international expertise.[9] The same structural limitations may, however, also dictate a Codex Member's active participation in negotiations of standards and consequently their affinity with decisions made by this body.[10] The relevance of an individual standard will also naturally vary according to a state's domestic food consumption, agricultural capacity and regulatory history. Moreover, even were we to assume WTO Members' full respect

[3] G de Búrca, 'Developing Democracy Beyond the State' (2008) 46 *Columbia Journal of Transnational Law* 221, 233.

[4] RA Pereira, 'Why Would International Administrative Activity Be Any Less Legitimate?—A Study of the Codex Alimentarius Commission' (2008) 9 *German Law Journal* 1694. See also Masson-Matthee (n 1) 277 (arguing that standards 'do not leave Codex Members with a high degree of discretion to respond to domestic concerns').

[5] In particular, the questionable legitimacy of Codex decision-making processes has been well documented. See T Hüller and ML Maier, 'Fixing the Codex?: Global Food-Safety Governance under Review' in C Joerges and E-U Petersmann (eds), *Constitutionalism, Multilevel Trade Governance and Social Regulation* 268 (Oxford, Hart Publishing, 2006); J Steffek and MP Ferretti, 'Accountability or "Good Decision"? The Competing Goals of Civil Society Participation in International Governance' (2009) 23 *Global Society* 37, 49–56; Masson-Matthee (n 1) Chap. V; Livermore (n 2); de Búrca (n 3); Pereira (n 4).

[6] One exception is D Livshiz, 'Updating American Administrative Law: WTO, International Standards, Domestic Implementation and Public Participation' (2007) 24 *Wisconsin International Law Journal* 961, 975–982 (noting at 977 that 'it is not immediately obvious whether international standards have altered the substance of US regulations').

[7] Codex STAN 192-1995. A regularly updated version of the GSFA is available at www.codexalimentarius.net/gsfaonline/index.html.

[8] CAC/GL 55–2005.

[9] T Josling, 'Norms and Standards' (Institute for International Studies, Stanford University 2003) 12, www.ycsg.yale.edu/documents/papers/Josling.doc.

[10] Hüller and Maier (n 5) 272–275 (discussing the dominance of rich states in Codex standard setting).

of SPS obligations, we would still expect the harmonisation process to be imperfect. Conformity to standards is not explicitly required by the SPS Agreement.[11]

While regulatory diversity would not therefore be surprising, it inevitably raises questions about the real influence of international standards. If international norms only partially infiltrate domestic law, should their role be considered significant, superficial or something in between? Addressing this complexity forces the international lawyer into difficult conceptual territory. As seen in Part I of this book, it is customary for lawyers to extrapolate the impact of international law by assuming its implementation in a domestic context. As demonstrated in Part II, this approach can lead to distorted expectations as to the anticipated consequences of the SPS regime. To deepen our understanding of Codex's influence, we clearly have to move beyond the limits imposed by the dichotomous compliance/non-compliance perspective of international law. Before turning to the empirical study of global regulation of food additives and food supplements in Sects. 7.3 and 7.4 respectively, Sect. 7.2 therefore first reflects on how the exercise of assessing the impact of international standards on domestic regulations can be conceptualised. After summarising existing scholarly explanations of norm dissemination, it draws from this work a categorisation that will facilitate the subsequent study of Codex norms.

7.2 Tracing the Influence of International Norms

In the late 1990s, the attention of a number of international relations and legal scholars shifted from demonstrating the importance of international law to explaining how it led to domestic political change.[12] In particular, constructivists sought to develop conceptual frameworks that would help analyse and empirically demonstrate the process of norm dissemination. The most widely discussed of these are the 'life cycle', the 'spiral model' and 'transnational legal process'. The 'life cycle' is Finnemore and Sikkink's description of the progress of norms through international society. It involves a three-stage process: the emergence of the norm, its 'cascade' across the global community, and finally an internalisation through which norms may become 'taken for granted' in a domestic context.[13] Risse and Sikkink subsequently developed a more complex 'spiral model' which elaborates on the intermediate stages in the acceptance of a norm. This involves a series of steps (including denial of the validity of a norm, and tactical concessions towards the norm) through which the international norm gradually insinuates itself in the domestic

[11] SPS Agreement Art 3.1, it will be remembered, only obliges Members to 'base' their sanitary measures on agreements reached by Codex.

[12] For an account of the intellectual backdrop to this work, see generally HH Koh, '*Why Do Nations Obey International Law*?' (1997) 106 *Yale Law Journal* 2599, 2616–2634.

[13] M Finnemore and K Sikkink, 'International Norm Dynamics and Political Change' (1998) 52 *International Organization* 887, 895–905.

setting.[14] Most relevant to legal norms, Koh's 'transnational legal process' describes the '"transmission belt," whereby norms created by international society infiltrate into domestic society'.[15] In a manner that parallels Finnemore and Sikkink's life-cycle, Koh outlines a four-phase process of interaction (when the norm is created), interpretation (which allows the norm to crystallise), internalisation (as domestic society adopts the new norm as its own), and ultimately obedience.[16]

Can these models serve as a structure for analysing the effect of international standards? Certainly, they have proved to be a valuable framework for the exploration of norms in a wide variety of fields.[17] However, the common weakness of these models for the purpose of studying Codex norms is that the outcome of normative dissemination (as opposed to the process) is under-conceptualised. While none of the authors would deny that the internalisation of norms may not occur,[18] alternative scenarios are not explored, creating a sense of inevitability around the norm-dissemination process.[19] The limited attention paid to non-internalisation is understandable. Firstly, the international relations (IR) models, and indeed the majority of the work on international norm dissemination, are dominated by consideration of human rights. The 'fundamental' nature of these rights, and thus the failure associated with them not being secured, reduces the relevance of normative change that falls short of internalisation. Secondly, in their respective fields, the work undertaken contributes to weightier theoretical ends, be they to counter realist scepticism about the limited explanatory value of norms in international relations[20]

[14] T Risse and K Sikkink, 'The Socialisation of International Human Rights Norms into Domestic Practices: Introduction' in T Risse, SC Ropp and K Sikkink (eds), *The Power of Human Rights: International Norms and Domestic Change* (Cambridge, CUP, 1999).

[15] Koh, 'Why Do Nations Obey International Law?' (n 12) 2651.

[16] HH Koh, 'The 1998 Frankel Lecture: Bringing International Human Rights Home' ('Bringing Rights Home') (1998) 35 Houston Law Review 623, 644.

[17] See, eg H Entwisle, 'Tracing Cascades: The Normative Development of the UN Guiding Principles of Internal Displacement' (2005) 19 *Georgetown Immigration Law Journal* 369; RP Alford, 'The Nobel Effect: Nobel Peace Prize Laureates as International Norm Entrepreneurs' (2008) 49 VJIL 61; A Peck, 'The New Imperialism: Toward an Advocacy Strategy for GMO Accountability' (2008) 21 *Georgetown International Environmental Law Review* 37; EC Lim, 'A Long "TRIP" Home: Intellectual Property Rights, International Law and the Constructivist Challenge' (2008) 4 *Journal of International Law and International Relations* 57.

[18] See Finnemore and Sikkink (n 13) 914 (noting that 'actors must choose which rules or norms to follow and which obligations to meet at the expense of others in a given situation...'); Koh (n 16) 675 (recognising the importance of the 'degree to which particular rules are or are not internalised into domestic infrastructure'). T Risse and SC Ropp, 'International Human Rights Norms and Domestic Change: Conclusions' in *Power of Human Rights* (n 14) 236 (acknowledging that '[w]e also need to account for the variation in the impact of principled ideas and norms on domestic actors').

[19] As Keohane notes, in practice 'there are barriers and blockages: norm internalization does not take place'. RO Keohane, 'When Does International Law Come Home?' (1998) 35 *Houston Law Review* 683, 701. Such lapses into determinism incite criticisms of naivety and a lack of explanatory rigour. For an example of the former, see TM Franck, 'Dr. Pangloss Meets The Grinch: A Pessimistic Comment on Harold Koh's Optimism' (1998) 35 *Houston Law Review* 683 and of the latter, see EA Posner, 'Transnational Legal Process and The Supreme Court's 2003–2004 Term: Some Skeptical Observations' (2004) 12 *Tulsa Journal of Comparative and International Law* 23.

[20] Finnemore and Sikkink (n 13) 889–890.

or to bolster claims of the relevance of international law even to the most powerful states.[21] Expanding on the exceptions to, and limitations of, norm internalisation might have undermined the clarity and force of the arguments presented. Critics have noted the failure of these models to take account of the local reception of international norms.[22] In particular, these frameworks do not envisage the type of dynamic interaction between international and domestic norms—the generation of new norms—which one may have expected to be at the forefront of this work, given their constructivist roots.[23] Such interactions are particularly pertinent to this study of SPS harmonisation, given the flexibility implicit in Article 3.1 over how standards are translated into sanitary measures. Models that can only capture the 'successes' of norm adoption are hardly better suited to tracing variations in normative influence than a 'compliance/non-compliance' analysis.

Stimulated in part by the post-9/11 climate, which brought into question fundamental rights previously deemed to be beyond contention, scholars have started to look more critically at domestic treatment of international norms.[24] For IR scholars, this has entailed a more rigorous application of constructivist principles in the scrutiny of norm dissemination. They discard any assumptions about the meaning of norms adopted internationally. Instead, they recognise that 'norms entail an inherently contested quality and therefore acquire meaning in relation to the specific context in which they are enacted'.[25] The prohibition of torture, sustainable development and the status of the enemy combatants have all been demonstrated to have different and shifting meanings over time and depending on domestic context: a norm's 'contestation is always a possibility'.[26] In a similar vein, legal scholars have sought to understand the significance of norms beyond their formal meaning in binding conventions. Brunnée and Toope have traced the evolution of internationally 'shared understandings' of norms relating to climate change, use of force and the prohibition of torture. They chart out periods of normative flux which challenge simpler expla-

---

[21] Koh (n 16) 635.

[22] See PS Berman, 'From International Law to Law and Globalisation' (2005) 43 *Columbia Journal of Transnational Law* 485, 545 (pointing to the need for a more nuanced understanding of how international norms influence actors on the ground). See also GA Sarfaty, 'International Norm Diffusion in the Pimicikamak Cree Nation: A Model of Legal Mediation' (2007) 48 *Harvard International Law Journal* 441, 445.

[23] See J Brunnée and SJ Toope, *Legitimacy and Legality in International Law* (Cambridge, CUP, 2010) 62. The failure of early IR constructivist accounts to acknowledge the mutual constitution of norms and the need to 'bring agency back in' was recognised by Checkel. See JT Checkel, 'The Constructivist Turn in International Relations Theory' (1998) 50 *World Politics* 323, 339–341.

[24] A Liese, 'Exceptional Necessity. How Liberal Democracies Contest the Prohibition of Torture and Ill-Treatment When Countering Terrorism' (2009) 5 *Journal of International Law and International Relations* 17, 24.

[25] A Wiener and U Puetter, 'The Quality of Norms Is What Actors Make of It' (2009) 5 *Journal of International Law and International Relations* 1, 7.

[26] I Venzke, 'Legal Contestation about "Enemy Combatants": On the Exercise of Power in Legal Interpretation' (2009) 5 *Journal of International Law and International Relations* 154, 162. See also S Park, 'The World Bank, Dams and the Meaning of Sustainable Development in Use' (2009) 5 *Journal of International Law and International Relations* 93.

nations of norm internalisation.[27] With their later work on normative acculturation, Goodman and Jinks have also sought to explain 'incomplete internalization'.[28] They identify a 'decoupling' between formal norm acceptance and state action which does not connote non-compliance as such, but is a way to 'avoid the substantial disruption and conflict that often accompany the wholesale adoption of global models ill-suited for many local contexts'.[29] The entry of international norms in domestic settings is increasingly recognised to be uncertain and complex.

It could be objected at this stage that concerns about contested meaning are peripheral to the analysis of international food standards. After all, the latter will most typically limit or prohibit the use of a given substance in food, provisions that are hardly likely to be ambiguous either in meaning or purpose. However, as we will see below, such standards are not simply the conclusions of scientific analysis, but reflect complex views about our relationship with food and the appointed role of government in managing consumer behaviour. Such views, like any other international norms, will give rise to 'shared understandings' that evolve over time and are subject to domestic contestation. This said, while more recent and sophisticated work on norm dissemination may indeed better reflect the dynamic processes at play in the development and subsequent use of standards, it does have its limitations. As scholars have refined their study of norm diffusion, this has generally not been accompanied by the type of simple descriptive tools found in the earlier models discussed above. A focus on norm contestation encourages insightful micro-analysis on a case-by-case basis, but for the purpose of a macro-level analysis of the SPS regime across countries, a method of categorising different degrees of normative influence is required.

One IR scholar who combines the more complex conceptualisation of norm dissemination with descriptive clarity is Amitav Acharya, in his study of the spread of norms in the Association of South East Asian Nations (ASEAN).[30] The following section describes and builds on Acharya's work to propose a categorisation of norm dissemination suitable for tracing the impact of international standards.

7.2.1 A Conceptual Framework for the Transnational Dissemination of Legal Norms

Acharya argues that local norms cannot be given up without social and political consequences and therefore that foreign norms are typically reshaped by the recipients in a way that adapts them to the latter's prior beliefs.[31] This is a dynamic,

---

[27] Their study concludes that '[i]n all cases... norms are not unidirectional projections; they are created and sustained in social interaction'. Brunnée and Toope (n 23) 351.

[28] R Goodman and D Jinks, 'Incomplete Internalization and Compliance with Human Rights Law' (2008) 19 EJIL 725.

[29] ibid 731.

[30] A Acharya, 'How Ideas Spread: Whose Norms Matter? Norm Localization and Institutional Change in Asian Regionalism' (2004) 58 *International Organization* 239.

[31] ibid 245–246.

creative process in which 'the existing normative order and an external norm are in a "mutually constitutive" relationship … [which] can only be fully understood in terms of both'.[32] The local policy paradigm is adapted to take into account the ideas emerging from a transnational interaction, without relinquishing what may be important domestic values and ideas.[33] Yet, while the author's primary focus is localisation, he recognises that new norms may not necessarily emerge from this interaction. He thus establishes a three-pronged framework that foresees, in addition to localisation, two alternative domestic responses to international norms:

Displacement An existing local norm will sometimes be rejected in favour of a new international norm. Ideas emanating from international rules can challenge the coherence of domestic policy paradigms, which are undermined and ultimately abandoned. This type of normative change is akin to the internalisation foreseen in the life cycle, spiral and 'transnational legal process' models, but contrary to its representation in the latter, is not viewed to be commonplace.[34] Nevertheless, celebrated examples such as the effective spread of norms against landmines[35] demonstrate that displacement is neither purely theoretical nor aspirational.

Resistance Alternatively, a local norm may be sufficiently robust and important to domestic society to withstand international pressure. In spite of formal state adherence to an international legal norm, there may therefore sometimes be a 'failure of norm transmission'.[36] Brunnée and Toope argue that this kind of normative conflict arises in particular where the international norm 'is markedly at odds with—or ahead of—social background understandings'.[37]

While more nuanced in its expectations for norm dissemination than earlier models, there are other scenarios potentially relevant to the study of international food standards that are not represented within Acharya's framework. Firstly, Acharya assumes the pre-existence of local norms. This assumption may not be appropriate in the context of Codex Alimentarius, given the body's aim of providing regulatory templates for developing countries. Secondly, Acharya envisages initial discrepancy between international and local norms. Again, this may not be the case

---

[32] ibid 251–252.

[33] For a detailed illustration of this process, see Twining's discussion of the adoption of the UK Human Rights Act of 1998, 'a story of complex borrowing from theories of human rights, public international law, national laws and the specific ideas of a British Draftsman.' W Twining, 'Diffusion of Law: A Global Perspective' (2004) 49 *Journal of Legal Pluralism and Unofficial Law* 1, 16.

[34] Acharya (n 30) 254 (describing displacement as 'a rarer occurrence'). This is echoed in Twining's criticisms of research into the transnational diffusion of law. Rather than displacing norms, '[n]early all modern detailed studies of reception recognise that it usually involves interaction with pre-existing normative orders'. ibid 29.

[35] L Wexler, 'The International Deployment of Shame, Second-Best Responses, and Norm Entrepreneurship: The Campaign to Ban Landmines and the Landmine Ban Treaty' (2003) 20 *Arizona Journal of International and Comparative Law* 561.

[36] Acharya (n 30) 254.

[37] Brunnée and Toope (n 23) 76.

in international fora such as Codex, where countries actively seek to 'share' their own regulatory experience. Taking these additional scenarios into account, Acharya's framework can be expanded to include two further forms of local reception of international norms, as follows:

Innovation Where domestic norms are not settled, international normative input can have what may be described as an innovative effect. Such innovation is most frequently associated with historical moments where events have left a normative vacuum.[38] But normative innovation may equally occur due to technological or scientific developments[39] or in cases, as mentioned above, where structural limitations have prevented a state's engagement in an issue. As normative innovation does not involve contestation of existing local norms, this process differs significantly from that of displacement.

Accentuation The establishment of international norms can sometimes have an effect on existing domestic norms without necessarily changing the content of norms. For example, transnational discussion and agreement can provide important support for fragile norms still contested domestically.[40] Even where the norm has been deliberately advanced by a given state, it can have particular force when re-entering the domestic sphere due to transnational reinforcement.[41]

In each of the above transnational norm dissemination scenarios (summarised in Fig. 7.1), international law plays a role in influencing domestic norms, although the extent of its impact may vary. With these distinctive scenarios in mind, we turn to the two case studies on Codex Alimentarius.

7.3 Case Study on Food Additives

The need for international coordination of the regulation of food additives has long been recognised. First discussed by Codex in 1965, a number of the core principles for managing the use of additives have survived largely unchallenged over sub-

[38] Farrell argues that this type of change, what he describes as 'radical norm diffusion' only occurs in specific conditions, usually as a result of an 'external shock to the local culture system with effective norm entrepreneurs and/or personnel change in the target community'. T Farrell, 'Transnational Norms and Military Development: Constructing Ireland's Professional Army' (2001) 7 *European Journal of International Relations* 63, 65.

[39] Consider, for example, the rapid consensus that developed around treaties governing the protection of the ozone layer and common understandings that swiftly extended to the international system. See JK Setear, 'Ozone, Iteration, and International Law' (1989) 40 VJIL 193.

[40] See JW Legro, 'Which Norms Matter? Revisiting the "Failure" of Internationalism' (1997) 51 *International Organization* 31, 35 (describing how states seek reaffirmation of norms during international negotiations).

[41] See SM Tarzi, 'International Norms, Trade, and Human Rights: A Perspective on Norm Conformity' (2002) 27 *The Journal of Social, Political, and Economic Studies* 187 (describing the additional power given to essentially US norms such as 'reciprocity', 'liberalisation' and 'nondiscrimination' when embodied in the GATT).

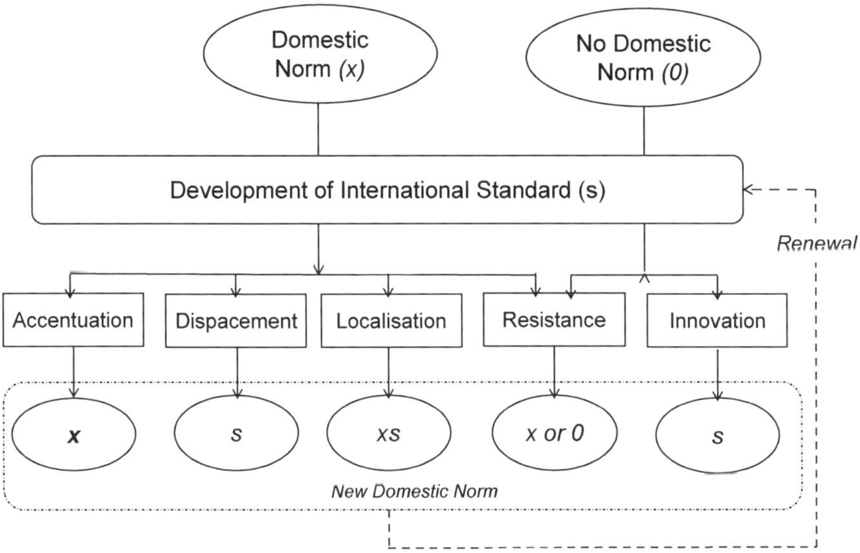

Fig. 7.1 Transnational norm dissemination

sequent decades.[42] Firstly, food additives may only be included in foods if safe. Secondly, use of food additives can only be justified for certain purposes: maintaining nutritional value, enhancing the quality and attractiveness of food and assisting in the manufacturing process of foods. Thirdly, their use must not mislead the consumer. Fourthly, additives must not be used at a level above that needed to achieve the technological effect required. National governments worldwide have few qualms about ascribing to these basic tenets: the difficulty arises in their local interpretation and application. For example, Codex additionally provides that '[t]he use of food additives is justified … only where these purposes cannot be achieved by other means which are economically and technologically practicable'.[43] What is economically and technologically practicable is contested, as it is dependent on a wide range of factors—raw materials, climate, stage of technological development, storage capacity and consumer expectations—which naturally diverge across different regions of the world. The use of additives on the Indian food market may be incomprehensible for Norwegian consumers and regulators and vice versa. The challenge for Codex has therefore been to develop a system of rules that manages these differing expectations while permitting efficient international trade in food. This case study evaluates the progress made, explaining the development of Codex's work and the main issues of contention, before analysing worldwide implementation of these norms.

[42] See, by way of comparison, the earlier Codex Alimentarius General Principles for the Use of Food Additives 1, CAC/MISC 1-1972, 6.a. and the Preamble of the Codex General Standard for Food Additives (GSFA) of 2005 (n 7).

[43] GSFA, Preamble, 3.2.

7.3.1 The Development of the General Standard for Food Additives (GSFA)

Until the 1990s, Codex's approach to facilitating food trade was based upon the development of 'vertical' standards for individual commodities.[44] These standards typically included detailed provisions on additive use, labelling, pesticides and other contaminants. While numerous, vertical standards did not cover a large quantity of 'non-standardised' foods, therefore limiting the effectiveness of Codex's work from both a consumer-protection and trade-facilitation perspective. Two factors propelled Codex towards a new approach. A review undertaken at the request of Codex by a UK consultant, WHB Denner, forthrightly exposed the limitations of Codex's work and set out a number of recommendations for change.[45] Most importantly, the Denner Paper advocated a more prominent role for international scientific expertise in additive assessment and recommended 'a major revision including a complete restructuring to accommodate provisions for non-standardised foods'.[46] An FAO/WHO and GATT conference held in March 1991 gave further impetus to these proposals, recommending Codex to adopt a more horizontal approach in order to provide the comprehensive framework necessary for international trade.[47]

The commencement of work on a GSFA in 1991, combined with the enhanced importance of Codex following the Uruguay Round, raised the stakes of international discussions on additives. How could Codex Members embrace the food-additive choices of others without undermining their own? Within the relevant Codex Committees,[48] Codex Members have consistently offered two broad lines of response. On the one hand, the US, strongly supported by Australia and China, has led a drive for pragmatism. From this viewpoint, Codex must fully acknowledge the varying requirements of different countries in the use of additives and work inclusively to incorporate all these needs.[49] On the other hand, in order to guard against an unnecessary escalation of additive use, some Codex Members, most notably the European Union (EU), have urged utmost respect of the agreed principles for managing additives. Taken literally, this would entail a detailed assessment of every individual additive, a process destined to lead Codex into an analytical quagmire, given the number of additive-food relationships implicated. While this debate

---

[44] See, for example, Codex Commodity standards 003-1981 (Canned Salmon), 012-1981 (Honey) and 013-1981 (Tinned Tomatoes) available at www.codexalimentarius.net/web/standard_list.jsp.

[45] This paper has been reproduced in WHB Denner, 'Food Additives: Recommendations for Harmonisation and Control' (1990) 1 *Food Control* 150.

[46] ibid 156 (recommendation 8).

[47] FAO/WHO, 'Report of the FAO/WHO Conference on Food Standards, Chemicals in Food and Food Trade' (ALICOM 91/22).

[48] This work has been carried out by the Codex Committee on Food Additives and Contaminants (CCFAC) reorganised and renamed in 2006 as the Codex Committee on Food Additives (CCFA).

[49] In support of this goal, the US has frequently evoked the flexibility advocated by the Denner Paper. See, eg CX/FAC 03/06, Add.1, 5. This is somewhat disingenuous as the relevant recommendation (number 7), unlike many of Denner's recommendations, was never formally adopted by Codex. For an overview of CCFAC's response to the Denner Paper, see CX/FAC 03/06, 23–24.

is most frequently couched in the language of Codex's own goals and principles, there is no disguising the underlying divergence in sentiments towards this category of foods. While the US has been forthcoming in acknowledging the merits of food additives,[50] the EU's stance reflects an underlying wariness towards unbridled additive use.[51] This cultural divide only adds to the complexity of what is already a copious technical exercise, one that has sometimes appeared close to collapse.[52]

The process whereby the GSFA has managed to contain these conflicting pressures and the nature of its 'completely different approach'[53] can best be illustrated by three issues that are central to regulating additives:

Which Additives Should Be Permitted and for Which Foods?

A basic question in the GSFA's compilation was which additives should be included. Scientific advice on the safety of additives is provided by the Joint FAO/WHO Expert Committee on Food Additives (JECFA). Prior to the development of the GSFA, no JECFA evaluation was required for the inclusion of an additive in a Commodity standard.[54] However, taking its lead from the Denner Paper,[55] the Codex Committee on Food Additives and Contaminants (CCFAC) established this scientific assessment as a prerequisite for the inclusion of an additive in the GSFA.[56] A more thorny issue was whether the consideration of each individual additive's technological justification should be required for inclusion in the GSFA. Pre-GSFA, one of Codex's guiding principles had been that an additive approval 'as far as possible be limited to specific foods for specific purposes and under specific conditions'.[57] The huge number of additives and non-standardised foods under discussion necessitated a change of approach.[58] Firstly, technological justification was determined for whole

[50] As the US reminded the CCFAC in 2003, 'food additives can preserve an additional quality, prolonged durability, improve the taste and texture, and ensure the safety of food'. CX/FAC 03/06–Add.1, 1.

[51] Although there are strong economic incentives for food producers to limit additive use as far as possible, the EU often appears to assume escalation in use. For example: 'Even if the use of an additive in the GSFA is governed by the GMP [ie lowest level to meet need] principle, it is very probable that the use of food additives in standardised foods will be increased.' CX/FAC 06/37, Add.1, 3.

[52] Discussions became particularly heated in 2004, when the Swiss delegation prepared a Discussion Paper which failed (in a manner untypical of Codex) to reflect the concerns of many Members, thus leading Australia to formally express concerns about Swiss behaviour. CX/FAC 04/36/6–Add.1, 1–3.

[53] This was the Swiss description included in Discussion Paper CX/FAC 04/36/6, para 9.

[54] Denner (n 45) 154.

[55] ibid (stressing that the 'only realistic way forward' was the establishment of a single source of scientific knowledge in which Codex Members could have confidence).

[56] ALINORM 93/12A, para 30. The US initially objected to this approach, fearing the list of additives would be far from comprehensive given that JECFA's work had been limited to standardised foods. ALINORM 91/12, para 32.

[57] 1 CAC/MISC 1-1972, 6.a.

[58] ALINORM 93/12, para 31.

additive function classes, eg preservatives or antioxidants, rather than on the additive-by-additive basis typically adopted for Commodity Standards.[59] Secondly, the GSFA introduced the Food Categorisation System as a new organising principle.[60] This classifies all foodstuffs into a hierarchical system of general food categories and sub-categories, with the effect that an additive approved in the general category is automatically permitted for all foods falling within any category below.[61] Additives are consequently indirectly approved for some foodstuffs for which their use has never specifically been investigated.

These decisions led to the retrospective complaint that Codex recommendations were 'broader than they would have been had … the General Principles been followed'.[62] In 2001, some Codex Members renewed efforts to rein in the liberalisation in additive approval perceived to be in progress.[63] A notable flashpoint in this respect is the (still ongoing) process of integrating Commodity Standards—developed according to the principle of specificity—into the horizontal GSFA. Given the GSFA's aim to be 'a single authoritative reference point for food additives,'[64] it was proposed in 2003 to replace the detailed additive provisions contained in Commodity Standards with a general indication of the food-additive classes permitted and reference to the GSFA.[65] The EU persistently objected to this step away from specificity,[66] arguing that 'not all the additives within the same functional class have the same efficacy in food'.[67] It therefore pressed for continued Commodity Committee work on individual additives.[68] After 4 years, a compromise was finally reached by allowing the listing of specific food additives in Commodity Standards, but 'only under exceptional circumstances'.[69]

How to Establish Technological Need?

As will already be apparent from the discussion above, establishing technological need is an essential criterion for permitting additive approval. But how should the validity of 'technological need' be determined? The issue is particularly tricky

---

[59] ALINORM 95/12A, para 44.

[60] ALINORM 93/12, para 31. This system was based on a pre-existing categorisation used by the European food industry.

[61] GFSA, Preamble, para 5. There is the possibility to make specific exceptions for individual foodstuffs or sub-categories.

[62] CX/FAC 04/36/6, para 18.

[63] For example, in 2001, the EU declared that the GSFA 'generally allows too many additives in too many food products'. CX/FAC 01/8, para 154.

[64] GFSA, Preamble, para 1.2.

[65] CX/FAC 03/06, 20 (amending the Codex Procedural Manual).

[66] See comments respectively in CX/FAC 03/06, Add.1, 8; CX/FAC 04/36/6, Add.1., 4; CX/FAC 06/38/7, Add.1, 2.

[67] CX/FAC 04/36/6, Add.1, 4

[68] CX/FAC 06/38/7, Add.1, 4.

[69] ALINORM 07/30/12, para 95.

in the light of differences between national approaches to the question that long predated the Codex debate on the GSFA.[70] Under Codex's 'vertical' process of establishing standards, Commodity committees were charged with evaluating technological need, a decision sensitive to both industrial demands and the specific quality of the commodity concerned. A move to horizontal standards therefore demanded a re-evaluation of this practice.

The general list of additives to be permitted in non-standardised foods by the GSFA was constructed on the basis of Codex Member recommendations. In discussions on technological need, pragmatism initially took the upper hand. Following a first proposal to accept as technologically necessary *any* additive for which national approval had been granted,[71] the CCFAC subsequently agreed in 1998 that food-additive use in a given food category in at least two Codex Member States should constitute adequate justification of need.[72] In 2002, the EU requested for this principle to be reconsidered.[73] The existence of national legislation for a given additive, it pointed out, did not demonstrate actual use or therefore any real need on the part of the industry.[74] Moreover, there was a growing concern among some Codex Members that additive recommendations in practice were only coming from a single Codex Member or sometimes an Observer NGO.[75] In spite of this criticism, the adopted GSFA retained an inclusive approach, resisting any need to demonstrate widespread use of an additive as a criterion for approval.[76] The EU's persistence did bear fruit in two respects. Firstly, the Preamble to the GSFA was revised in a way that reasserted technological need as a key principle in additive approvals.[77] Secondly, as the exercise of reconciling commodity standards with the GSFA advanced, the systematic consultation of commodity committees as a source of expertise on establishing technological justifications was reinstated in the working principles.[78]

[70] In their assessment of new additives, the tendency among West European countries was to interpret need in the context of the existing additive market. In other words, an applicant seeking authorisation of a new additive would typically have to demonstrate a technological purpose not yet served by an existing additive. In the US, by contrast, the emphasis was on demonstrating that an overall need was met, or rather that the additive was 'effective'. See J Abraham and E Millstone, 'Food Additive Controls: Some International Comparisons' (1989) 14 Food Policy 43, 46–49.

[71] This proposal was set out in a discussion paper prepared by New Zealand, Australia and Iceland. See ALINORM 97/12A, para 35.

[72] ALINORM 99/12, para 47.

[73] ALINORM 03/12, para 50.

[74] CX/FAC 03/06, Add.1, 6. The EU therefore proposed greater scrutiny of Member proposals and also unsuccessfully attempted to shift the goalposts by suggesting that support from two or more Codex *regions* rather than individual Members should be required. CX/FAC 05/37/7, Add. 1, 3.

[75] CX/FAC 04/36/6, para 37.

[76] A Working Group had proposed that only additives 'which are widely permitted for use in the food' be included in line with the existing rules set out in Codex Procedure Manual. This was supported by the EU on the basis that it demonstrated international trade, but rejected by the US as an 'obsolete practice' reflecting pre-GSFA thinking. See CX/FAC 03/06, Add.1, 7 and 2 respectively. The latter view prevailed.

[77] The EU noted its satisfaction at this revision. CX/FAC 05/37/7, Add.1, 2.

[78] ALINORM 07/30/12 Rev, para 84.

The principle of demonstrating technological need was therefore maintained, albeit in a somewhat diluted form.

How Much of an Additive Should Be Permitted?

To ensure the safe use of additives in food, JECFA evaluates and establishes, where possible, Acceptable Daily Intakes (ADI) for each additive, taking into account consumption across the whole diet. Even with these safety parameters established, the difficult question remains how much of an additive should be permitted in a given food, not least as using only the amounts needed to fulfil the technological function is a long-standing principle of Good Manufacturing Practice (GMP). The question of maximum levels has proved divisive over the years. For additives for which no numerical ADI (ie no identifiable risk) could be assigned by JECFA, it was agreed that GMP should explicitly apply.[79] A more contested question was how to treat additives with a JECFA numerical ADI. Some Codex Members argued that all such additives should have a numerical maximum level in the GSFA. The US, in particular, argued against categorical application of this principle, arguing that in some instances, maximum levels were unnecessary or impractical.[80] By way of solution, the basic principle of establishing a numerical level was maintained with the possibility of establishing exemptions in exceptional circumstances.[81]

The most significant source of disagreement among Members arose around the setting of maximum levels in cases where Codex Members proposed different values. Once more, the initial approach (led by Australia) was inclusive: CCFAC should opt for the highest level, unless another Member can satisfactorily demonstrate that the level poses a public-safety concern, could mislead the consumer or is technologically unnecessary.[82] The EU was particularly opposed to this procedure, which placed the burden of proof on those objecting to higher levels rather than on those applying for those levels. This ran counter to the basic principle of aiming to limit additive use to that amount which is technologically needed. Instead, the EU suggested that the lowest level should be taken, with the onus on other countries requiring a higher use to substantiate their demands.[83] However, this proposal was rebuffed by other Members, in part due to the burden it would place on developing countries.[84] Recognising the practical implications of pursuing its position, the

[79] ALINORM 91/12A, para 36.

[80] It cited the example of caramel colours, for which the intensity of the colouring can vary greatly and high intensity sweeteners whose use in food is self-limiting for reasons of taste. CX/FAC 03/06, Add.1, 3.

[81] ALINORM 91/12A, para 44.

[82] ALINORM 99/12, para 47. This is not the case where the food is an obscure or unrepresentative one. In such cases, a specific level could be given for that food and a more representative one for the whole food category.

[83] See EU recommendations in CX/FAC 03/06–Add.1, 7. The Swiss took up the recommendation in its controversial Discussion Paper in December of the same year. See CX/FAC 04/36/6, 19.

[84] ALINORM 03/12A, para 46.

EU grudgingly backed down,[85] consoled in part by a clarification of the Preamble which emphasised that the 'the maximum level will not usually correspond to the optimum, recommended, or typical level of use'.[86]

Considerable time and effort has been invested by international regulators to find a common platform for the trade of food-containing additives. Where has it left Codex? Although the more theoretical debate on the principles underlying the GFSA may have run its course, the tension between different standpoints has far from disappeared.[87] Yet a mode of working has developed that seeks to accommodate both perspectives. On the one hand, leaning towards the pragmatic, reservations on additive use will not prevent the adoption of an additive provision.[88] On the other hand, adhering to basic principles, the acceptance of an additive's technological need is far from automatic. Consideration of the use of a class of additive in a given food category can be discontinued where inadequate technical justification has been provided.[89]

The case can certainly be made that the ongoing transition from detailed vertical standards to more general horizontal ones has opened up permitted additive use. As seen above, under hierarchical food categorisation, the appropriateness of the use of an additive for every food is not evaluated. Yet, a counter-case for Codex's increased stringency over additive use can also be made.[90] JECFA evaluation is now required for all additives, the principles of good manufacturing practice have been introduced even for additives for which no specific safety concerns have been identified, and specific numerical limits have replaced reference to GMP where an additive has a numerical ADI. These plausible contrasting perspectives confirm in many ways that hard-fought compromise lies at the core of the GSFA. Perhaps the

[85] The debate, however, was far from over. In subsequent discussion on reconciling the GSFA and Commodity standards, the issue was played out once more in similar terms. See the pragmatic proposal of China for an inclusive approach in CX/FAC 06/38/7, para 13(m) and the EU's critical response in CX/FAC 06/38/7, Add.1, 4. The compromise found on this occasion was to accept the Chinese approach, but place all the information from Commodity standards into an Annex to the GSFA as a list of exceptions to be subjected to further reflection. See ALINORM 07/30/12 Rev, para 85.

[86] GSFA, Preamble, para 2 (d) (amended in 2005). See EU comments, CX/FAC 05/37/7–Add.1.

[87] For example, in its 2010 meeting, the Committee resisted requests for a fundamental rediscussion of the place of consumer perception in the Preamble. ALINORM 10/33/12, para 100. Nevertheless, at the same meeting EU representatives continued a recent tendency to adopt the use of individual additives with a caveat, known as 'note 161' (see Codex General Standard for Food Additives, Codex Stan 192-1995, 246). In this way, the EU accepts a substance only 'subject to national legislation'. The practice threatens to paralyse discussions and has caused considerable frustration among other Codex Members. See Codex Alimentarius Commission Document ALINORM 10/33/12, para 70–75. See generally C Downes, 'Only a Footnote? The Curious Codex Battle for Control of Additive Regulations' (2012) 7 *European Food and Feed Law Review* 232.

[88] For instance, additives have been approved for use in pre-cooked pasta in spite of the EU's persistent objections to this practice, such as those in ALINORM 08/31/12, para 68.

[89] See, for instance, the Committee's work on food additives containing aluminium. ALINORM 09/32/12, para 64.

[90] DL Post, 'Food Fights: Who Shapes International Food Safety Standards and Who Uses Them?' (PhD Thesis, University of California Berkeley, 2005) 63–64.

most remarkable element of the GSFA, given the cyclical battles that have occurred during its development, is that in spite (or perhaps because) of its halting progress, Codex Members remain fully engaged in the process. While quarrels over the appropriate management of individual additives will undoubtedly persist, Codex has largely succeeded in creating a working structure for the management of all food additives used in international trade.

Yet have these considerable efforts moved Codex Members a meaningful step closer to achieving compatible regulatory systems? The next section will consider what effect the establishment of the GSFA has had on the development of national measures to regulate additives.

7.3.2 The Impact of the GSFA

As noted in the introduction to this chapter, extensive academic attention to Codex has not led to significant analysis of the substantive impact of its standards on national regulations.[91] In addition to the conceptual obstacles discussed above, there are a number of factors that discourage this type of evaluation.[92] Firstly, notwithstanding WTO Members' efforts to meet transparency obligations,[93] tracking down and ensuring adequate understanding of the relevant legislation can be a time-consuming and linguistically challenging task.[94] On occasions, secondary references to legislation must suffice.[95] Secondly, the number of additives regulated internationally defies a comprehensive review of their uptake by national authorities even where this information is available. Thirdly, international standards will often be exploited by scientific and technical experts in the development of national lists of approved additives, but the weight given to Codex standards in such deliberations will not necessarily be apparent to the external observer. In short, an assessment

[91] For the most elaborate attempt to assess the impact of international standards, see DL Post, ibid and DL Post, 'Diffusion of International Food Safety Standards: Food Additive Regulation and the Codex Alimentarius Commission' ('Diffusion of Food Standards') (American Political Science Association annual meeting, Philadelphia, August 2003).

[92] The first and third set of factors are equally relevant to the study below on food supplements.

[93] A fair number of changes to food additive measures have been notified under SPS Agreement Article 7 (and under the Agreement on Technical Barriers to Trade (TBT Agreement)), but not all legislation is therefore necessarily easily accessible to the general public.

[94] The FAO's Legal Office provides a very useful service—FAOLEX, available at faolex.fao.org—in this respect, although inevitably this is not comprehensive in coverage or fully up to date. This type of research, unthinkable just a few years ago, is now viable due to online translation facilities, although this only remains suitable for the type of broad brush approach taken here—identifying the replication of standards in national legislation—and clearly not more fine-grained textual analysis. In some instances, national authorities were contacted with requests for information, but this generally proved ineffective. The survey strove to be as comprehensive as possible.

[95] Some national standards eg Russia, Guatemala must be (but were not!) purchased. In such instances, the US Department of Agriculture's (USDA) Foreign Agricultural Services Global Agriculture Information Network (GAIN) can often provide extremely helpful overviews of food legislation. The GAIN reports referred to below are available at gain.fas.usda.gov.

of the overall impact of the GSFA will at best be partial. With these limitations in mind, this study was confined to assessing to what extent the GSFA constitutes a reference point in national legislation, and if so, which of the primary features of the GSFA—its basic principles, food categorisation, International Numbering System (INS),[96] GMP requirements or the food-additive provisions—have shaped these texts. The survey is organised according to the transnational norm dissemination framework described in Sect. 7.2.[97]

Innovation

The comprehensive nature of the GSFA makes it a particularly valuable source for domestic regulatory innovation in those countries with limited scientific and technical capacities. Such innovation can take different forms. Some countries, such as Uganda, Bahrain and the Dominican Republic, choose to reproduce the GSFA in its entirety in national legislation.[98] Others like Laos, Nicaragua and Myanmar prefer to develop their own legal frameworks and simply refer to Codex Standards as an authoritative source on the acceptability of additives.[99] Still others use Codex standards in practice as a defining reference point whenever queries on food additives arise, although the precise legal basis for doing so may not always be clear.[100] It is therefore possible that Codex's reach is more significant in many countries than can always be ascertained in a survey of legislation.[101]

In spite of the numerous examples of domestic regulatory innovation drawing on Codex norms, more extensive use of the GSFA might have been expected in

[96] The INS, first adopted by Codex in 1989, aims to simplify the labelling of foods by providing a numerical alternative to lengthy additive names. See CAC/GL 36-1989.

[97] Given that the exercise undertaken in the GSFA was the result of pragmatic compromise rather than the implementation of an existing national approach, the category 'accentuation' is less relevant in this case study.

[98] See, for example, Ugandan Standard US 45: 2009, reported in G/TBT/N/UGA/123 (18 May 2010). Similar examples are offered by Bahrain and the Dominican Republic. See respectively G/SPS/GEN/537 (18 January 2005); Draft Proposal for Food Sanitary Regulations for the Dominican Republic (2009), in particular Title VII, otcasea.gob.do/wp-content/uploads/2009/06/propuesta-regl-sanitario-alimentos-rd.pdf, as notified to the SPS Committee under G/SPS/N/DOM/20 (7 July 2006). For a detailed discussion on the development of additive rules in the latter, see Post, 'Diffusion of Food Standards' (n 91) 18–21.

[99] See Laos Ministry of Health, Regulation No. 586/MoH, Art 5 (12 May 2006); Nicaraguan Ministry of Agriculture and Forestry, Ministerial Agreement No. 23-2000, Art 1, paras (b) and (c) (2000) (establishing the legality of those additives accepted by Codex Alimentarius); Myanmar Ministry of Livestock and Fisheries, Directive No. (9/96), November 6 1996, 1.1 (specifically relating to fishery products).

[100] In Pakistan, there is no food additive legislation as such, but the Ministry of Commerce is reported to allow the entry of imported food additives on the basis of Codex standards. See USDA, 'GAIN Report' (PK:9012, August 2009) 5–6.

[101] For instance, Mali also reports a high level of harmonisation of food standards with Codex standards (see CX/AFRICA 09/18/6, 1), although it has not been possible to confirm this in the case of food additives.

developing countries. After all, one of Codex's goals is to assist its under-resourced Members in the attainment of adequate food standards. Accounts of regulatory practice in Africa offer one explanation of why Codex's influence is confined. Although many African countries are actively committed to the harmonisation process,[102] limited technical competence among officials and insufficient monitoring and enforcement capacity put a brake on regulatory innovation.[103] In addition, a greater concern in some parts of Africa is to focus administrative resources explicitly on specific product sectors with latent export capacity, a strategy stimulated by developed countries.[104] Where this is the case, tailoring local legislation to the regulatory demands of relevant export markets takes priority over the type of comprehensive framework envisaged by the GSFA.[105]

Displacement

While regulatory innovation can clearly be extremely important to countries lacking administrative resources, for the purposes of measuring the 'bite' of Codex standards, these arguably represent soft examples. Can Codex be influential in the same way where regulatory systems are already established? The answer is that it can, although the significant displacement of local policy by the GSFA can only really be considered to have taken place in two settings, as summarised below.[106]

China

In the wake of a number of food-safety scandals, China has looked to reassure the international community by undertaking an ambitious review of its food-safety regulations.[107] Prior to this process, China had maintained its own positive list of food additives. In 2007, China introduced a National Standard on Food Additives which

---

[102] Following a survey of use of Codex standards by African countries, FAO/WHO Coordinating Committee for Africa reported that 'many countries based their national food standards/regulations on Codex standards or used them as reference'. ALINORM 09/32/28, para 47.

[103] See CX/AFRICA 09/18/6.

[104] One such programme is the EU's 'Strengthening Fishery Products' Health Conditions in ACP/OCT Countries Programme' running since 2002. See sfp.acp.int/.

[105] See Congo Ministry of Forestry Economy and Fisheries, Decree 3642 (29 September 2000) (establishing a list of food additives permitted in fish products); Eritrean Government Legal Notice No. 65/2003 Fishery Products Additives Regulations (30 April 2003). Both laws refer to the EU numbering system for additives with the former citing explicitly EU Directive 95/2/EC on food additives other than colours and sweeteners.

[106] Given that China, Australia and New Zealand do not entirely replicate the GSFA, it could be argued that their regulations represent examples of localisation. However, the significance of their changes in policy particularly marks out these cases. Strictly speaking there is a third case, as Hong Kong China has pursued a very similar course to China.

[107] See European Commission, DG Trade, *SPS Newsletter* (July 2010) trade.ec.europa.eu/doclib/docs/2010/august/tradoc_146404.pdf.

largely replicates the GSFA in both format and content.[108] The Standard therefore introduces a number of new concepts into Chinese legislation, namely the basic principles as to the permitted use of additives, international additive numbering and the application of the food categorisation system adopted in the GSFA. The permitted conditions for individual additives in the Chinese standard do not necessarily replicate Codex standards, but China has shown itself to be willing to bring its rules into line where trade disruptions occur.[109]

Australia and New Zealand

In 2000, Australia and New Zealand developed a Joint Standard for food additives that replaced their respective codes.[110] This evolution echoed developments in Codex, replacing systems primarily oriented towards food-commodity standards with horizontal standards for all foods, thus embracing the flexibility underpinning the GSFA.[111] The GSFA's influence on the new code is evident, although the 'world's best practice'[112] is a fair description of the inclusive approach taken by the two countries. The risk analysis of additives and the establishment of their technological functions is informed not only by the GSFA and regional precedents, but also by regulatory frameworks in the EU, Canada and the US.[113] Nevertheless, the organisational structure of the Standard draws heavily on the GSFA, introducing the INS and the format and hierarchical logic of the Codex food-categorisation system.[114] The most innovative feature of the new Standard was the introduction of the requirement to manufacture in accordance with GMP, a significant departure from early

[108] Chinese Ministry of Health National Standard GB-2760-2007 (27 August 2007), an unofficial translation of which is available in USDA, 'GAIN Report' (CH8018 20, March 2008). The notable exceptions are that the Standard also incorporates flavouring agents and processing aids in addition to other additives and does not spell out the concept of good manufacturing practice.

[109] Following complaints in 2008 by the EU as to quantitative restrictions on the use of sulphur dioxide in sweet white wines, China raised the maximum level from 250 to 400 mg/l in 2010, thus opening the Chinese market to these wines. See European Commission DG Trade, *Market Access Flash Note 36* (19 May 2009). For the relevant discussion on this topic within the WTO TBT Committee, see G/TBT/M/48 (29 September 2009) paras 199–200.

[110] Australia New Zealand Food Standard 1.3.1, *Commonwealth of Australia Gazette* No. P 10 (22 June 2000). For an account of this process, see S Brooke-Taylor et al., 'Reforms to Food Additive Regulation in Australia and New Zealand' (2003) 14 *Food Control* 375.

[111] See Australia and New Zealand Food Authority (ANZFA), User Guide to Standard 1.3.1—Food Additives (July 2001) ('ANZFA's User Guide') 4–5 (drawing attention to the new Code's aim of 'eliminating unnecessary prescriptiveness').

[112] See Brooke-Taylor (n 110) 381.

[113] The permitted justifications for use of additives established by Codex are not found in Australia New Zealand Food Standard 1.3.1, but are included in the 'ANZFA's User Guide' (n 111).

[114] Australia New Zealand Food Standard 1.3.1, Schedule 1. It should be noted that Australian and New Zealand have introduced some amendments into the categorisation. See Brooke-Taylor (n 110) 380.

rules which permitted additives to be used without limit.[115] The Codex GMP criteria are directly reproduced in the Standard as guidance to manufacturers.[116]

In both these instances, GSFA offered Codex Members a valuable template which significantly shaped the measures introduced in a period of regulatory renewal.

Resistance

At other end of the spectrum lie those countries on which the GSFA has made no or very little impression. Such regulatory systems, as found in the US, Canada, Malaysia or South Africa, are typically characterised by an established practice of managing food additives, with detailed legislation and substantial scientific risk-evaluation capacity.[117] Where science-based regulatory systems prevail, these countries may feel relatively confident about compatibility with SPS norms and therefore not vulnerable to new and potentially divergent standards emerging in Codex.[118] Let us consider three examples:

South Korea

South Korea's legal basis for regulating food additives is found in its 1986 Food Sanitation Act.[119] This creates a 'Deliberation Council' within the Korean Food and Drug Administration (KFDA) that assesses the safety and appropriate use of additives.[120] The fruit of this work is a Code covering in excess of 600 additives, a comprehensive compendium of information including identification, chemical formula, content, purity, assay and permitted use.[121] In spite of the many amendments to both the Act and Code since the adoption of the GSFA, no reference at all is made to the

[115] ibid 378.

[116] Australia New Zealand Food Standard 1.3.1, Clause 3.

[117] See Appendix II for an overview of these countries. For a comprehensive account of the US's 50-year experience of regulating food additives, see L Noah and R Merrill, 'Starting from Scratch?: Reinventing the Food Additive Approval Process' (1990) 78 *Boston University Law Review* 329. Some other countries such as Egypt and Morocco appear to have maintained positive lists of functional classes of additives without reference to Codex. See USDA, 'GAIN Report' (EG9014 July 2009) and USDA 'GAIN Report' (MO8011 June 2008). However, unfortunately the legislation is not publicly available to verify their precise relationship with Codex norms.

[118] The US, for one, does not appear unduly concerned about such divergences. Although the sweeteners cyclamates have long been banned in the US, during the Codex adoption process for the inclusion of the sweeteners into the GSFA, the US delegation simply noted 'that they had not approved cyclamates and ponceau 4R, but respected the Codex process and would not block adoption.' ALINORM 10/10 /33/REP, para 40.

[119] Korean Food Sanitation Act No 3823 (10 May 1986). This Act has been amended on several occasions, most recently in 2009 by Law No. 9692.

[120] Korean Food Sanitation Act No 3823, Art 6.

[121] Korea Food Additive Code 2004, fa.kfda.go.kr/foodadditivescode.html. See also Guidelines for Designation of Food Additives fa.kfda.go.kr/process/food1_5_4.html.

Codex work.[122] In practice, moreover, the existence of a Codex standard is of little help to a food exporter where it is not included within the Korean code.[123]

Japan

A similar situation is found in Japan, the country with the longest tradition of regulating additives.[124] The country's Additives Standard comprises, at the time of writing, a list of 345 additives. The addition of internationally used substances to this list is possible through an internal review process.[125] Salzer predicts that given the long legacy of management of food additives, Japan 'will take time to get harmonisation to international guidelines'.[126] Certainly, this is the view of the EU, which has been vocal in its criticism of Japan's slow uptake of international standards.[127] More fundamentally, the major GSFA innovations—the food-categorisation system, INS identification and GMP principles[128]—have not been incorporated into the Japanese standard.

EU

The EU has enjoyed an ambivalent relationship with Codex as regards food additives. The first of the EU's two major initiatives on food-additive legislation was strongly influenced by international discussions. In 1989, the EU expanded the coverage of its legislation to include all categories of additives, introduced harmonised labelling (in the form of E numbers), and provided a mechanism for adopting new additives which required the support of the European Parliament.[129] The definition

[122] The only reference to international standards is an oblique one, a provision allowing the Deliberational Council to appoint 'research commissioners' to study such standards. Korean Food Sanitation Act No 3823, Art 43.

[123] See USDA, 'GAIN Report' (KS8044, 31 July 2008).

[124] Japan's first Ministerial decree on food colouring dates back to 1878. The first specifications for food additives were produced in 1960. For the latest edition adopted in 1999 (including a history of the standard's development), see The Ministry of Health and Welfare, 'Japan's Specifications and Standards for Food Additives' (English translation, 7th edn, September 2000) www.ffcr.or.jp/zaidan/FFCRHOME.nsf/pages/spec.stand.fa.

[125] For an overview of Japanese regulatory activity on additives, see the Ministry of Health, Labour and Welfare website: www.mhlw.go.jp/english/topics/foodsafety/foodadditives/index.html.

[126] U-J Salzer, 'Legislation/Toxicology' in H Ziegler (ed), *Flavourings* (Weinheim, Wiley-VCH, 2007) 786.

[127] In particular, the EU bemoaned the 7 years taken by Japan to assess only 25 of 46 active submitted by the EU for authorisation, in spite of their international approval, WT/TPR/M/179/Add.1 (22 June 2007) 54. In addition, both the US and India have challenged Japan's regulatory practices. See respectively G/SPS/R/28 (5 February 2003) 7 and WT/TPR/M/179/Add.1, 153.

[128] Additives not subject to specific numerical limits are simply left blank within the Japanese standards without reference to GMP or *quantum satis*.

[129] Council Directive 89/107/EEC on the approximation of the laws of the Member States concerning food additives authorized for use in foodstuffs [1989] OJ L40/27.

of a food additive, the criteria governing the purposes of additives and the conditions of approval almost entirely replicated the 1972 Codex principles.[130] In 2006, a second major review set in motion a re-evaluation programme for all food additives and replaced the cumbersome inter-institutional method of additive approval with a centralised authorisation system permitting the Commission to approve additives with the support of Member States.[131] Tellingly perhaps, neither the Commission's impact assessment of the 2006 proposal[132] nor the final legislation makes significant mention of the work of Codex.[133] Indeed, in recent years the EU has taken a course that runs contrary to the more pragmatic approach reflected in the GSFA. Firstly, the new Regulation introduced new criteria into the evaluation of approval—'other legitimate factors, including environmental factors'[134]– which depart from existing Codex principles. Secondly, the EU is developing a food-categorisation system that draws on Codex, but neither fully respects its categories nor its hierarchical logic.[135] The ultimate impact on trade of these developments is still unclear, but the seeming disregard by the EU for the GSFA increases the potential for trade conflict.

Notwithstanding the limited enthusiasm among these countries for harmonisation with the GSFA, the characterisation of them as 'resisting' Codex's work should be treated with a little caution. As the discussion in Sect. 7.3.1 suggests, these countries have not shied away from participation in Codex. Nor has their respective management of food additives been entirely impervious to its effects.[136] However,

[130] Council Directive 89/107/EEC, Annex II.

[131] See respectively Regulation (EC) No 1333/2008 of the European Parliament and of the Council on food additives [2008] OJ L354/16 and Regulation (EC) No 1331/2008 of the European Parliament and of the Council establishing a common authorisation procedure for food additives, food enzymes and food flavourings [2008] OJ L354/1.

[132] Acknowledgement of Codex's work is limited to the discussion of whether the EU should revise the definition of processing aids. Its evaluation on the impact of the proposal on third countries and international relations simply reads: 'This proposal will further harmonise the legislation on additives and will create a uniform market within the EU.' European Commission, 'Staff Working Document, Annex to the proposal for a European Parliament and Council Regulation on food additives: Impact Assessment' SEC (2006) 1040 (19 and 22 respectively).

[133] The lack of reference to Codex or the EU's international commitments in the context of food additives stands in obvious contrast to the specific recognition of the body's work in the EU's contaminants legislation. See, for example, Commission Regulation (EC) No 1881/2006 setting maximum levels for certain contaminants in foodstuffs [2006] OJ L364/5, recital 1.

[134] Regulation (EC) No 1333/2008, Art 6.

[135] See Commission Regulation (EU) No 1129/2011 of 11 November 2011 amending Annex II to Regulation (EC) No 1333/2008 of the European Parliament and of the Council by establishing a Union list of food additives [2011] OJ L 295/1, especially rec 4 (explaining the Regulation's relationship to the GSFA).

[136] For example, in its 2004 WTO Trade Policy Review, Korea reported: 'The KFDA approves new food additives generally twice a year, and continues to relax usage level provisions, in order to harmonize KFDA's standards and usage levels with international standards.' WTO Document WT/TPR/M/137/Add.1 (20 December 2004) 4. Likewise, Japan has moved to incorporate Codex criteria on technological justification into its guidelines for the designation of food additives and acknowledges Codex standards as a source for scientific assessments. See Japanese Ministry of Health and Welfare Guidelines for designation of food additives and for revision of standards for use of food additives (2006) www.mhlw.go.jp/english/topics/foodsafety/foodadditives/index.html.

failure to embrace either the structure or the content of the GSFA leaves WTO Members vulnerable to WTO challenge.[137]

Localisation

In many countries, the relationship between the GSFA and domestic legislation is less pronounced than in the situations outlined above. Involvement in and acknowledgement of Codex standards is sometimes evident even where there is no simple replication of Codex's work. Some have introduced fairly cosmetic GSFA-based changes to national legislation, such as the adoption of the INS.[138] Others retain specific commodity standards in line with pre-GSFA Codex work, but in addition, permit the use of food additives approved by Codex where they fall outside existing national standards.[139] Some examples of localised use of Codex norms are given below:

Latin America

The Mercosur[140] has had a common list of additives[141] permitted on the Common Market since 1993, and it has been updated on a regular basis.[142] The general principles, predating as they do the establishment of the GSFA, reflect the Codex principles established in 1972, most notably the requirement to approve additives for use in specific foods and in specific conditions.[143] Consistent with this practice, for certain food categories, Mercosur does not permit the use of additives, even where

[137] By way of illustration, when Korea threatened to ban 'tar colours' permitted by international standards, it came under immediate pressure from the US and abandoned the initiative. See United States Trade Representative, '2010 Report on Sanitary and Phytosanitary Measures', www.ustr.gov/sites/default/files/SPS%20Report%20Final(2).pdf.

[138] See the Mexican Ministry of Health, Agreement determining the substances permitted as additives and processing aids in food, beverages and nutritional supplements, *Diaro Oficial* (July 17 2006) 8, www.salud.gob.mx/unidades/cdi/nom/compi/a170706.pdf.

[139] Kenya is one example of this approach. See Food, Drugs and Chemical Substances (Food Labelling, Additives and Standards) (Amendment) Regulations 2010, www.kenyalaw.org.

[140] Mercosur stands for Mercado Común del Sur or Southern Common Market, the political and economic agreement signed in 1991 by Argentina, Brazil, Paraguay and Uruguay.

[141] Mercosur standards are intended to serve as a basis for domestic regulations adopted by its Members and are as such a reasonable indication of the influence of Codex in the region. However, the rate of incorporation into national law of Mercosur standards may be slow. For example, while the standard MERCOSUR/GMC/RES N°51/00 on additives and their maximum concentration levels was due to be incorporated by January 1 2000, the relevant Argentinean legislation was only published in January 2004, See G/TBT/N/ARG/154 (23 January 2004). All the Mercosur standards cited are available at www.mercosur.int.

[142] The last major overhaul of the General List of Additives permitted can be found in MERCOSUR/GMC/RES N°11/06.

[143] MERCOSUR/GMC/RES N°31/92, Art 1(c).

Codex has approved them for general use in foods.[144] Indeed, while Codex's work is clearly highly pertinent to the market's management of additives, both national and international reference points of expertise can be influential, depending on the aspect under consideration. The justification of technical need required for an additive's approval can be drawn from either Codex, the EU, the US, or a Mercosur Member's domestic law, if acceptable to other Members.[145] For the purposes of introducing an additive to the general list of permitted additives, either Codex or EU approval is required, with the possibility of using US regulations as a source of 'additional information'.[146] By contrast, for the setting of maximum levels, a clear hierarchy is established, with Codex being the preferred reference point, followed by EU and US regulations respectively.[147] This rather idiosyncratic approach reflects a delicate balance between international obligations and the demands of the most significant export markets.

Thailand

Prior to its engagement in Codex, food additives in Thailand could only be placed on the market with the approval of the Thai Food and Drug Administration.[148] This system was amended in 2004 by a ministerial decree which permitted the use of all additives and related conditions of use as found in the Codex Alimentarius.[149] While internationally approved additives may be sold in Thailand, the criteria employed by the Thai Food and Drug administration in assessing new additives remain entirely safety-oriented,[150] and as such, unaffected by the Codex discussion on technological need. In other words, Thailand appears to accept international constraints imposed by Codex, but does not necessarily adhere to the overall philosophy embraced by the international body.

The Philippines

From the mid-1980s, the Philippines had an overall approach towards additives modelled on US regulations, maintaining a positive list of food additives which

[144] By way of example, Mercosur updated the list of food additives permitted for use according to GMP, but retained restrictions for certain food categories eg breads made only with flour wheat, water, raising agents and salt (7.1.1 and 7.1.2), a category of products for which Codex does not foresee specific restrictions. See GSFA, Table III, Annex; MERCOSUR/GMC/RES N°34/10, Annex (c).

[145] MERCOSUR/GMC/RES N°52/98, Annex, para 3.

[146] MERCOSUR/GMC/RES N°17/93, Annex A, point 1.

[147] MERCOSUR/GMC/RES N°52/98, Annex A, footnote.

[148] See Salzer (n 126) 798.

[149] Thailand Ministry of Public Health Notification, No. 281 B.E. 2547 (2004) Art 6.

[150] ibid Art 4.

could be amended at the request of a petitioner.[151] Most strikingly, there was no requirement for petitioners to demonstrate a technical need for an additive. Rather, it was necessary to demonstrate that 'the food additive will have intended physical or other technical effect … and the amount necessary to accomplish this'.[152] In its revision of its regulatory guideline in 2006,[153] the Philippines incorporated wholesale the Codex principles on permitted technological functions and GMP. Under this new guideline, the Philippines automatically include any food additive adopted by Codex.[154] However, in the management of the levels permitted in additives, not only Codex standards, but also Philippines commodity standards and requests by interested parties are taken into account.[155] Equally, the food-categorisation system used to allocate additive uses is largely a copy of Codex, but has some additions included to reflect local diet.[156]

As the above survey and the overview in Appendix II demonstrate, the impact of Codex's GSFA on regulatory measures worldwide is significant, but far from homogeneous. The often assumed impact of international standards, namely the wholesale displacement of national rules, is rare. This survey suggests that domestic innovation on the basis of the GSFA, localisation of Codex norms and resistance to its influence are equally common outcomes. Notably, the GSFA has been largely sidelined by those WTO Members with long regulatory experience in managing additive use in food. The result is that in spite of the extensive negotiation of the GSFA, and its undoubted influence in many countries, a patchwork of regulatory systems for food additives remains that is deeply coloured by local mores.

7.4 Case study on Vitamin and Mineral Food Supplements

Barely extending beyond two pages, one could be forgiven for finding the Codex Guidelines for Vitamin and Mineral Food Supplements (VMS Guidelines) an unexceptional document. It contains a general description of vitamin and mineral supplements ('concentrated forms of those nutrients'), the substances that may be used (but without naming them), the levels that may be used (but without defining them), and a handful of packaging and labelling recommendations.[157] Yet, this vague and

[151] Republic of Philippines, Department of Health, Administrative Order No. 88-A s (1984). US regulations served as a basis approach for this list of permitted additives and conditions. See Salzer (n 126) 794.

[152] Administrative Order No. 88-A s, Art 3.2(d).

[153] Republic of Philippines, Department of Health, Bureau of Food and Drugs Circular 2006-016 (18 October 2006).

[154] Circular 2006-016, para VII.

[155] Circular 2006-016, para III.A.3.

[156] See, for example, the inclusion of soya bean curd into food category 04.2.2.6, Circular 2006-016, Table 1.

[157] CAC/GL 55–2002 ('VMS Guidelines').

slender document took more than 10 years to negotiate. Moreover, it propelled Codex from obscurity to notoriety, merited a star-led documentary[158] and has offered a bountiful source for conspiracy theorists worldwide.[159] The conspiracy element—the claim of collusion between an international organisation and the pharmaceutical industry—simply embellished the central concern of those that have campaigned vociferously against the Guidelines, namely that Codex will 'take away our liberty to use dietary supplements in effective doses'.[160] That controversy is not central to this case study, although through it, the validity of such claims will probably become clearer. From the perspective of this book, a more striking feature of the anti-Codex movement is its seemingly unerring belief in international law. Underneath the vitriol and angst lies a conviction that decisions taken by Codex have the capacity to sweep away national practices governing the use of food supplements. This second case study examines to what extent these expectations have been fulfilled. Their infamy aside, the generality and brevity of the Guidelines make them an interesting point of comparison to the case of the elaborate GSFA studied above. This study firstly discusses the development of the Codex Guidelines and then assesses to what extent a process of global regulatory harmonisation for these products has occurred.

7.4.1 The VMS Guidelines

Before turning to the content of the VMS Guidelines, it is worth briefly explaining their status. While set out in a form identical to that of a standard, the Codex Committee on Nutrition and Foods for Special Dietary Uses' (CCNFSDU) explicit intention from the opening of discussions in 1991 was to establish a Guideline.[161] The choice not to opt for a standard was significant. At the time, Codex Members could choose formally to accept standards (and Maximum Residue Levels),[162] but not other Codex texts, which remained purely 'of an advisory nature'.[163] The lowered ambition associated with Guidelines, while not allaying the fears of all Members,[164]

[158] See KP Miller's 2005 documentary 'We Become Silent: *The Last Days of Health Freedom'*, *narrated by Dame Judi Dench.*

[159] A quick enquiry using any Internet search engine, using the keywords 'Codex' and 'supplements' will provide a wealth of material on this topic. From mainstream journalism, see J Blythman, 'Health supplement: RIP' *The Guardian* (14 September 2002) www.guardian.co.uk/society/2002/sep/14/medicineandhealth.lifeandhealth.

[160] 'Health Threat from the EU and UN' *The New American* (4 February 2008).

[161] See ALINORM 91/26, para 126. The format of the document was confirmed by the CCNFSDU in 1995 (see ALINORM 95/26, 48), although the question as to whether to proceed at all with the Guideline rumbled on until 2000. See ALINORM 01/26, para 38.

[162] The acceptance procedure, which never really operated effectively, was abandoned in 2005. For a discussion of this procedure, see Masson-Matthee (n 1) 83–85.

[163] Joint WHO/FAO Food Standards Program, *Codex Alimentarius Commission*, Procedural Manual (Rome, FAO/WHO, 16th ed, 2006) 30.

[164] The US, UK (ALINORM 95/26, para 45), later joined by Japan (ALINORM 97/26, para 42) were particularly vocal in their opposition to the development of Guidelines.

was essential to permitting work on the issue. The notion that the choice for Guidelines reduced their legal significance was questionable at the time, given the non-mandatory nature of all Codex texts. This is more evidently so today given the amendment of the Codex Procedural Manual, in line with the SPS Agreement,[165], to remove any distinction between standards and 'related texts'.[166] Nevertheless, the ambiguity of the document's legal weight throughout negotiations has left its mark on both the content and coherence of the document. Since it took the form of Guidelines, the Committee considered it appropriate to remove many of the sections—on additives, contaminants and hygiene—common to Codex standards,[167] and thus diminished its immediate relevance as a basis for nascent national legislation. At the same time, underlying fear of the Guidelines' potential implications for national legislation discouraged Members from developing detailed provisions. The inclusion of, for example, lists of names and sources of vitamins and minerals would have greatly enhanced the Guidelines' practical value to many countries. Ambivalence about the status of the document is moreover reflected in the use of tenses, which vacillates between 'should' and 'shall'.[168] The result is a text that arguably falls short in many respects.[169] To understand the reluctance of many delegations towards the development of the VMS Guidelines and why discussions were so protracted, it is necessary to trace the principal themes that dominated the debate.

Food Supplements: What Are They?

From the outset, the elaboration of the VMS text was mired in diverging conceptions of the products under discussion. There are essentially three rationales for taking food supplements. Firstly, a person may suffer from an identified medical problem, eg a vitamin deficiency, for which supplementation is required. Secondly, inadequate vitamin and mineral intake due to unbalanced or inadequate diets can be compensated through the nutritional use of supplements. Thirdly, regardless of the actual adequacy of their diets, consumers may choose to supplement their diet on a regular basis due to the perceived health benefits of doing so.[170] Many Codex

[165] The fact that the SPS and TBT Agreements did not draw a distinction between 'mandatory' and 'advisory' Codex texts was a central counter-argument to those countries such as Malaysia who were intent on maintaining two tiers of Codex texts. See ALINORM 07/30/33, paras 143–145.

[166] Whatever their form, the Manual now clarifies that Codex texts are 'not a substitute for, or alternative to national legislation.' Joint WHO/FAO Food Standards Program, *Codex Alimentarius Commission*, Procedural Manual (Rome, FAO/WHO, 19th ed, 2010) 17.

[167] ALINORM 01/26, para 53.

[168] This discrepancy was noted by the Committee at one point, but not rectified. ALINORM 04/27/26, para 52.

[169] This sentiment, in particular that the document does not contain 'any indication of its purpose', was expressed in the Codex Alimentarius Commission even at the moment of its adoption. See ALINORM 05/28/41, para 52.

[170] The 2000 discussion paper produced by Brazil, Canada, the EU, Mexico and the USA elaborates helpfully on these issues. See CX/NFSDU 00/5, 5.

Members had regulations in place prior to 1991 which firmly embraced one of these rationales for supplementation. A central struggle in the ensuing Codex debate was how strongly each rationale—medicinal, nutritional, consumer health—would be reflected in the Guideline. Unhelpfully, perhaps, the quasi-philosophical aspects of regulating supplements were brought to the fore through the insertion of a Preamble that aimed to set the context for the Guidelines.[171] In this Preamble, predominantly developing countries sought a text that played down the need for supplementation. India, for example, unsuccessfully attempted to include the statement that 'people *who do not have access to balanced diets* may need vitamins and minerals supplements'.[172] India's concerns that supplementation might undermine policies promoting good dietary practices drew vocal support from Brazil[173] and Malaysia.[174] This more paternalistic approach inevitably clashed with the views of those states whose regulatory systems entrusted the consumer with decisions on supplementation. Most significantly, the developing-country prescriptions were viewed as threatening consumers' 'choice', indeed their 'right', to dietary supplements, a leitmotif of the US regulatory system in particular.[175] Ultimately, it was necessary to develop a wording sufficiently abstract to appease both sides. Thus, the Preamble noted that 'people should … be encouraged to select a balanced diet from food before considering any vitamin and mineral supplement', but also, tritely, 'where consumers consider their diet requires supplementation, vitamin and mineral supplements serve to supplement the daily diet.'[176]

While reconciling nutritional and health conceptions of supplementation, this compromise did not satisfy the many Codex Members, from both developing and developed countries, who considered supplements to be medicines.[177] With Codex only governing the regulation of food, those regimes constructed according to this view were by definition excluded from the scope of the Guidelines. Yet, the concern remained that by providing an international framework for trade of supplements as food, countries that continued to treat supplements as drugs would be vulnerable to international challenge. To dissipate those worries, the Scope clarified that the Guidelines 'only apply in those jurisdictions where products … are regulated as foods'.[178] The impact of the medicinal perspective on the VMS Guidelines was sig-

[171] ALINORM 95/26, para 44 (introduced at the request of Codex Observer, Consumers International).

[172] ALINORM 97/26, para 45 (emphasis added).

[173] CX/NFSDU 02/06, 5 (fearing use of supplements 'without control by consumers').

[174] CX/NFSDU 02/06, 8 (arguing that supplements were 'required only in cases when the intake of food is insufficient').

[175] Consumer 'rights' and 'choice' arguments were put forward in ALINORM 99/26, para 43 and ALINORM 01/26, para 38 respectively.

[176] 'VMS Guidelines', Preamble.

[177] This was the view of Australia (ALINORM 93/26, para 100), Canada, India and Kenya (ALINORM 01/26, para 38).

[178] 'VMS Guidelines', 1.2. The Codex Commission included the word 'only' at the very end of negotiations to firmly rule out any ambiguity as to the requirements of medicine-oriented Codex Members. See ALINORM 05/28/41, para 54.

nificant in two respects. Firstly, by excluding certain countries from the Guidelines' application, the text establishes a caveat which, as South Africa noted, 'creates a potential barrier to trade', one that is fundamentally at odds with Codex's harmonisation goals.[179] Secondly, and perversely, the detailed discussions on the Guidelines were often complicated and delayed by precisely those delegations who asserted their irrelevance to their national situation.[180] While still relevant to the majority of Codex Members, the exemption from application that the Guidelines condones undoubtedly limits the overall authority of the document.

Which Food Supplements?

On the European market alone, around 400 substances are estimated to be marketed as food supplements.[181] From the outset, the CCNFSDU limited the scope of its work to vitamins and minerals.[182] This reflects in part the relative economic dominance of this sub-category of products,[183] but also pressure from an industry deeply concerned about the implications of regulating other substances, in particular herbal products.[184] Yet even agreeing to what constitutes a vitamin or mineral suitable for supplementation proved problematic. Germany initially proposed a list of 25 nutrients, but this list was too long for some,[185] and too prescriptive for others.[186] In essence, the debate on which substances to permit concealed a more sensitive one, on the appropriate relationship between regulators and the consumer. Should the consumer be able to make a choice between all nutrients known to be essential to humans, or should only vitamins and minerals not already abundant in the diet be permitted in food supplements (thereby saving unnecessary expenditure by consumers)? Moreover, were one to favour the latter approach, could the pres-

[179] CX/NFSDU 02/6, 11.

[180] This irony was not lost on Germany who rather tetchily recommended in 2003 'that all countries in the jurisdiction of which vitamin and mineral supplements are regulated as drugs should from now on refrain from participating in the discussion'. CX/NFSDU 03/5, 7.

[181] European Commission, 'Staff Working Document, Characteristics and Perspectives of the Market for Food Supplements Containing Substances other than Vitamins and Minerals' (SEC (2008) 2976) 2.

[182] The Russian Federation belatedly and unsuccessfully tried to extend the discussion to other substances. ALINORM 03/26A, para 94.

[183] A report undertaken at the request of the European Commission found that vitamin and mineral supplements account for 50% of the European Market. European Advisory Services, 'The Use of Substances with Nutritional or Physiological Effect other than Vitamins and Minerals in Food Supplements' (28 March 2007) ec.europa.eu/food/food/labellingnutrition/supplements/documents/2007_A540169_study_other_substances.pdf.

[184] See C Aschwanden, 'Herbs for Health, but How Safe Are They?' (2001) 79 *Bulletin of the World Health Organization* 692 (in particular the view of Dr Alan Randell, formerly working for the FAO/WHO Codex Secretariat, that the food supplement industry is 'out of control and has been for a very long time. By and large, the people running the industry want it to stay that way').

[185] ALINORM 93/26, para 104. The original list can be found in CX/NFSDU 92/11, 5–6.

[186] ALINORM 97/26, para 55.

ence of vitamins and minerals in the diet be accurately determined worldwide?[187] Recognising the considerable difficulties involved in establishing a definitive list, delegations relatively quickly opted to replace a list with two criteria: that a vitamin or mineral's 'nutritional value for human beings has been proven by scientific data'; and that their 'status' is 'recognised by the FAO and WHO'.[188] It remains unclear today which substances have achieved this status. The Codex Guidelines on Nutrition Labelling (explicitly referenced under labelling provisions in the VMS Guidelines, but notably not in relation to composition), provides a list of 14 vitamins and minerals, which differs from the 19 nutrients recognised by a Joint FAO/WHO Expert Consultation,[189] which in turn is surpassed by the 26 substances discussed by the CCNFSDU in 2010.[190] Until this issue is resolved, the relevance of the text for evaluating the validity of a country's decision not to permit trade of VMS is questionable, even in those countries that regulate these products under food law.

How Much of these Vitamins and Minerals?

A third point of controversy, and one considered to be the primary cause of the lengthy 'deadlock' in Codex discussions,[191] centred on the limits to nutrient content permitted in supplements. The question of maximum levels reflects the practical implications of the philosophical disagreements about supplementation outlined above. A nutritional view of supplementation dictates that no individual needs to be consuming through supplementation more than what is recommended by nutritionists (as expressed in reference daily intakes or RDI).[192] For those that associate health benefits with higher intakes of nutrients, limiting supplement content to the RDI levels represents an unjustifiable constraint on the individual's attempt to optimise health. From such a perspective, content should be limited only by considerations of consumer safety, the assessment of which has been extensively developed by various international scientific bodies.[193] Whereas careful wording, as seen above, could finesse the conceptual disagreements between Codex Members, in the case of maximum levels, this was a battle that had to be fought to a conclusion.

At the outset, the emphasis was placed on a restrictive, nutritional approach. Germany, drafter of the first working paper on supplements in 1992, proposed a

[187] See CX/NFSDU 00/5, 7–8.

[188] 'VMS Guidelines', para 3.1.1. This provision is softened still further by including the conditional 'should', compared to 'shall' elsewhere in the Guidelines.

[189] See this WHO/FAO, Vitamin and Mineral Requirements in Human Nutrition (Sun Feng, 2nd ed, 2004).

[190] See ALINORM 10/33/26, para 84, Appendix IV.

[191] 'Codex Breakthrough on Risk Assessment for Max Nutrient Levels' ('Codex Breakthrough') *Nutraceuticals International* (November 2003).

[192] In other words, food supplements should contain a maximum amount of 100% of the RDI.

[193] For a fuller discussion of these options, see CX/NFSDU, 8–11.

100% RDI content limit for VMS.[194] This position was permitted to stand until 1996, at which point the UK and Canada introduced an alternative option based on safety and risk assessment.[195] The two options—nutritional need and safety—squarely split the Committee. Brazil, China, Denmark, Hungary, Malaysia, Norway, Spain and Thailand were among those advocating the former approach, while the latter found favour with Australia, Cuba, New Zealand, South Africa, the US and (ultimately shifting from their original standpoint) Germany.[196] After four meetings with polarised discussion, the divide appeared insurmountable.[197] New momentum came in 2002 with the introduction of the wording based on the EU Directive on food supplements (itself the fruit of considerable negotiation).[198] This proposal was primarily safety-oriented, but suggested that 'due account should be taken to (*sic*) the reference intake values'.[199] But the real breakthrough occurred the following year when the German Chair of the Committee pushed through the European compromise in the face of remaining resistance.[200] While acceptable to European ears, the ambiguous relationship between maximum levels and RDI remained a cause of concern for more liberal Codex Members. Nutritional criteria as a basis for supplement content were consequently finally banished from the text in 2005 through an additional sentence clarifying that any mention of reference intakes 'should not lead to setting of maximum levels that are solely based' on these levels.[201] Rather than verbal finesse, the unifying of the EU position, together with determined chairmanship and sheer attrition served to force a resolution of the issue, one that entirely reversed the original proposal based on RDIs. This shift was heralded as 'the single most important development in the ongoing effort to open the world's market to safe, healthy products'.[202]

Equally lengthy although less bitterly contested discussions were held on the minimum content level of supplements. The difficulty for the Committee was to fulfil consumer expectations, while accommodating the nutritional and technical

[194] CX/NFSDU 95/6, 16 (Germany arguing that 'there are no objective reasons for supplementing the ordinary diet with more than 100% of the recommended daily intake').

[195] ALINORM 97/26, para 58.

[196] See CX/NFSDU 02/06; CX/NFSDU 03/5; 01/4-Add.2; CX/NFSDU 03/5; ALINORM 04/27/26.

[197] Indeed, it seemed that for some time the Committee was not prepared to discuss the issue, with the Chair of the CCNFSDU in the 2000 session reported to have 'moved the subject swiftly through the agenda'. See 'Differences Continue at Codex on Vitamins and Mineral Supplement Guidelines' *Nutraceuticals International* (August 2000).

[198] Directive 2002/46/EC of the European Parliament and of the Council on the approximation of the laws of the Member States relating to food supplements [2002] OJ L183/51 (EU Food Supplement Directive).

[199] ALINORM 03/26A, Appendix IV, 3.2.2.

[200] See ALINORM 04/27/26, para 46; 'Codex Breakthrough' (n 191).

[201] See 'VMS Guidelines' 3.2.2 and ALINORM 05/28/26, para 31.

[202] US Council of Responsible Nutrition Board member MA Le Doux, cited in 'Codex Breakthrough' (n 191).

differences between vitamins and minerals.[203] There being no particularly compelling argument for a given minimum level, the discussion swayed for almost a decade between the various numerical preferences of different delegations, ranging from 15% of the RDI to 33%.[204] Ultimately, the lower level was accepted on the grounds that it was the figure already established in the Guidelines for Use of Nutrition Claims as justifying a claim that a food constituted a 'source' of vitamins and minerals.[205]

Labelling

Labelling issues were never likely to arouse the same level of passion among delegates as some of the issues above. Nevertheless, differing views on supplementation were once more present in these discussions. Those countries sharing a nutritional or medicinal perspective on supplementation sought to reflect this in the information provided to consumers. Among the unsuccessful proposals in this respect were statements that 'intake of a nutrient above the recommended daily intake does not result in benefits on health or wellbeing'[206] and that supplements should be taken on the basis of qualified advice,[207] and warnings not to exceed the recommended daily quantity.[208] In the light of the compromises described above, it is not surprising that such proposals were either neutralised (advice replacing warnings) or replaced with provisions primarily aimed at simply clarifying the content of the product.[209] In this respect, the Committee again ultimately drew heavily on the provisions of the EU Food Supplement Directive.[210]

With the regulatory approach to supplementation varying so widely across nations, transcending these divergences in Guidelines was inevitably a complex exercise. As regards certain aspects—the purpose of supplements, their labelling and the selection of nutrients—compromises could be found. The paradigmatic struggle

---

[203] In particular, establishing minimum levels for minerals, such as calcium and magnesium, could lead to excessively bulky products in the case of multivitamin and mineral products. See CX/NFSDU 00/5, 11.

[204] For example, Australia, Germany, Spain, Malaysia supported a level of 15%, Norway 25%, Denmark 25–30%, Cuba 30%, Hungary 33% and Brazil a range of 15–33%. See CX/NFSDU 01/4 Add.1; CX/NFSDU 01/4-Add.2; CX/NFSDU 02/06; CX/NFSDU 03/5.

[205] ALINORM 04/27/26, para 44.

[206] This was the original German proposal presented in CX/NFSDU 92/11, 9.

[207] See ALINORM 01/26, para 56; ALINORM 04/27/26, para 59.

[208] See, for example, Australia's proposal in CX/NFSDU, 4.

[209] The one remaining piece of nutritional advice is provision 5.8 requiring labelling that 'supplements cannot be used for the replacement of meals or a varied diet'.

[210] Only one provision in the labelling section of the 'VMS Guidelines' (proposing labelling on how the product is used) is not contained in the Articles 6–8 of the EU Food Supplement Directive 2002/46/EC. However, the Commission was not successful in removing a reference to nutrient information per 'single use' which it deemed to be confusing. See CCNFSDU Twenty-sixth Session, CRD 6 (October 2004) 9.

of permitted content, by contrast, had to be resolved. The particular irony of the public backlash against Codex is that the Guidelines, whilst reputed to be restrictive, undoubtedly favoured a more liberal approach to supplementation. As they stand—and no further elaboration is currently foreseen—these Guidelines prohibit no more than those supplements established to be dangerous to consumers. What then, if any, has been their impact on national regulations?

7.4.2 Impact of Codex VMS Guidelines on Domestic VMS Rules

In stark contrast to the GSFA, whose influence is plainly identifiable across regulatory systems worldwide, the direct impact of the Codex VMS Guidelines is not immediately discernible in the vast majority of countries regulating food supplements. As noted above, even if countries were inclined to do so, the unelaborated content of the Guidelines does not permit national authorities to *displace* existing regulations in the manner identified in the additives case study. Nor is regulatory *innovation* inspired by the VMS Guidelines obviously evident, even in the legislation that has emerged after the finalisation of the Guidelines in 2005. Certainly, it can be argued that the regulatory needs of governments faced with a much broader range of supplements on the market have surpassed the limited scope of the Guidelines.[211] Nevertheless, even those aspects of the document to which national administrations could easily comply have not always been incorporated. Most notably, where minimum levels for nutrient content are established in domestic legislation, they range from 20 % (Argentina and Costa Rica) to 100 % (Chile), rather than the 15 % agreed in the Guidelines. Equally, while the agreed Codex nomenclature of 'food supplements' has been adopted in a number of countries (Chile, Indonesia and Thailand) the category name 'dietary supplements' (eg in Colombia, Argentina and Costa Rica) and other alternatives persist.[212] Most strikingly, in the few instances where WTO Members have notified new supplement rules to the SPS Committee, they have indicated that no international document is relevant to the development of their measures.[213]

Some WTO Members have been explicit in expressing their *resistance* to the Codex Guidelines—largely, one suspects, in order to manage much of the public backlash to the Codex work. Health Canada's website informs readers that 'the Guidelines are not applicable to the Canadian regulatory system' due to the clas-

[211] Legislation typically covers a wide range of substances including botanical ingredients. Of the countries surveyed, only Brazil, Chile and Venezuela limit the scope of food supplement legislation to VMS. See Appendix III.

[212] See Appendix III.

[213] See the SPS notifications by Colombia (G/SPS/N/COL/123, 30 November 2006) and Korea (G/SPS/N/KOR/206, 9 June 2006). A number of countries do not notify new supplement measures to the WTO, or only do so to the TBT Committee. See, for example, Argentina's notification in G/TBT/N/ARG/221 (1 August 2007).

sification of supplements as natural health products.[214] The Australian authorities are even more emphatic: 'The proposed Codex Guidelines for Vitamin and Mineral Food Supplements will NOT apply in Australia and will have NO IMPACT on the way these types of products are regulated in Australia.'[215] In the US, where they are regulated as foods and therefore fall within the scope of the Guidelines, the Food and Drug Administration (FDA) adopts an alternative approach to reassuring its citizens, arguing that as US legislation is not restrictive, it is unlikely to be challenged by third countries.[216]

In the light of the above, can the VMS Guidelines be shown to have been of any relevance at all to the work of national regulators? Given the incompleteness of the VMS Guidelines, regulatory bodies looking beyond their borders when developing new supplement rules are practically obliged to draw on international practice outside Codex. The diversity of regulatory models (as seen in Appendix III) does not therefore demonstrate domestic rejection as such of the VMS Guidelines. Indeed, the trend in regulation towards the establishment of food-supplement rules under food law (in Thailand, India, Colombia, Argentina, Costa Rica and Korea)[217] and the tendency to move away from a nutritional approach to establishing supplement content (in Colombia, Argentina, Costa Rica and Korea) could be construed as broadly following the overall direction set by Codex.[218] There is therefore some merit in the assessment of market operators that 'while there continue to be many different approaches to regulating dietary supplements, the principles that form the basis of these are increasingly consistent around the world'.[219] Yet clear evidence of the impact of Codex norms on domestic regulation remains fleeting. One instance is the use of the Codex definition of a supplement in Japanese rules on food with nutrient function claims.[220] Another is Denmark's invocation of Codex Guidelines in its calls for establishing minimum content levels in supplements in Europe.[221]

---

[214] See the Health Canada website at www.hc-sc.gc.ca/fn-an/intactivit/codex/activit/vit_min_sup-eng.php.

[215] See the Australia Department of Health Ageing Therapeutic Goods Administration website at www.tga.gov.au/archive/cm-codex-050504.htm.

[216] See the US FDA website, 'Responses to Questions about Codex and Dietary Supplements', www.fda.gov/Food/GuidanceRegulation/GuidanceDocumentsRegulatoryInformation/DietarySupplements/ucm113860.htm.

[217] See Appendix III.

[218] These trends are ambiguous however. Since 2005, Thailand and India have introduced new rules limiting VMS content to nutritional levels.

[219] B Bouckley, 'IADSA: diverse regulations hinder Latin America food supplement markets' *NUTRAingredients.com*. (12 November 2010) (citing P Zambetti, Chair of the International Alliance of Dietary Supplement Associations (IADSA)) www.nutraingredients.com/Industry/IADSA-diverse-regulations-hinder-Latin-America-food-supplement-markets.

[220] H Tanaka et al., 'Current System for Regulation of Health Foods in Japan' (2004) 47 *Japan Medical Association Journal* 436, 441.

[221] 'Comments from The Danish Veterinary and Food Administration to the Discussion Paper, June 2006, on the setting of maximum and minimum amounts for vitamins and minerals in foodstuffs' (29 September 2006) 4, ec.europa.eu/food/food/labellingnutrition/supplements/documents/denmark_en.pdf 26 September 2011.

But it may also be the case that the grand debates in Codex on safety levels have left a greater mark on regulatory trends than is immediately apparent. For example, the ASEAN is harmonising the regulation of supplements across the region. This involves Thailand and Malaysia, two of the countries who argued most actively within Codex for a nutritional approach to food safety.[222] However, efforts led by Thailand to establish upper levels of vitamins and minerals have nonetheless followed the risk-assessment orientation advocated by Codex.[223]

In the case of the EU, Codex VMS Guidelines serve as an example of norm *accentuation*, the reinforcement of domestic norms through international recognition. As seen above, the EU's labelling provisions and compromise on supplement content form the basis of the Codex text. At the very least, the proximity of Codex Guidelines to EU law significantly reduces the chance of a WTO challenge of EU legislation. The Codex discussion has also arguably cemented a trend away from an RDI-based approach to food-supplement levels. The EU compromise—an ambiguous mixture of safety and nutritional principles—was agreed only with some reluctance by Member States, many of whom still favoured a purely nutritional approach to supplement content.[224] The international debate on the VMS Guidelines may well have further undermined the case of those Member States who remain highly resistant to discarding their nutrition-based policy.[225] Certainly, in the most recent round of EU discussions on this issue, fervour for nutritional limits has been somewhat dampened.[226] While the precise role of Codex in this more tempered discourse is difficult to discern, the Codex Guidelines provide an additional buttress to the safety-based orientation of the EU Directive.[227]

In the absence of norm innovation and displacement, and with blatant resistance by a number of WTO Members, one might anticipate trade tensions of the type reported in the case of additives. Interestingly, in spite of the regulatory disharmony that remains for VMS, no WTO Member has yet formally criticised the supplement measures of another Member. There are various explanations for this. Given their vagueness, the VMS Guidelines are possibly not considered to form a strong legal

[222] See n 196 and related text.

[223] ASEAN, 'Minutes of the Fourth Meeting of the ASEAN Traditional Medicines and Herbal Supplements Scientific Committee (ATSC)' (12–13 January 2009) para 30 (on file with author).

[224] At the outset of discussions, only the UK was significantly opposed to the proposal then under discussion to limit VMS content to 1.5 times the RDI. See P Berry Ottoway, 'The Promised European Supplements Directive—10 Years On' *Nutraceuticals International* (May 1999) 8–9.

[225] The reluctance of some Member States to relinquish their traditional policy on VMS is demonstrated through the number of continuing trade problems for these products. See European Commission, 'Discussion Paper on the Setting of Maximum and Minimum Amounts for Vitamins and Minerals in Foodstuffs' (June 2006) para 15, ec.europa.eu/food/food/labellingnutrition/supplements/discus_paper_amount_vitamins.pdf.

[226] In response to the Commission's Discussion Paper (ibid) only Ireland explicitly called for limits related to nutritional intake. See Member State responses ec.europa.eu/food/food/labellingnutrition/supplements/.

[227] The failure of the Commission to present maximum levels 6 years after the completion of its consultation process gives some indication of the lingering controversy surrounding the topic.

basis for any potential formal challenge in a WTO context.[228] It may be that because the general trend in regulation, as noted above, increasingly follows the path established by Codex, the harmonisation process, however imperfect, is considered to have a momentum that would make any WTO confrontation redundant. The lack of challenge may equally suggest that regulatory diversity itself is not always an insurmountable barrier to trade.[229] If the latter is true, a more focused discussion on those specific technical aspects of regulation that do pose real trading problems for operators may be preferable to the broader and more culturally divisive interchanges that dogged the VMS Guidelines.

7.5 Conclusion

This chapter sought to further our knowledge of the role played by Codex standards in transnational food governance. A complete picture of domestic use of Codex norms would require analysis over a broader range of issues than the two cases studied here. Nevertheless, at the very least, this survey casts doubt over commonly held assumptions about the influence of Codex standards. International standardisation and harmonisation do not, as these case studies have shown, inexorably lead to regulatory homogeneity. Rather, the relationship between international norms and domestic policies is complex and unpredictable. Domestic incorporation of Codex norms differs widely both between countries and according to the field under discussion. Countries that have adopted the GSFA in its entirety appear to have paid little attention to VMS Guidelines. Existing regulatory practices and the perceived need for regulation have a considerable impact on the uptake of international norms, but so will the nature of the norm itself, its quality, completeness and relevance to the products with which regulators are confronted. In spite of the hubbub generated by the VMS Guidelines, their impact on the way that national regulators manage food supplements is largely imperceptible. By contrast, albeit to differing degrees across states, the GSFA has been highly influential.

These case studies suggest that assumptions, both among academics and the general public, of global norm convergence and diminished domestic influence are misplaced. Even where harmonisation rather than resistance occurs, localisation can ensure that a broad convergence of norms does not entail major and potentially culturally disruptive normative shifts. In areas where international standardisation is highly advanced, the regulatory landscape nonetheless remains diverse. Moreover, notwithstanding the methodological limitations of the surveys, it would appear that

[228] However, it should be noted that the legal basis for trade complaints made to the SPS Committee is often not clearly articulated and would not necessarily dissuade complaints.

[229] The latter point reflects the views of the staff of IADSA as expressed in an interview in December 2010. Even where supplements require registration under medicinal law, the regulatory demands are often not such as to create a true barrier to a market, although they will require additional efforts on the part of the exporter.

Codex's reach is still far from comprehensive. This both underlines the argument that claims about Codex's power are overstated and raises broader questions as to the extent that standards can secure the WTO's goal of enhancing trade.

Finally, in the light of the relatively few WTO trade complaints about additives and food supplements, these case studies also suggest that localisation of, or even resistance to, Codex norms may not necessarily hinder trade in a way that requires WTO intervention. As Codex Members build up experience in localising food standards without international challenge, the fears and suspicions of Codex's norm setting may well diminish. This finding should also provoke further reflection on the focus of international standardisation discussions. If localisation does indeed not unduly inhibit international trade, precisely what degree of harmonisation is required, and in which areas, in order to have a meaningful impact on global trade? Such reflection could accelerate the work of standardisation bodies and potentially reduce the cultural conflicts that have beleaguered international discussions on additives and food supplements.

References

Abraham J and Millstone E, 'Food Additive Controls: Some International Comparisons' (1989) 14 *Food Policy* 43.

Acharya A, 'How Ideas Spread: Whose Norms Matter? Norm Localization and Institutional Change in Asian Regionalism' (2004) 58 *International Organization* 239.

Alford RP, 'The Nobel Effect: Nobel Peace Prize Laureates As International Norm Entrepreneurs' (2008) 49 VJIL 61.

Aschwanden C, 'Herbs for Health, But How Safe Are They?' (2001) 79 *Bulletin of the World Health Organization* 692.

Berman PS, 'From International Law to Law and Globalisation' (2005) 43 *Columbia Journal of Transnational Law* 485.

Brooke-Taylor S, Baines J, Goodchap J, Gruber J and Hambridge T, 'Reforms to Food Additive Regulation in Australia and New Zealand' (2003) 14 *Food Control* 375.

Brunnée J and Toope SJ, *Legitimacy and Legality in International Law* (Cambridge, CUP, 2010).

Checkel JT, 'The Constructivist Turn in International Relations Theory' (1998) 50 *World Politics* 323.

De Búrca G, 'Developing Democracy Beyond the State' (2008) 46 *Columbia Journal of Transnational Law* 221.

Denner WHB, 'Food Additives: Recommendations for Harmonisation and Control' (1990) 1 *Food Control* 150.

Entwisle H, 'Tracing Cascades: The Normative Development of the UN Guiding Principles of Internal Displacement' (2005) 19 *Georgetown Immigration Law Journal* 369.

Farrell T, 'Transnational Norms and Military Development: Constructing Ireland's Professional Army' (2001) 7 *European Journal of International Relations* 63.

Finnemore M and Sikkink K, 'International Norm Dynamics and Political Change' (1998) 52 *International Organisation* 887.

Franck TM, 'Dr. Pangloss Meets The Grinch: A Pessimistic Comment on Harold Koh's Optimism' (1998) 35 *Houston Law Review* 683.

Goodman R and Jinks D, 'Incomplete Internalization and Compliance with Human Rights Law' (2008) 19 EJIL 725.

Hüller T and Maier ML, 'Fixing the Codex? Global Food-Safety Governance under Review' in C Joerges and E-U Petersmann (eds), *Constitutionalism, Multilevel Trade Governance and Social Regulation* (Oxford, Hart Publishing, 2006).

Josling T, 'Norms and Standards' (Institute for International Studies, Stanford University, 2003).

Keohane RO, 'When Does International Law Come Home?' (1998) 35 *Houston Law Review* 683.

Koh HH, 'Why Do Nations Obey International Law?' (1997) 106 *Yale Law Journal* 2599.

Koh HH, 'The 1998 Frankel Lecture: Bringing International Human Rights Home' (1998) 35 *Houston Law Review* 623.

Legro JW, 'Which Norms Matter? Revisiting the "Failure" of Internationalism' (1997) 51 *International Organization* 31.

Liese A, 'Exceptional Necessity. How Liberal Democracies Contest the Prohibition of Torture and Ill-Treatment When Countering Terrorism' (2009) 5 *Journal of International Law and International Relations* 17.

Lim EC, 'A Long "TRIP" Home: Intellectual Property Rights, International Law and the Constructivist Challenge' (2008) 4 *Journal of International Law and International Relations* 57.

Livermore MA, 'Authority and Legitimacy in Global Governance: Deliberation, Institutional Differentiation, and the Codex Alimentarius' (2006) 81 *New York University Law Review* 766.

Livshiz D, 'Updating American Administrative Law: WTO, International Standards, Domestic Implementation and Public Participation' (2007) 24 *Wisconsin International Law Journal* 961.

Masson-Matthee MD, *The Codex Alimentarius Commission and its Standards* (The Hague, TMC Asser Press, 2007).

Noah L and Merrill R, 'Starting from Scratch?: Reinventing the Food Additive Approval Process' (1990) 78 *Boston University Law Review* 329.

Park S, 'The World Bank, Dams and the Meaning of Sustainable Development in Use' (2009) 5 *Journal of International Law and International Relations* 93.

Peck A, 'The New Imperialism: Toward an Advocacy Strategy for GMO Accountability' (2008) 21 *Georgetown International Environmental Law Review* 37.

Pereira RA, 'Why would International Administrative Activity Be Any Less Legitimate?—A Study of the Codex Alimentarius Commission' (2008) 9 *German Law Journal* 1693.

Posner EA, 'Transnational Legal Process and The Supreme Court's 2003–2004 Term: Some Skeptical Observations' (2004) 12 *Tulsa Journal of Comparative and International Law* 23.

Post DL, 'Diffusion of International Food Safety Standards: Food Additive Regulation and the Codex Alimentarius Commission' (American Political Science Association annual meeting, Philadelphia, August 2003).

Post DL, 'Food Fights: Who Shapes International Food Safety Standards and Who Uses Them?'(Ph.D Thesis, University of California Berkeley 2005).

Risse T and Ropp SC, 'International Human Rights Norms and Domestic Change: Conclusions' in T Risse, SC Ropp and K Sikkink (eds), *The Power of Human Rights: International Norms and Domestic Change* (Cambridge: CUP 1999).

Risse T and Sikkink K, 'The Socialisation of International Human Rights Norms into Domestic Practices: Introduction' in T Risse, SC Ropp and K Sikkink (eds), *The Power of Human Rights: International Norms and Domestic Change* (Cambridge: CUP 1999).

Salzer U-J, 'Legislation/Toxicology' in H Ziegler (ed), *Flavourings* (Weinheim, Wiley-VCH, 2007).

Sarfaty GA, 'International Norm Diffusion in the Pimicikamak Cree Nation: A Model of Legal Mediation' (2007) 48 *Harvard International Law Journal* 441, 445.

Setear JK, 'Ozone, Iteration, and International Law' (1989) 40 VJIL 193.

Steffek J and Ferretti MP, 'Accountability or "Good Decision"? The Competing Goals of Civil Society Participation in International Governance' (2009) 23 *Global Society* 37.

Tanaka H, Kaneda F, Suguro R and Baba H, 'Current System for Regulation of Health Foods in Japan' (2004) 47 *Japan Medical Association Journal* 436.

Tarzi SM, 'International Norms, Trade, and Human Rights: A Perspective on Norm Conformity' (2002) 27 *The Journal of Social, Political, and Economic Studies* 187.

Twining W, 'Diffusion of Law: A Global Perspective' (2004) 49 *Journal of Legal Pluralism and Unofficial Law* 1.

Venzke I, 'Legal Contestation about "Enemy Combatants": On the Exercise of Power in Legal Interpretation' (2009) 5 *Journal of International Law and International Relations* 154.

Wexler L, 'The International Deployment of Shame, Second-Best Responses, and Norm Entrepreneurship: The Campaign to Ban Landmines and the Landmine Ban Treaty' (2003) 20 *Arizona Journal of International and Comparative Law* 561.

Wiener A and Puetter U, 'The Quality of Norms Is What Actors Make of It' (2009) 5 *Journal of International Law and International Relations* 1.

Winickoff DE and Bushey DM, 'Science and Power in Global Food Regulation: The Rise of the Codex Alimentarius' (2010) 35 *Science, Technology and Human Values* 356.

Chapter 8
Conclusion

Abstract This final chapter draws together the analysis of previous chapters to summarise the main findings on the influence of the SPS Agreement on EU food regulations. It reflects on the potential limitations of this research for drawing broader conclusions about the operation of the SPS regime and, finally, considers possible areas of future research on the Agreement.

Let us return to where we started this study: to Rue Breydel, and the day-to-day trials of administrators who manage the panoply of interests and concerns that underlie European Union (EU) food policy. It was posited that there is discordance between the dominant narrative found in legal commentaries, which portray the Agreement on the Application of Sanitary and Phytosanitary Measures (SPS Agreement) as intrusive and constraining, and the actual experience of regulators, for whom SPS norms form one, but hardly a determining aspect of their work. The challenge set was to understand these divergent perspectives and reassess the impact of international rules on domestic food regulations. These concluding remarks summarise the findings of this book, reflect on the extent to which it has provided useful insights into the Agreement's functioning and finally consider where future research on the regime may focus.

8.1 Too Much Anxiety about the SPS Agreement …

The SPS Agreement is predominantly considered by legal commentators to be a restraining force on the regulatory choices of World Trade Organisation (WTO) Members. Although bringing discipline to the development and management of sanitary measures is the very purpose of the SPS regime, the outcome of such discipline is commonly expressed in critical and emotive terms. Judging by both the weight and tone of the writing, public sensitivities about the regulation of food both stimulate and infuse the work of legal commentators. An extensive review of the legal literature found little empirical underpinning for the claim that national regulators are inhibited by international legal obligations. Instead, Part I concluded that this characterisation of the Agreement was the direct consequence of a series of common analytical choices made by commentators. Notably, a primary focus on formal sources (the text of the Agreement and dispute-settlement reports), an

C. Downes, *The Impact of WTO SPS Law on EU Food Regulations,* Studies in European Economic Law and Regulation 2, DOI 10.1007/978-3-319-04373-9_8,

assumption that law has a regulative effect on domestic policy, and a tendency to evaluate the regime from the ascending perspective of the state combine to anticipate, but not necessarily demonstrate, an intrusive role for international rules. Part I thus provided some explanation for the contrast between the significant academic disquiet and the marginal administrative interest in the SPS Agreement.

This study sought to revaluate the expectations of constraint, through a more empirical review of the Agreement's impact, firstly focusing on the development of EU food regulations (Part II) and then tracing the procedural and substantive impact of norms generated in international fora (Part III). In both contexts, while the Agreement is highly pertinent in many instances to domestic policy-making, its reach is often overstated by legal commentators. This is particularly the case with regard to the two of the major argumentative threads that have contributed to criticism of the SPS framework. The first contention is, to paraphrase, that the SPS Agreement significantly reduces sovereign control over food policies, an outcome that is particularly worrying in light of their often culturally sensitive nature. In the EU context, the international constraints placed on policy choices cannot be entirely dismissed. Most notably, as Chap. 5 illustrated, the spectre of possible legal challenge in Geneva over food from cloned animals incited the European Commission to steer the Novel Foods Regulation in a different direction to that favoured by the EP and Council. However, neither in this case, nor the other areas of EU policy examined in Chap. 4, is there evidence of fundamental EU long-term policy goals being compromised by SPS obligations. Likewise, as illustrated in Chap. 4, international standards do form a reference point for EU policy and sometimes come to replace existing EU rules. Permitted levels of contaminants and acceptable maximum pesticide residue levels are two areas where the outcomes of international agreements have clearly infiltrated EU law. Yet there is nothing automatic or unconsidered about this process. The European Food Safety Authority (EFSA) and the Standing Committee are called to reflect on the appropriateness of international standards and may legitimately draw conclusions entirely different from those of its international counterparts.[1] Where, as in the EU, the regulatory system is established and strongly supported by scientific expertise, the 'threat' of norm-making beyond the sovereign state does not appear particularly potent. Even the most prominent examples of SPS influence on EU food policy presented in this study cannot therefore substantiate stronger claims of relinquished sovereign control.

The second predominant argument emerging from the legal literature is that the Agreement has instituted a science-led style of policy-making to the exclusion of important social concerns. Picked up and repeated by academics over the last decade, this characterisation has come to seem almost self-evident, a defining feature of the Agreement. The evidence presented here suggests that it deserves to be treated with greater scepticism, or at least nuance, than is generally the case. To a certain

[1] For example, following discrepancies between EFSA and JECFA proposals for a guidance value for permitted cadmium intake in food drawing on the same database, EFSA reviewed and confirmed the validity of its lower values. See EFSA, Comparison of the Approaches Taken by EFSA and JECFA to Establish a HBGV for Cadmium (2011) 9 *EFSA Journal* 2006.

extent, the Agreement's role in enhancing the status of science in policy-making is undeniable: it has provoked a rigorous reappraisal of scientific principles in Codex and encouraged institutional reform worldwide. Yet there is scant evidence to conclude that this evolution is synonymous with the impoverishment of policy and the subjection of important societal interests. As Chap. 4 argued, the impact of science on food policy must be put in perspective. Even where the tension between scientific evidence and SPS disciplines is apparent, domestic policymakers must not necessarily abandon their central goals. Moreover, there is mutual interest among WTO Members, none of whom develops food regulation in a political vacuum, not to be over-zealous in their pursuit of purely science-based policy. Most significantly, Chap. 4 demonstrated that, in spite of the prominent place of science in EU policy, much of the existing EU food legislation clearly reflects social-value judgements, sometimes at odds with scientific findings. This is no different in international fora. As the analyses of Codex discussions on food additives and supplements in Chap. 7 exposed, competing visions of the appropriate role of certain foods in today's diets are constantly reasserted. In many areas of Codex's work there remains a battle of ideas that directly challenges the notion that 'the risk analysis framework … has marginalized environmental, economic, and other potential factors in food safety regulation'.[2] In practice, while the SPS Agreement can create additional dilemmas for regulators, as in the EU's management of novel foods described in Chapter 5, the widely feared scientific conquest of food policy has not yet occurred.

8.2 … But Not to be Ignored

Yet, although this study found that expectations of SPS-imposed regulatory constraint are inflated, it also illustrated the considerable importance of SPS disciplines beyond the dispute settlement arena, namely for the transnational governance of food.[3] The SPS Agreement has prompted routine communication of new regulations between WTO Members, opening up domestic rules to scrutiny by third countries and providing a common language for discussing SPS measures. As seen in Chap. 6's review of the EU's implementation of procedural SPS obligations, WTO Members may not, often for practical reasons, fully adhere to these rules. Nevertheless, this account of the EU's experience suggests that through regular discussion of notified policy proposals, evaluation of the equivalence of third-country measures and technical assistance, WTO Members are increasingly enmeshed in a dynamic

[2] DE Winickoff and DM Bushey, 'Science and Power in Global Food Regulation: The Rise of the Codex Alimentarius' (2010) 35 *Science, Technology and Human Values* 356, 364.

[3] Wolfe has appropriately captured this impact through the image of a 'great pyramid', with the 'Appellate Body [as] merely the small tip of a substantial pyramid of WTO activity, and most of the real action in holding Members accountable for their obligations … lower down towards the base'. R Wolfe, 'Letting the Sun Shine in at the WTO: How Transparency Brings the Trading System to Life' (2013) WTO Economic Research and Statistics Division, Staff Working Paper, ERSD-2013-03, www.wto.org/english/res_e/reser_e/ersd201303_e.pdf.

transnational process of dialogue and self-reflection on SPS measures. As was illustrated by the case of the EU Novel Food Regulation in Chap. 5, this can, sometimes inconspicuously, lead to meaningful policy change for exporting countries.

The survey of Codex norms in Chap. 7 presents a similar picture. In many countries, including the EU, the negotiation and agreement of international standards does not have the dramatic effect on national policy choices that some legal commentators and the general public seem to fear. The domestic treatment of Codex standards can vary significantly, not only among different WTO Members, but depending on the food category under discussion. Yet, international norms are rarely completely irrelevant to national administrators who will fiercely contest their content. Even for Members such as the EU with the scientific and regulatory capacity to be autonomous, Codex norms can find their way into legislation.

The SPS Agreement does then exert an influence on domestic policy-makers, but not in the way generally envisaged. It does not unduly constrain the overall course of domestic food policy in the manner anticipated by a regulative account of international law. However, it does generate transnational practices that bring to the fore the interests of trading partners and can facilitate the alignment of technical regulations. This dynamic can remove obstacles to trade, but its impact should not be overstated. It would be naive to expect such interaction between trading partners to resolve, for example, the deep-seated cultural conflicts that prevent the free trade of meat containing hormones or GM foods. Yet, lest we forget in the clamour that these issues generate, international agricultural trade consists of much more than such products. Cooperation on the minutiae of SPS measures can make the difference between trading and not trading for operators worldwide. Whatever the SPS regime's shortcomings and imperfections, the discipline, transparency and common thinking surrounding SPS measures has attained a level inconceivable under the former GATT Standards Code.

8.3 How Representative Is This Study of the SPS Regime?

By adopting a different analytical approach—empirically oriented, more attentive to the generative possibilities of SPS law and, in Part III at least, using a predominantly descending perspective focused on the regime's goals—this book has offered alternative insights into the SPS Agreement. But has it furthered our overall understanding of the influence of SPS obligations?

There are three possible concerns that could be raised about the characterisation of the SPS regime presented in this study.

The first is that this account has underplayed the intrusiveness of the SPS Agreement by presenting, in Parts II and III, cases that are not necessarily representative. An extraordinary number of food regulations are generated each year in the EU and internationally. Inevitably, the cases chosen can provide only a sketch of EU regulatory activity and thus the study is vulnerable to the charge of selectivity. Could it be that analysis in other areas of food law would tell an entirely different story, one that confirms the WTO's suppression of domestic preferences and valid consumer concerns? This cannot be entirely ruled out. For example, the imposition of a Codex contaminant level, characterised in this account as a relatively insignificant measure in political terms, could, from another perspective or with greater scrutiny, be demonstrated to have far-reaching consequences for domestic consumers.[4] Yet, this study deliberately sought out such 'hard' cases, in areas of food law that have proved particularly highly charged for EU citizens, where SPS-led constraint would thus cut closest to sovereign concerns. One would therefore expect those areas of EU food law not touched upon in this book to be, if anything, less rather than more likely to demonstrate the intrusive impact of the Agreement. With regard to the Codex norms investigated, it is possible that a comprehensive review of other areas of Codex standards may give rise to examples of more homogenous and intrusive harmonisation. Yet, given the relatively advanced and comprehensive nature of Codex's additive work, a more consistent uptake of Codex norms in other fields seems improbable.[5]

An alternative criticism could be that the importance attached to regulatory interaction between national administrators in Part III of this study overstates the regime's influence. Does such exchange between technical experts, whether at the margins of SPS Committee meetings or as a result of transparency initiatives, really amount to a tangible impact on domestic regulation? This is the tenor of Steinberg's criticism of Lang and Scott's account of the 'hidden world' of the SPS Committee. In particular, Steinberg considers that, whatever the level of interaction reported, it is 'hard to see [a US civil servant] advancing an agenda which deviates far from that of the United States of America'.[6] While undoubtedly true in a simple sense, this presupposes that major 'deviations' in policy are what is foreseen or required by the SPS Agreement in order to attain its trade-enhancement goals. The reality is less dramatic. Accommodating the trade concerns of third countries—re-evaluating assessment processes, permitting transition periods, providing assistance—may often require a modification of practices rather than a decisive change of policy. Without the transnational exchanges galvanised by the SPS Agreement's mechanisms, it is precisely these opportunities for identifying and addressing obstacles to trade that would be missed.

Thirdly, doubt could be cast over the relevance of this EU-dominated survey to the overall influence of the SPS Agreement. As has been seen, the relationship between EU policy-making and the SPS Agreement is an ambivalent and probably atypical one. On the one hand—as seen in Chap. 6's account of the vigorous ap-

[4] We need only to consider the demise of the 'meat-glue' additive thrombin recounted in Chap. 4 above.

[5] Indeed a recent OECD survey on pesticide residue policies points to an inconsistent response to Codex MRLs which mirror the findings in ch 7 above on the GSFA. See OECD, 'Survey on Pesticide Maximum Residue Limit (MRL) Policies: Survey Results, Series on Pesticides No. 51' (ENV/JM/MONO(2010)2312), in particular 25 and 86–87 (explaining how Codex Maximum Residue Levels are incorporated into national regulations)

[6] RH Steinberg, 'The Hidden World of WTO Governance: A Reply to Andrew Lang and Joanne Scott' (2009) 20 EJIL 1063, 1071.

plication of the principles of transparency and equivalence—the EU is very much an active partner in the transnational governance mechanisms established by the Agreement. Moreover, with access to a well-resourced and credible scientific body, the EU is well placed to meet the high scientific demands of the SPS Agreement and provide a robust grounding for its SPS measures. On the other hand, as seen in Chap. 4, policy choices on a range of food issues—GMOs, hormones, irradiation, novel foods, use of food additives—remain strongly guided by European social value choices that can collide with scientific advice. As such, the EU is perhaps unusually exposed to WTO challenge, and this is a danger—as was seen in discussion on novel foods in Chap. 5—of which the European Commission (if not other EU institutions) is acutely aware. Yet there are few signs of EU policy changing course in this respect. If anything, the ratification of the Lisbon treaty has enabled an enhanced role for the European Parliament in more technical decisions. The consequence, as seen in the thrombin 'meat glue' case referred to in Chap. 4, is sanitary measures in which scientific rationale is discarded in the face of popular concerns. The EU is therefore at once one of the SPS regime's most dynamic participants and one of its greatest challengers.

This idiosyncratic European response to SPS requirements may therefore have its limitations as a reference point for understanding the impact of the Agreement. Moreover, the EU's political and economic weight allows it to withstand the demands of the WTO, as in the case of *Hormones,* in a way that may be beyond the organisation's smaller and less economically advanced Members. Yet the continued diversity of regulatory models portrayed in Chap. 7 at least provides a preliminary indication that the EU is not alone in continuing to pursue its domestic policy preferences. Only detailed empirical studies of regulatory practices in other regions would be able to confirm whether the EU's experience of the SPS Agreement, as portrayed here, is truly representative.

8.4 Where Next?

In some senses, a finding that the SPS Agreement exerts influence unpredictably and largely out of sight does not lend itself to strong conclusions. Yet it may at least encourage us to think again about some of the standard criticisms of the regime. If we believe (or hope) that the work of legal commentators contributes meaningfully to understanding the functioning of international bodies, and is in turn instrumental in their improvement, an accurate diagnosis of their strengths and weaknesses is important. The recurrent argument that the SPS Agreement is structurally unresponsive to legitimate non-scientific concerns begets calls for reform. Ensuring that the Dispute Settlement Body shows greater deference to domestic regulatory processes, or restructures its approach to scientific fact-finding are possible options.[7]

[7] See respectively M Trebilcock and J Soloway, 'International Trade Policy and Domestic Food Safety Regulation: The Case for Substantial Deference by the WTO Dispute Settlement Body under the SPS Agreement' in DLM Kennedy and JD Southwick (eds), *The Political Economy of*

An entirely new approach to interpreting the SPS Agreement, to include a broader understanding of the precautionary principle, is another.[8] Yet how much energy and political capital should states invest in such ideas, if in practice, WTO Members can continue to implement sanitary measures that reflect the ethical or environmental preferences of its citizens? Likewise, how relevant is the clamour for a rethink to public participation in the Codex system, if, as suggested by Chap. 7, domestic regulatory systems can successfully process international norms in a manner consistent with local interests? Should time or resources be invested, for example, in increasing stakeholder participation[9] or introducing majority voting in the Codex Commission?[10] Rather than being swept along by popular misconceptions of the power of global bodies (clearly illustrated in the case study of Codex work on vitamin and mineral supplements), legal commentators must acknowledge and embrace the complexity of the relationship between international and domestic legal norms.[11]

This study has suggested that the real influence of the SPS Agreement lies in its contribution towards truly transnational food governance, that is, its capacity to subject domestic policy-making to scrutiny and to contribute to constructive reflection and dialogue among food regulators around the globe. If so, perhaps the focus of future research and institutional innovation should rather be in evaluating and improving these elements of its functioning.[12] What further SPS disciplines will improve WTO Members' capacity to identify and communicate potential obstacles to trade? Can exporter groups with the relevant technical knowledge and experience to contribute to their governments' transnational activity be more closely involved in that process? Is Codex's norm-setting process sufficiently attuned to the real problems of the global market or is too much time lost in developing standards that will not facilitate trade?

International Trade Law: Essays in Honour of Robert E. Hudec (Cambridge, CUP, 2002) 549–552 and VR Walker, 'Keeping the WTO from Becoming the "World Trans-Science Organisation": Scientific Uncertainty, Science Policy, and Fact-Finding in the Growth Hormones Dispute' (1998) 31 *Cornell International Law Journal* 251, 281.

[8] J Bohanes, 'Risk Regulation in WTO Law: A Procedure-Based Approach to the Precautionary Principle' (2002) 40 *Columbia Journal of Transnational Law* 323, 376–399.

[9] D Livshiz, 'Updating American Administrative Law: WTO, International Standards, Domestic Implementation and Public Participation' (2007) 24 *Wisconsin International Law Journal* 961.

[10] See MA Livermore, 'Authority and Legitimacy in Global Governance: Deliberation, Institutional Differentiation, and the Codex Alimentarius' (2006) 81 *New York University Law Review* 766, 795–96; T Hüller and ML Maier, 'Fixing the Codex? Global Food-Safety Governance under Review' in C Joerges and E-U Petersmann (eds), *Constitutionalism, Multilevel Trade Governance and Social Regulation* (Oxford, Hart Publishing, 2006) s IV.

[11] De Búrca, herself impressed it would seem by the ultimately fallacious claims surrounding the Codex Guidelines on vitamin and mineral supplements, points to popular opposition as a driver of reform. G De Búrca, 'Developing Democracy beyond the State' 46 *Columbia Journal of Transnational Law* 221, 240 (2008). Of course, it may be argued that the perception of illegitimacy well founded or not, is sufficient to justify reform of the body.

[12] For a recent example of this type of research is H Horn, PC Mavroidis and EN Wijkstrom, 'In the Shadow of the DSU: Addressing Specific Trade Concerns in the WTO SPS and TBT Committees' (2013) 47 JWT 729.

We must not abandon critical analysis of the SPS Agreement. A global regulatory system in thrall to scientific rationality and deaf to the needs and concerns of citizens is indeed something worth rallying against. But a decade and a half after the Agreement's implementation, there is little prospect of this situation occurring. If the efficient international trade of food envisioned by the Agreement remains a desirable goal, it may be time to set aside those fears and deepen our understanding of the SPS regime' contribution to transnational food governance, paying due attention to its successes as well as its deficiencies. This book is one modest step in that direction.

References

Bohanes J, 'Risk Regulation in WTO Law: A Procedure-Based Approach to the Precautionary Principle' (2002) 40 *Columbia Journal of Transnational Law* 323.

De Búrca G, 'Developing Democracy beyond the State' 46 *Columbia Journal of Transnational Law* 221, 240 (2008).

Horn H, Mavroidis PC and Wijkstrom EN, 'In the Shadow of the DSU: Addressing Specific Trade Concerns in the WTO SPS and TBT Committees' (2013) 47 JWT 729.

Hüller T and Maier ML, 'Fixing the Codex? Global Food-Safety Governance under Review' in C Joerges and E-U Petersmann (eds), *Constitutionalism, Multilevel Trade Governance and Social Regulation* (Oxford, Hart Publishing, 2006).

Livermore MA, 'Authority and Legitimacy in Global Governance: Deliberation, Institutional Differentiation, and the Codex Alimentarius' (2006) 81 *New York University Law Review* 766.

Livshiz D, 'Updating American Administrative Law: WTO, International Standards, Domestic Implementation and Public Participation' (2007) 24 *Wisconsin International Law Journal* 961.

Steinberg RH, 'The Hidden World of WTO Governance: A Reply to Andrew Lang and Joanne Scott' (2009) 20 EJIL 1063.

Trebilcock M and Soloway J, 'International Trade Policy and Domestic Food Safety Regulation: The Case for Substantial Deference by the WTO Dispute Settlement Body under the SPS Agreement' in DLM Kennedy and JD Southwick (eds), *The Political Economy of International Trade Law: Essays in Honour of Robert E. Hudec* (Cambridge, CUP, 2002).

Walker VR, 'Keeping the WTO from Becoming the "World Trans-Science Organisation": Scientific Uncertainty, Science Policy, and Fact-Finding in the Growth Hormones Dispute' (1998) 31 *Cornell International Law Journal* 251.

Appendix

Appendix I: SPS Measures Adopted by the European Union in 2008 and Not Notified to the WTO SPS Committee

This table was first published in Downes 'The Impact of WTO Transparency Rules: Is the 10,000th SPS Notification a Cause for Celebration?—A Case Study of EU Practice' published in (2012) 15 JIEL 503.

Field of food law	Measures
Approval of residue monitoring transmitted by third countries	Commission Decision 2008/105/EC, 2008 OJ L 38/9; Commission Decision 2008/222/EC, 2008 OJ L 70/17; Commission Decision 2008/407/EC, 2008 OJ L 143/49; Commission Decision 2008/772/EC, 2008 OJ L 263/20.
Authorization of the placing on the market of products containing genetically modified material	Commission Decision 2008/730/EC, 2008 OJ L 247/50; Commission Decision 2008/280/EC, 2008 OJ L 87/19; Commission Decision 2008/279/EC, 2008 OJ L 87/17; Commission Decision 2008/993/EC, 2008 OJ L 333/7; Proposal for a Council Decision, COM/2008/0678
Food additives	Common Position 7/2008, OJ 2008 C 111E/10; Common Position (EC) No 9/2008, OJ 2008 C 111E /46; Common Position (EC) No 8/2008; OJ 2008 C 111E /532; Commission Directive 2008/60/EC, OJ 2008 L 158/ 18.617; Corrigendum to 95/45, OJ 2008 L 345/116
Hygiene of foodstuffs	Commission Regulation 1020/2008, 2008 OJ L 277/ 8; Commission Regulation 1019/2008, 2008 OJ L 277/7; Proposal for a Council Regulation, COM/2008/0430 final; Commission Regulation 1023/2008, 2008 OJ L 277/21.
Novel food applications	Commission Decision 2008/36/EC, 2008 OJ L 8/15; Commission Decision 2008/413/EC, 2008 OJ L 146/12; Commission Decision 2008/559/EC, 2008 OJ L 180/20; Commission Decision 2008/558/EC, 2008 OJ L 180/17; Commission Decision 2008/575/EC, 2008 OJ L 183/38; Commission Decision 2008/968/EC, 2008 OJ L 344/123; Commission Decision 2008/985/EC, 2008 OJ L 352/46.

C. Downes, *The Impact of WTO SPS Law on EU Food Regulations*, Studies in European Economic Law and Regulation 2, DOI 10.1007/978-3-319-04373-9,

Field of food law	Measures
Residues and contaminants	Commission Decision 2008/47/EC, 2008 OJ L 11/12; Commission Regulation 61/2008/EC, 2008 OJ L 22/8; Commission Regulation 203/2008/EC, 2008 OJ L 60/18; Commission Regulation 542/2008/EC, 2008 OJ L 157/43; Commission Regulation 565/2008, 2008 OJ L 160/20; Commission Directive 2008/76, 2008 OJ L 198/37; Corrigendum 807/2001, 2008 OJ L 307/21.
Rules governing the production/ processing/ distribution and the introduction of products of animal origin of human consumption/ Amendments of lists of third countries from which imports of specific products of animal origin are permitted	Commission Decision 2008/61/EC, 2008 OJ L 15/33; Commission Decision 2008/156/EC, 2008 OJ L 50/65; Commission Decision 2008/388/EC, 2008 OJ L 115/35; Commission Regulation 439/2008, 2008 OJ L 132/16; Commission Decision 2008/642/EC, 2008 OJ L 207/36; Commission Decision 2008/804/EC, 2008 OJ L 215/1; Commission Decision 2008/641/EC, 2008 OJ L 207/34; Commission Decision 2008/660/EC, 2008 OJ L 215/6; Commission Decision 2008/817/EC, 2008 OJ L 283/49; Commission Decision 2008/883/EC, 2008 OJ L 316/14; Commission Decision 2008/638/EC, 2008 OJ L 207/24; Commission Regulation 798/2008, 2008 OJ L 226/1; Commission Decision 2008/592/EC, 2008 OJ L 190/27.
Specific measures to combat a risk to health (rice from the US, fish from Gabon, crustaceous from Bangladesh, molluscs from Peru)	Commission Decision 2008/162/EC, 2008 OJ L 52/25; Commission Decision 2008/289/EC, 2008 OJ L 96/29; Commission Regulation 601/2008, 2008 OJ L 165/3; Commission Decision 2008/630/EC, 2008 OJ L 205/49; Commission Decision 2008/866, 2008 OJ L 307/9.

Appendix II: Relationship Between Codex Alimentarius GSFA and National/Regional Regulatory Frameworks

	Do national additive regulatory frameworks take into account the following? *(Y = Yes, N = No, ± = partially, blank = information not available)*						
	Principles of technological justification	Food categorisation	INS numbers	Acceptance of GSFA additives	GSFA as reference point in additive evaluation	GMP provisions	Impact of Codex on domestic regulation
Australia/NZ[a]	Y	Y	Y		Y	Y	Displacement
Bahrain[b]				Y			Innovation
Bolivia[c]				Y			Innovation
Canada[d]	N	N	N	N	±	N	Resistance
Chile[e]	±	N	Y	Y		±	Localisation
China[f]	Y	Y	Y	Y		±	Displacement
Colombia[g]	Y	N	N	N	Y	Y	Localisation
Congo[h]	N	N	N	N	N	N	Resistance
Costa Rica[i]				Y			Innovation
Dominican Republic[j]				Y			Innovation
Egypt[k]	N	N	N	N			Resistance
El Salvador[l]				Y			Localisation
Eritrea[m]	N	N	N	N		N	Resistance
EU[n]	±	N	±	N	±	N	Resistance
Guatemala[o]				±	Y		Innovation
Hong Kong, China[p]	Y	Y	Y	Y			Displacement
India[q]	N	N	Y	Y		Y	Localisation
Indonesia[r]	N	N	N	N	Y	N	Localisation
Japan[s]	Y	N	N		±		Resistance
Kenya[t]	N	N	N	N	Y		Localisation
Korea[u]	N	N	N	N	Y	N	Resistance
Laos[v]				Y			Innovation
Malaysia[w]	N	N	N	N	N	N	Resistance
Mexico[x]	N	N	Y	N		N	Localisation
Morocco[y]				N	N		Resistance
Myanmar[z]				Y			Innovation
Nicaragua[aa]				Y			Innovation
Peru[ab]				Y			Innovation
Philippines	Y	Y		N	Y		Localisation
Russia[ac]	N	N	N	N			Resistance
South Africa[ad]	N	N	N	N		N	Resistance
Tanzania[ae]	N	N	Y	N		N	Localisation
Thailand[af]	N	N	N	Y		N	Localisation
Uganda[ag]				Y			Innovation
Vietnam[ah]	N	N	Y	N		N	Localisation

[a] Australia New Zealand Food Standard 1.3.1, *Commonwealth of Australia Gazette* No. P 10 (22 June 2000) www.comlaw.gov.au/Series/F2008B00614
[b] See G/SPS/GEN/537 (18 January 2005)
[c] Bolivian Ministry of Rural Development, Agriculture and Environment, National Service for Animal Health, Plant Protection and Food Safety (SENASAG) Administrative Resolution 019/2003 (12 March 2003)
[d] Canadian, Food and Drug Regulations (CRC, c. 870laws.justice.gc.ca/eng/regulations/C.R.C.,_c._870/index.html
[e] Chilean Regulation on providing for healthy food, Decree 977 (6 August 1996)
[f] Chinese Ministry of Health National Standard GB-2760-2007 (27 August 2007), an unofficial translation of which is available in GAIN Report No: CH8018 (20 March 2008)
[g] Colombia Ministry of Social Protection, Decree 2106 (26 July 1983)
[h] Congo Ministry of Forestry Economy and Fisheries, Decree 3642 (29 September 2000)
[i] Costa Rican Ministry of Health, Executive Decree 35353-S, *La Gaceta, Diario Oficial* (25 August 2009)
[j] Proposal for Food Sanitary Regulations for the Dominican Republic (2009) (otcasea.gob.do/wp-content/uploads/2009/06/propuesta-regl-sanitario-alimentos-rd.pdf 26 September 2011) as notified to the SPS Committee under G/SPS/N/DOM/20 (9 April 2009). Publication of the final legislation has not yet been notified to the WTO
[k] See Gain Report No. EG9014 (July 2009)
[l] El Salvador maintains commodity standards generally based on Codex standards. See, for example, General Standard for Cheese Specifications, NSO 67.01.14:06, *Diario Oficial* (23 January 2008)
[m] Eritrean Government Legal Notice No. 65/2003 Fishery Products Additives Regulations (30 April 2003)
[n] Regulation (EC) No 1333/2008 of the European Parliament and of the Council on food additives [2008] OJ L354/16
[o] See GAIN report no (GT9011 July 2009)
[p] See G/SPS/N/HKG/25/Add.1 (25 May 2008)
[q] Indian Ministry of Health and Family Welfare, 'Food Safety and Standards (Licensing and Registration of Food Businesses) 2011' *Gazette of India* (1 August 2011) 65
[r] Decision of the Director General of Drug and Food Control No. 02592/B/SK/VIII/91 (14 August 1991)
[s] The Ministry of Health and Welfare, 'Japan's Specifications and Standards for Food Additives' (Seventh Edition English translation, Sep. 2000) http://www.ffcr.or.jp/zaidan/ffcrhome.nsf/pages/spec.stand.fa
[t] Kenya Food, Drugs and Chemical Substances (Food Labelling, Additives and Standards) (Amendment) Regulations 2010, www.kenyalaw.org
[u] Korea Food Additive Code 2004, fa.kfda.go.kr/foodadditivescode.html
[v] Laos Ministry of Health, Regulation No. 586/MoH (12 May 2006)
[w] Malaysian Food Regulations 1985, as last amended 24 September 2009. Available at faolex.fao.org
[x] Mexican Ministry of Health Agreement determining the substances permitted as additives and processing aids in food, beverages and nutritional supplements, *Diaro Oficial* (17 July 2006)
[y] See GAIN Report no. MO8011 (June 2008)
[z] Myanmar Ministry of Livestock and Fisheries, Directive No. (9/96) (6 November 6 1996)
[aa] Nicaraguan Ministry of Agriculture and Forestry, Ministerial Agreement No. 23-2000
[ab] Peruvian Environmental Health Department, Directorial Resolution 0775/2003/DIGESA/SA, *El Peruano* (16 July 2003) p248210
[ac] Ministry of Health of The Russian Federation Chief State Sanitary Inspector of the Russian Federation Resolution No. 36 on Implementing Sanitary Rules (14 November 14 2001) registered with the Ministry of Justice of the RF, No. N 3326 (22 March 2002)
[ad] See, for example, Regulation relating to food colorants 1008/1996, published under Government Notice No. R 1008 (21 June 1986)

[ae] Tanzania Food (Food Additives) Regulations of 1998 (amending The Food (Control of Quality) Act of 1978, Government Notice No. 370 (19 June 1998)
[af] Notification of the Ministry of Public Health, No. 281 B.E. 2547 (2004)
[ag] Ugandan Standard US 45: 2009, reported in G/TBT/N/UGA/123 (18 May 2010)
[ah] Vietnamese Ministry of Health, Decision No. 3742/2001/QD-BYT (31 August 2001)

Appendix III: Relationship Between Codex Alimentarius Guidelines on Vitamin and Mineral Supplement Guidelines and National/Regional Regulatory Frameworks

Do national food supplement regulatory frameworks take into account the following?
(Y = Yes, N = No, blank = not specified)

Country	Year	Under food law	Name: '(V&M) food supplement'	Minimum level: 15 % RDI	Maximum level: safety, not RDI-based	Codex Scope of VMS?	Labelling per portion as recommended for daily consumption %RDI Stored out of reach of children How to be used advice not to exceed maximum 1 day amount not imply replacement for food					
							a.	b.	c.	d.	e.	f.
Singapore[a]	1965	N				*Health Supplements under medicinal law*						
Malaysia[b]	1984	N				*Medicines*						
Paraguay	1984	N				*Medicines*						
New Zealand	1985	Y	Dietary supplement		Safety—levels where necessary		Y	Y	N	Y	N	N
El Salvador[c]	1988	N				*Medicines*						
Australia[d]	1989	N				*Complementary medicines*						
US[e]	1994	Y	Dietary supplement			VMS & herb/botanical, amino acid, dietary substances	Y	Y	N	N	N	N
Bolivia[f]	1996	N				*Medicines*						
Brazil[g]	1998	Y	Vitamin and Mineral supplements	25 %	N (< 100 % RDI)	Vitamins and minerals	Y	Y	N	Y	N	N

	Do national food supplement regulatory frameworks take into account the following? (Y = Yes, N = No, blank = not specified)											
Country	Year	Under food law	Name: '(V&M) food supplement'	Minimum level: 15 % RDI	Maximum level: safety, not RDI-based	Codex Scope of VMS?	Labelling per portion as recommended for daily consumption %RDI Stored out of reach of children How to be used advice not to exceed maximum 1 day amount not imply replacement for food					
							a.	b.	c.	d.	e.	f.
Chile[h]	2002	Y	Food supplement	100 %	Y	Vitamins and minerals						
EU[i]	2002	Y	Food supplement		Y—safety oriented	Vitamins and minerals	Y	Y	Y	N	Y	Y
Canada[j]	2003	N				*Natural health product*						
Vietnam[k]	2003	Y	Functional food		N (<300 % RDI)		Y	Y	N	Y	N	N
Indonesia[l]	2004	Y	Food supplement		Y	vitamins, minerals, amino acids and other materials	Y	N	N	Y	N	N
Thailand[m]	2005	Y	Food supplement	Y	N (<Thai RDI)	Vitamins, amino acids, fatty acids, minerals, plant/animal substances	Y	N	N	Y	N	Y
Colombia[n]	2006	Y	Dietary supplement		Y	Vitamins, minerals, proteins, amino acids, plant extracts, where accepted by international bodies	Y	Y	Y	Y	N	Y

	Do national food supplement regulatory frameworks take into account the following? (Y = Yes, N = No, blank = not specified)											
Country	Year	Under food law	Name: '(V&M) food supplement'	Minimum level: 15 % RDI	Maximum level: safety, not RDI-based	Codex Scope of VMS?	Labelling per portion as recommended for daily consumption %RDI Stored out of reach of children How to be used advice not to exceed maximum 1 day amount not imply replacement for food					
							a.	b.	c.	d.	e.	f.
India[o]	2006	Y	Foods for special Dietary Uses/Functional Foods/Nutraceuticals/Health supplements		N (<RDI)	Minerals/vitamins/proteins/metals/amino acids/enzymes						
Argentina[p]	2008	Y	N—Dietary supplement	20 %	Y	Peptides, proteins, lipids, amino acids, carbohydrate, vitamins, minerals, dietary fibre, herbs	Y	Y	Y	Y	Y	Not for pregnant women, or children
Costa Rica[q]	2010	Y	Dietary supplement	20 %	Y	Vitamins, minerals, proteins, amino acids, plant extracts (not exhaustive)	Y	N	Y	N	N	N

	Do national food supplement regulatory frameworks take into account the following? (Y=Yes, N=No, blank=not specified)											
Country	Year	Under food law	Name: '(V&M) food supplement'	Minimum level: 15% RDI	Maximum level: safety, not RDI-based	Codex Scope of VMS?	Labelling per portion as recommended for daily consumption %RDI Stored out of reach of children How to be used advice not to exceed maximum 1 day amount not imply replacement for food					
							a.	b.	c.	d.	e.	f.
Korea[r]	2010	Y	Health Functional Food	30%	Y	Wide range of ingredients					Specific to nutrient	

[a] Singapore Medicines Act 1975. See Health Sciences Authority, Health Supplements Guidelines, www.hsa.gov.sg
[b] Malaysia Control of Drugs and Cosmetics Act 1984, PU (A)223/84, www.bpfk.gov.my/Quest2/body_help_reg.htm
[c] El Salvador, Legislative Decree No. 955 of 28 April 1988 *Diaro Oficial* 86: 299 (11 May 1988)
[d] Australian Therapeutic Goods Act 1989, Act No. 21 of 1990
[e] US Dietary Supplement Health and Education Act of 1994, Public Law 103-417, 103rd Congress
[f] Bolivian Medicinal Law 1737 (17 December 1996)
[g] Brazil Ministry of Health, Ordinance No. 32 (13 January 1998)
[h] Chile Ministry of Health, Resolution 394/2002, *Diaro Oficial* (1 March 2002)
[i] Directive 2002/46/EC of the European Parliament and of the Council on the approximation of the laws of the Member States relating to food supplements [2002] OJ L183/51
[j] Canada Natural Health Products Regulation SOR/2003-196 (3 June 2006)
[k] Vietnam Ministry of health Decision No. 6289/2003/QD-BTY (9 December 2003)
[l] Indonesia Food and Drug Supervisory Board Decision Number HK00.05.23.3644 (4 August 2004)
[m] Notification of Thailand Ministry of Public Health (No. 293) BE2548 (2005), *Government Gazette*, Vol. 122, Special Part 150 Ngor (28 December 2005)
[n] Colombia Ministry of Social Protection, Act 3496, *Official Journal* No. 46395 (18 September 2006)
[o] Indian Food Safety and Standards Act 2006, No. 34 (23 August 2006)
[p] Argentina Food Code, Article 1381 incorporated by Joint Resolution of the Secretariat of Health Policy, Regulation and Institutions (SPRI) No. 118/2008 and of the Secretariat of Agriculture, Livestock, Fisheries and Food (SAGPA) No. 474/2008
[q] Costa Rica Ministry of Health, Executive Decree 436:2009, la Gaceta Diario Ofical No. 186 (24 September 2010)
[r] Korea Health Functional Food Act, Enacted by Act No. 6727 (26 August 2002); Korea Food and Drug Administration, Health Functional Food Code (2010)

Index

C. Downes, *The Impact of WTO SPS Law on EU Food Regulations,* Studies in European Economic Law and Regulation 2, DOI 10.1007/978-3-319-04373-9,

Printed by Printforce, the Netherlands